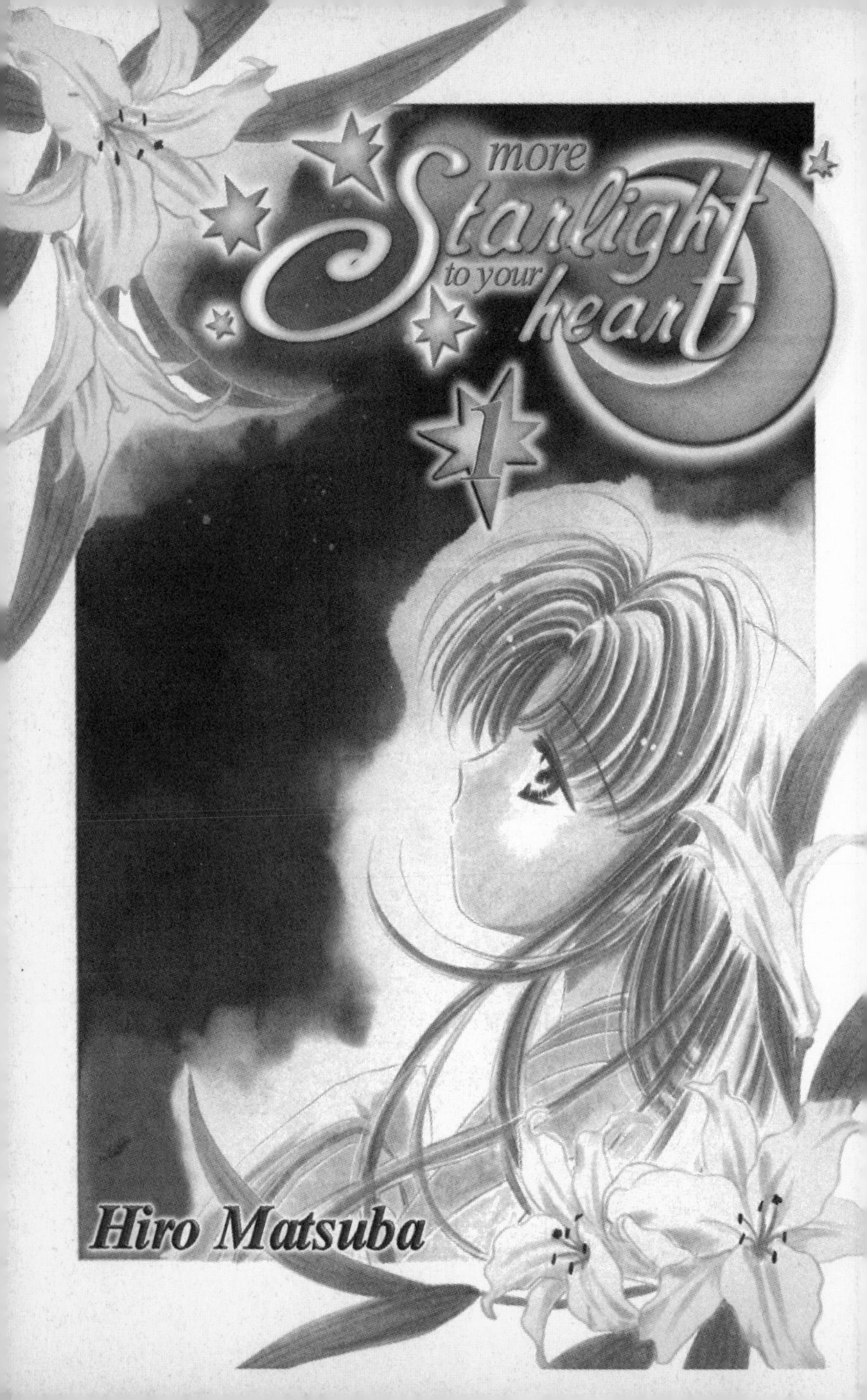
more Starlight to your heart
1
Hiro Matsuba

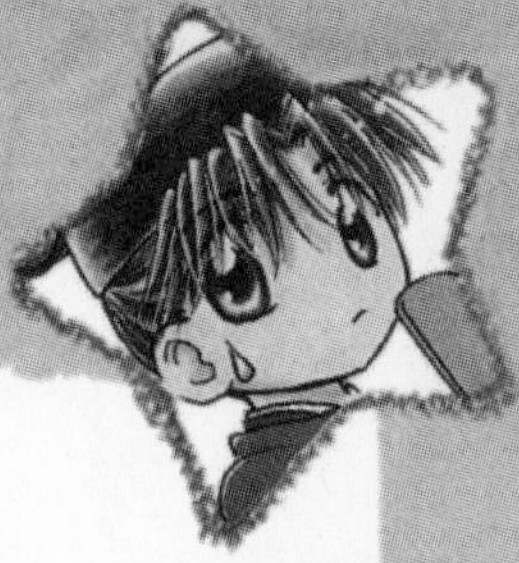

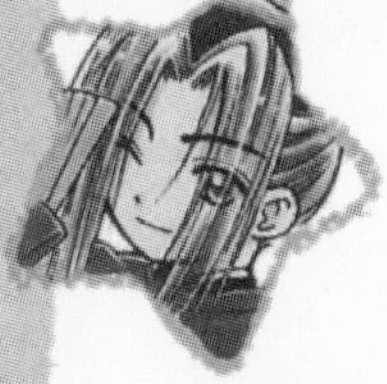

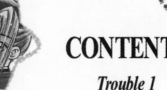

CONTENTS

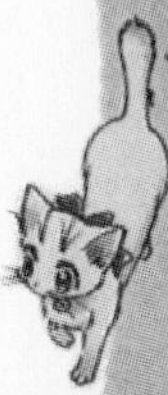

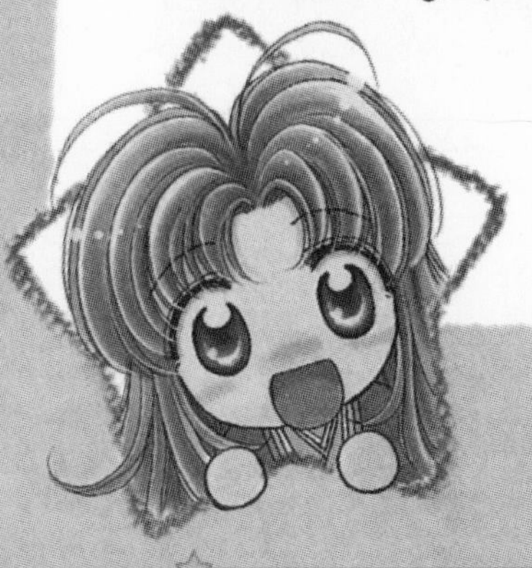

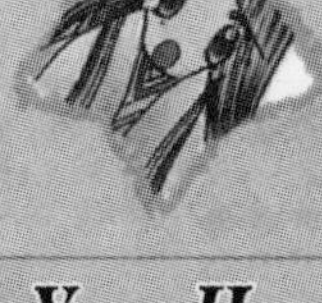

More Starlight to Your Heart

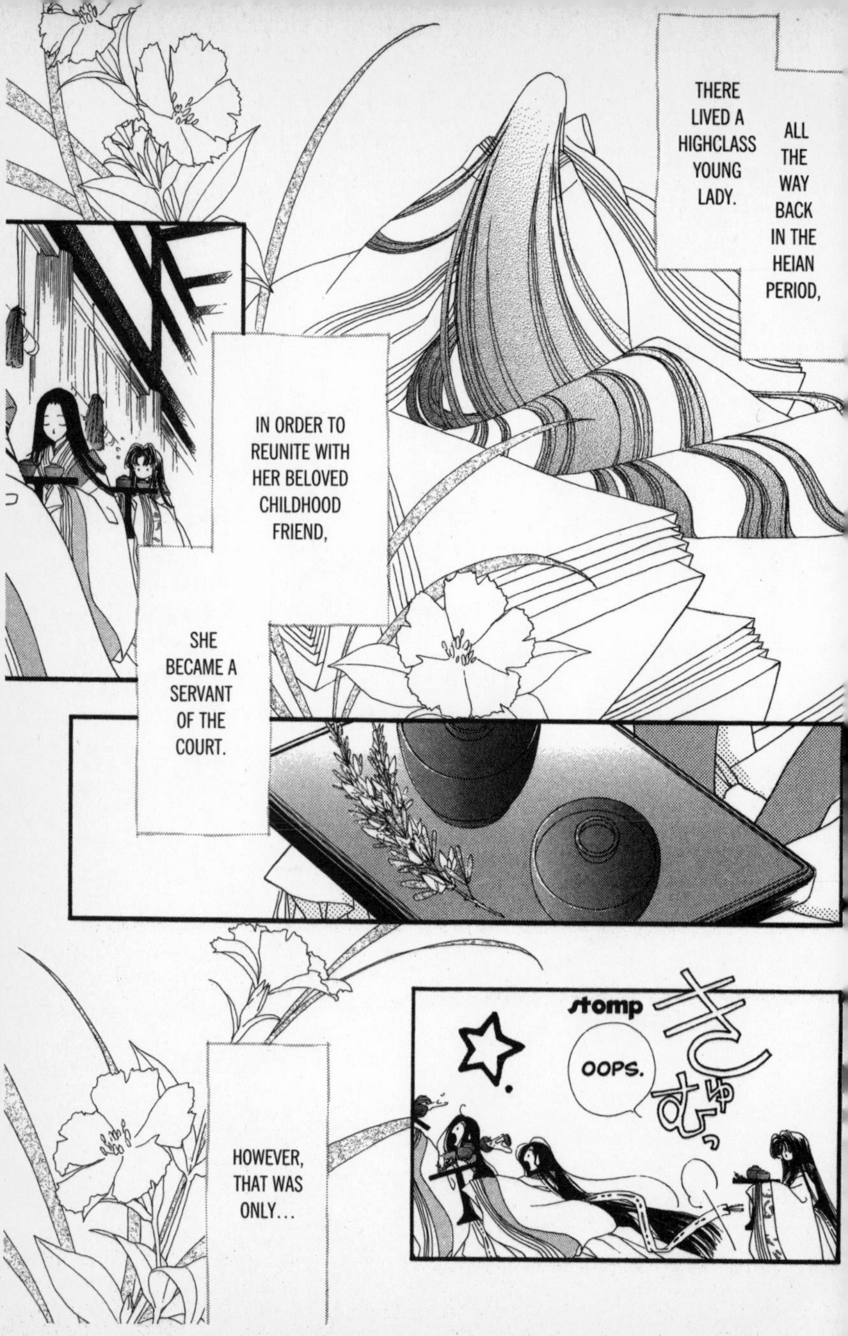
ALL THE WAY BACK IN THE HEIAN PERIOD,
THERE LIVED A HIGHCLASS YOUNG LADY.
IN ORDER TO REUNITE WITH HER BELOVED CHILDHOOD FRIEND,
SHE BECAME A SERVANT OF THE COURT.
きゅむっ
stomp
OOPS.
HOWEVER, THAT WAS ONLY...

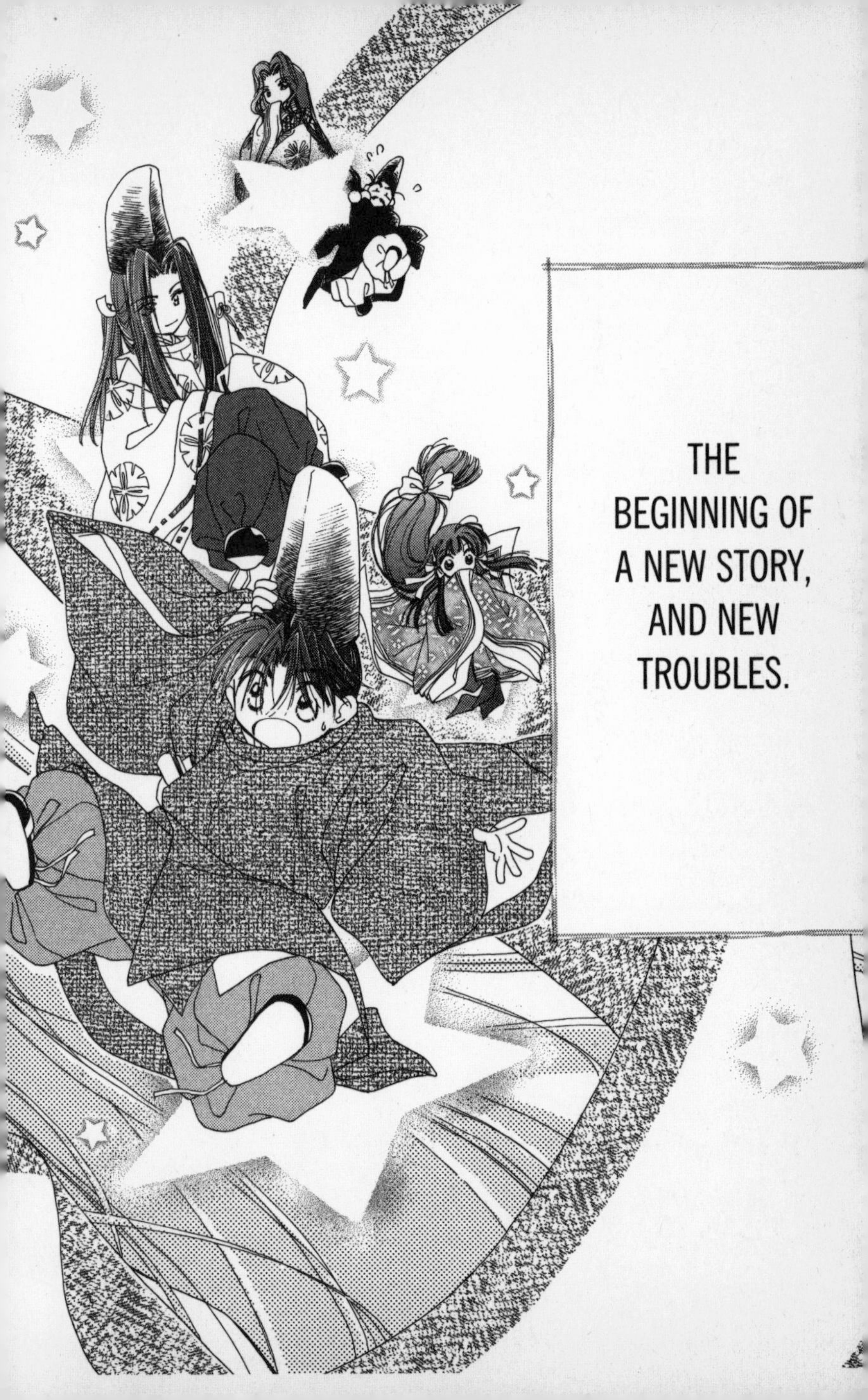
THE BEGINNING OF A NEW STORY, AND NEW TROUBLES.

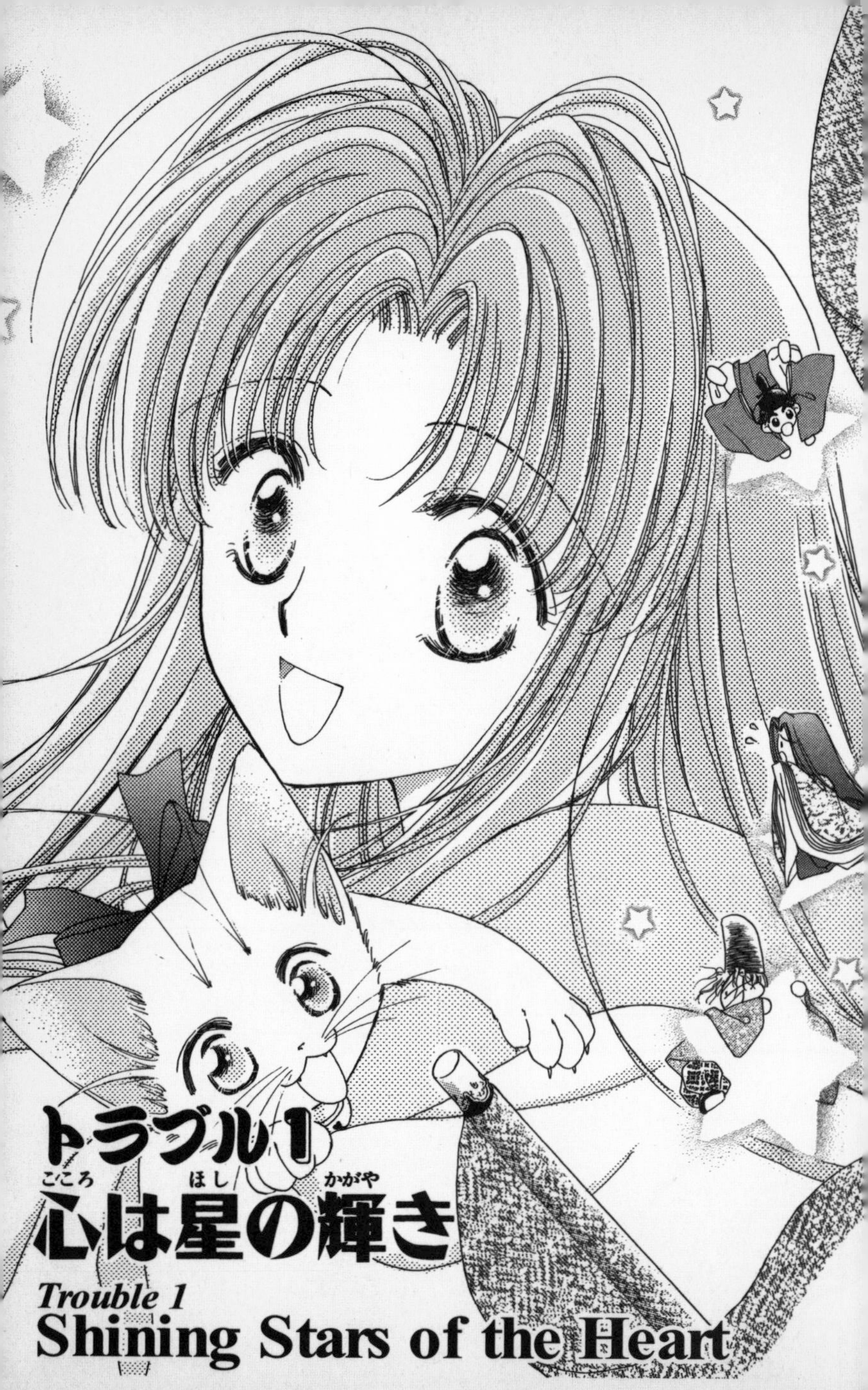
トラブル1
こころ ほし かがや
心は星の輝き
Trouble 1
Shining Stars of the Heart

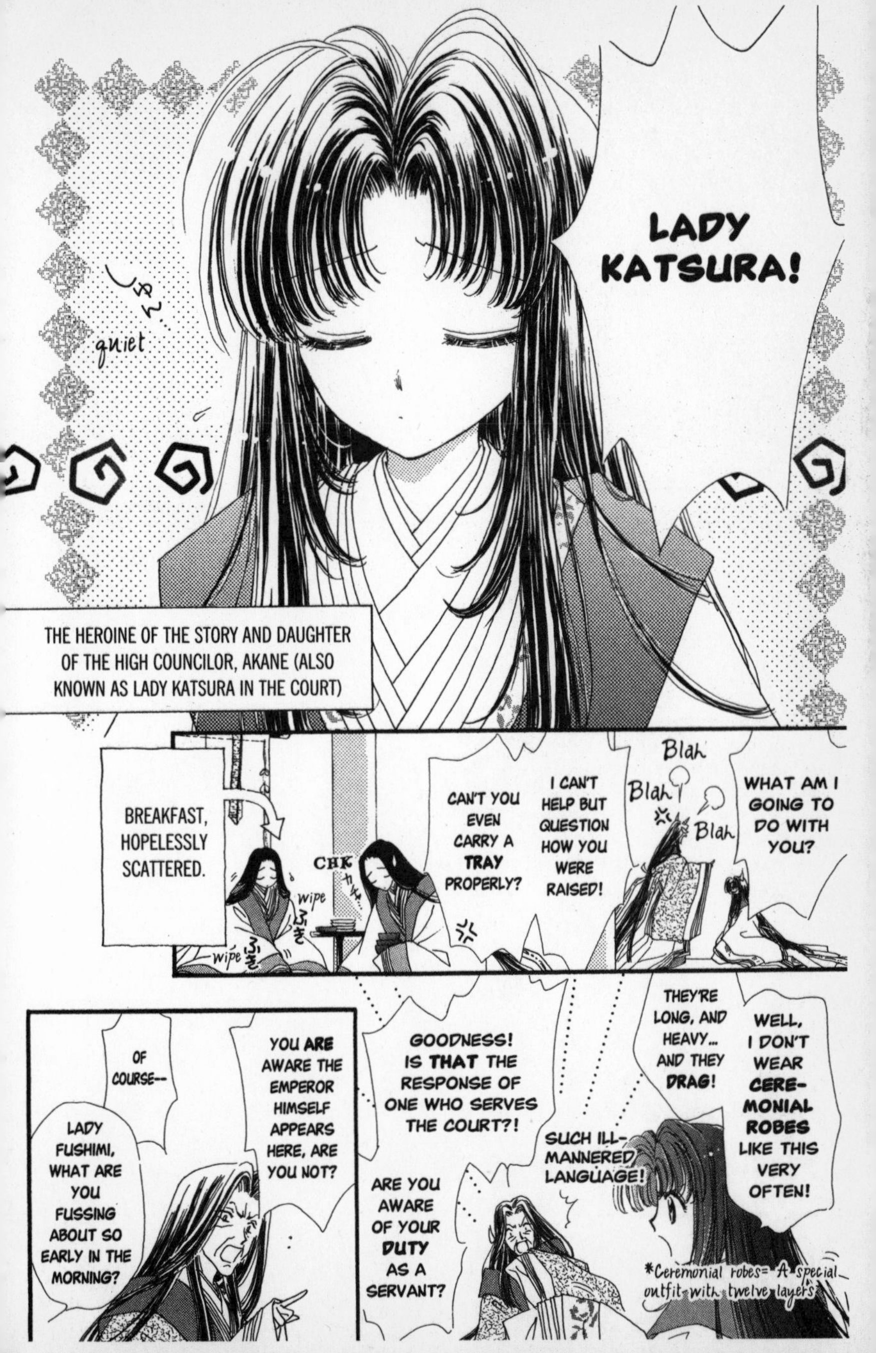
LADY KATSURA!
quiet
THE HEROINE OF THE STORY AND DAUGHTER OF THE HIGH COUNCILOR, AKANE (ALSO KNOWN AS LADY KATSURA IN THE COURT)
WHAT AM I GOING TO DO WITH YOU?
Blah Blah Blah
I CAN'T HELP BUT QUESTION HOW YOU WERE RAISED!
CAN'T YOU EVEN CARRY A TRAY PROPERLY?
CHK
BREAKFAST, HOPELESSLY SCATTERED.
wipe
wipe
WELL, I DON'T WEAR CEREMONIAL ROBES LIKE THIS VERY OFTEN!
THEY'RE LONG, AND HEAVY... AND THEY DRAG!
GOODNESS! IS THAT THE RESPONSE OF ONE WHO SERVES THE COURT?!
SUCH ILL-MANNERED LANGUAGE!
ARE YOU AWARE OF YOUR DUTY AS A SERVANT?
*Ceremonial robes= A special outfit with twelve layers
YOU ARE AWARE THE EMPEROR HIMSELF APPEARS HERE, ARE YOU NOT?
OF COURSE--
LADY FUSHIMI, WHAT ARE YOU FUSSING ABOUT SO EARLY IN THE MORNING?

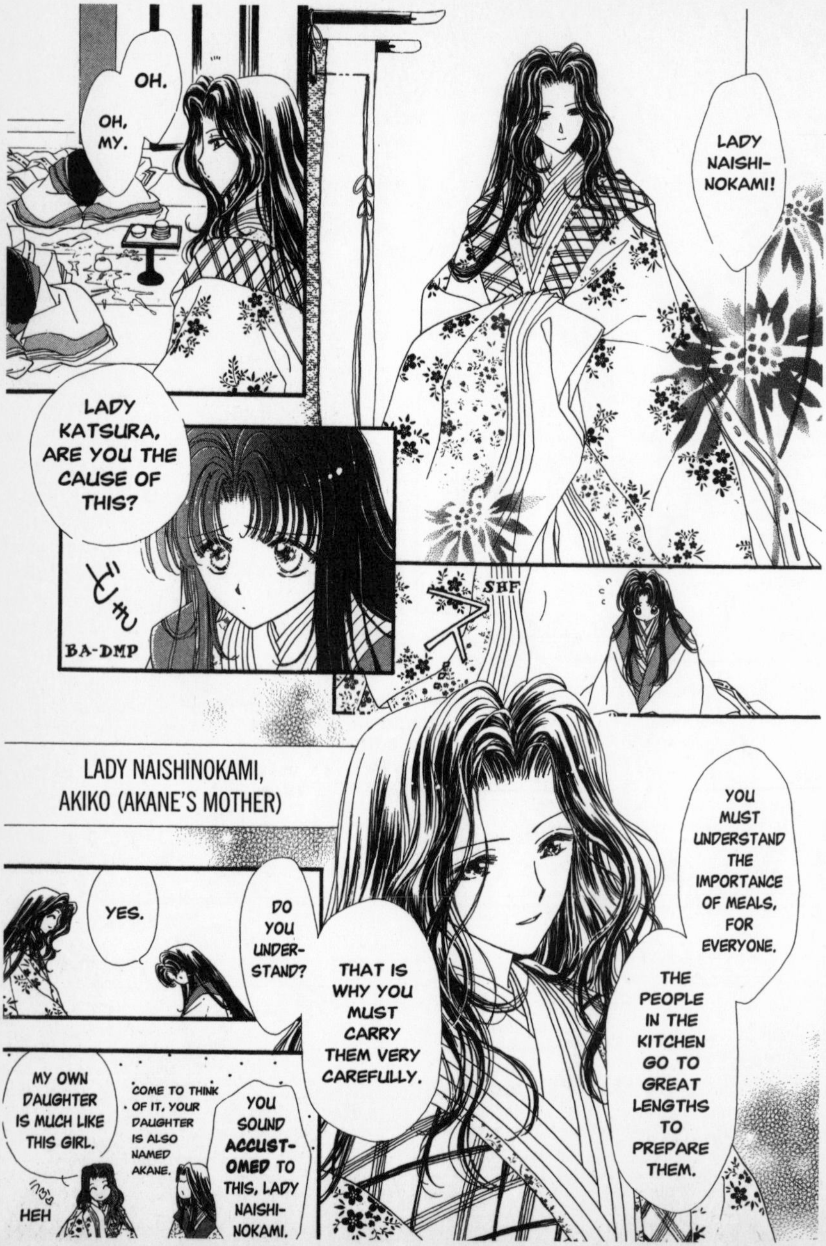
LADY NAISHI-NOKAMI!
OH.
OH, MY.
LADY KATSURA, ARE YOU THE CAUSE OF THIS?
BA-DMP
SHF
LADY NAISHINOKAMI, AKIKO (AKANE'S MOTHER)
YOU MUST UNDERSTAND THE IMPORTANCE OF MEALS, FOR EVERYONE.
THE PEOPLE IN THE KITCHEN GO TO GREAT LENGTHS TO PREPARE THEM.
THAT IS WHY YOU MUST CARRY THEM VERY CAREFULLY.
DO YOU UNDER-STAND?
YES.
YOU SOUND **ACCUST-OMED** TO THIS, LADY NAISHI-NOKAMI.
COME TO THINK OF IT, YOUR DAUGHTER IS ALSO NAMED AKANE.
MY OWN DAUGHTER IS MUCH LIKE THIS GIRL.
HEH

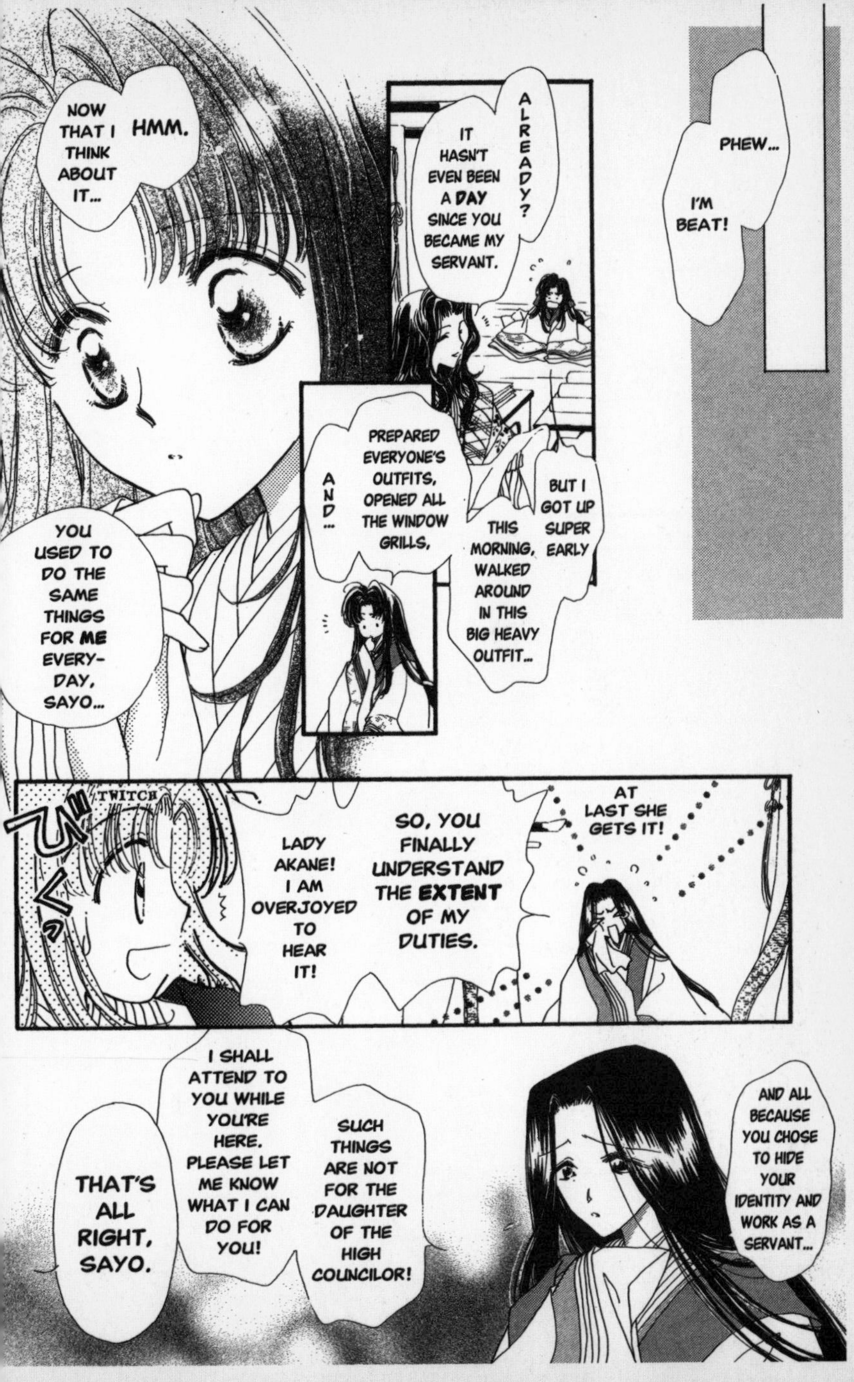
PHEW... I'M BEAT!
ALREADY? IT HASN'T EVEN BEEN A DAY SINCE YOU BECAME MY SERVANT.
BUT I GOT UP SUPER EARLY THIS MORNING, WALKED AROUND IN THIS BIG HEAVY OUTFIT...
PREPARED EVERYONE'S OUTFITS, OPENED ALL THE WINDOW GRILLS,
AND...
HMM.
NOW THAT I THINK ABOUT IT...
YOU USED TO DO THE SAME THINGS FOR ME EVERY-DAY, SAYO...
AT LAST SHE GETS IT!
SO, YOU FINALLY UNDERSTAND THE EXTENT OF MY DUTIES.
LADY AKANE! I AM OVERJOYED TO HEAR IT!
TWITCH
AND ALL BECAUSE YOU CHOSE TO HIDE YOUR IDENTITY AND WORK AS A SERVANT...
SUCH THINGS ARE NOT FOR THE DAUGHTER OF THE HIGH COUNCILOR!
I SHALL ATTEND TO YOU WHILE YOU'RE HERE. PLEASE LET ME KNOW WHAT I CAN DO FOR YOU!
THAT'S ALL RIGHT, SAYO.

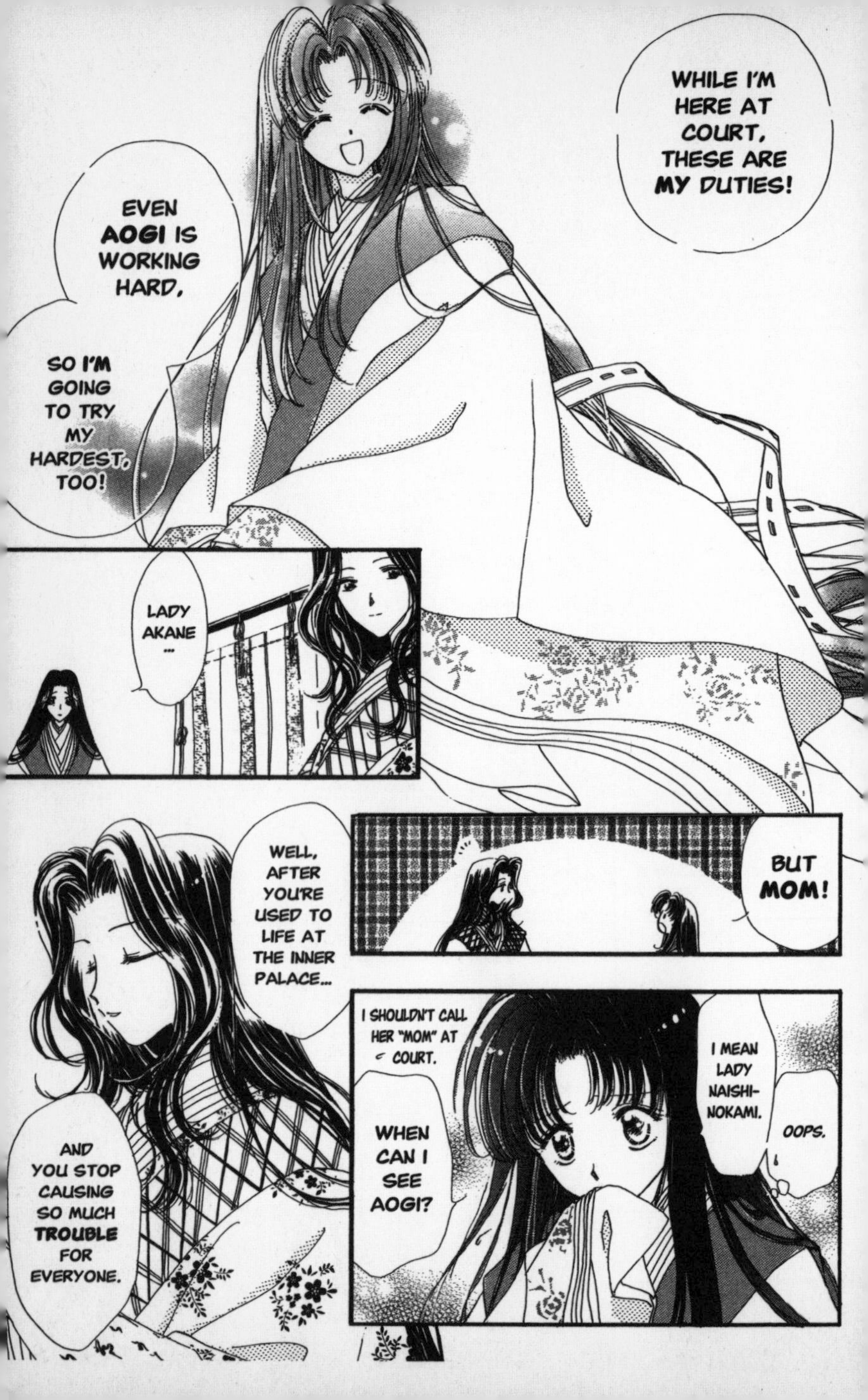

WHILE I'M HERE AT COURT, THESE ARE MY DUTIES!
EVEN AOGI IS WORKING HARD,
SO I'M GOING TO TRY MY HARDEST, TOO!
LADY AKANE...
BUT MOM!
WHEN CAN I SEE AOGI?
OOPS.
I SHOULDN'T CALL HER "MOM" AT COURT.
I MEAN LADY NAISHI-NOKAMI.
WELL, AFTER YOU'RE USED TO LIFE AT THE INNER PALACE...
AND YOU STOP CAUSING SO MUCH TROUBLE FOR EVERYONE.

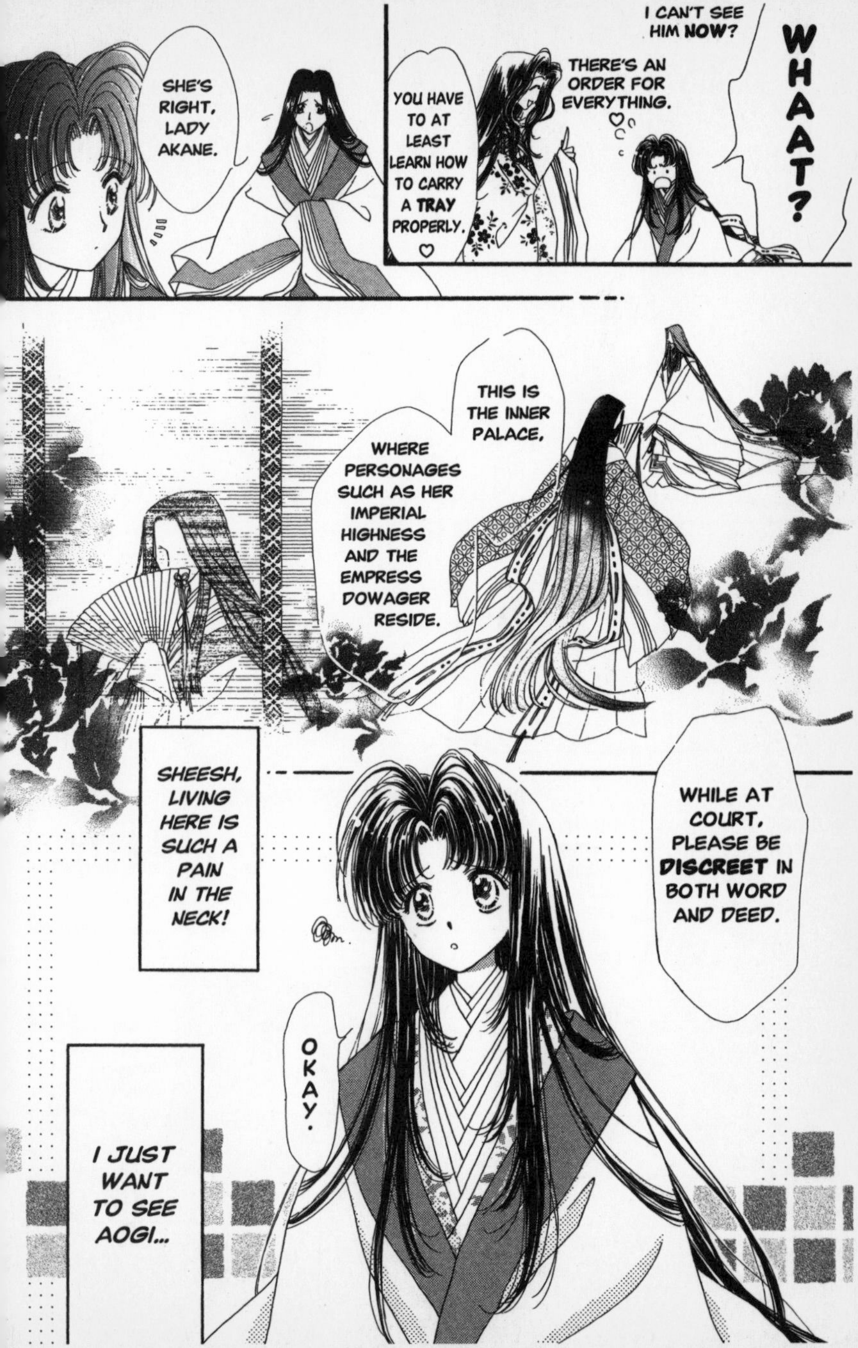

WHAAT?
I CAN'T SEE HIM NOW?
THERE'S AN ORDER FOR EVERYTHING.
YOU HAVE TO AT LEAST LEARN HOW TO CARRY A TRAY PROPERLY.
SHE'S RIGHT, LADY AKANE.
THIS IS THE INNER PALACE,
WHERE PERSONAGES SUCH AS HER IMPERIAL HIGHNESS AND THE EMPRESS DOWAGER RESIDE.
WHILE AT COURT, PLEASE BE DISCREET IN BOTH WORD AND DEED.
OKAY.
SHEESH, LIVING HERE IS SUCH A PAIN IN THE NECK!
I JUST WANT TO SEE AOGI...

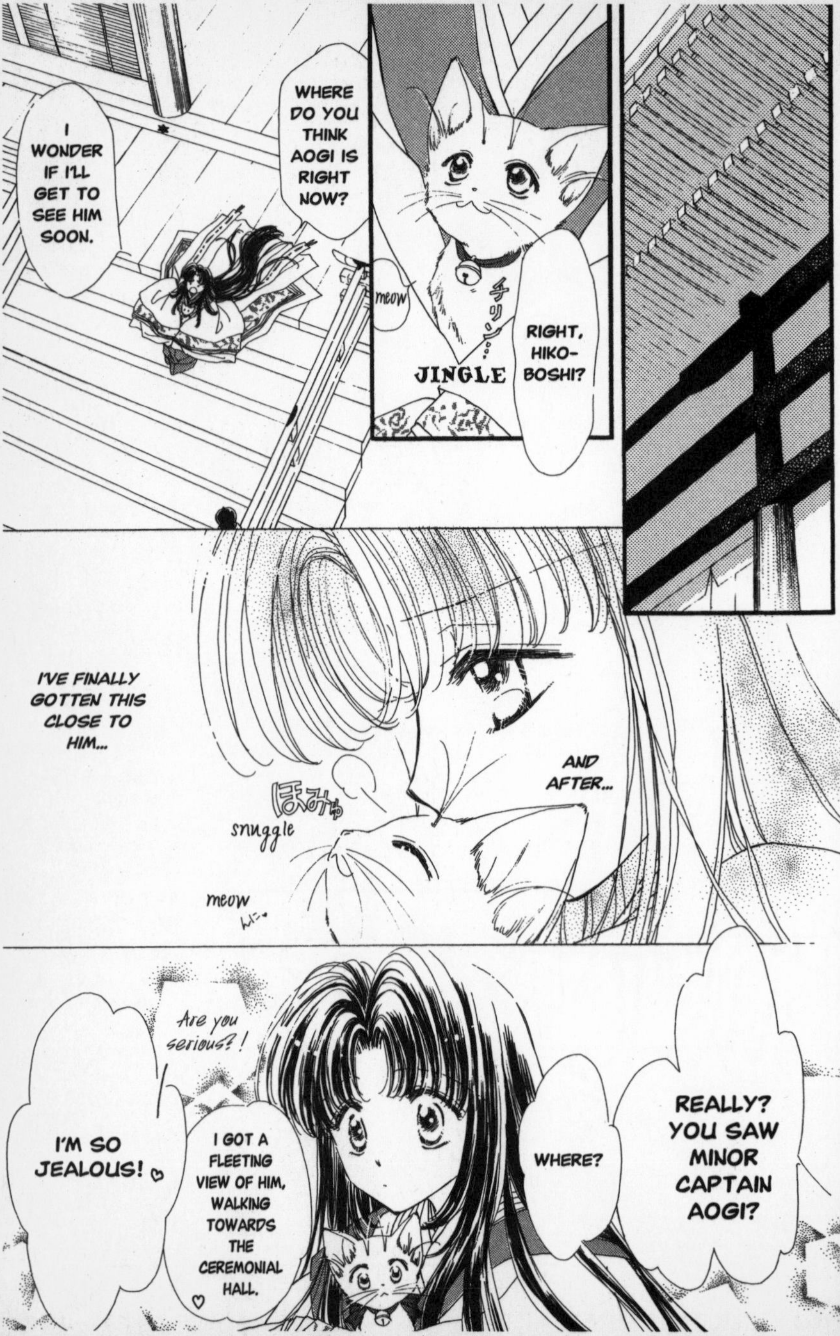
WHERE DO YOU THINK AOGI IS RIGHT NOW?
meow
チリン…
JINGLE
RIGHT, HIKO-BOSHI?
I WONDER IF I'LL GET TO SEE HIM SOON.
AND AFTER...
I'VE FINALLY GOTTEN THIS CLOSE TO HIM...
ほみゅ
snuggle
meow
REALLY? YOU SAW MINOR CAPTAIN AOGI?
WHERE?
I GOT A FLEETING VIEW OF HIM, WALKING TOWARDS THE CEREMONIAL HALL.
Are you serious?!
I'M SO JEALOUS!

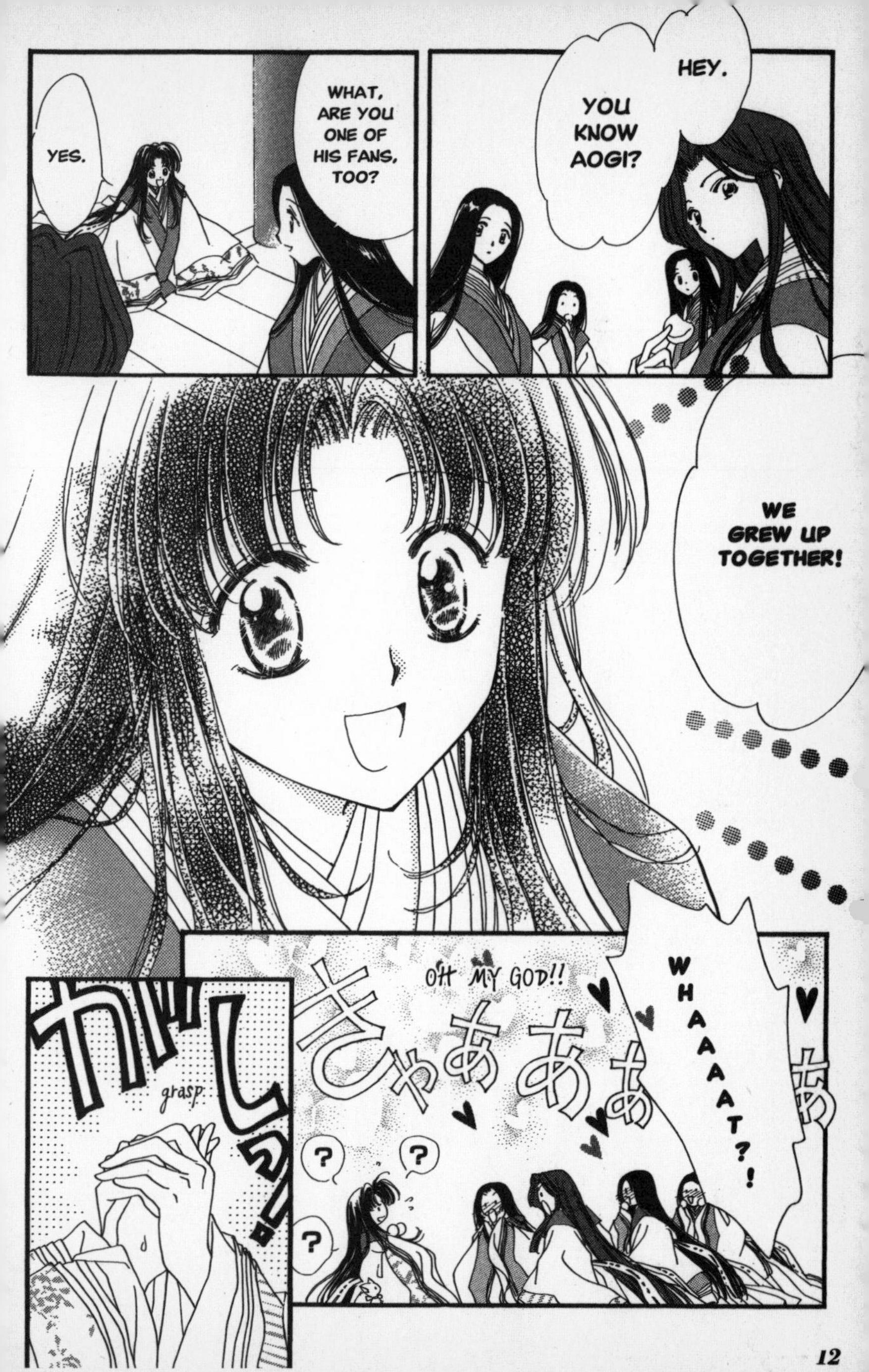
HEY.
YOU KNOW AOGI?
WHAT, ARE YOU ONE OF HIS FANS, TOO?
YES.
WE GREW UP TOGETHER!
WHAAAAT?!
OH MY GOD!!
きゃああああ
?
?
?
がしっ!
grasp.

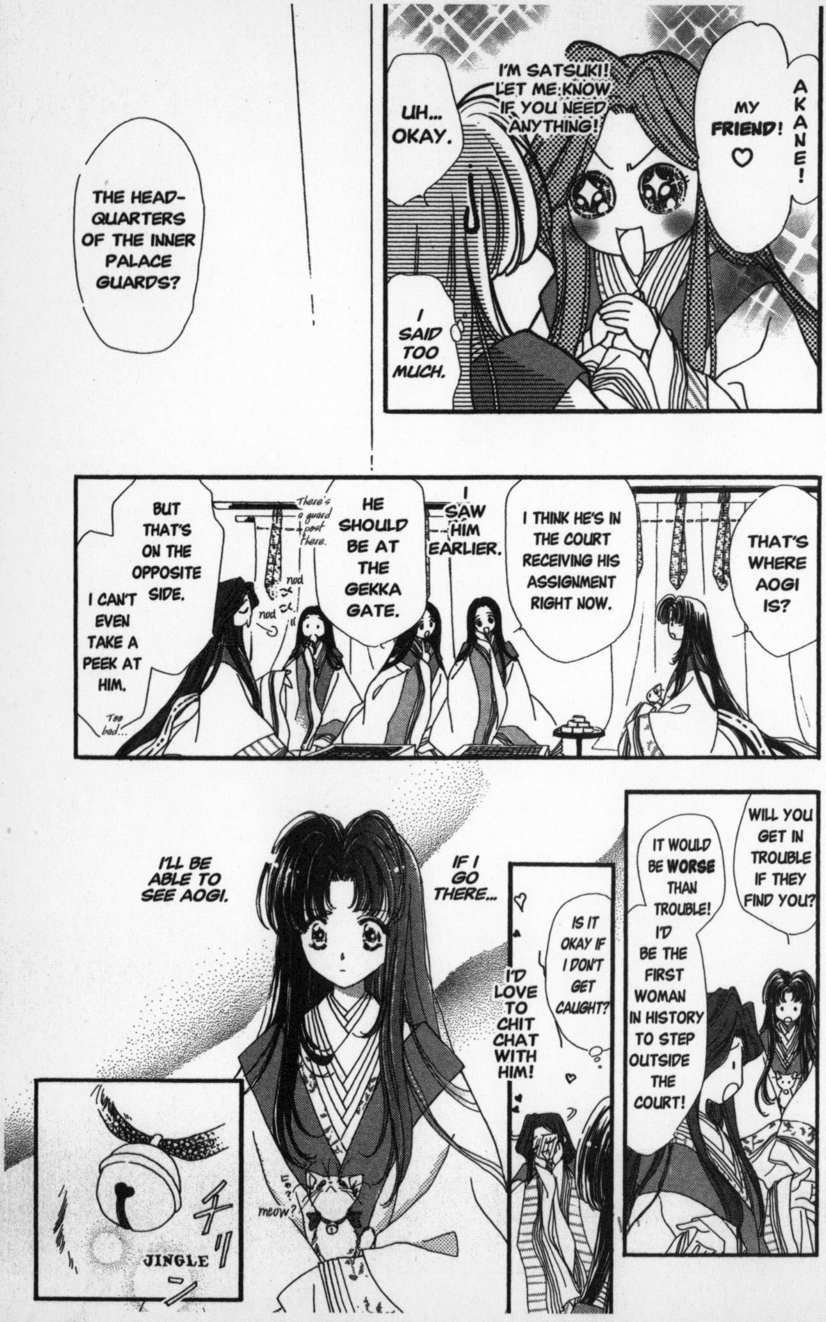

AKANE!
MY FRIEND! ♡
I'M SATSUKI! LET ME KNOW IF YOU NEED ANYTHING!
UH... OKAY.
I SAID TOO MUCH.
THE HEAD-QUARTERS OF THE INNER PALACE GUARDS?
THAT'S WHERE AOGI IS?
I THINK HE'S IN THE COURT RECEIVING HIS ASSIGNMENT RIGHT NOW.
I SAW HIM EARLIER.
HE SHOULD BE AT THE GEKKA GATE.
There's a guard post there.
BUT THAT'S ON THE OPPOSITE SIDE.
nod
nod
I CAN'T EVEN TAKE A PEEK AT HIM.
Too bad...
WILL YOU GET IN TROUBLE IF THEY FIND YOU?
IT WOULD BE WORSE THAN TROUBLE!
I'D BE THE FIRST WOMAN IN HISTORY TO STEP OUTSIDE THE COURT!
IS IT OKAY IF I DON'T GET CAUGHT?
I'D LOVE TO CHIT CHAT WITH HIM!
IF I GO THERE...
I'LL BE ABLE TO SEE AOGI.
meow?
JINGLE

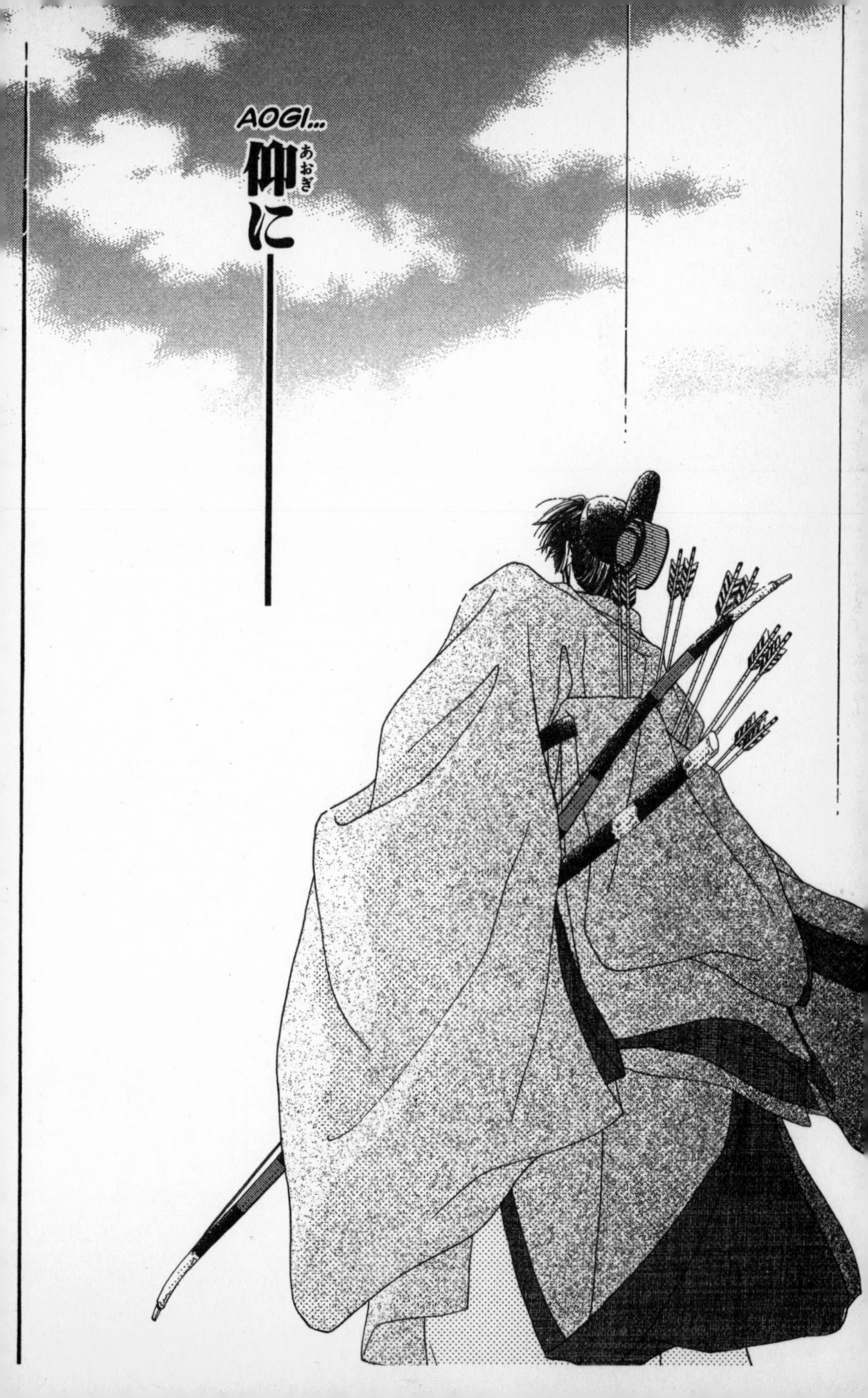
AOGI...
仰に——

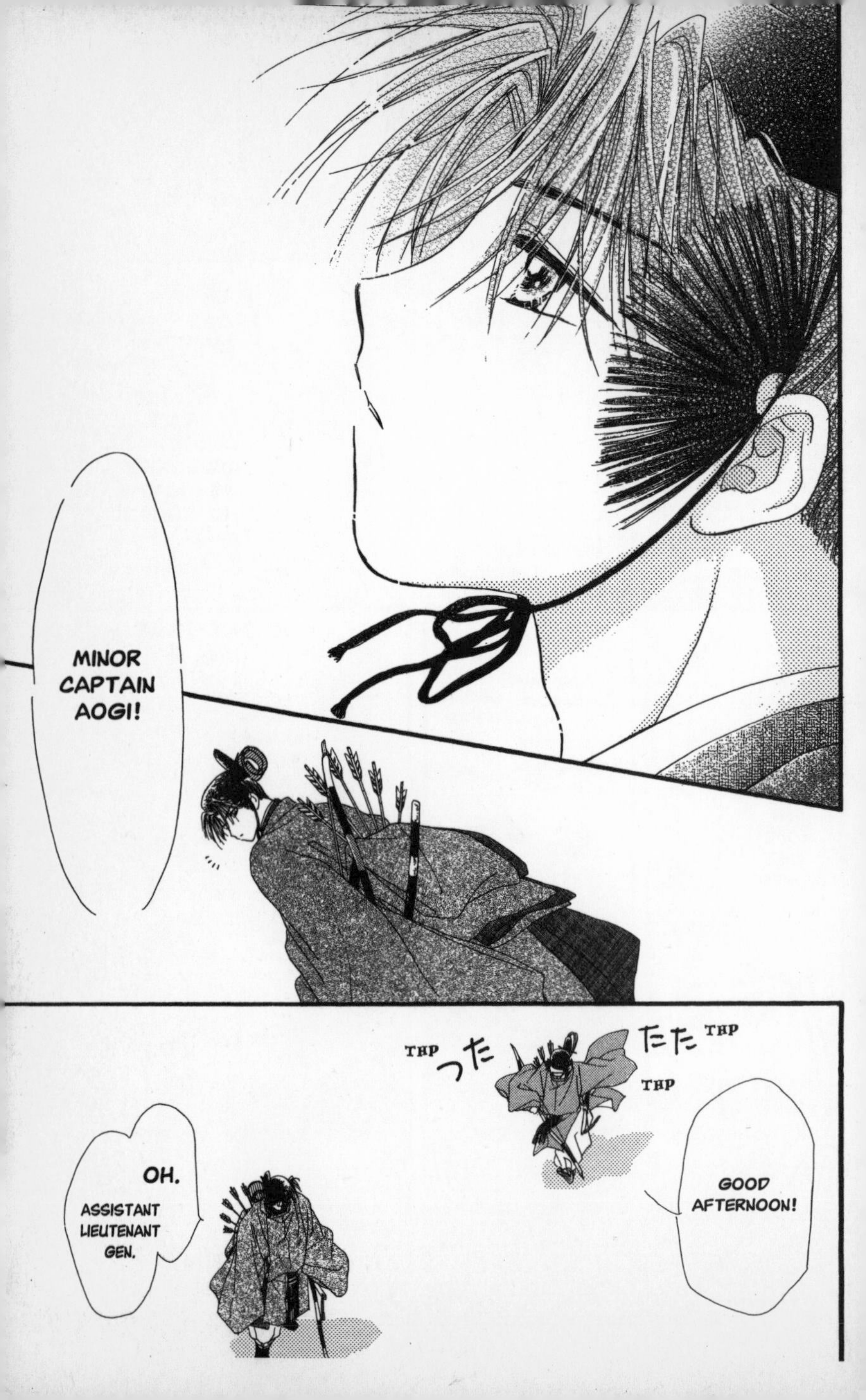
MINOR CAPTAIN AOGI!
たた THP
THP つた
THP
GOOD AFTERNOON!
OH.
ASSISTANT LIEUTENANT GEN.

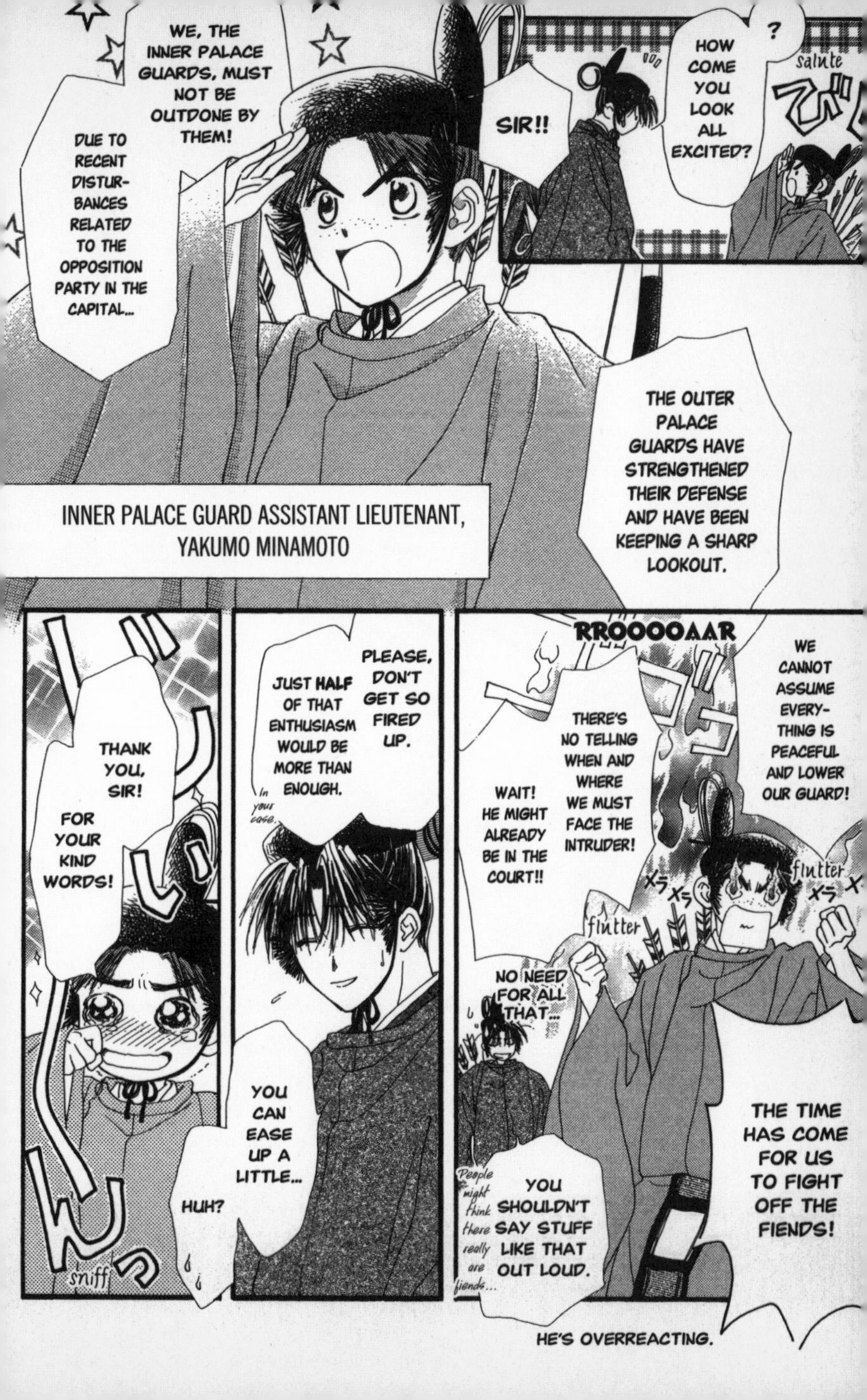

?
HOW COME YOU LOOK ALL EXCITED?
SIR!!
salute
DUE TO RECENT DISTURBANCES RELATED TO THE OPPOSITION PARTY IN THE CAPITAL...
THE OUTER PALACE GUARDS HAVE STRENGTHENED THEIR DEFENSE AND HAVE BEEN KEEPING A SHARP LOOKOUT.
WE, THE INNER PALACE GUARDS, MUST NOT BE OUTDONE BY THEM!
INNER PALACE GUARD ASSISTANT LIEUTENANT, YAKUMO MINAMOTO
RROOOOAAR
WE CANNOT ASSUME EVERYTHING IS PEACEFUL AND LOWER OUR GUARD!
THERE'S NO TELLING WHEN AND WHERE WE MUST FACE THE INTRUDER!
WAIT! HE MIGHT ALREADY BE IN THE COURT!!
flutter
flutter
NO NEED FOR ALL THAT...
THE TIME HAS COME FOR US TO FIGHT OFF THE FIENDS!
YOU SHOULDN'T SAY STUFF LIKE THAT OUT LOUD.
People might think there really are fiends...
HE'S OVERREACTING.
PLEASE, DON'T GET SO FIRED UP.
JUST HALF OF THAT ENTHUSIASM WOULD BE MORE THAN ENOUGH.
In your case.
YOU CAN EASE UP A LITTLE...
HUH?
THANK YOU, SIR!
FOR YOUR KIND WORDS!
sniff

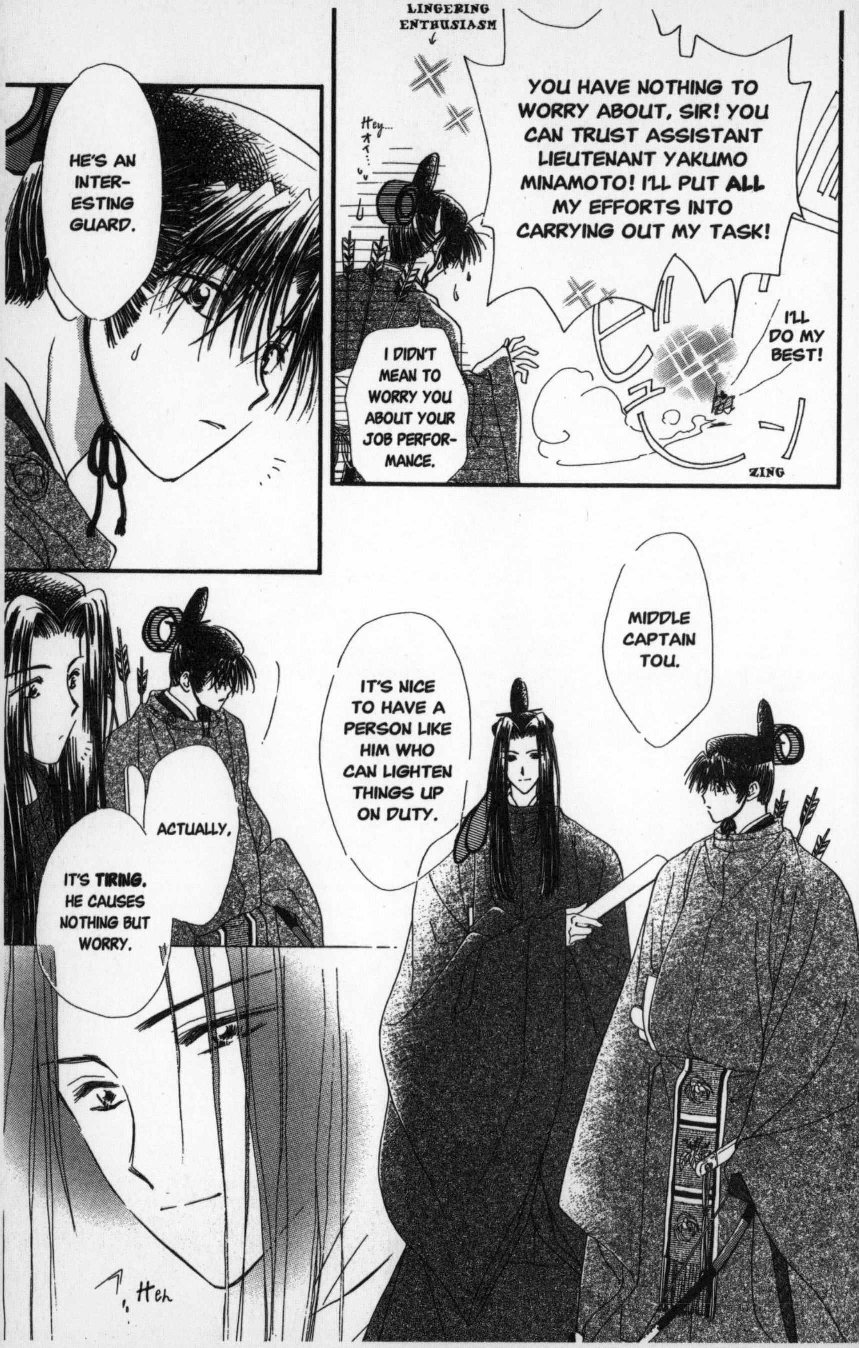

LINGERING ENTHUSIASM
YOU HAVE NOTHING TO WORRY ABOUT, SIR! YOU CAN TRUST ASSISTANT LIEUTENANT YAKUMO MINAMOTO! I'LL PUT ALL MY EFFORTS INTO CARRYING OUT MY TASK!
Hey...
I DIDN'T MEAN TO WORRY YOU ABOUT YOUR JOB PERFORMANCE.
I'LL DO MY BEST!
ZING
HE'S AN INTERESTING GUARD.
MIDDLE CAPTAIN TOU.
IT'S NICE TO HAVE A PERSON LIKE HIM WHO CAN LIGHTEN THINGS UP ON DUTY.
ACTUALLY,
IT'S TIRING. HE CAUSES NOTHING BUT WORRY.
Heh

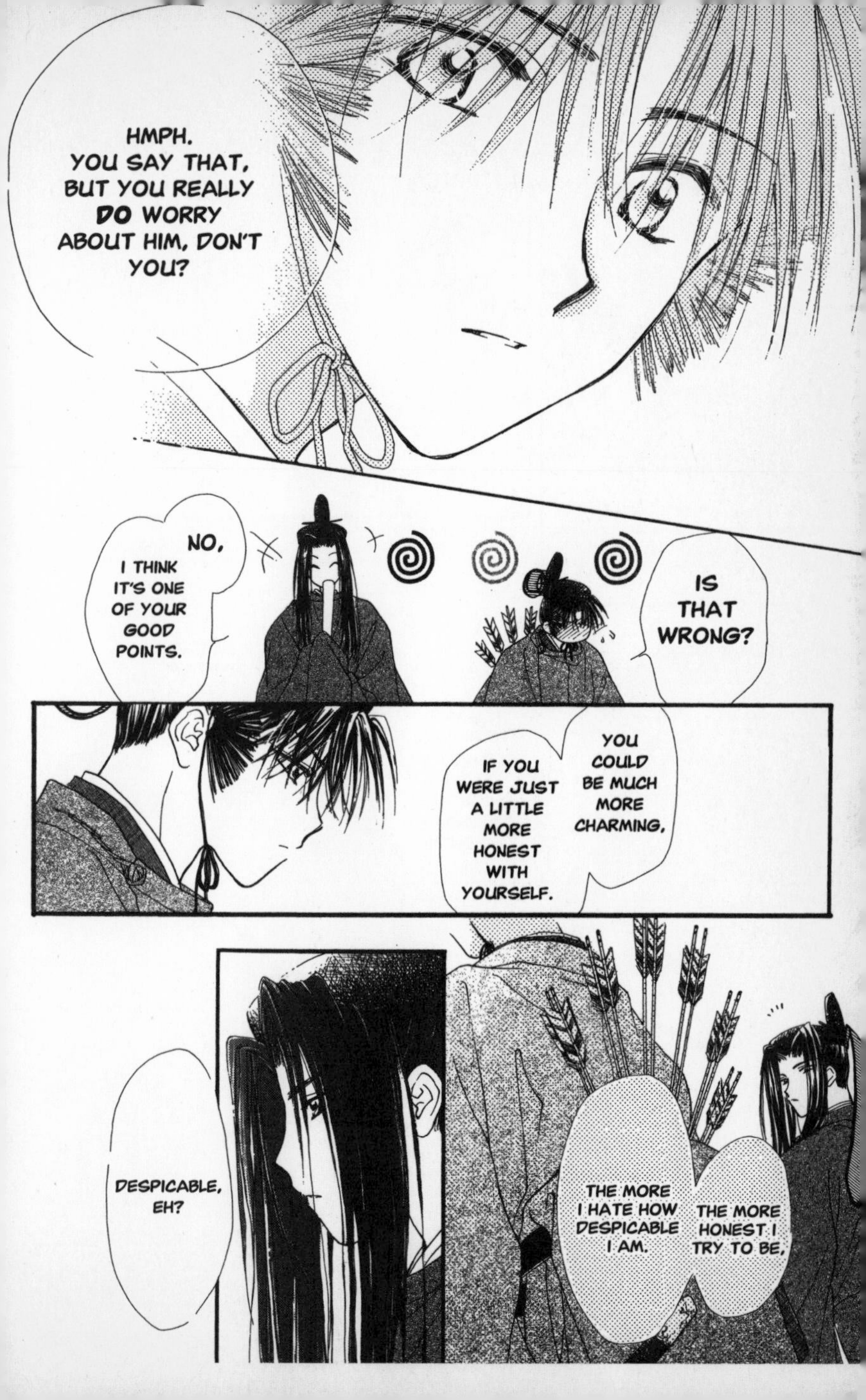
HMPH. YOU SAY THAT, BUT YOU REALLY DO WORRY ABOUT HIM, DON'T YOU?
IS THAT WRONG?
NO, I THINK IT'S ONE OF YOUR GOOD POINTS.
YOU COULD BE MUCH MORE CHARMING,
IF YOU WERE JUST A LITTLE MORE HONEST WITH YOURSELF.
THE MORE HONEST I TRY TO BE,
THE MORE I HATE HOW DESPICABLE I AM.
DESPICABLE, EH?

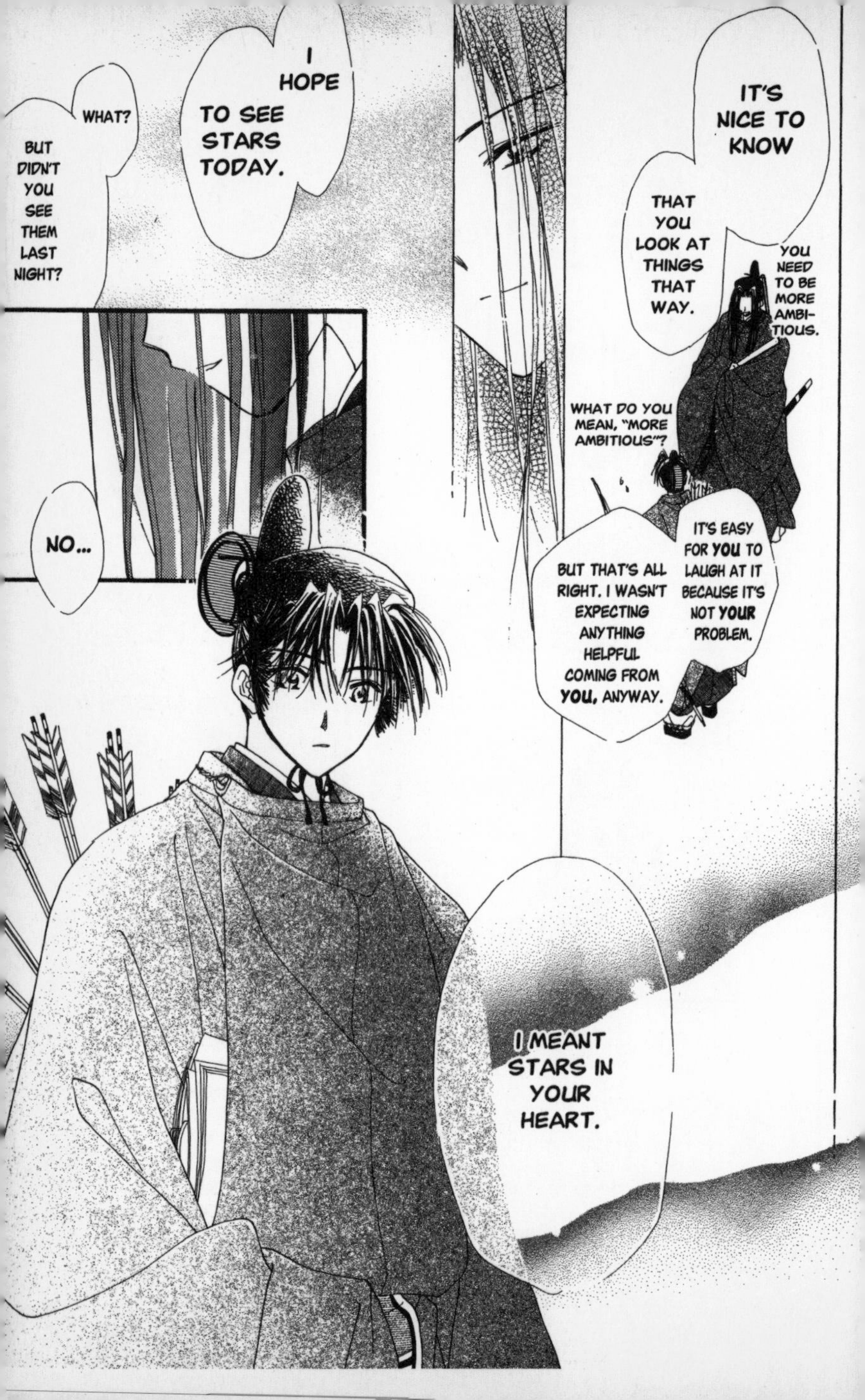
IT'S NICE TO KNOW
THAT YOU LOOK AT THINGS THAT WAY.
YOU NEED TO BE MORE AMBITIOUS.
WHAT DO YOU MEAN, "MORE AMBITIOUS"?
IT'S EASY FOR YOU TO LAUGH AT IT BECAUSE IT'S NOT YOUR PROBLEM.
BUT THAT'S ALL RIGHT. I WASN'T EXPECTING ANYTHING HELPFUL COMING FROM YOU, ANYWAY.
I HOPE TO SEE STARS TODAY.
WHAT?
BUT DIDN'T YOU SEE THEM LAST NIGHT?
NO...
I MEANT STARS IN YOUR HEART.

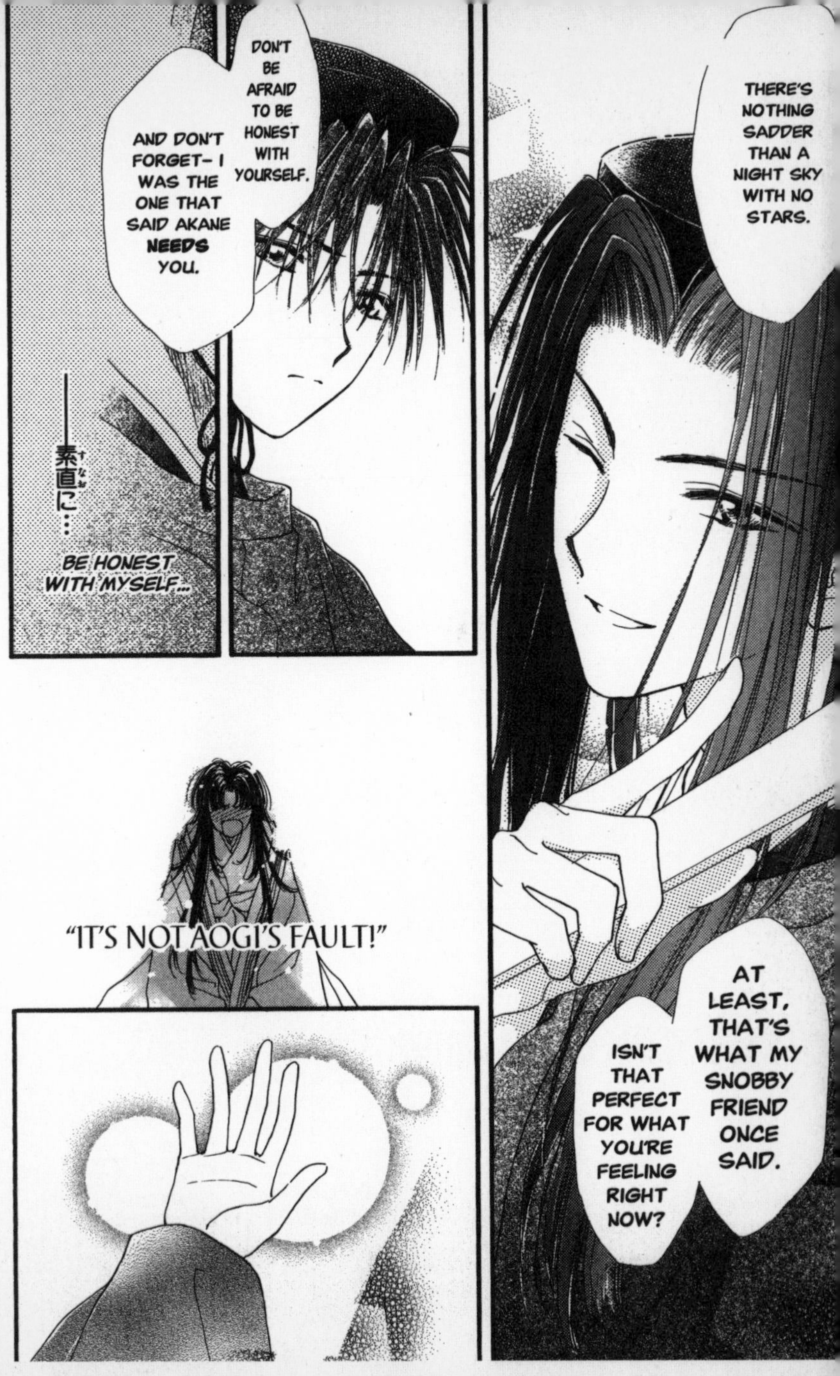
THERE'S NOTHING SADDER THAN A NIGHT SKY WITH NO STARS.
AT LEAST, THAT'S WHAT MY SNOBBY FRIEND ONCE SAID.
ISN'T THAT PERFECT FOR WHAT YOU'RE FEELING RIGHT NOW?
DON'T BE AFRAID TO BE HONEST WITH YOURSELF.
AND DON'T FORGET– I WAS THE ONE THAT SAID AKANE NEEDS YOU.
――素直に…
BE HONEST WITH MYSELF...
"IT'S NOT AOGI'S FAULT!"

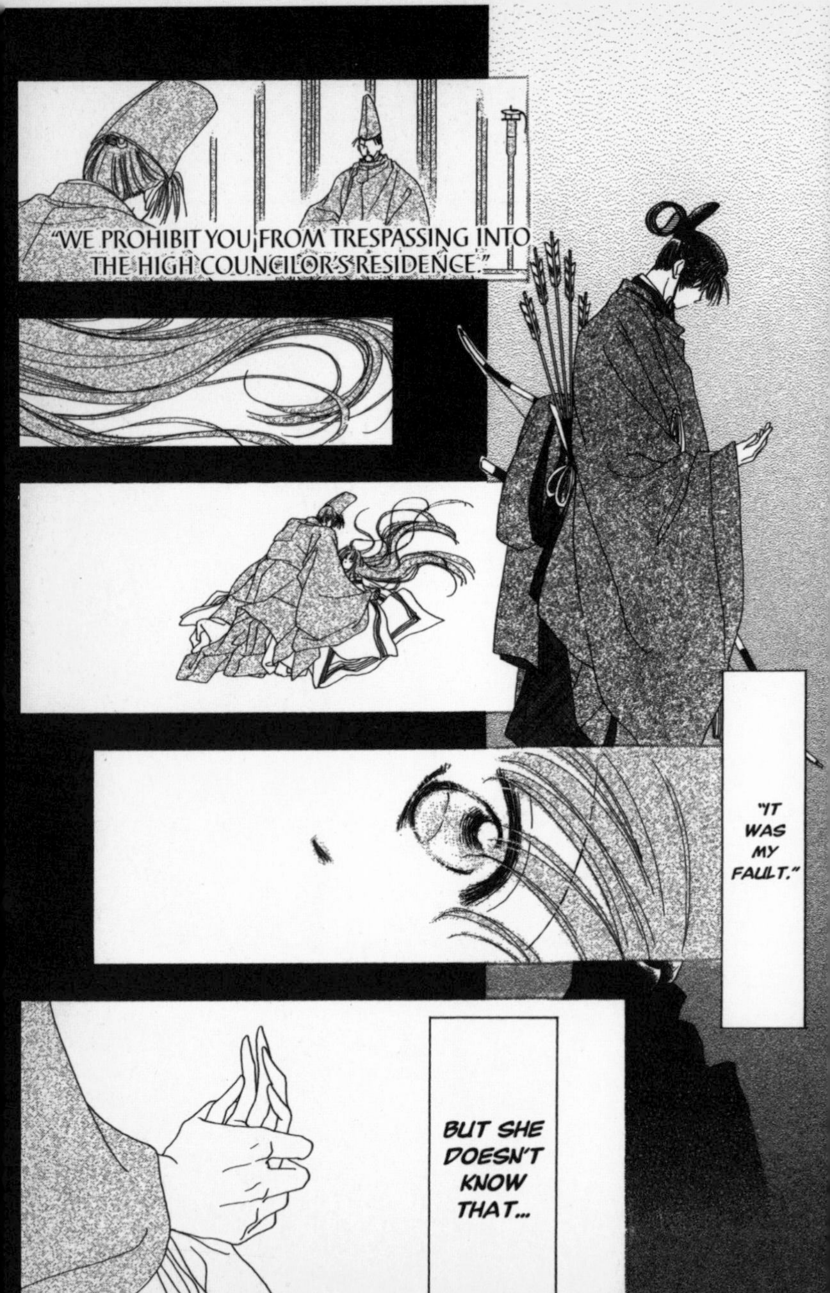
"IT WAS MY FAULT."
"WE PROHIBIT YOU FROM TRESPASSING INTO THE HIGH COUNCILOR'S RESIDENCE."
BUT SHE DOESN'T KNOW THAT...

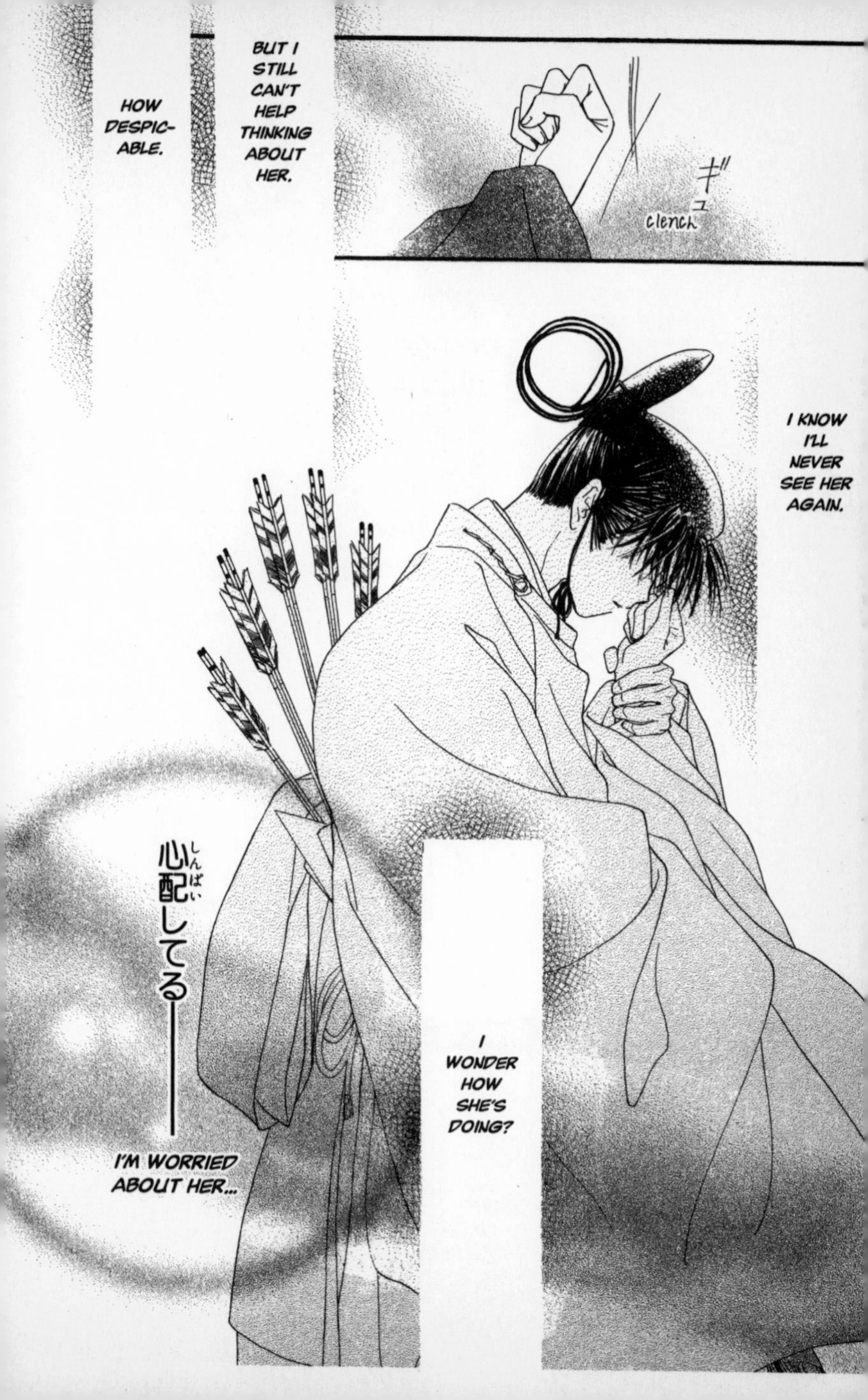
ギュ
clench
BUT I STILL CAN'T HELP THINKING ABOUT HER.
HOW DESPICABLE.
I KNOW I'LL NEVER SEE HER AGAIN.
I WONDER HOW SHE'S DOING?
心配してる——
I'M WORRIED ABOUT HER...

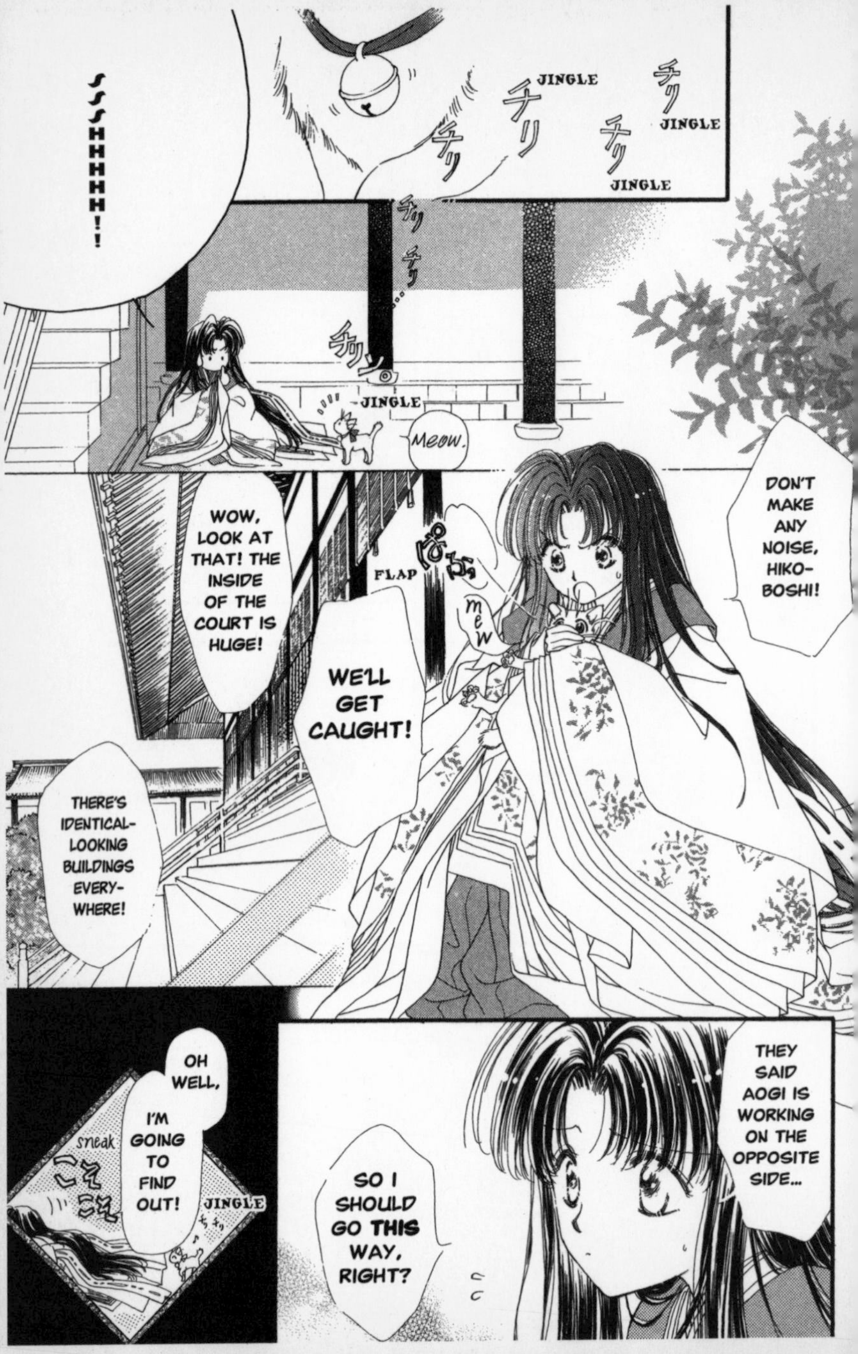

チリ
JINGLE
チリ
JINGLE
チリ
JINGLE
SSSHHHHHH!!
チリ
チリ...
チリ
JINGLE
Meow.
DON'T MAKE ANY NOISE, HIKO-BOSHI!
FLAP
mew
WE'LL GET CAUGHT!
WOW, LOOK AT THAT! THE INSIDE OF THE COURT IS HUGE!
THERE'S IDENTICAL-LOOKING BUILDINGS EVERY-WHERE!
THEY SAID AOGI IS WORKING ON THE OPPOSITE SIDE...
SO I SHOULD GO THIS WAY, RIGHT?
OH WELL,
I'M GOING TO FIND OUT!
sneak
こそこそ
JINGLE

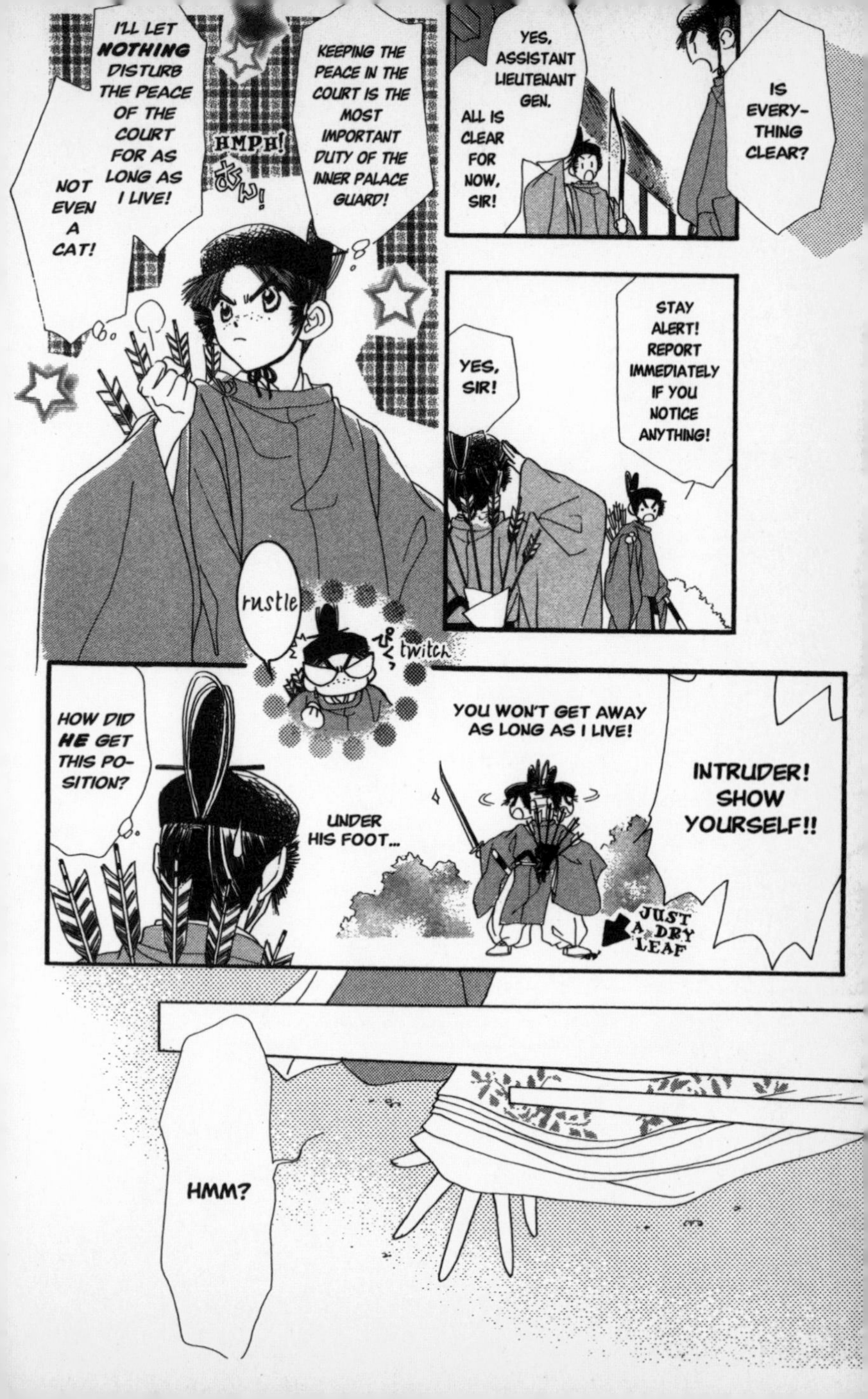

IS EVERYTHING CLEAR?
YES, ASSISTANT LIEUTENANT GEN.
ALL IS CLEAR FOR NOW, SIR!
STAY ALERT! REPORT IMMEDIATELY IF YOU NOTICE ANYTHING!
YES, SIR!
KEEPING THE PEACE IN THE COURT IS THE MOST IMPORTANT DUTY OF THE INNER PALACE GUARD!
HMPH!
あん!
I'LL LET NOTHING DISTURB THE PEACE OF THE COURT FOR AS LONG AS I LIVE!
NOT EVEN A CAT!
rustle
ぴく
twitch
INTRUDER! SHOW YOURSELF!!
YOU WON'T GET AWAY AS LONG AS I LIVE!
UNDER HIS FOOT...
HOW DID HE GET THIS POSITION?
JUST A DRY LEAF
HMM?

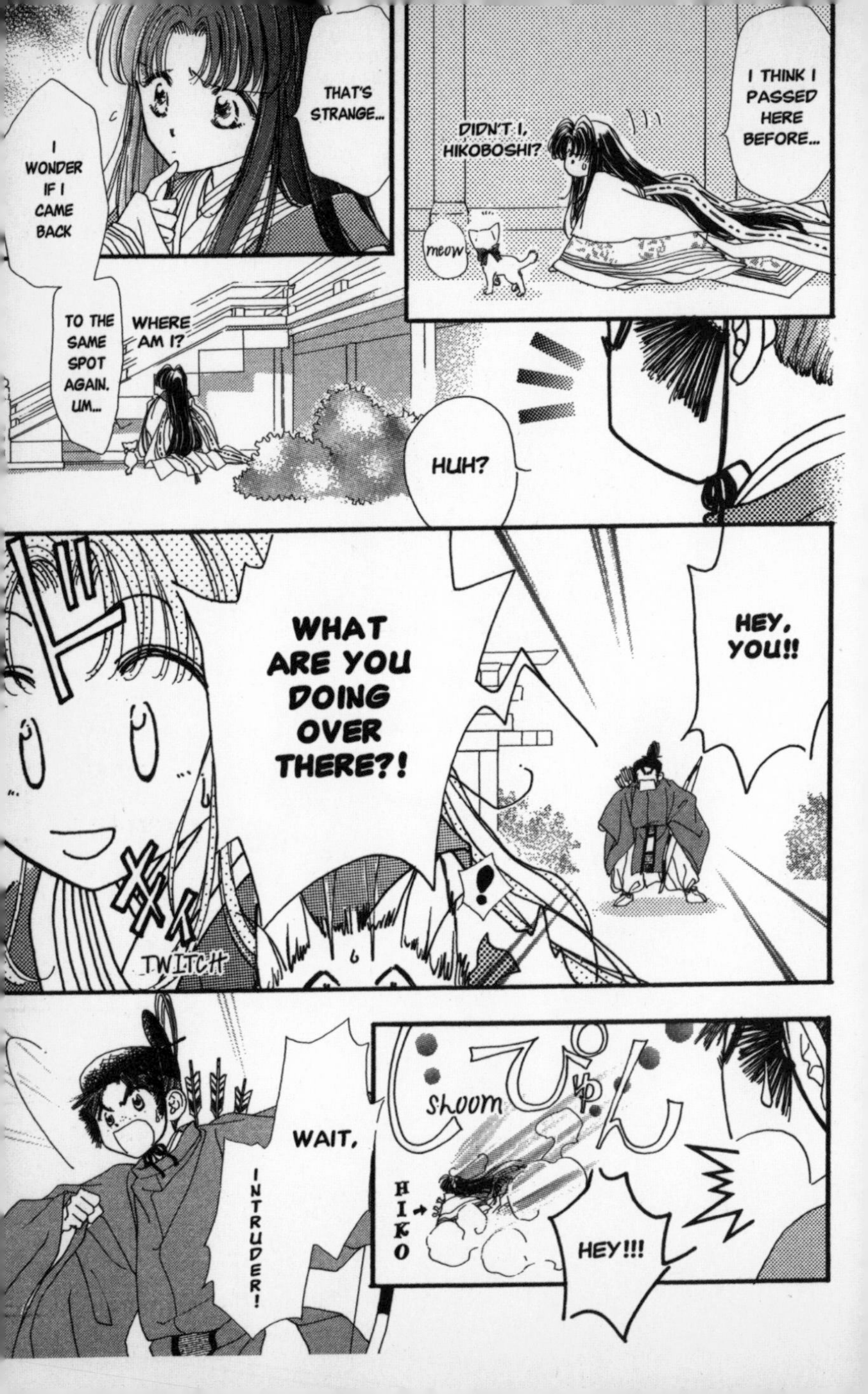
I THINK I PASSED HERE BEFORE...
DIDN'T I, HIKOBOSHI?
meow
THAT'S STRANGE...
I WONDER IF I CAME BACK
TO THE SAME SPOT AGAIN. UM...
WHERE AM I?
HUH?
HEY, YOU!!
WHAT ARE YOU DOING OVER THERE?!
TWITCH
shoom
HIKO
HEY!!!
WAIT,
INTRUDER!

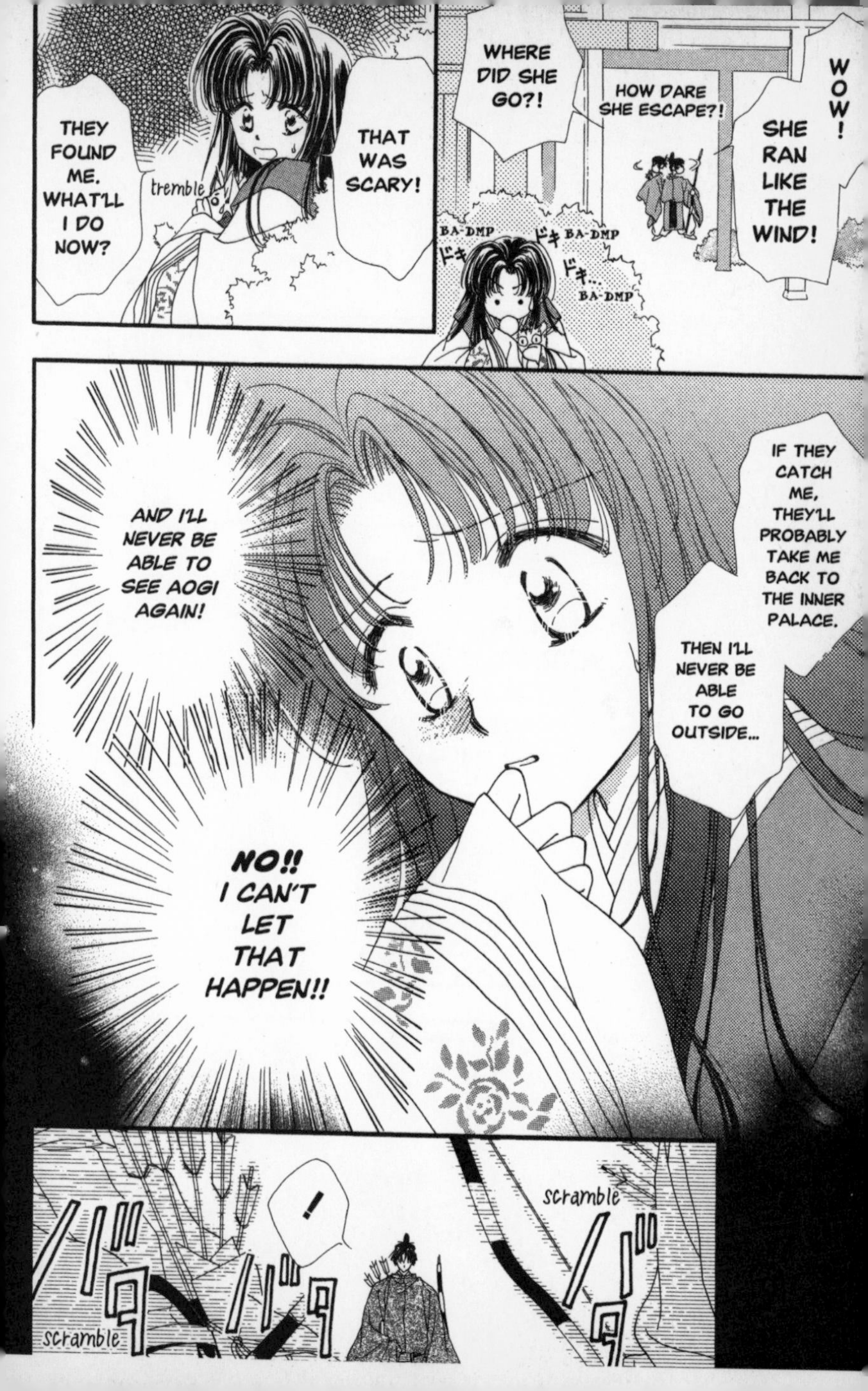
WOW! SHE RAN LIKE THE WIND!
WHERE DID SHE GO?!
HOW DARE SHE ESCAPE?!
ドキ BA-DMP
ドキ BA-DMP
ドキ... BA-DMP
THAT WAS SCARY!
tremble
THEY FOUND ME. WHAT'LL I DO NOW?
IF THEY CATCH ME, THEY'LL PROBABLY TAKE ME BACK TO THE INNER PALACE.
THEN I'LL NEVER BE ABLE TO GO OUTSIDE...
AND I'LL NEVER BE ABLE TO SEE AOGI AGAIN!
NO!! I CAN'T LET THAT HAPPEN!!
scramble
!
scramble

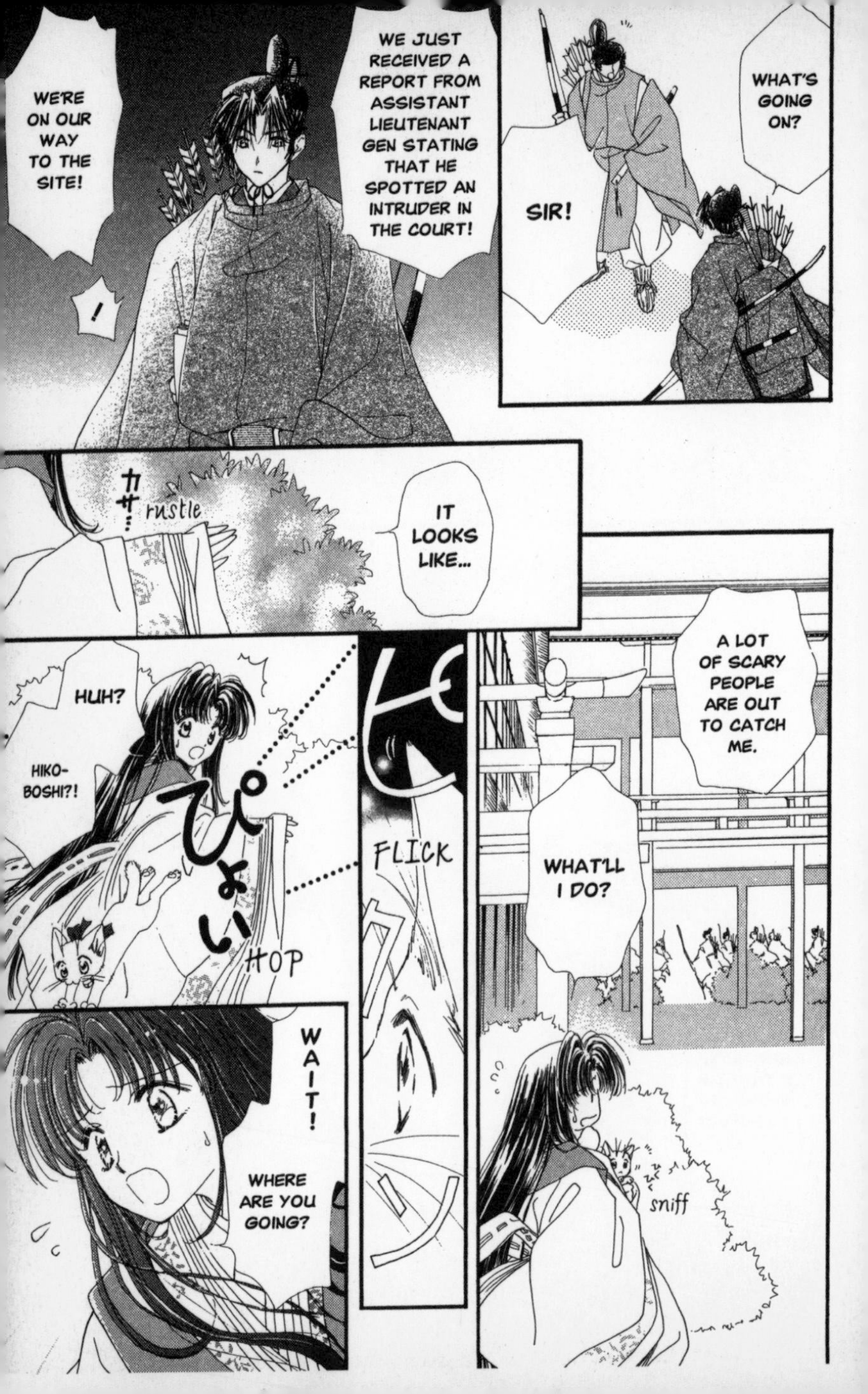
WHAT'S GOING ON?
SIR!
WE JUST RECEIVED A REPORT FROM ASSISTANT LIEUTENANT GEN STATING THAT HE SPOTTED AN INTRUDER IN THE COURT!
WE'RE ON OUR WAY TO THE SITE!
!
IT LOOKS LIKE...
カサ… rustle
A LOT OF SCARY PEOPLE ARE OUT TO CATCH ME.
WHAT'LL I DO?
sniff
FLICK
HUH?
HIKO-BOSHI?!
ぴょい HOP
WAIT!
WHERE ARE YOU GOING?

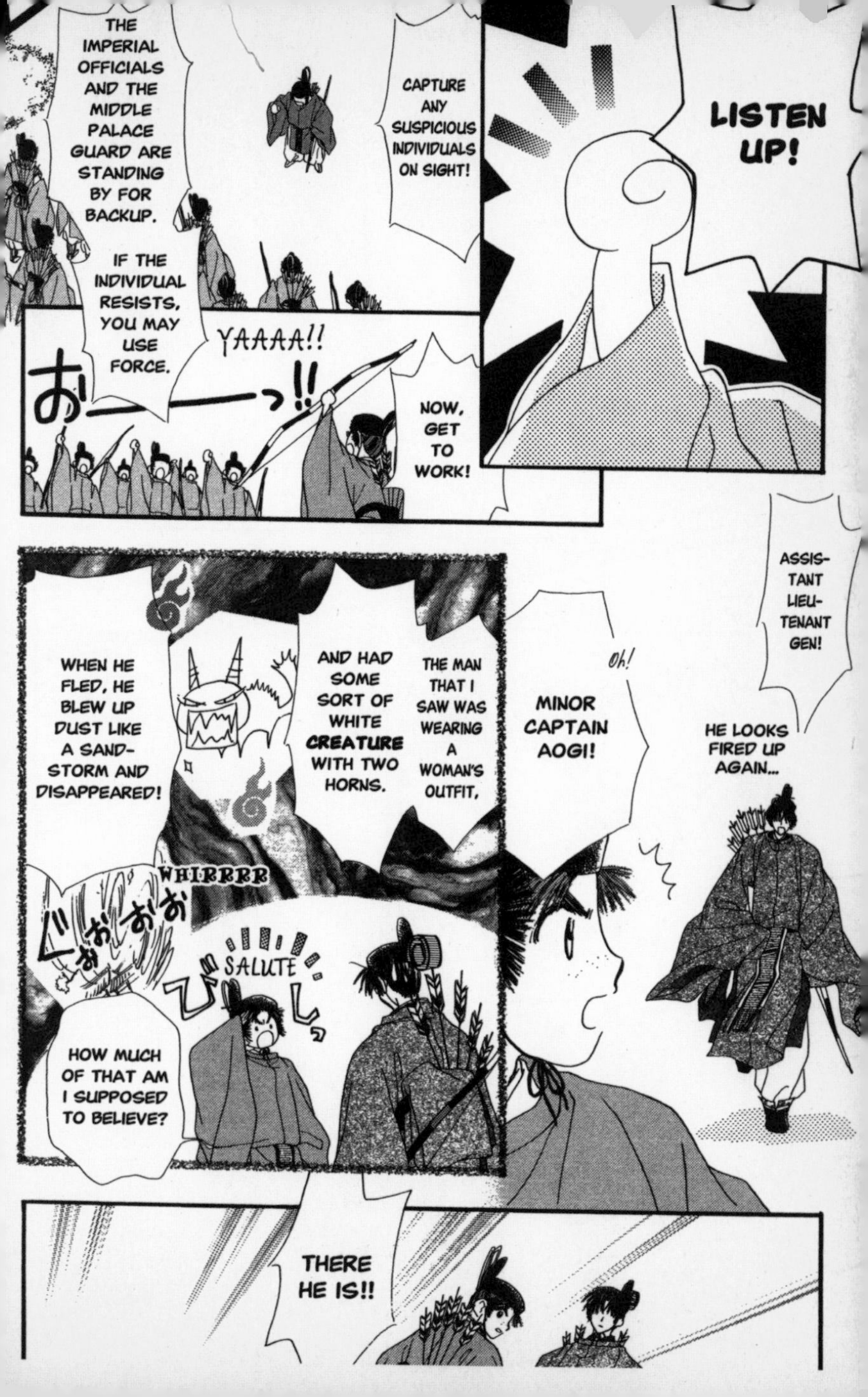
LISTEN UP!
CAPTURE ANY SUSPICIOUS INDIVIDUALS ON SIGHT!
THE IMPERIAL OFFICIALS AND THE MIDDLE PALACE GUARD ARE STANDING BY FOR BACKUP.
IF THE INDIVIDUAL RESISTS, YOU MAY USE FORCE.
NOW, GET TO WORK!
YAAAA!!
おーーーっ!!
ASSISTANT LIEUTENANT GEN!
HE LOOKS FIRED UP AGAIN...
Oh!
MINOR CAPTAIN AOGI!
THE MAN THAT I SAW WAS WEARING A WOMAN'S OUTFIT,
AND HAD SOME SORT OF WHITE **CREATURE** WITH TWO HORNS.
WHEN HE FLED, HE BLEW UP DUST LIKE A SANDSTORM AND DISAPPEARED!
WHIRRRR
ぐおおおお
SALUTE
びしっ
HOW MUCH OF THAT AM I SUPPOSED TO BELIEVE?
THERE HE IS!!

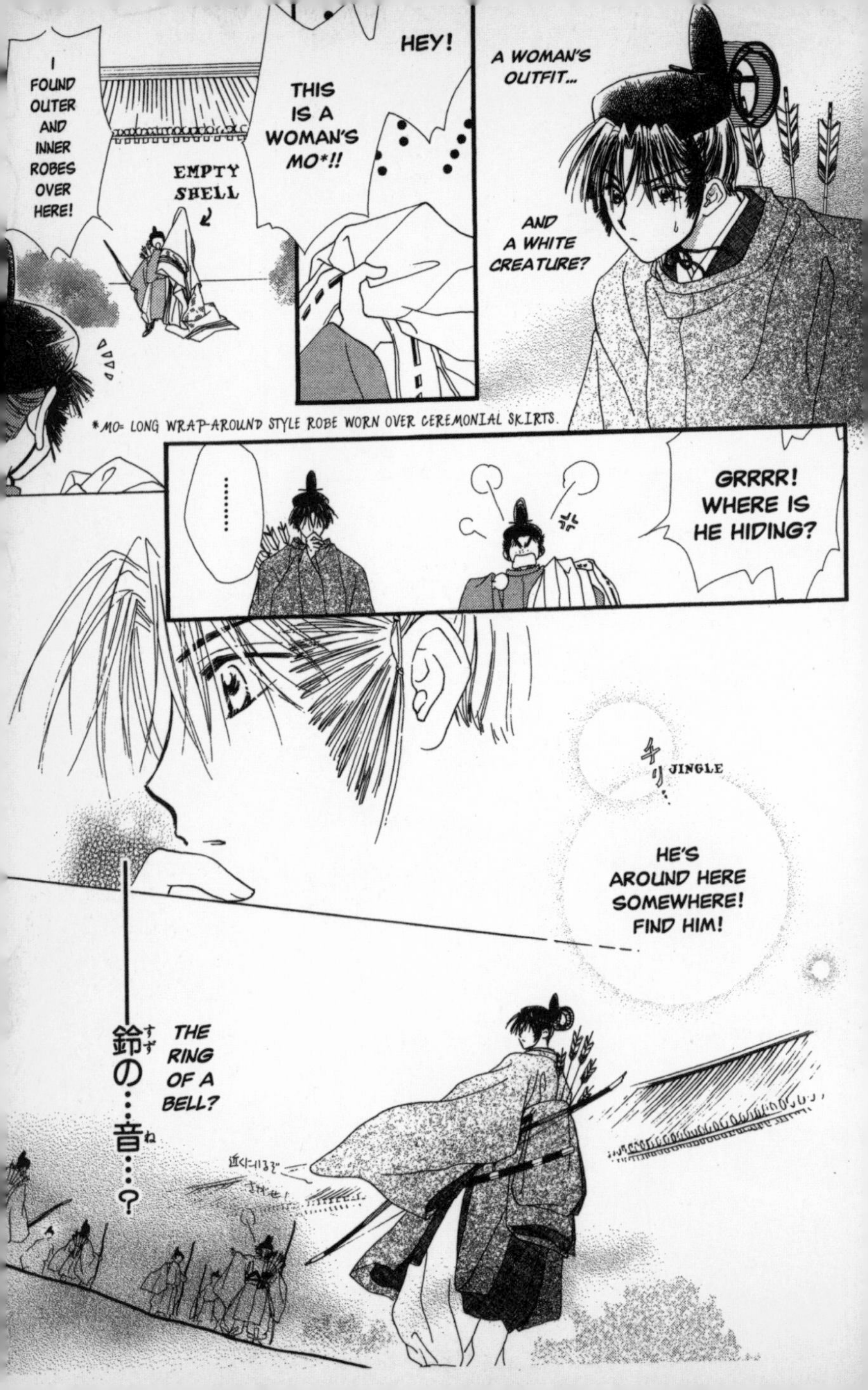
A WOMAN'S OUTFIT...
AND A WHITE CREATURE?
HEY!
THIS IS A WOMAN'S MO*!!
I FOUND OUTER AND INNER ROBES OVER HERE!
EMPTY SHELL
*MO= LONG WRAP-AROUND STYLE ROBE WORN OVER CEREMONIAL SKIRTS.
GRRRR! WHERE IS HE HIDING?
....
チリ
JINGLE
HE'S AROUND HERE SOMEWHERE! FIND HIM!
鈴の…音…?
THE RING OF A BELL?

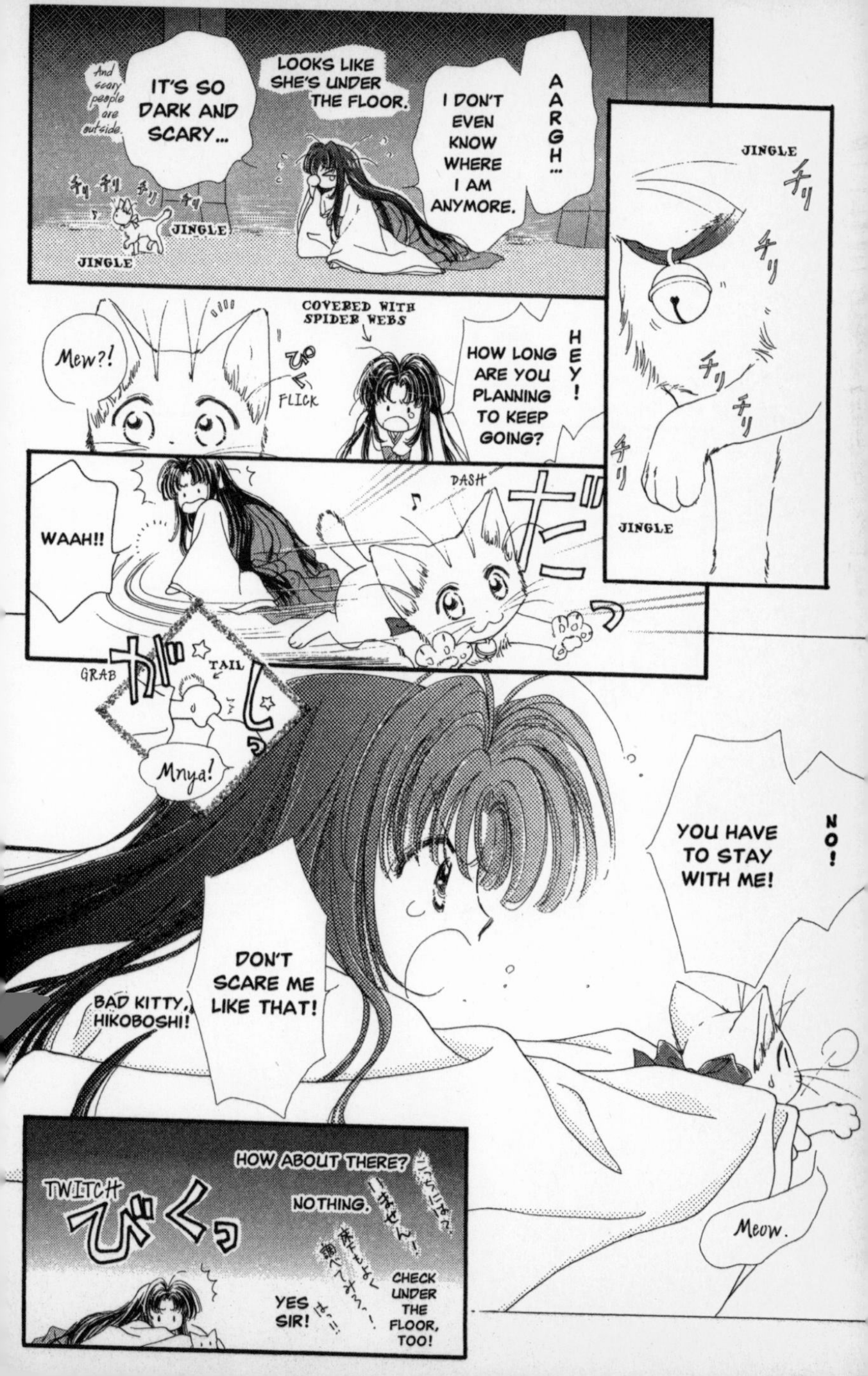
AARGH...
I DON'T EVEN KNOW WHERE I AM ANYMORE.
LOOKS LIKE SHE'S UNDER THE FLOOR.
IT'S SO DARK AND SCARY...
And scary people are outside.
チリ チリ チリ チリ
JINGLE
JINGLE
JINGLE
チリ チリ チリ チリ チリ
JINGLE
HEY!
HOW LONG ARE YOU PLANNING TO KEEP GOING?
COVERED WITH SPIDER WEBS
FLICK
Mew?!
DASH
WAAH!!
NO!
YOU HAVE TO STAY WITH ME!
Meow.
DON'T SCARE ME LIKE THAT!
BAD KITTY, HIKOBOSHI!
TAIL
GRAB
がしっ
Mnya!
CHECK UNDER THE FLOOR, TOO!
YES SIR!
NOTHING.
HOW ABOUT THERE?
TWITCH
びくっ

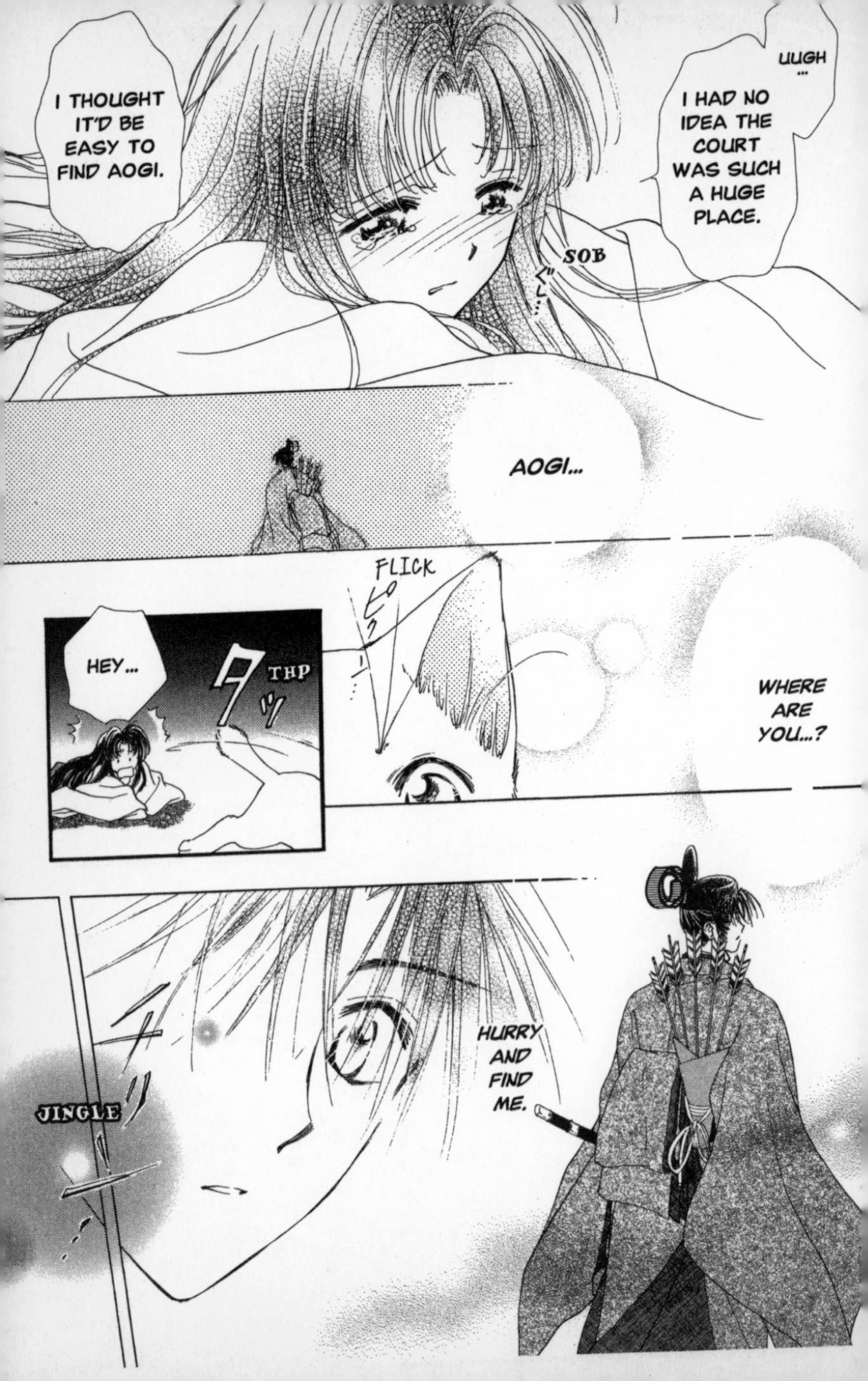
UUGH ...
I HAD NO IDEA THE COURT WAS SUCH A HUGE PLACE.
SOB
I THOUGHT IT'D BE EASY TO FIND AOGI.
AOGI...
WHERE ARE YOU...?
FLICK
HEY...
THP
HURRY AND FIND ME.
JINGLE

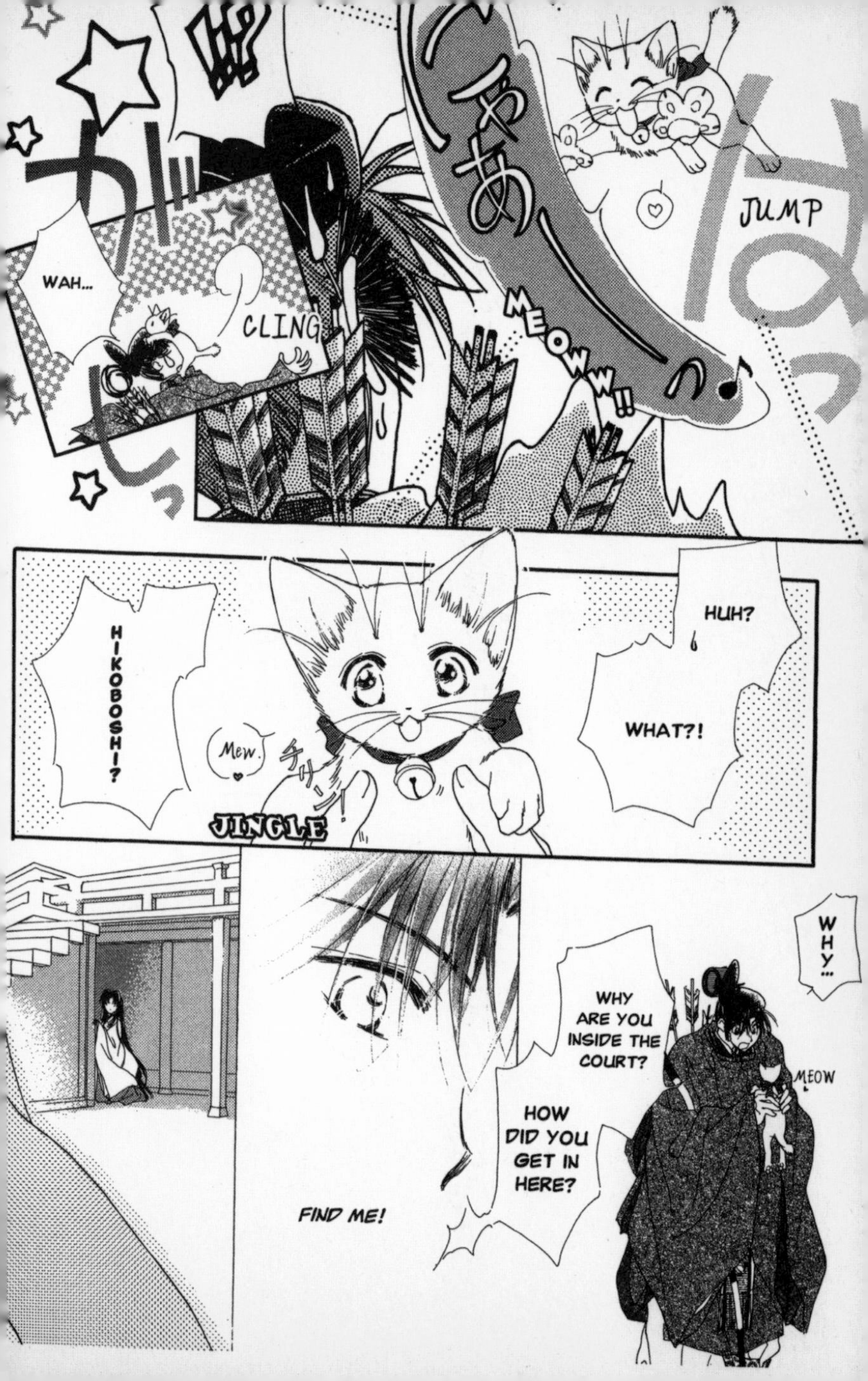
はっ
JUMP
にゃあーん♪
MEOWWW!!
!!?
わしっ
WAH...
CLING
HUH?
WHAT?!
Mew.
チリーン
JINGLE
HIKOBOSHI?
WHY...
MEOW
WHY ARE YOU INSIDE THE COURT?
HOW DID YOU GET IN HERE?
FIND ME!

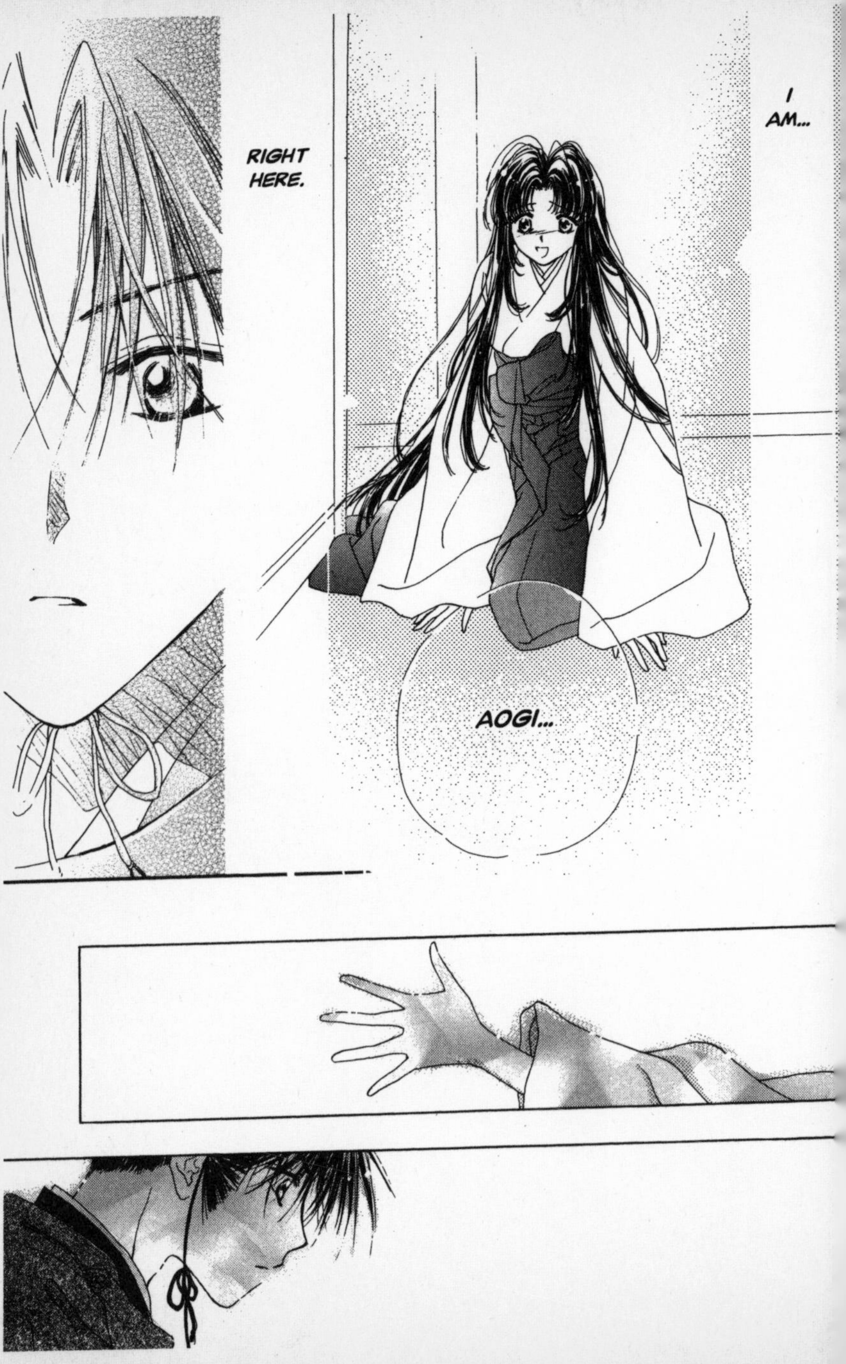
I AM...
RIGHT HERE.
AOGI...

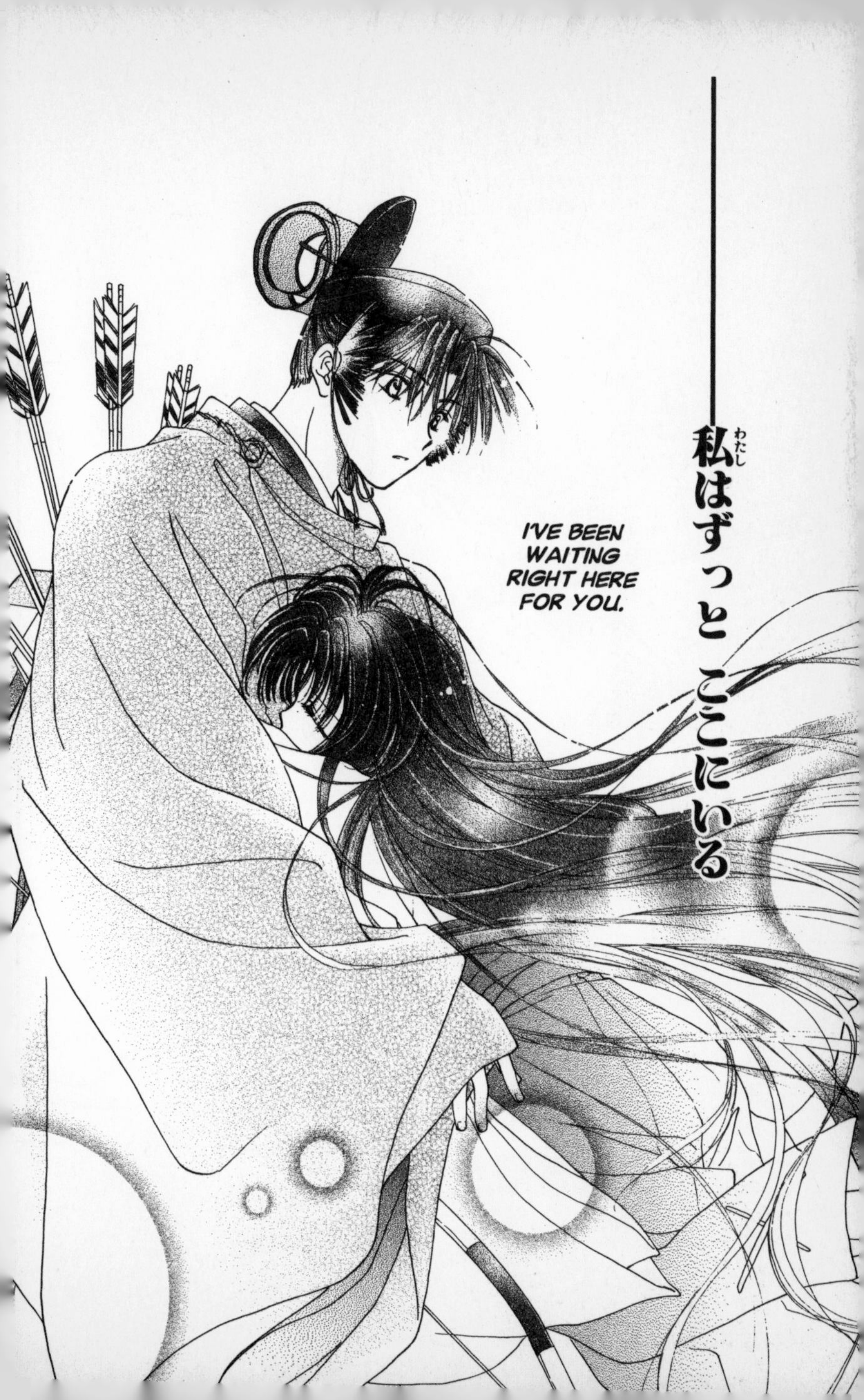
私はずっと　ここにいる
I'VE BEEN WAITING RIGHT HERE FOR YOU.

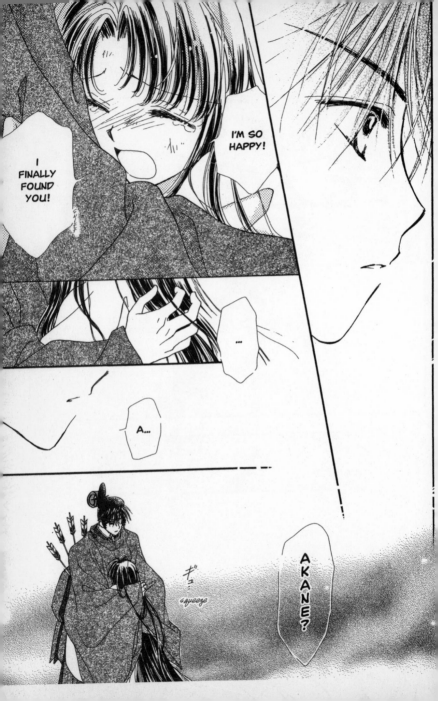

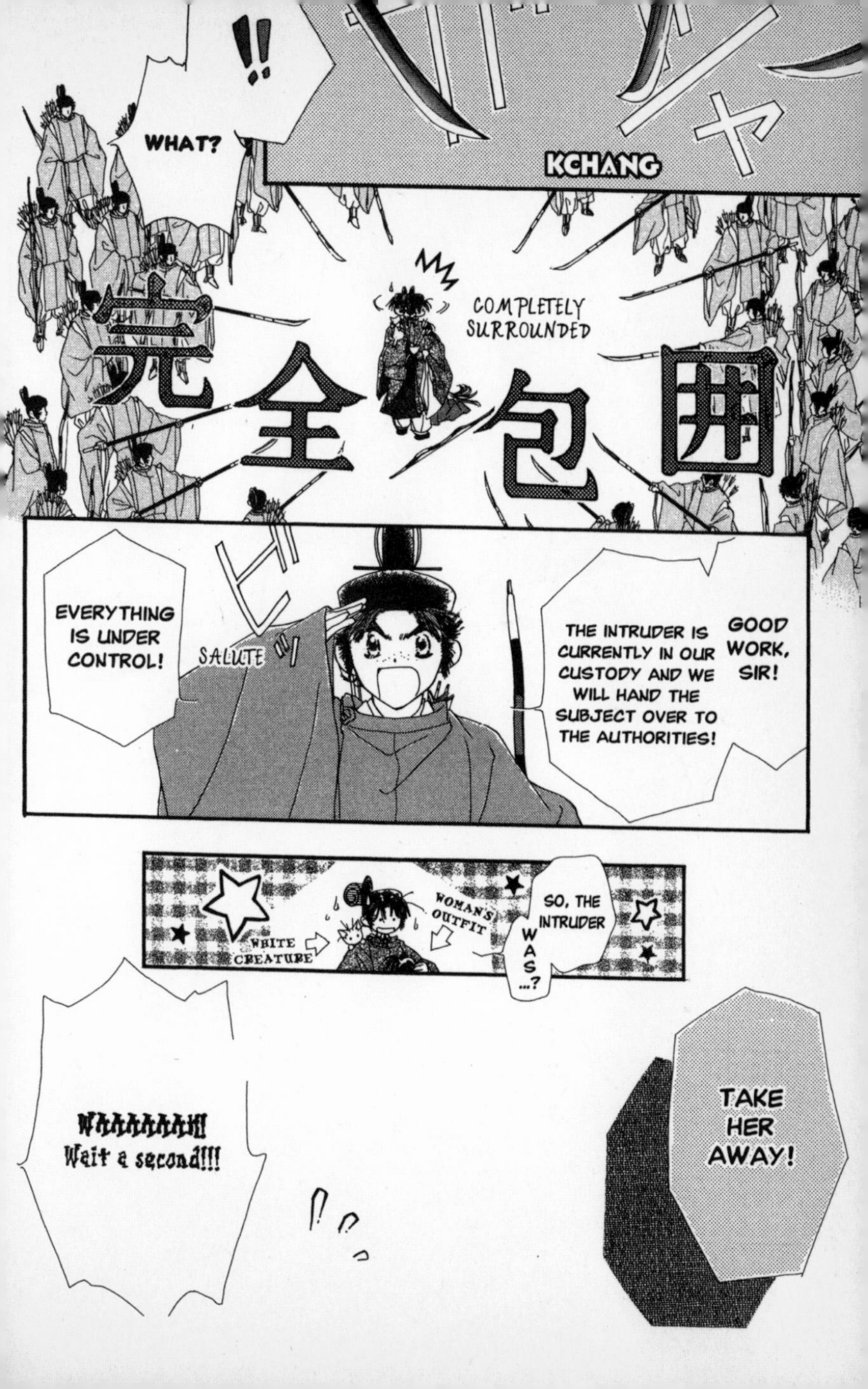
KCHANG
!!
WHAT?
完全包囲
COMPLETELY SURROUNDED
GOOD WORK, SIR!
THE INTRUDER IS CURRENTLY IN OUR CUSTODY AND WE WILL HAND THE SUBJECT OVER TO THE AUTHORITIES!
EVERYTHING IS UNDER CONTROL!
SALUTE
SO, THE INTRUDER WAS ...?
WOMAN'S OUTFIT
WHITE CREATURE
TAKE HER AWAY!
WAAAAAAH! Wait a second!!!

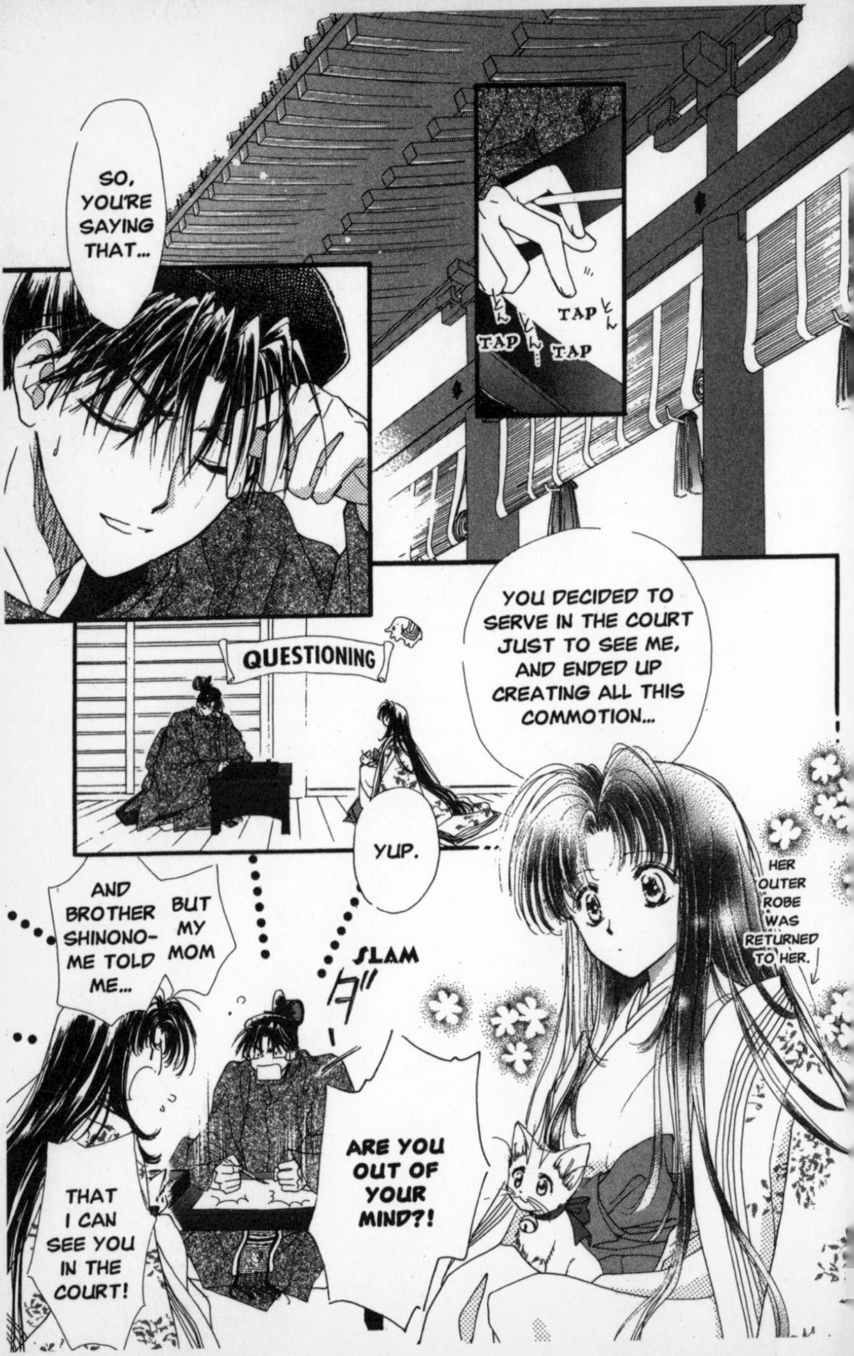

TAP
とん
TAP
とん
TAP
とん
SO, YOU'RE SAYING THAT...
YOU DECIDED TO SERVE IN THE COURT JUST TO SEE ME, AND ENDED UP CREATING ALL THIS COMMOTION...
HER OUTER ROBE WAS RETURNED TO HER.
QUESTIONING
YUP.
SLAM
ダ
ARE YOU OUT OF YOUR MIND?!
BUT MY MOM
AND BROTHER SHINONOME TOLD ME...
THAT I CAN SEE YOU IN THE COURT!

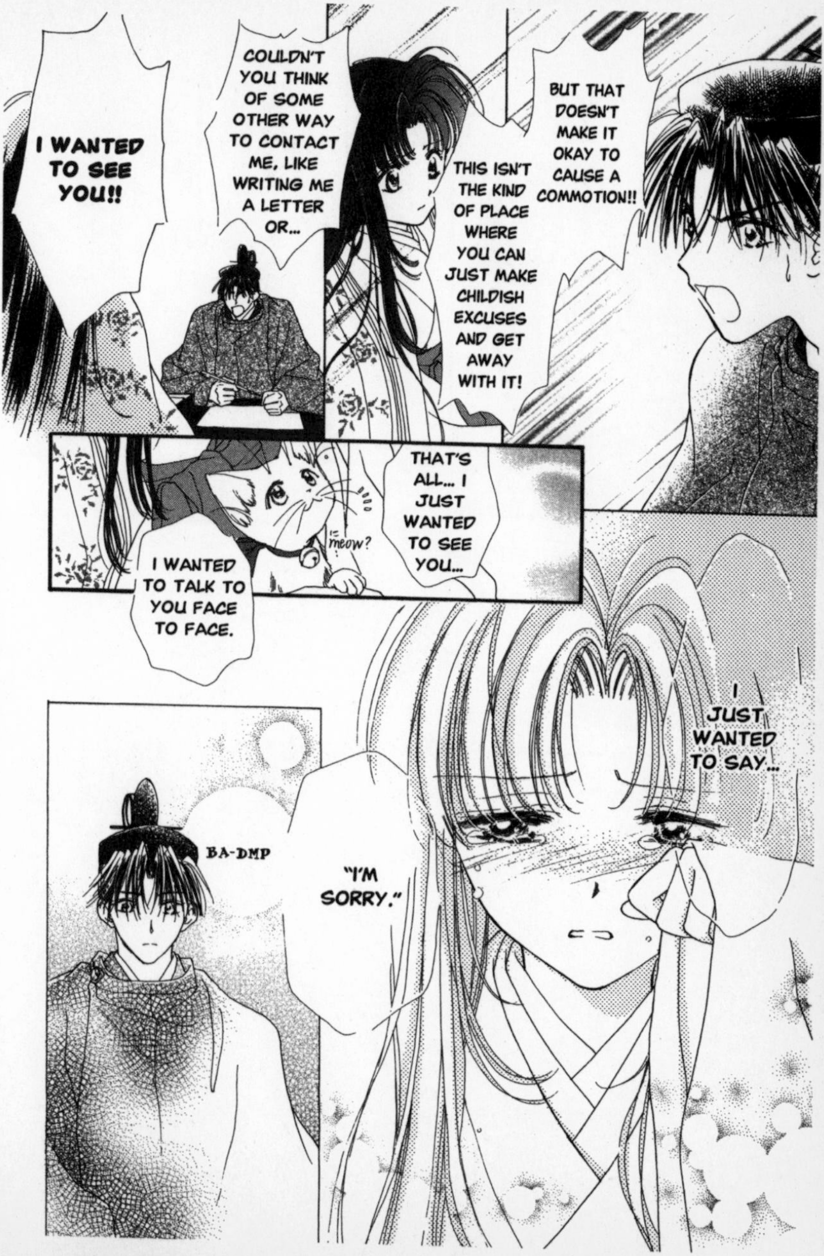
BUT THAT DOESN'T MAKE IT OKAY TO CAUSE A COMMOTION!!
THIS ISN'T THE KIND OF PLACE WHERE YOU CAN JUST MAKE CHILDISH EXCUSES AND GET AWAY WITH IT!
COULDN'T YOU THINK OF SOME OTHER WAY TO CONTACT ME, LIKE WRITING ME A LETTER OR...
I WANTED TO SEE YOU!!
THAT'S ALL... I JUST WANTED TO SEE YOU...
meow?
I WANTED TO TALK TO YOU FACE TO FACE.
I JUST WANTED TO SAY...
"I'M SORRY."
BA-DMP

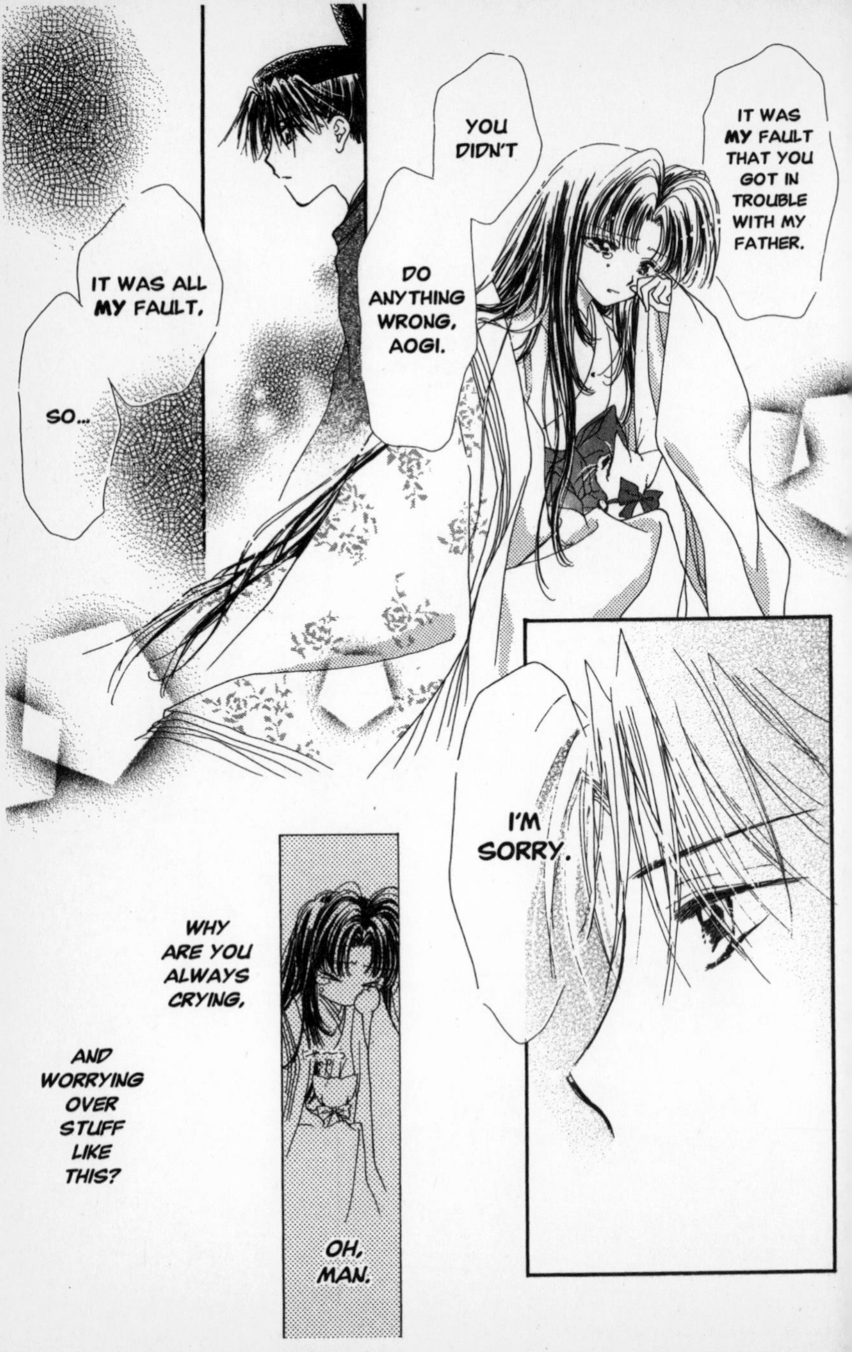
IT WAS MY FAULT THAT YOU GOT IN TROUBLE WITH MY FATHER.
YOU DIDN'T
DO ANYTHING WRONG, AOGI.
IT WAS ALL MY FAULT,
SO...
I'M SORRY.
WHY ARE YOU ALWAYS CRYING,
AND WORRYING OVER STUFF LIKE THIS?
OH, MAN.

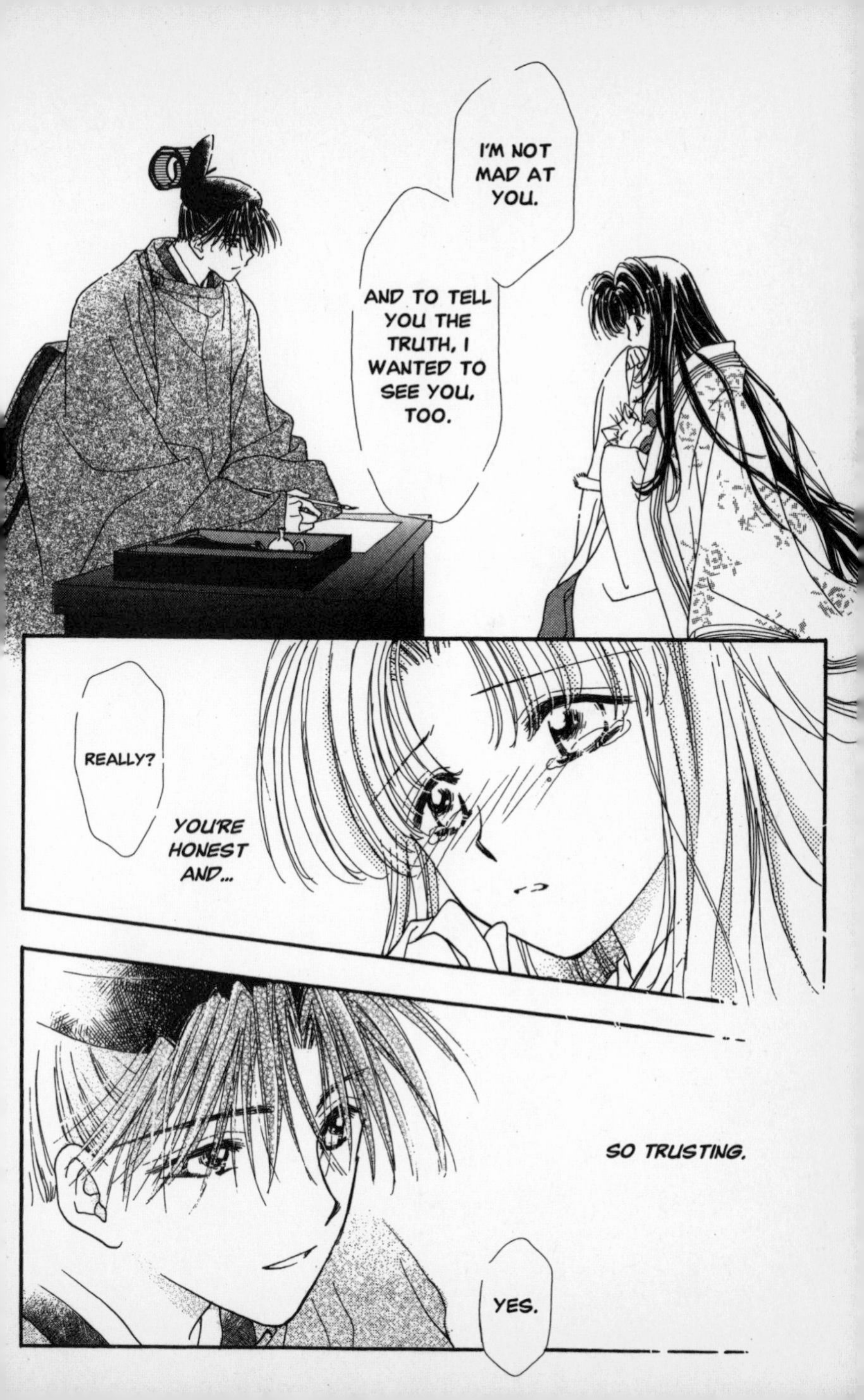
I'M NOT MAD AT YOU.
AND TO TELL YOU THE TRUTH, I WANTED TO SEE YOU, TOO.
REALLY?
YOU'RE HONEST AND...
SO TRUSTING.
YES.

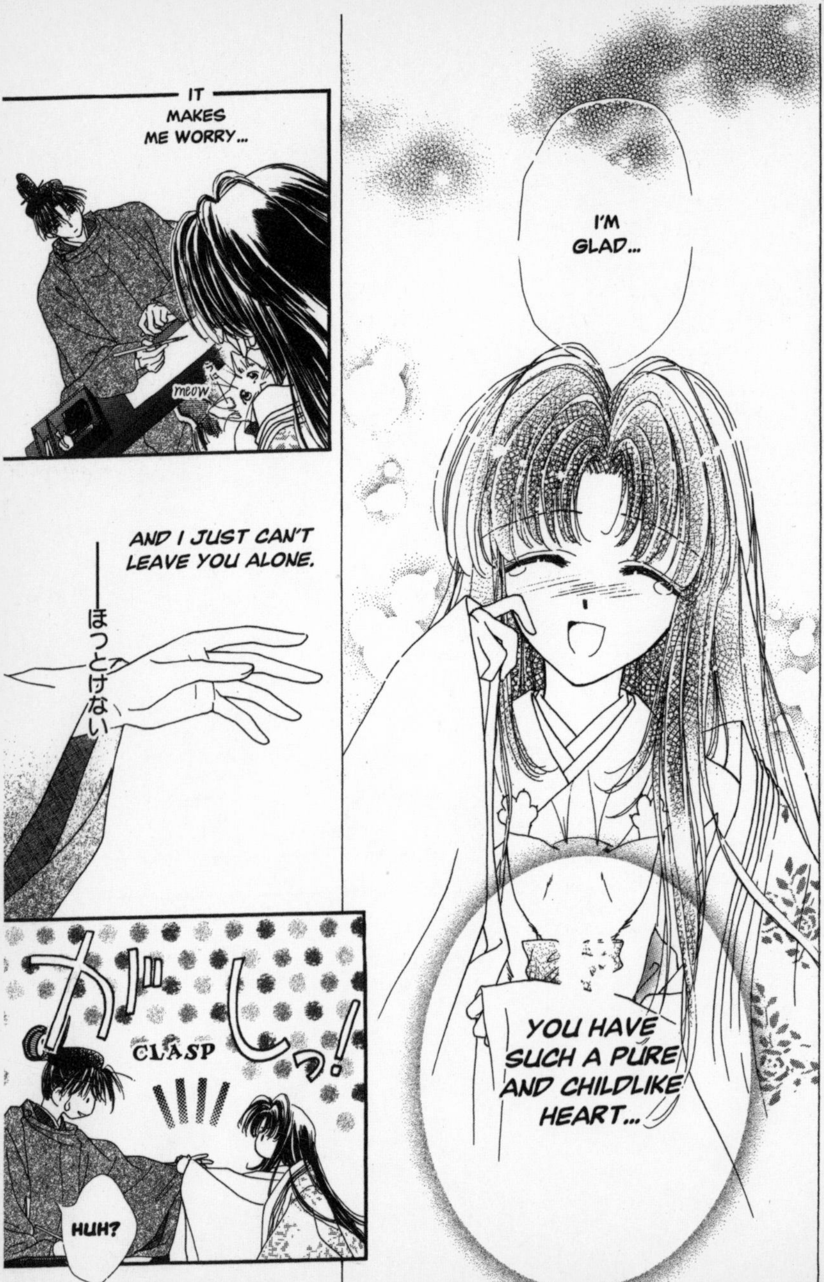
I'M GLAD...
YOU HAVE SUCH A PURE AND CHILDLIKE HEART...
IT MAKES ME WORRY...
meow
AND I JUST CAN'T LEAVE YOU ALONE.
ほっとけない
がしっ!
CLASP
HUH?

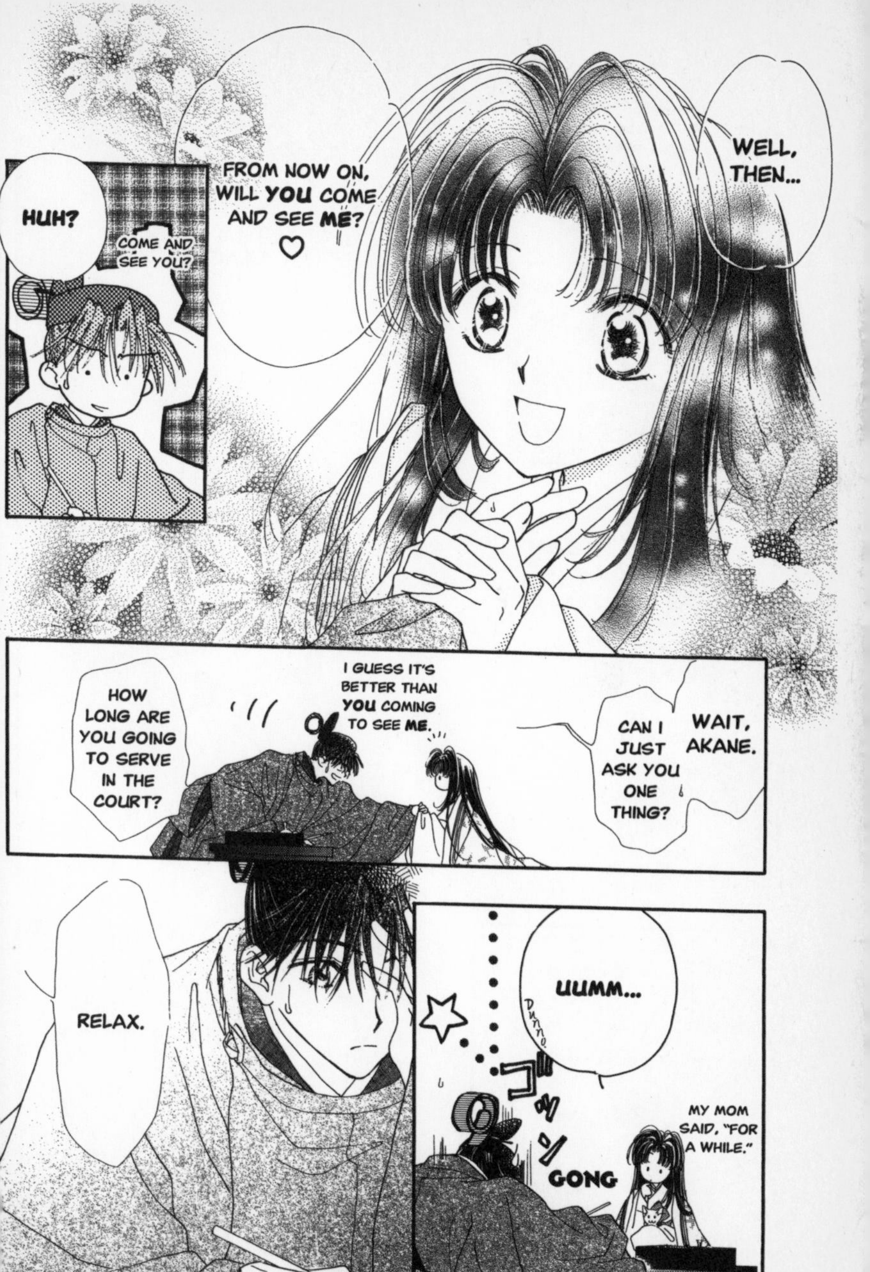
WELL, THEN...
FROM NOW ON, WILL YOU COME AND SEE ME? ♡
HUH?
COME AND SEE YOU?
I GUESS IT'S BETTER THAN YOU COMING TO SEE ME.
WAIT, AKANE.
CAN I JUST ASK YOU ONE THING?
HOW LONG ARE YOU GOING TO SERVE IN THE COURT?
UUMM...
Dunno.
GONG
MY MOM SAID, "FOR A WHILE."
RELAX.

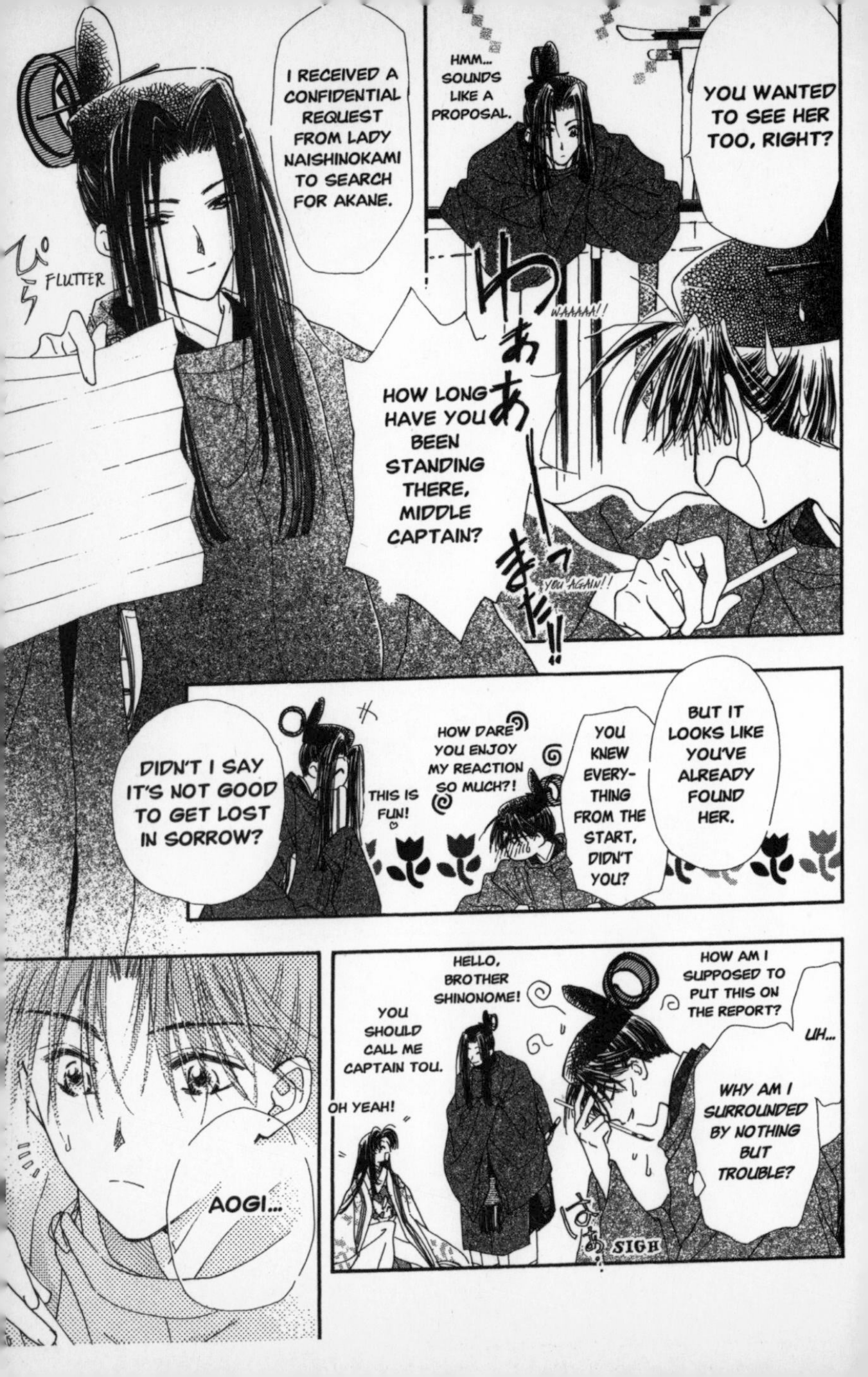
YOU WANTED TO SEE HER TOO, RIGHT?
HMM... SOUNDS LIKE A PROPOSAL.
わぁぁーっ
WAAAAAA!!
HOW LONG HAVE YOU BEEN STANDING THERE, MIDDLE CAPTAIN?
まだっ!!
YOU AGAIN!!
I RECEIVED A CONFIDENTIAL REQUEST FROM LADY NAISHINOKAMI TO SEARCH FOR AKANE.
ぴら
FLUTTER
BUT IT LOOKS LIKE YOU'VE ALREADY FOUND HER.
YOU KNEW EVERYTHING FROM THE START, DIDN'T YOU?
HOW DARE YOU ENJOY MY REACTION SO MUCH?!
THIS IS FUN!
DIDN'T I SAY IT'S NOT GOOD TO GET LOST IN SORROW?
HOW AM I SUPPOSED TO PUT THIS ON THE REPORT?
UH...
HELLO, BROTHER SHINONOME!
YOU SHOULD CALL ME CAPTAIN TOU.
WHY AM I SURROUNDED BY NOTHING BUT TROUBLE?
OH YEAH!
SIGH
AOGI...

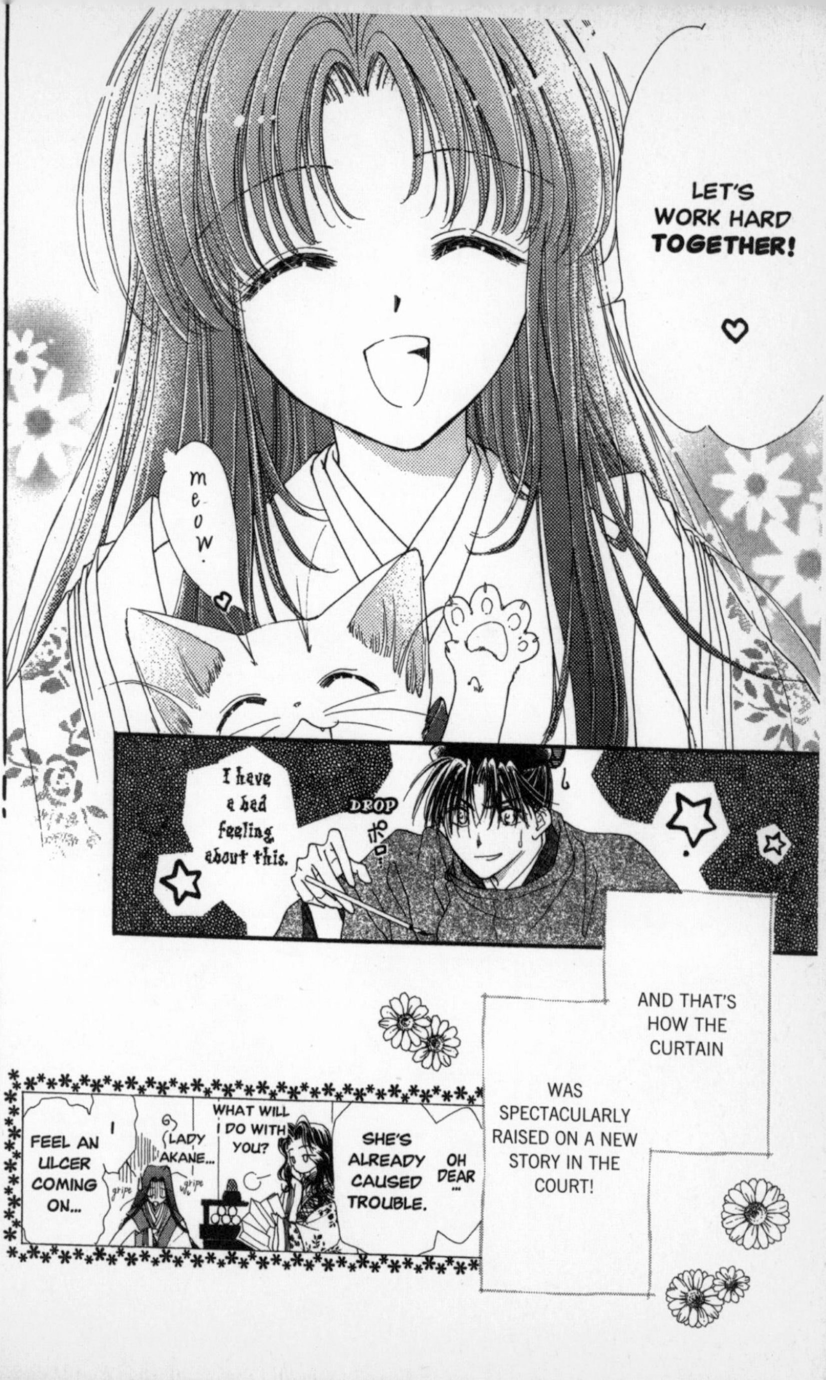
LET'S WORK HARD TOGETHER!
meow.
I have a bad feeling about this.
DROP
ポロ
AND THAT'S HOW THE CURTAIN
WAS SPECTACULARLY RAISED ON A NEW STORY IN THE COURT!
OH DEAR ...
SHE'S ALREADY CAUSED TROUBLE.
WHAT WILL I DO WITH YOU?
LADY AKANE...
gripe
I FEEL AN ULCER COMING ON...
gripe

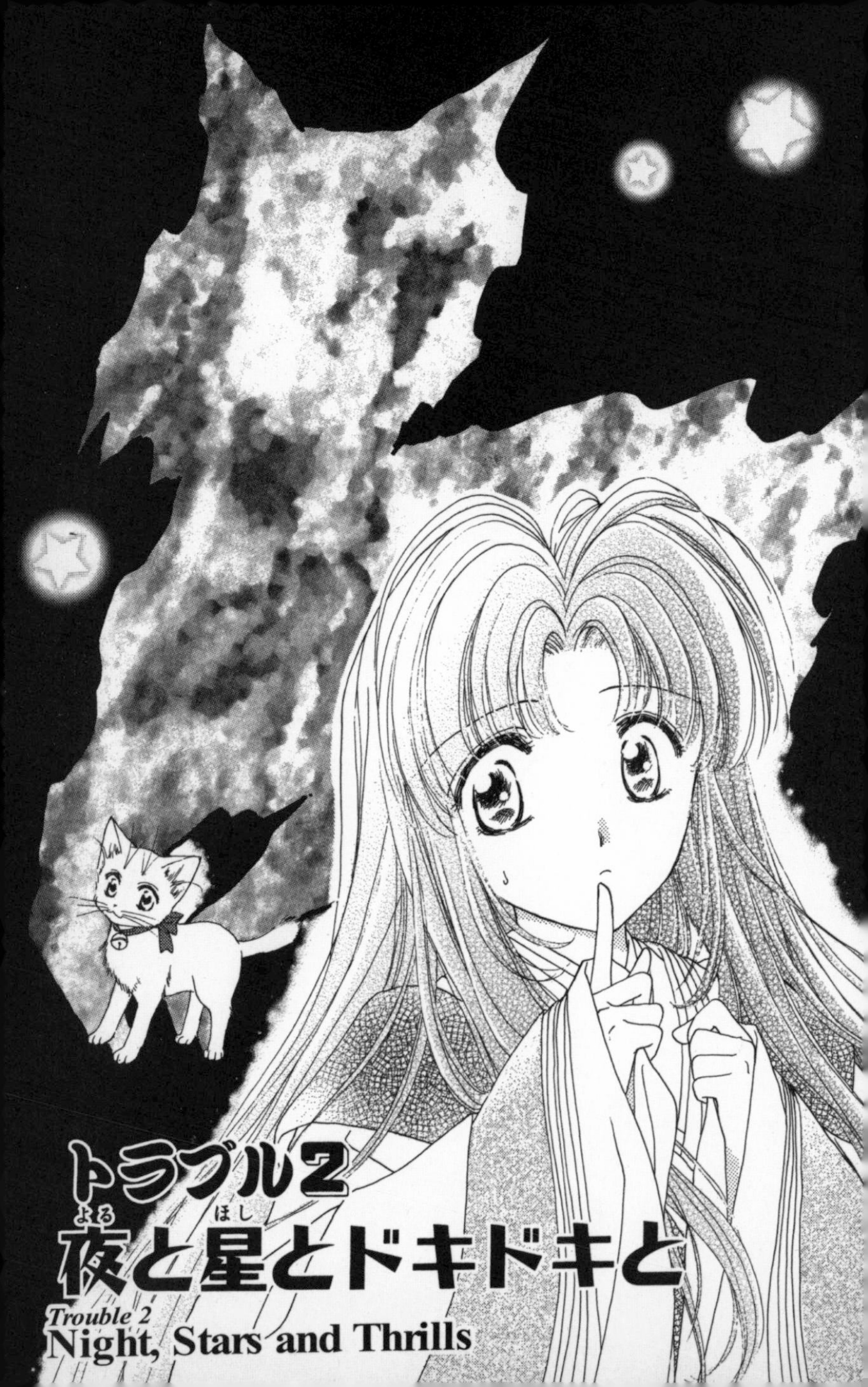
トラブル2
夜と星とドキドキと
Trouble 2
Night, Stars and Thrills

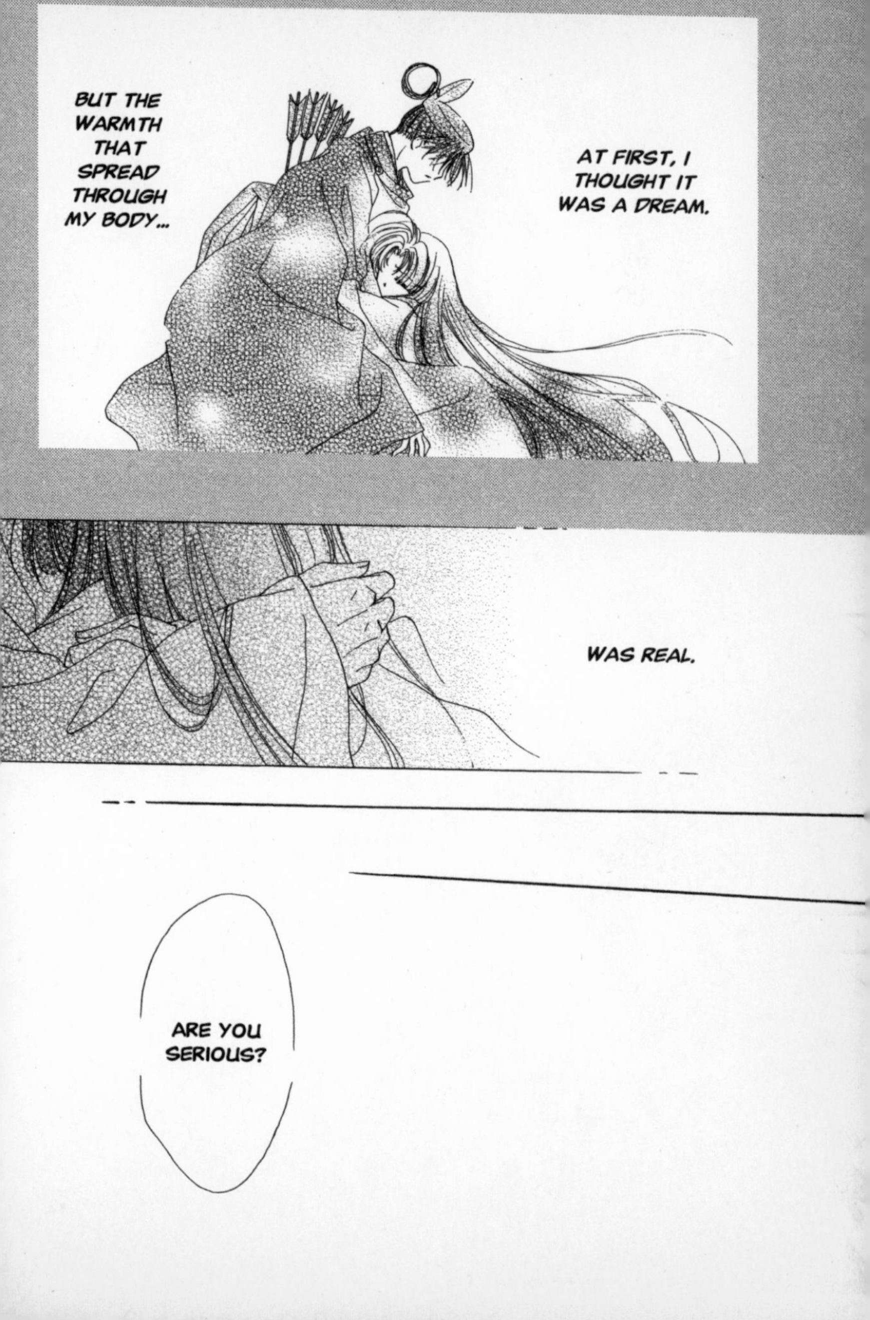
AT FIRST, I THOUGHT IT WAS A DREAM.
BUT THE WARMTH THAT SPREAD THROUGH MY BODY...
WAS REAL.
ARE YOU SERIOUS?

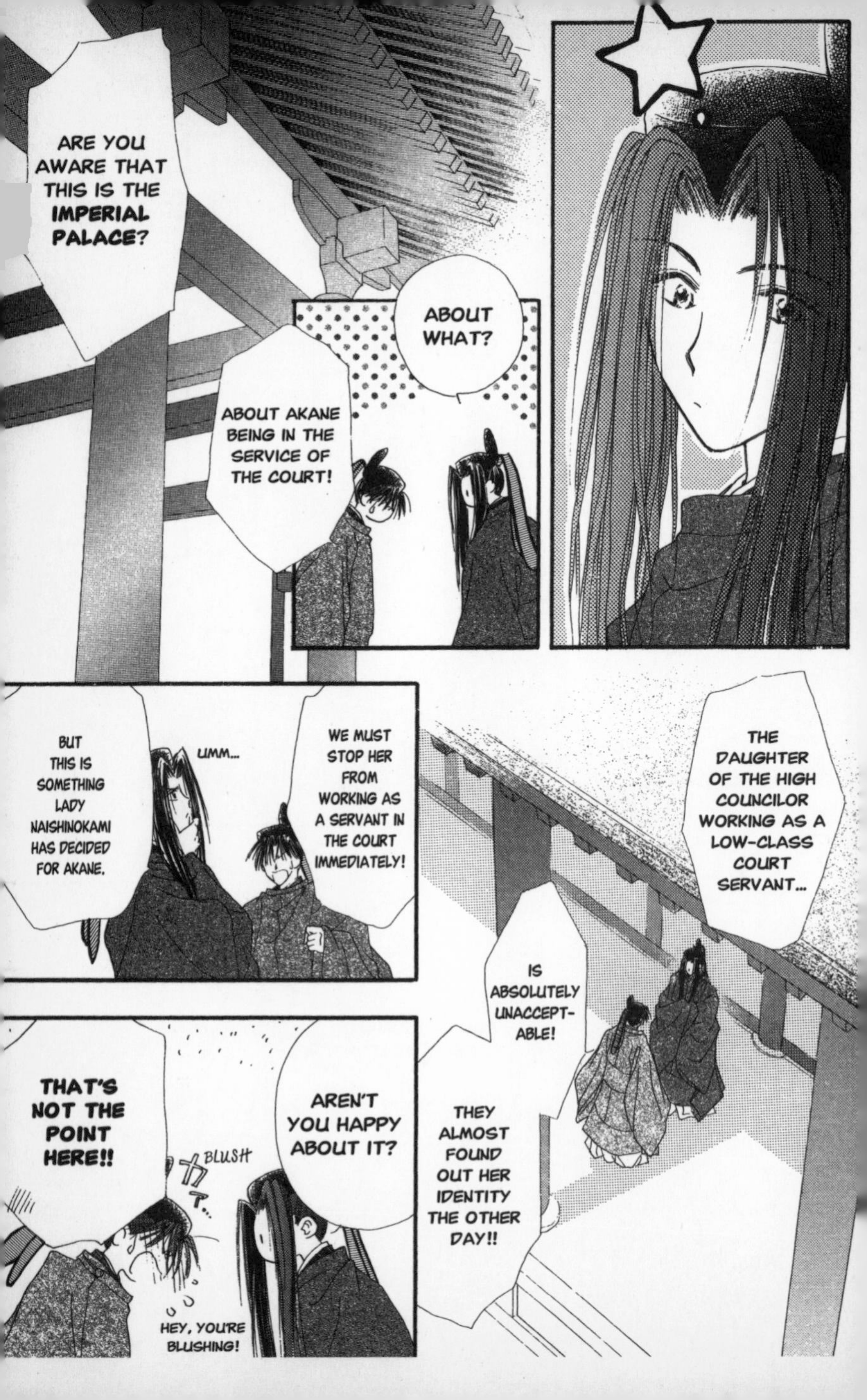

ARE YOU AWARE THAT THIS IS THE IMPERIAL PALACE?
ABOUT WHAT?
ABOUT AKANE BEING IN THE SERVICE OF THE COURT!
THE DAUGHTER OF THE HIGH COUNCILOR WORKING AS A LOW-CLASS COURT SERVANT...
IS ABSOLUTELY UNACCEPT-ABLE!
THEY ALMOST FOUND OUT HER IDENTITY THE OTHER DAY!!
WE MUST STOP HER FROM WORKING AS A SERVANT IN THE COURT IMMEDIATELY!
UMM...
BUT THIS IS SOMETHING LADY NAISHINOKAMI HAS DECIDED FOR AKANE.
AREN'T YOU HAPPY ABOUT IT?
BLUSH
THAT'S NOT THE POINT HERE!!
HEY, YOU'RE BLUSHING!

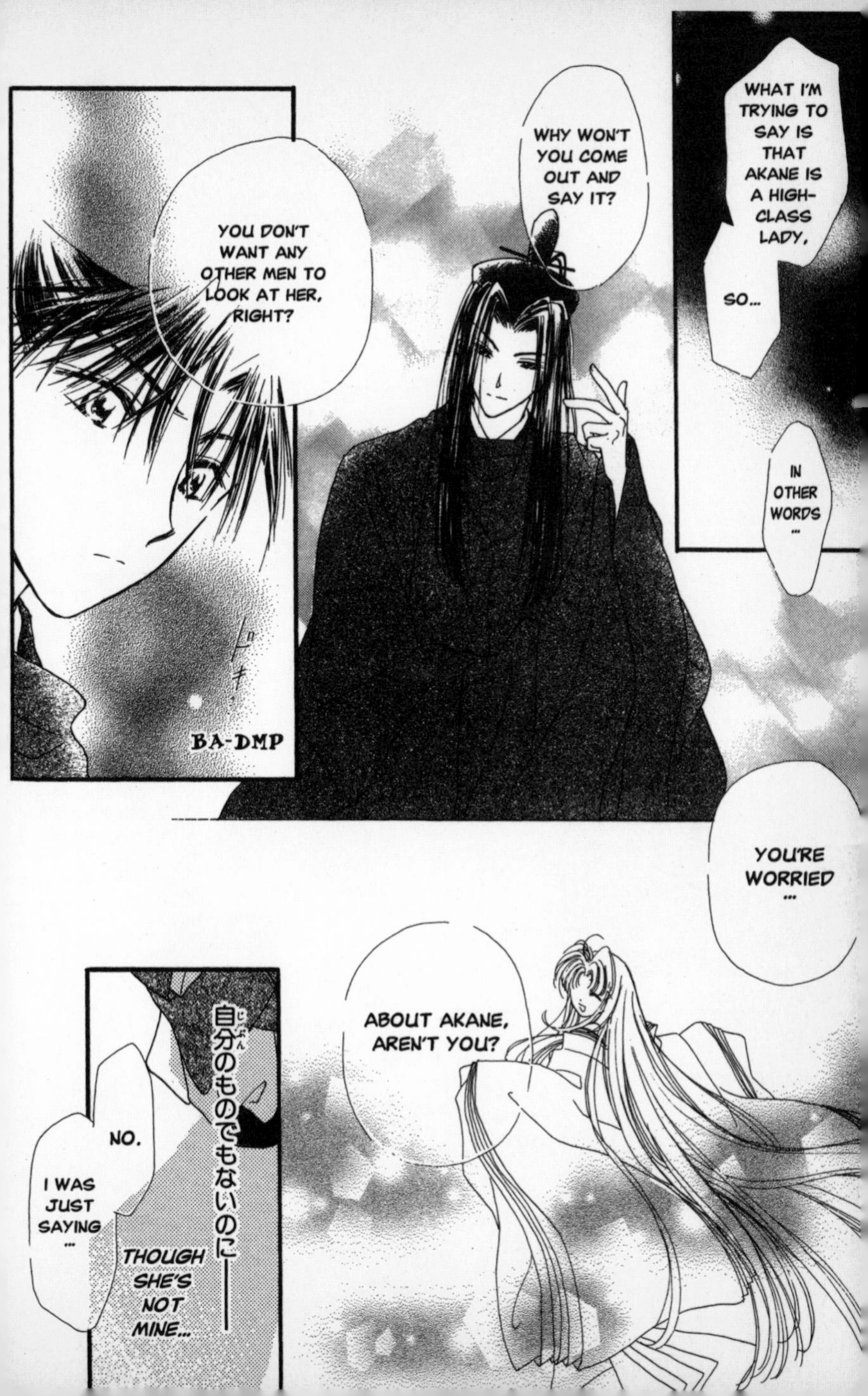
WHAT I'M TRYING TO SAY IS THAT AKANE IS A HIGH-CLASS LADY,
SO...
IN OTHER WORDS...
WHY WON'T YOU COME OUT AND SAY IT?
YOU DON'T WANT ANY OTHER MEN TO LOOK AT HER, RIGHT?
BA-DMP
YOU'RE WORRIED...
ABOUT AKANE, AREN'T YOU?
NO.
I WAS JUST SAYING...
自分のものでもないのに——
THOUGH SHE'S NOT MINE...

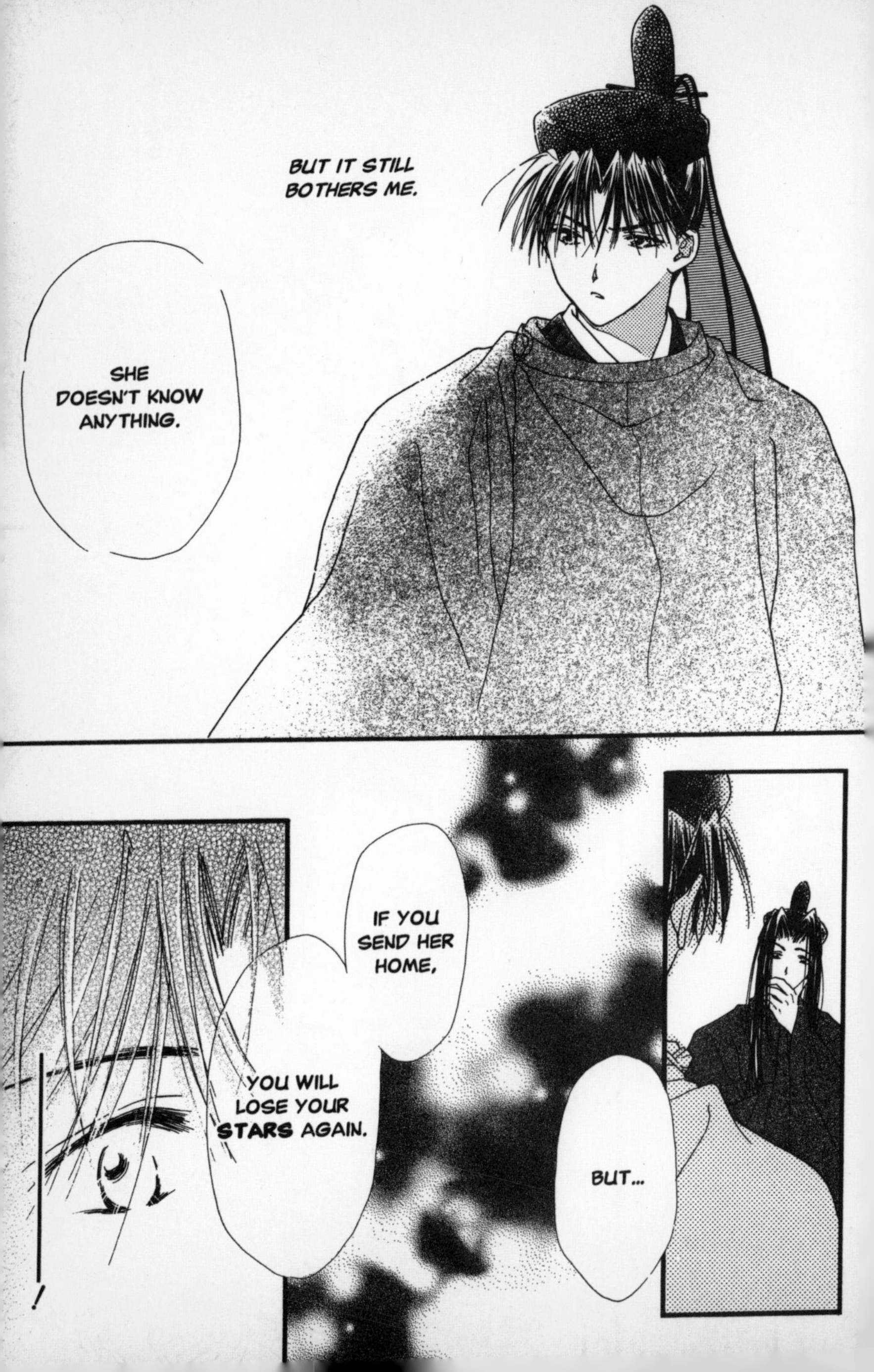
BUT IT STILL BOTHERS ME.
SHE DOESN'T KNOW ANYTHING.
IF YOU SEND HER HOME,
YOU WILL LOSE YOUR STARS AGAIN.
BUT...
!

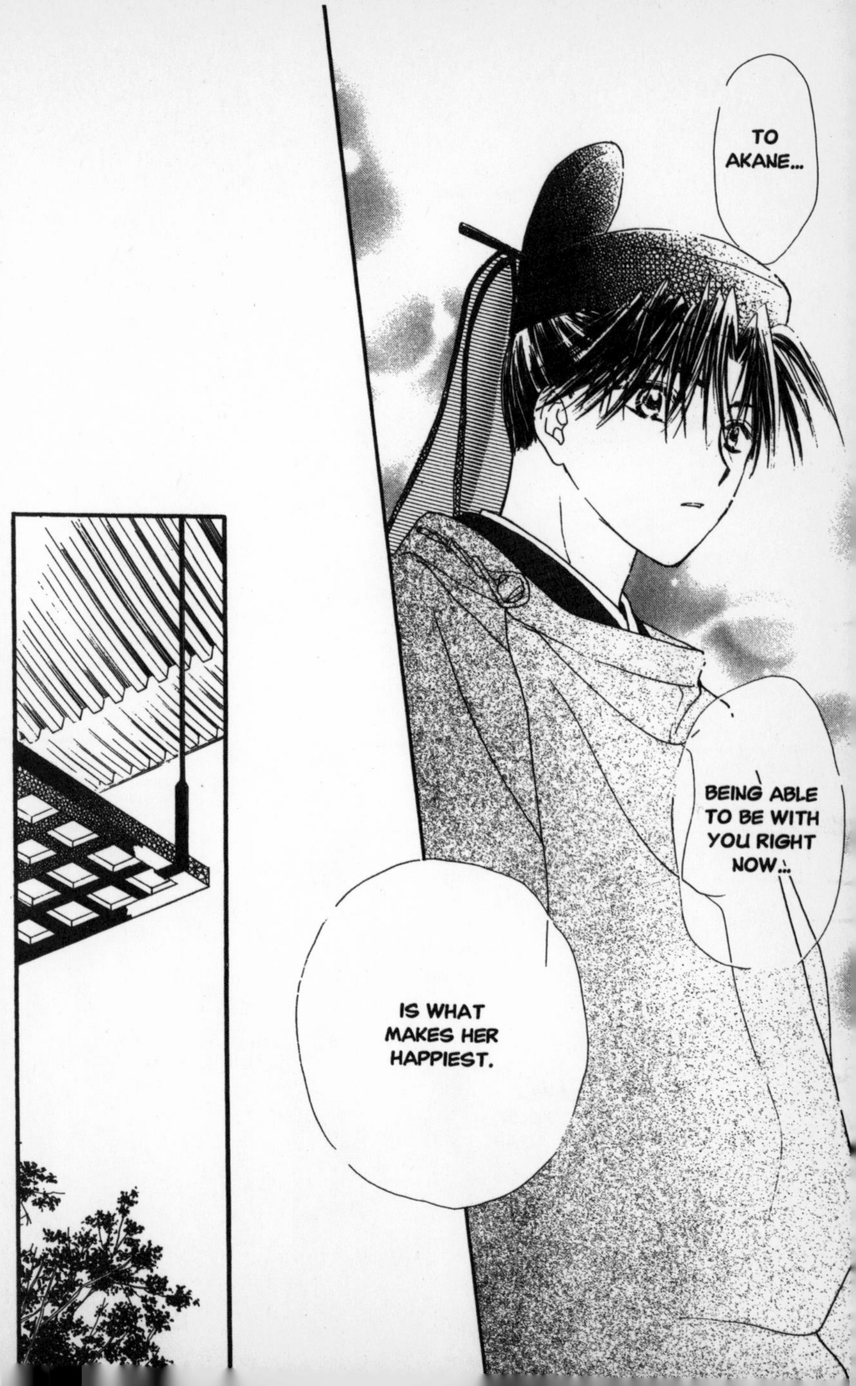
TO AKANE...
BEING ABLE TO BE WITH YOU RIGHT NOW...
IS WHAT MAKES HER HAPPIEST.

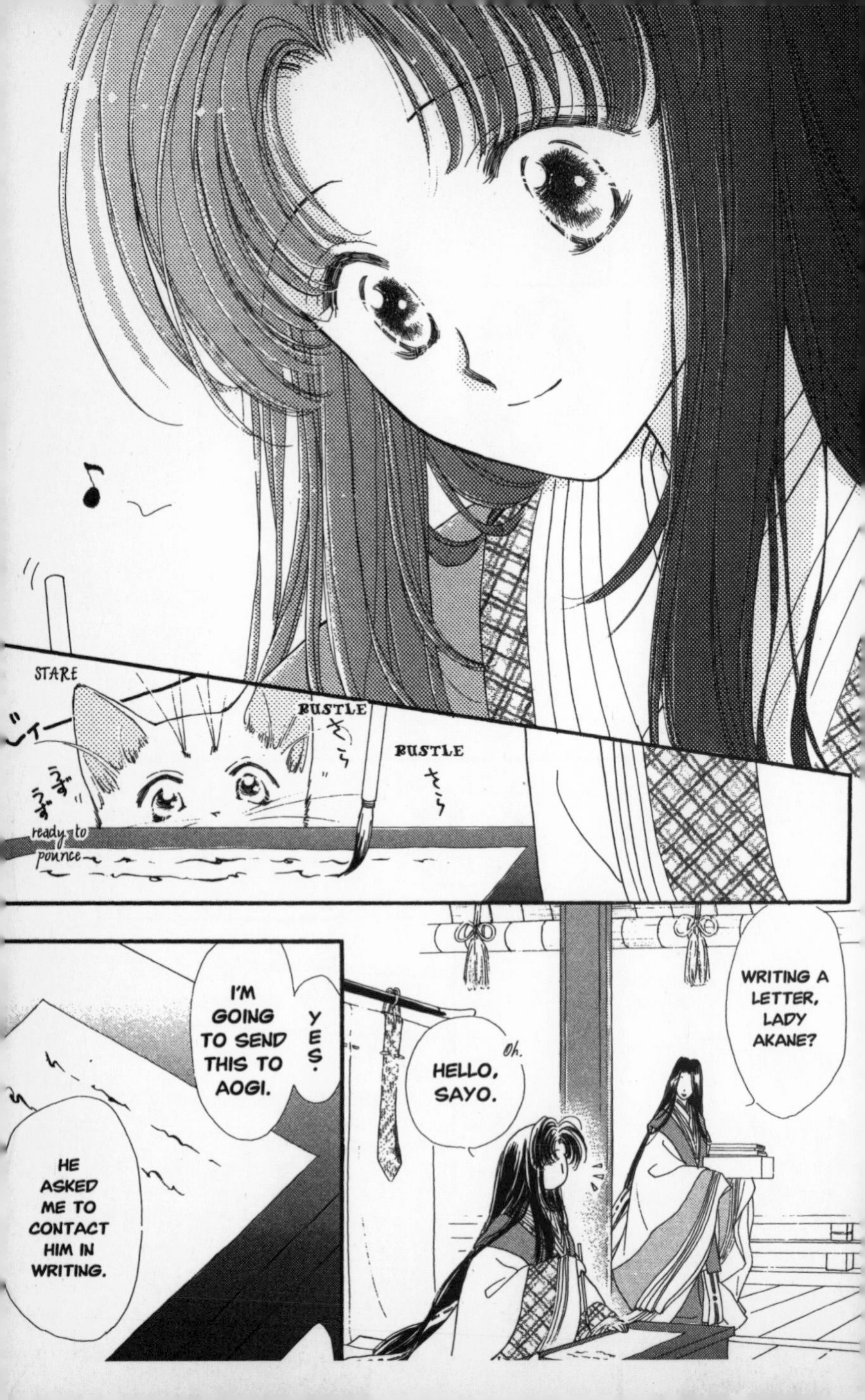
BUSTLE
さら
BUSTLE
さら
STARE
ジー
うずうず
ready to pounce
WRITING A LETTER, LADY AKANE?
Oh.
HELLO, SAYO.
YES.
I'M GOING TO SEND THIS TO AOGI.
HE ASKED ME TO CONTACT HIM IN WRITING.

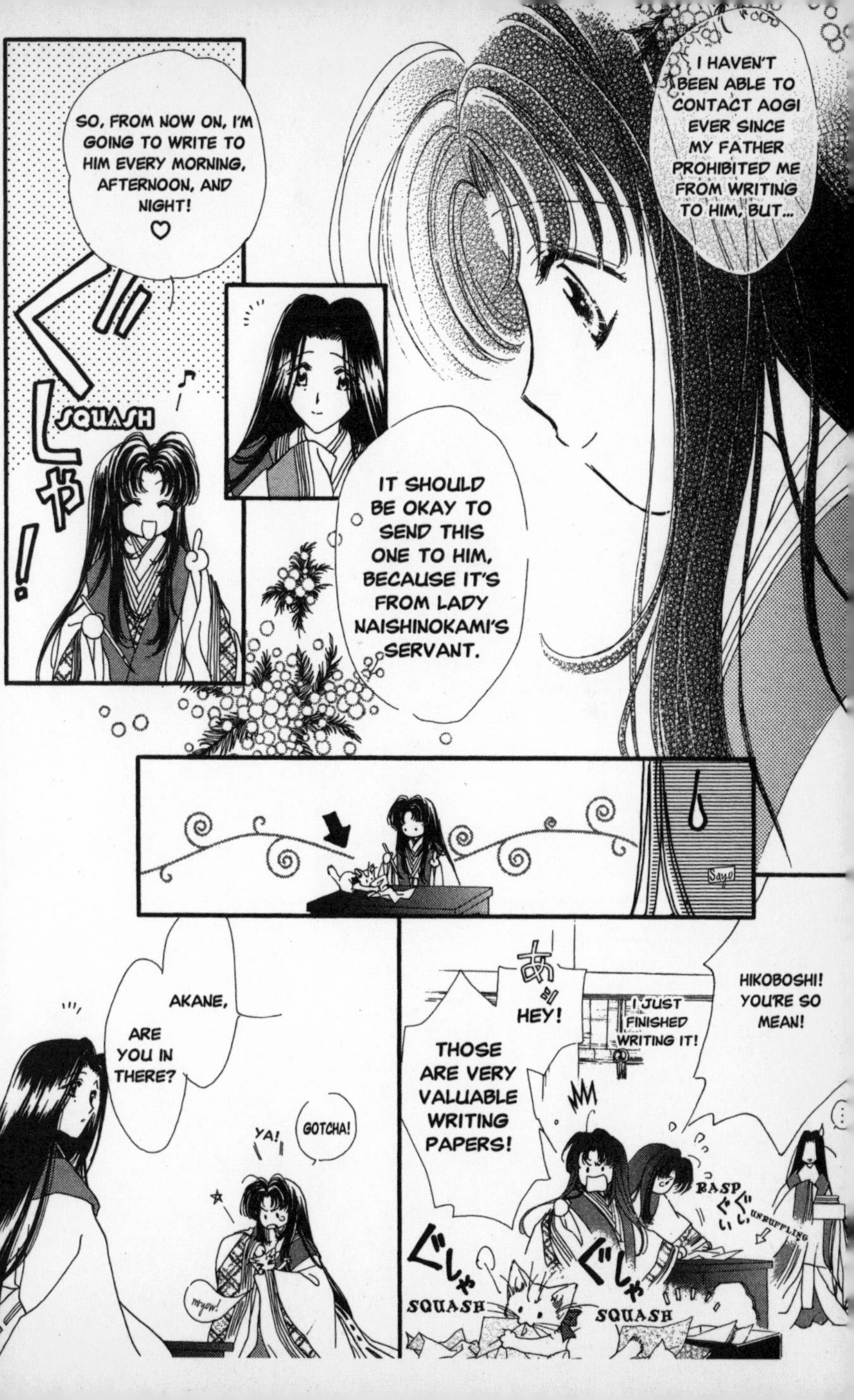

I HAVEN'T BEEN ABLE TO CONTACT AOGI EVER SINCE MY FATHER PROHIBITED ME FROM WRITING TO HIM, BUT...
IT SHOULD BE OKAY TO SEND THIS ONE TO HIM, BECAUSE IT'S FROM LADY NAISHINOKAMI'S SERVANT.
SO, FROM NOW ON, I'M GOING TO WRITE TO HIM EVERY MORNING, AFTERNOON, AND NIGHT! ♡
ぐしゃ!
SQUASH
Sayo
HIKOBOSHI! YOU'RE SO MEAN!
I JUST FINISHED WRITING IT!
あっ
HEY!
THOSE ARE VERY VALUABLE WRITING PAPERS!
RASP
ぐぐい
UNRUFFLING
ぐしゃ
SQUASH
ぐしゃ
SQUASH
AKANE,
ARE YOU IN THERE?
GOTCHA!
YA!
mryow!

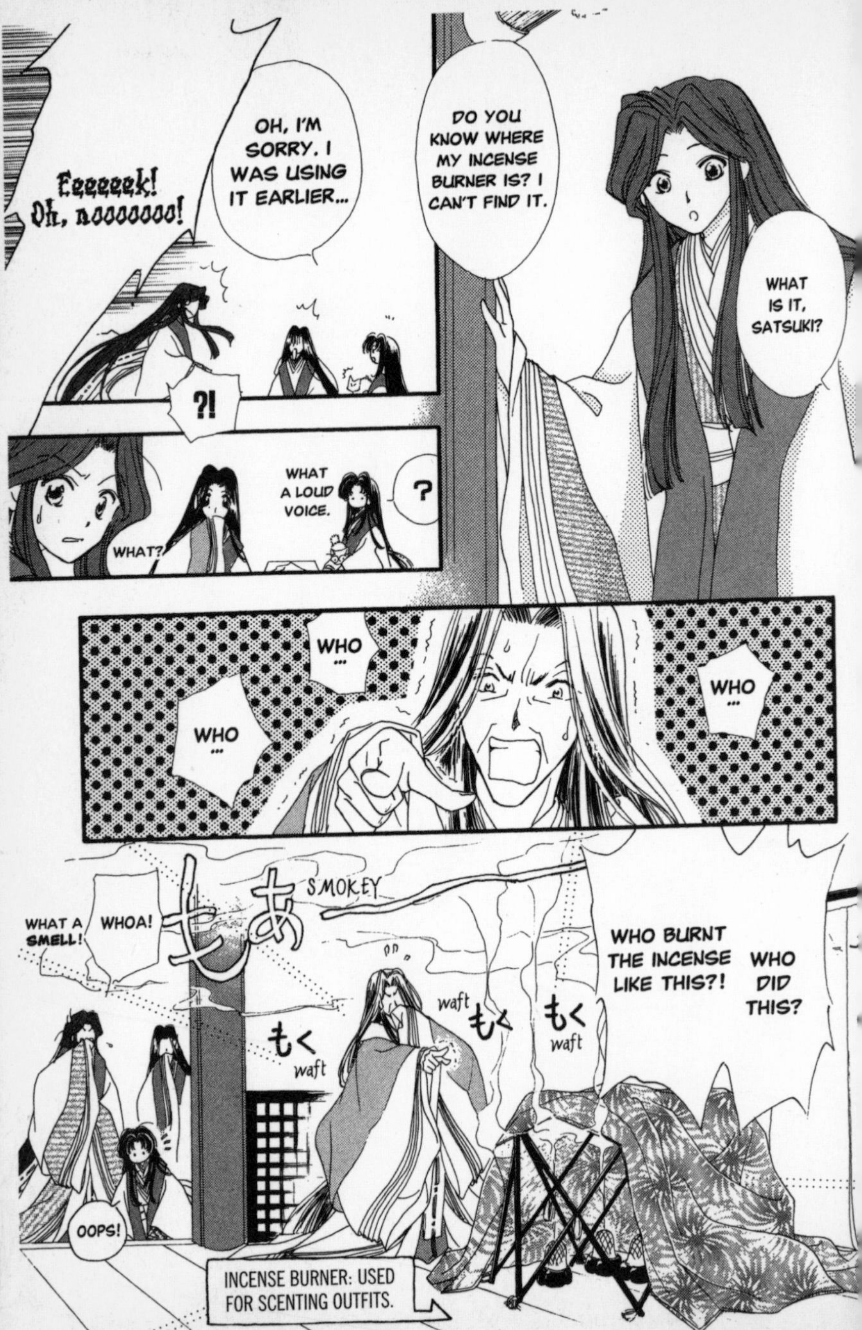
WHAT IS IT, SATSUKI?
DO YOU KNOW WHERE MY INCENSE BURNER IS? I CAN'T FIND IT.
OH, I'M SORRY. I WAS USING IT EARLIER...
Eeeeeek! Oh, noooooooo!
?!
?
WHAT A LOUD VOICE.
WHAT?
WHO ...
WHO ...
WHO ...
WHO DID THIS?
WHO BURNT THE INCENSE LIKE THIS?!
もく waft
もく waft
もく waft
もあ SMOKEY
WHOA!
WHAT A SMELL!
OOPS!
INCENSE BURNER: USED FOR SCENTING OUTFITS.

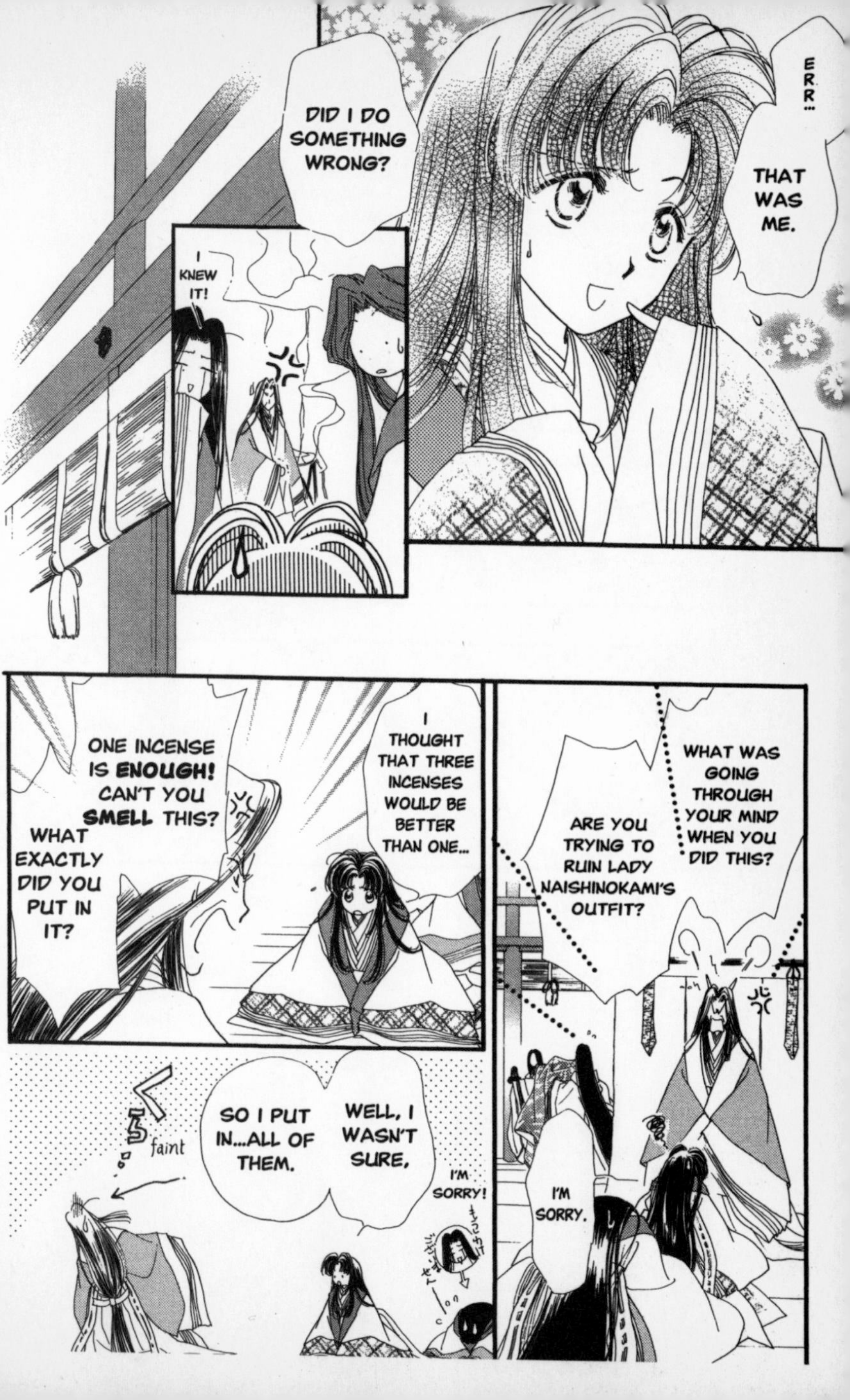
ERR...
THAT WAS ME.
DID I DO SOMETHING WRONG?
I KNEW IT!
WHAT WAS GOING THROUGH YOUR MIND WHEN YOU DID THIS?
ARE YOU TRYING TO RUIN LADY NAISHINOKAMI'S OUTFIT?
I'M SORRY.
I THOUGHT THAT THREE INCENSES WOULD BE BETTER THAN ONE...
ONE INCENSE IS ENOUGH! CAN'T YOU SMELL THIS?
WHAT EXACTLY DID YOU PUT IN IT?
WELL, I WASN'T SURE,
SO I PUT IN...ALL OF THEM.
I'M SORRY!
faint

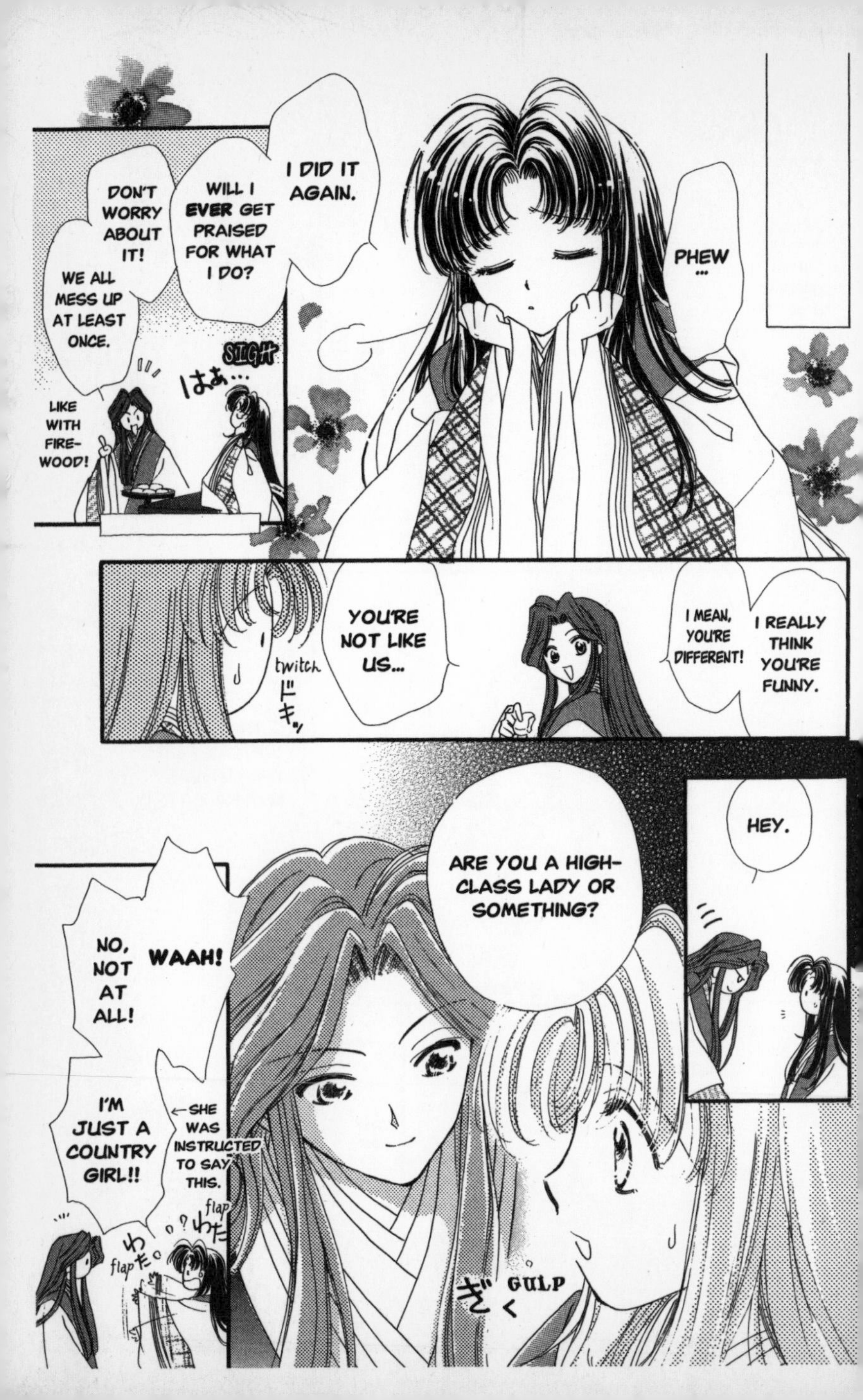
PHEW...
I DID IT AGAIN.
WILL I EVER GET PRAISED FOR WHAT I DO?
SIGH
はぁ…
DON'T WORRY ABOUT IT!
WE ALL MESS UP AT LEAST ONCE.
LIKE WITH FIRE-WOOD!
I REALLY THINK YOU'RE FUNNY.
I MEAN, YOU'RE DIFFERENT!
YOU'RE NOT LIKE US...
twitch
ドキッ
HEY.
ARE YOU A HIGH-CLASS LADY OR SOMETHING?
GULP
ぎく
WAAH!
NO, NOT AT ALL!
I'M JUST A COUNTRY GIRL!!
←SHE WAS INSTRUCTED TO SAY THIS.
flap
わた
flap
わた

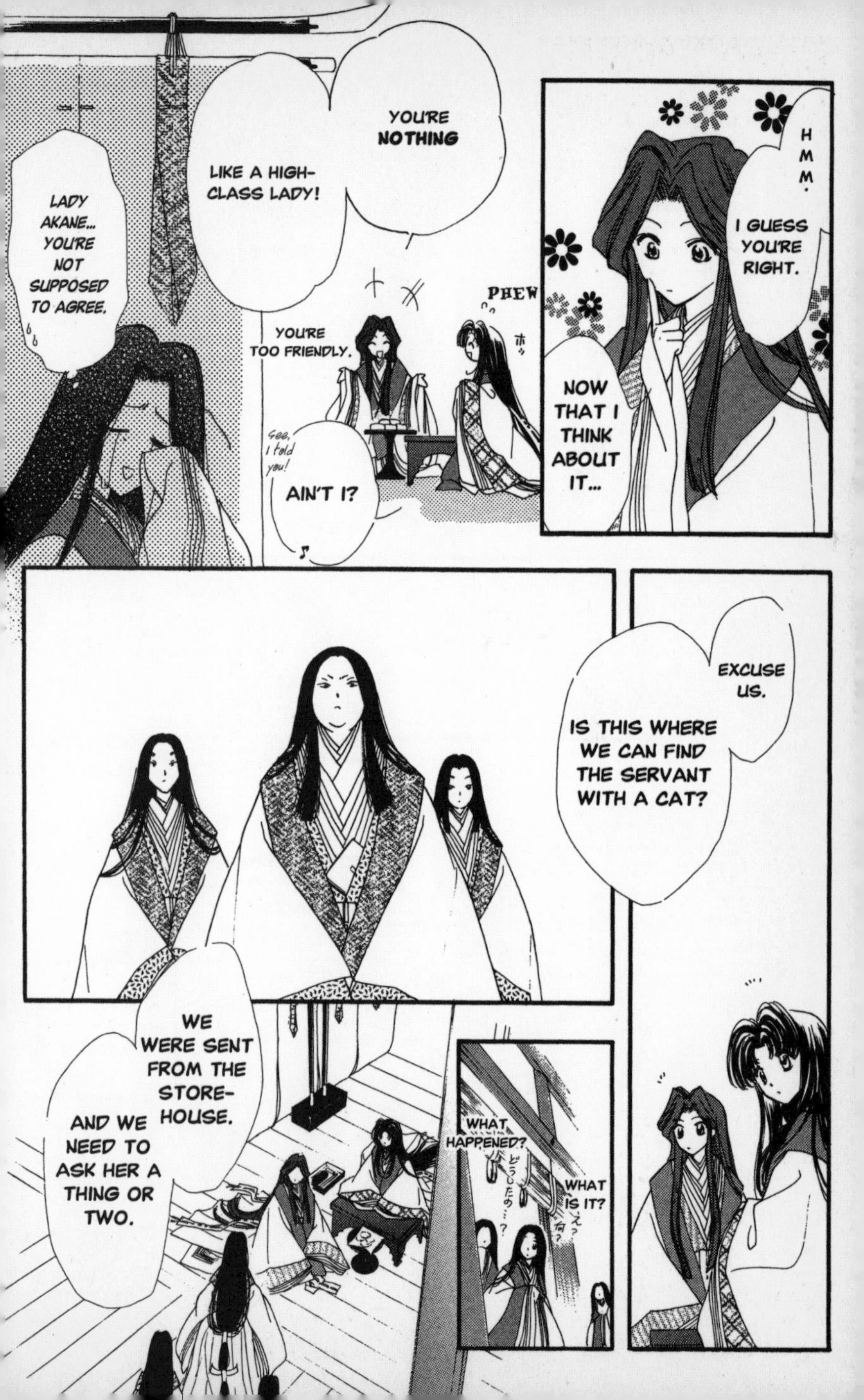
HMM.
I GUESS YOU'RE RIGHT.
NOW THAT I THINK ABOUT IT...
YOU'RE NOTHING LIKE A HIGH-CLASS LADY!
PHEW
YOU'RE TOO FRIENDLY.
AIN'T I?
See, I told you!
LADY AKANE... YOU'RE NOT SUPPOSED TO AGREE.
EXCUSE US.
IS THIS WHERE WE CAN FIND THE SERVANT WITH A CAT?
WHAT HAPPENED?
WHAT IS IT?
WE WERE SENT FROM THE STOREHOUSE.
AND WE NEED TO ASK HER A THING OR TWO.

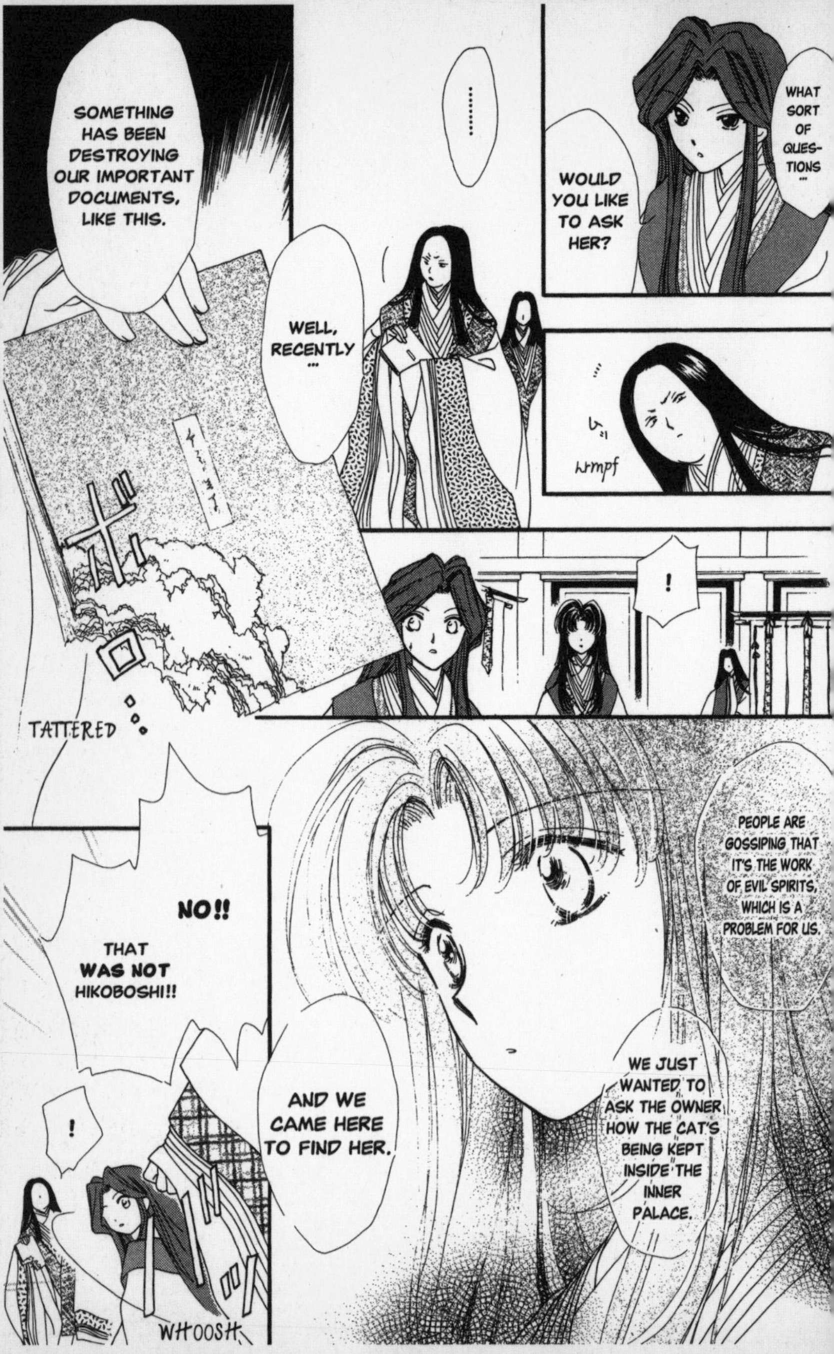
WHAT SORT OF QUESTIONS...
WOULD YOU LIKE TO ASK HER?
...
HRMPF
....
WELL, RECENTLY...
SOMETHING HAS BEEN DESTROYING OUR IMPORTANT DOCUMENTS, LIKE THIS.
TATTERED
!
PEOPLE ARE GOSSIPING THAT IT'S THE WORK OF EVIL SPIRITS, WHICH IS A PROBLEM FOR US.
WE JUST WANTED TO ASK THE OWNER HOW THE CAT'S BEING KEPT INSIDE THE INNER PALACE.
AND WE CAME HERE TO FIND HER.
NO!!
THAT WAS NOT HIKOBOSHI!!
!
WHOOSH

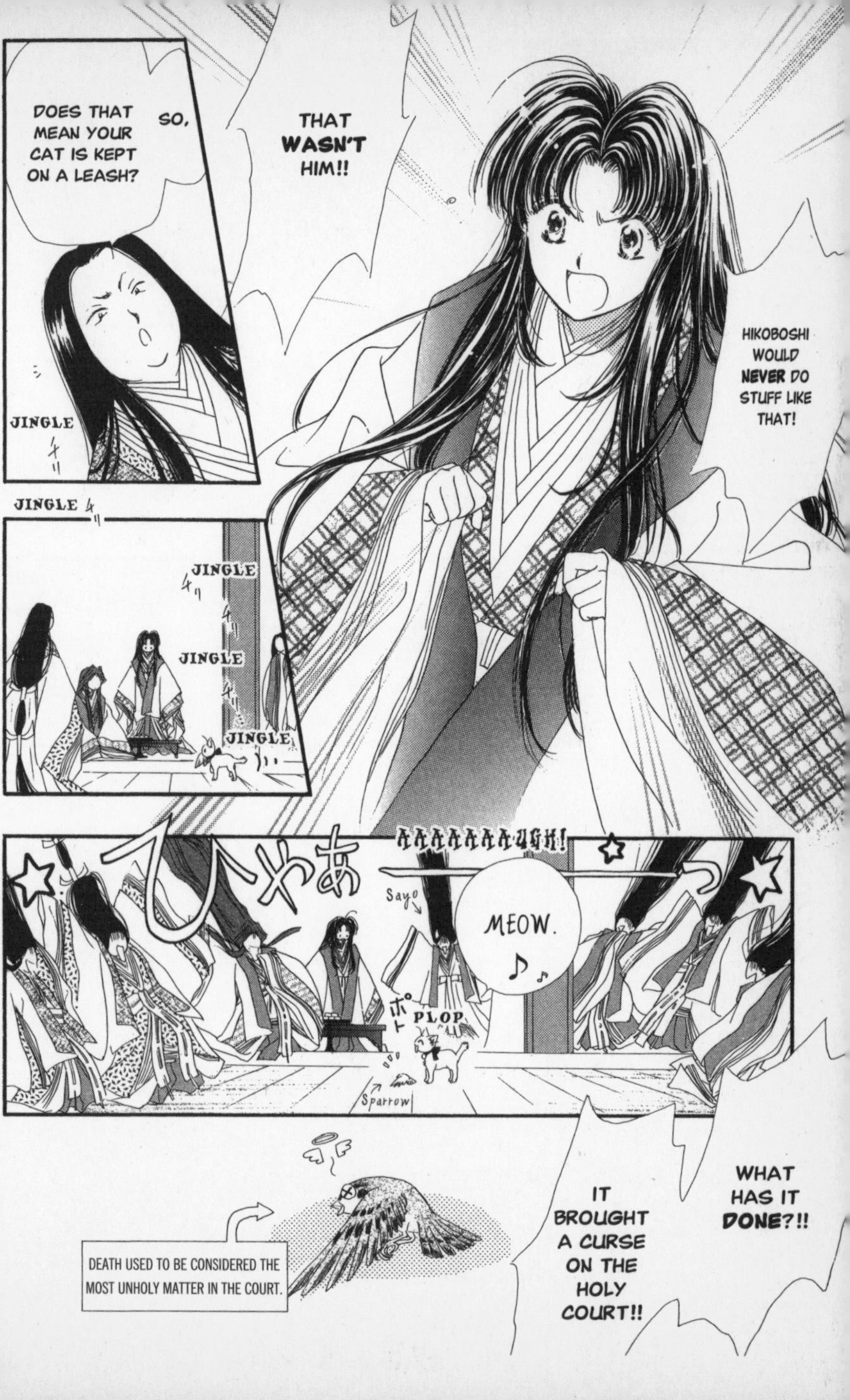
THAT WASN'T HIM!!
HIKOBOSHI WOULD NEVER DO STUFF LIKE THAT!
SO, DOES THAT MEAN YOUR CAT IS KEPT ON A LEASH?
JINGLE
JINGLE
JINGLE
JINGLE
JINGLE
AAAAAAAAUGH!
ひゃあ
MEOW. ♪
Sayo
ポト
PLOP
Sparrow
WHAT HAS IT DONE?!!
IT BROUGHT A CURSE ON THE HOLY COURT!!
DEATH USED TO BE CONSIDERED THE MOST UNHOLY MATTER IN THE COURT.

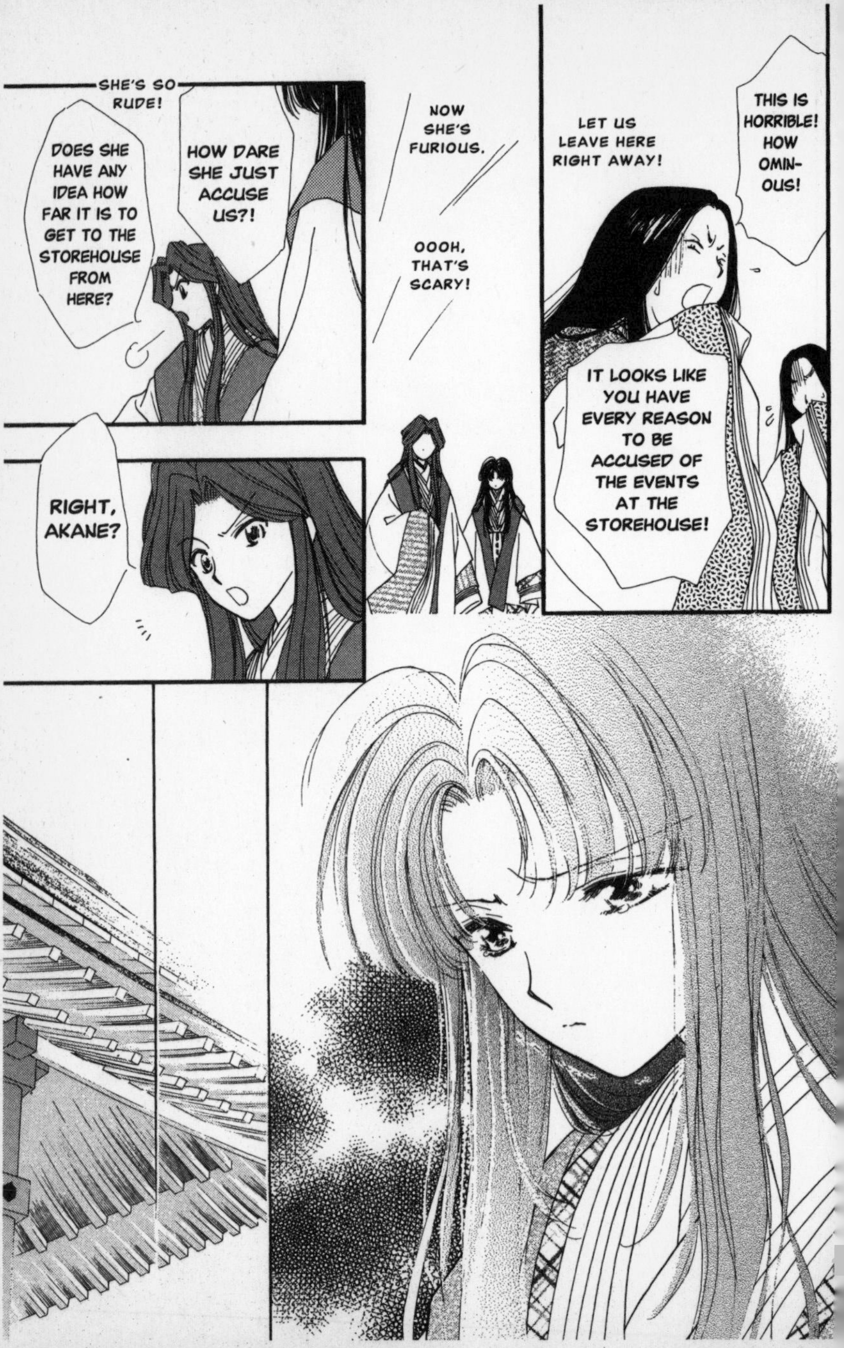
THIS IS HORRIBLE! HOW OMIN-OUS!
LET US LEAVE HERE RIGHT AWAY!
IT LOOKS LIKE YOU HAVE EVERY REASON TO BE ACCUSED OF THE EVENTS AT THE STOREHOUSE!
NOW SHE'S FURIOUS.
OOOH, THAT'S SCARY!
SHE'S SO RUDE!
HOW DARE SHE JUST ACCUSE US?!
DOES SHE HAVE ANY IDEA HOW FAR IT IS TO GET TO THE STOREHOUSE FROM HERE?
RIGHT, AKANE?

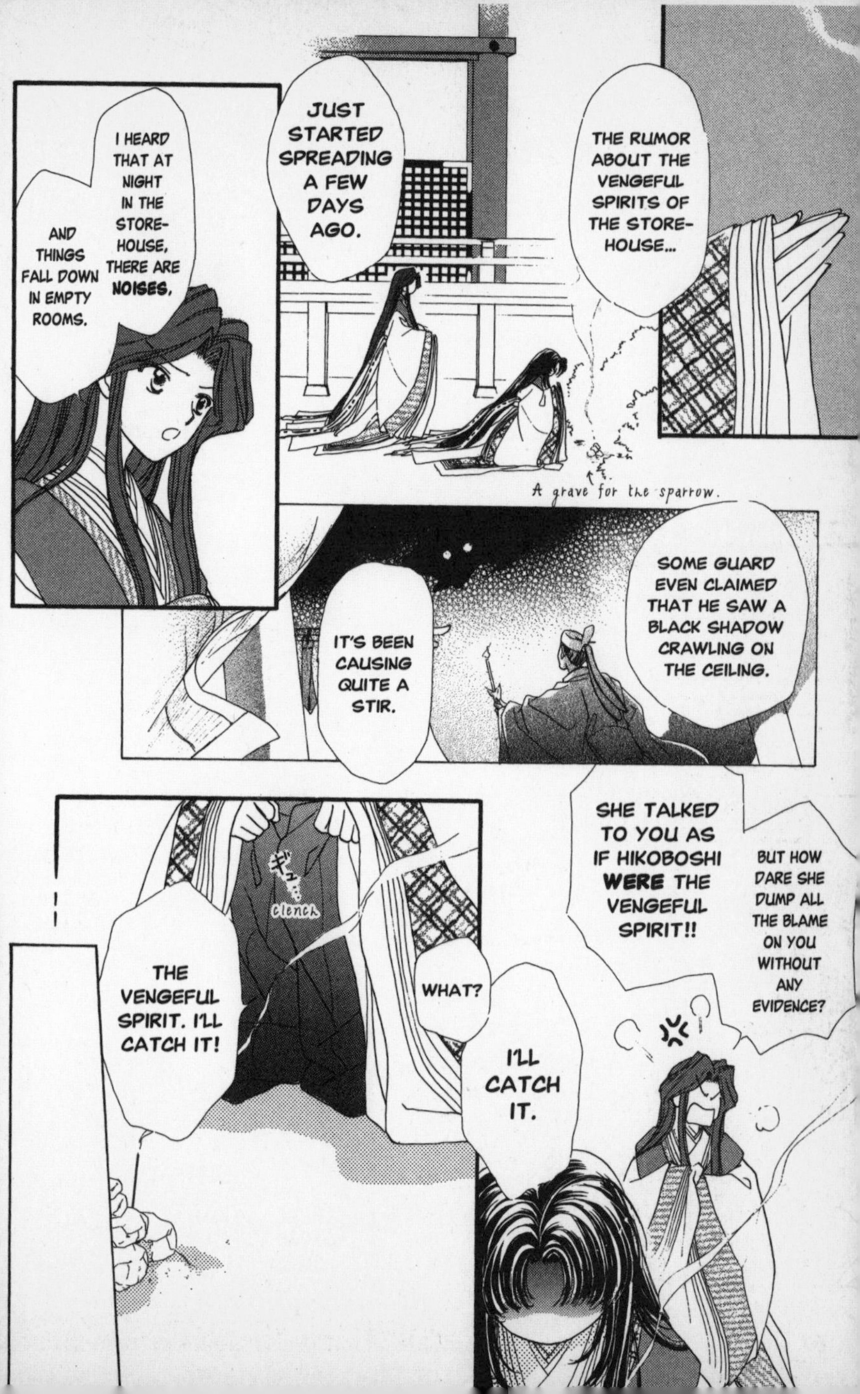
THE RUMOR ABOUT THE VENGEFUL SPIRITS OF THE STORE-HOUSE...
JUST STARTED SPREADING A FEW DAYS AGO.
A grave for the sparrow.
I HEARD THAT AT NIGHT IN THE STORE-HOUSE, THERE ARE NOISES,
AND THINGS FALL DOWN IN EMPTY ROOMS.
SOME GUARD EVEN CLAIMED THAT HE SAW A BLACK SHADOW CRAWLING ON THE CEILING.
IT'S BEEN CAUSING QUITE A STIR.
BUT HOW DARE SHE DUMP ALL THE BLAME ON YOU WITHOUT ANY EVIDENCE?
SHE TALKED TO YOU AS IF HIKOBOSHI WERE THE VENGEFUL SPIRIT!!
I'LL CATCH IT.
WHAT?
clench
THE VENGEFUL SPIRIT. I'LL CATCH IT!

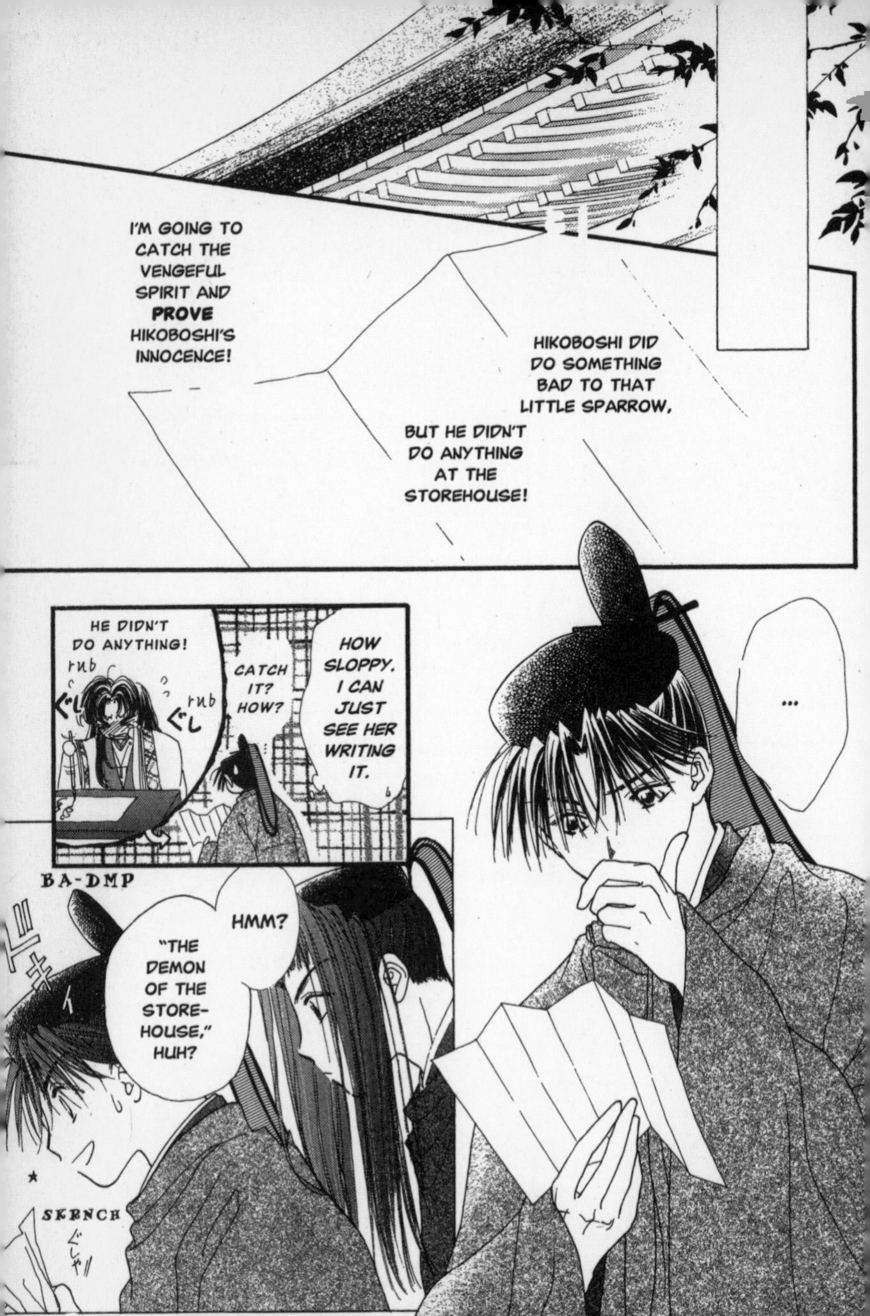

HIKOBOSHI DID DO SOMETHING BAD TO THAT LITTLE SPARROW,
BUT HE DIDN'T DO ANYTHING AT THE STOREHOUSE!
I'M GOING TO CATCH THE VENGEFUL SPIRIT AND PROVE HIKOBOSHI'S INNOCENCE!
...
HOW SLOPPY. I CAN JUST SEE HER WRITING IT.
CATCH IT? HOW?
HE DIDN'T DO ANYTHING!
rub
rub
HMM?
"THE DEMON OF THE STORE-HOUSE," HUH?
BA-DMP
SKRNCH

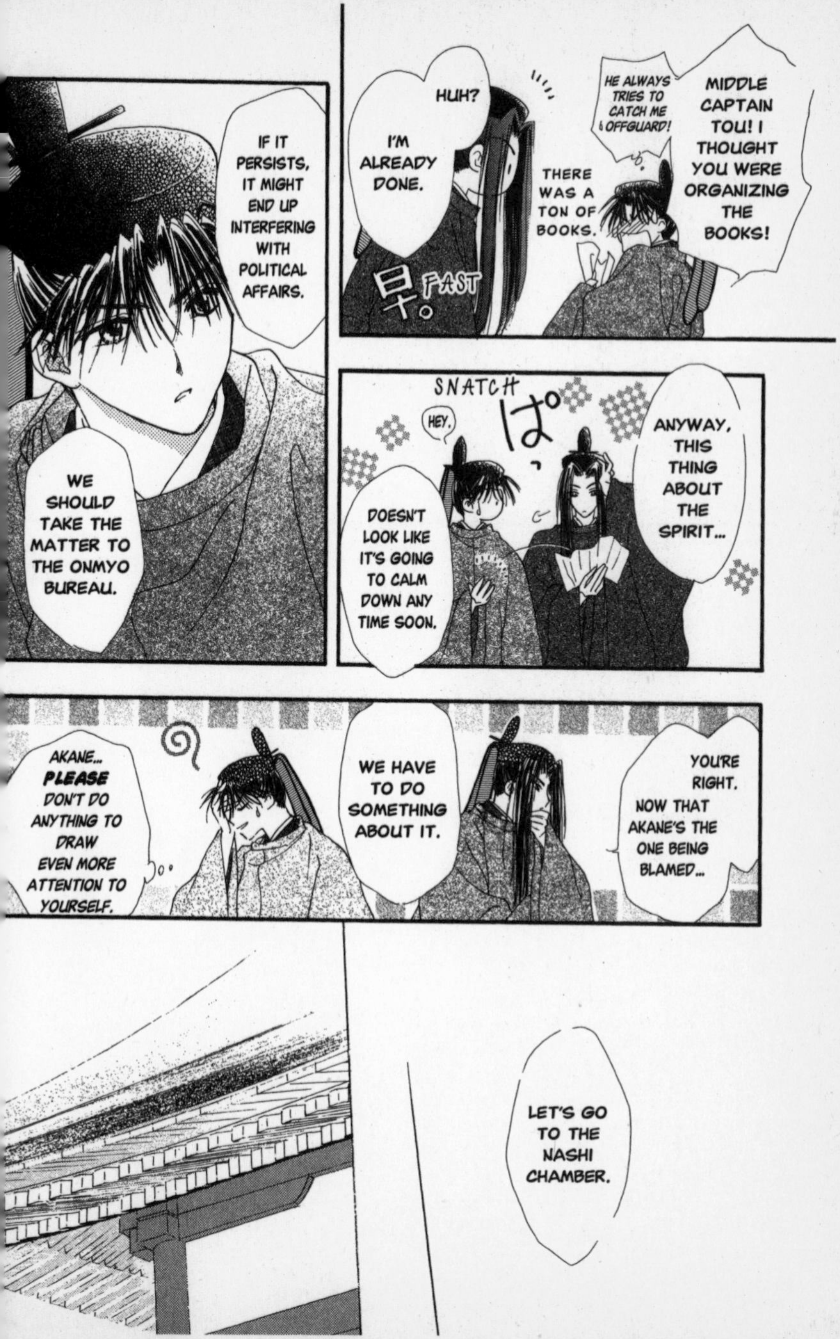
MIDDLE CAPTAIN TOU! I THOUGHT YOU WERE ORGANIZING THE BOOKS!
HE ALWAYS TRIES TO CATCH ME OFFGUARD!
THERE WAS A TON OF BOOKS.
HUH?
I'M ALREADY DONE.
早。 FAST
ANYWAY, THIS THING ABOUT THE SPIRIT...
SNATCH
ぱ
HEY.
DOESN'T LOOK LIKE IT'S GOING TO CALM DOWN ANY TIME SOON.
IF IT PERSISTS, IT MIGHT END UP INTERFERING WITH POLITICAL AFFAIRS.
WE SHOULD TAKE THE MATTER TO THE ONMYO BUREAU.
YOU'RE RIGHT. NOW THAT AKANE'S THE ONE BEING BLAMED...
WE HAVE TO DO SOMETHING ABOUT IT.
AKANE... PLEASE DON'T DO ANYTHING TO DRAW EVEN MORE ATTENTION TO YOURSELF.
LET'S GO TO THE NASHI CHAMBER.

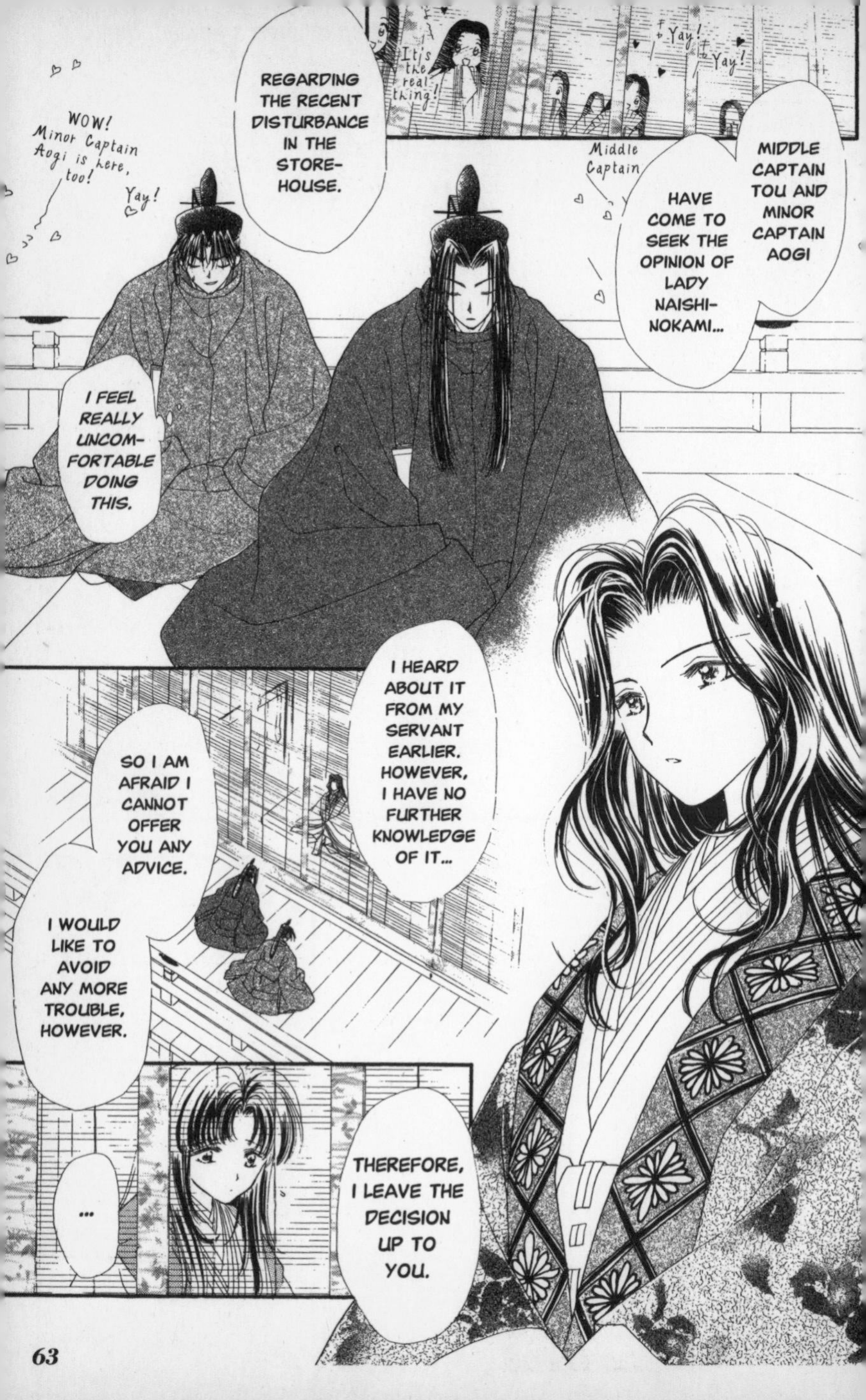
It's the real thing!
Yay!
Yay!
Middle Captain
MIDDLE CAPTAIN TOU AND MINOR CAPTAIN AOGI
HAVE COME TO SEEK THE OPINION OF LADY NAISHI-NOKAMI...
REGARDING THE RECENT DISTURBANCE IN THE STORE-HOUSE.
WOW! Minor Captain Aogi is here, too!
Yay!
I FEEL REALLY UNCOM-FORTABLE DOING THIS.
I HEARD ABOUT IT FROM MY SERVANT EARLIER. HOWEVER, I HAVE NO FURTHER KNOWLEDGE OF IT...
SO I AM AFRAID I CANNOT OFFER YOU ANY ADVICE.
I WOULD LIKE TO AVOID ANY MORE TROUBLE, HOWEVER.
THEREFORE, I LEAVE THE DECISION UP TO YOU.
...

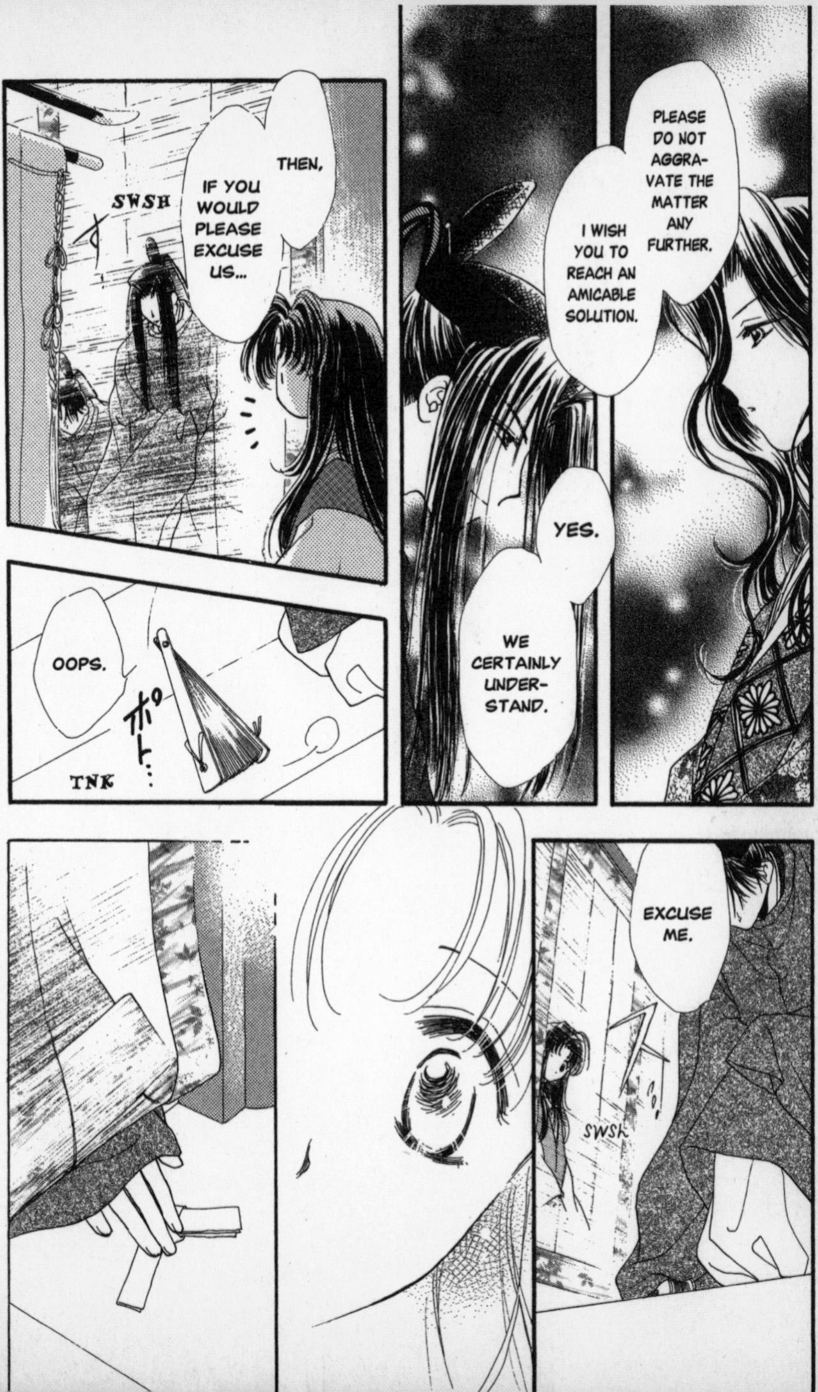
PLEASE DO NOT AGGRAVATE THE MATTER ANY FURTHER.
I WISH YOU TO REACH AN AMICABLE SOLUTION.
YES.
WE CERTAINLY UNDERSTAND.
THEN,
IF YOU WOULD PLEASE EXCUSE US...
SWSH
OOPS.
TNK
EXCUSE ME.
SWSH

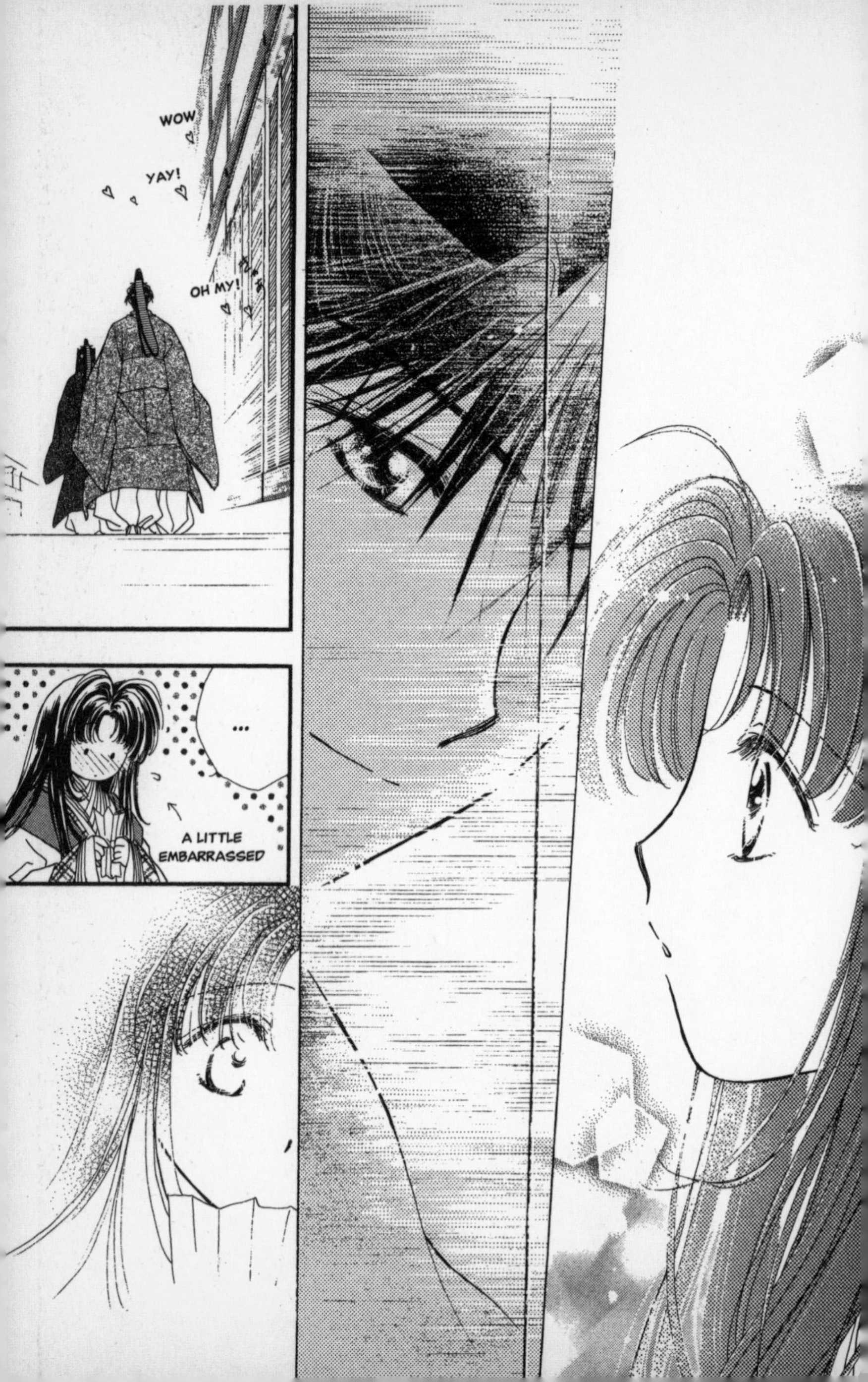
WOW
YAY!
OH MY!
...
A LITTLE EMBARRASSED

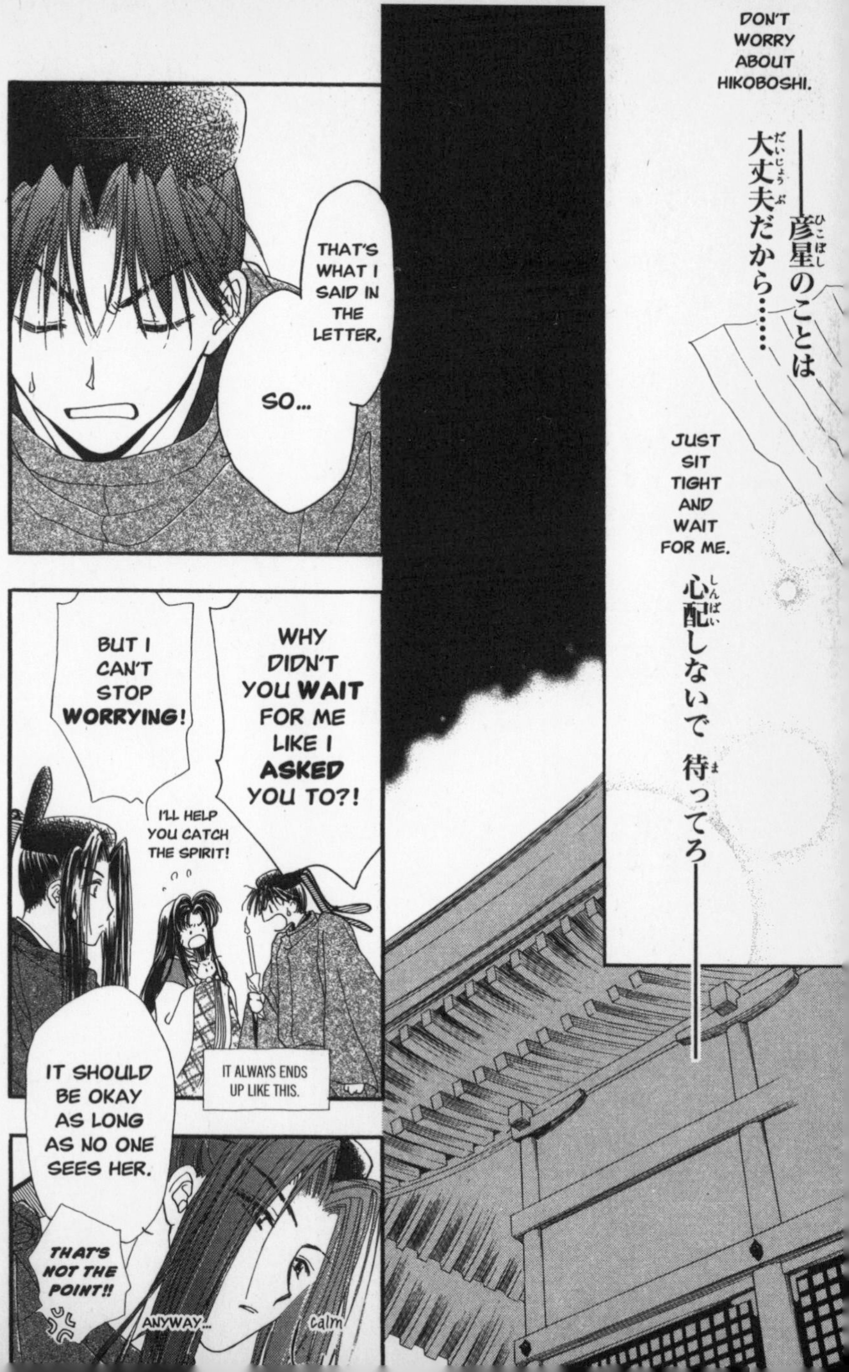
DON'T WORRY ABOUT HIKOBOSHI.
——彦星のことは 大丈夫だから……
JUST SIT TIGHT AND WAIT FOR ME.
心配しないで 待ってろ——
THAT'S WHAT I SAID IN THE LETTER,
SO...
WHY DIDN'T YOU WAIT FOR ME LIKE I ASKED YOU TO?!
BUT I CAN'T STOP WORRYING!
I'LL HELP YOU CATCH THE SPIRIT!
IT ALWAYS ENDS UP LIKE THIS.
IT SHOULD BE OKAY AS LONG AS NO ONE SEES HER.
calm
THAT'S NOT THE POINT!!
ANYWAY...

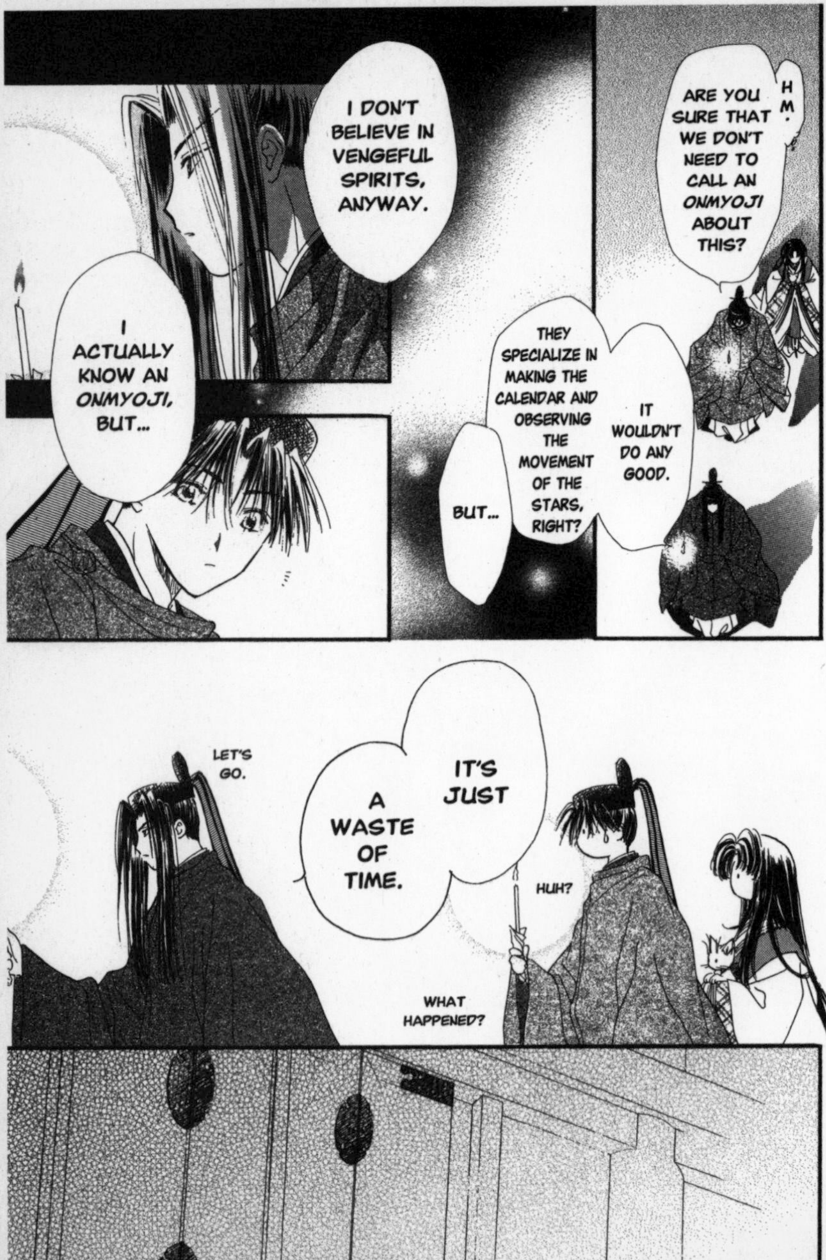
HM.
ARE YOU SURE THAT WE DON'T NEED TO CALL AN *ONMYOJI* ABOUT THIS?
IT WOULDN'T DO ANY GOOD.
THEY SPECIALIZE IN MAKING THE CALENDAR AND OBSERVING THE MOVEMENT OF THE STARS, RIGHT?
BUT...
I DON'T BELIEVE IN VENGEFUL SPIRITS, ANYWAY.
I ACTUALLY KNOW AN *ONMYOJI*, BUT...
IT'S JUST A WASTE OF TIME.
LET'S GO.
HUH?
WHAT HAPPENED?

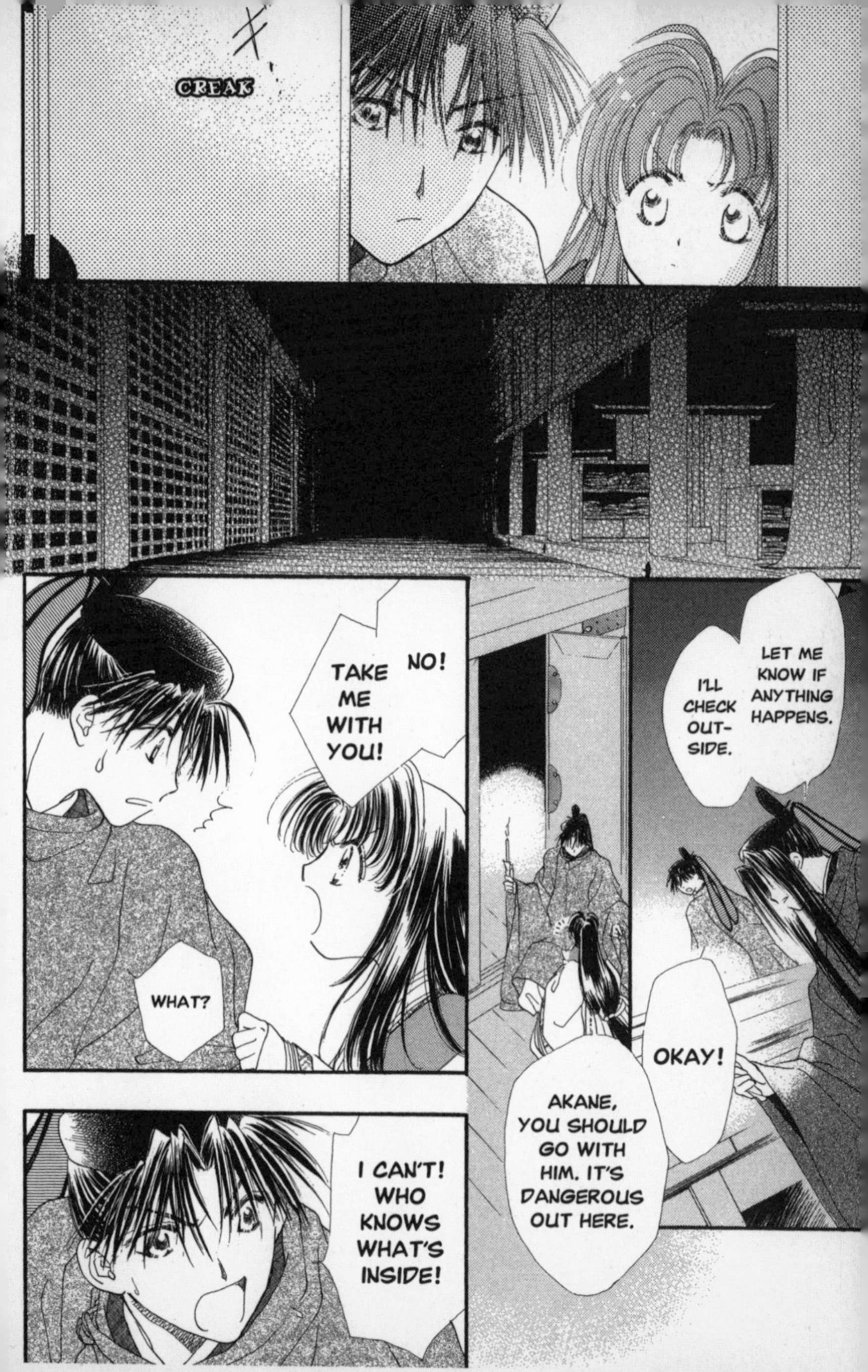
CREAK
LET ME KNOW IF ANYTHING HAPPENS.
I'LL CHECK OUT-SIDE.
OKAY!
AKANE, YOU SHOULD GO WITH HIM. IT'S DANGEROUS OUT HERE.
NO!
TAKE ME WITH YOU!
WHAT?
I CAN'T! WHO KNOWS WHAT'S INSIDE!

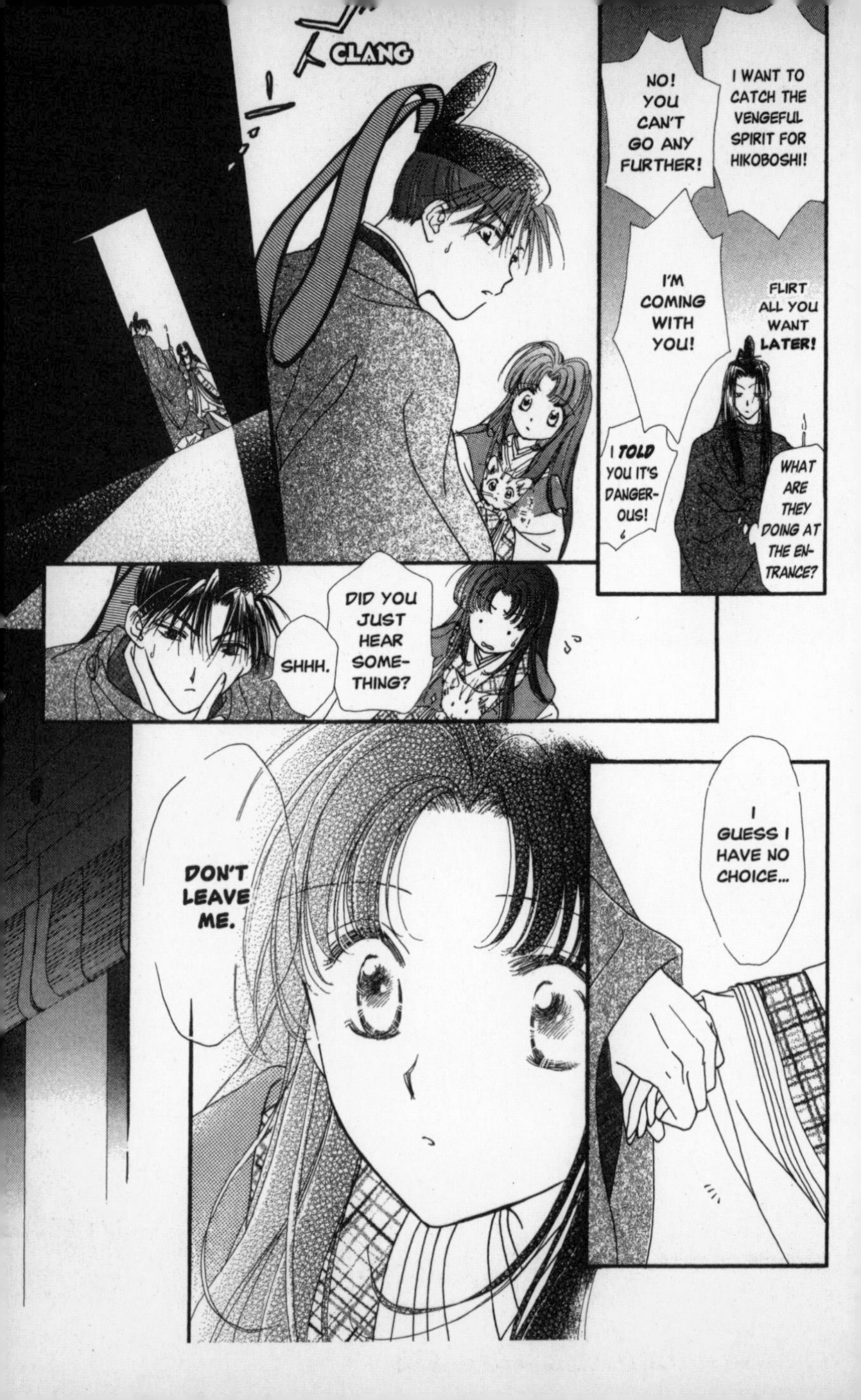
I WANT TO CATCH THE VENGEFUL SPIRIT FOR HIKOBOSHI!
NO! YOU CAN'T GO ANY FURTHER!
FLIRT ALL YOU WANT **LATER!**
I'M COMING WITH YOU!
WHAT ARE THEY DOING AT THE EN-TRANCE?
I ***TOLD*** YOU IT'S DANGER-OUS!
CLANG
DID YOU JUST HEAR SOME-THING?
SHHH.
I GUESS I HAVE NO CHOICE...
DON'T LEAVE ME.

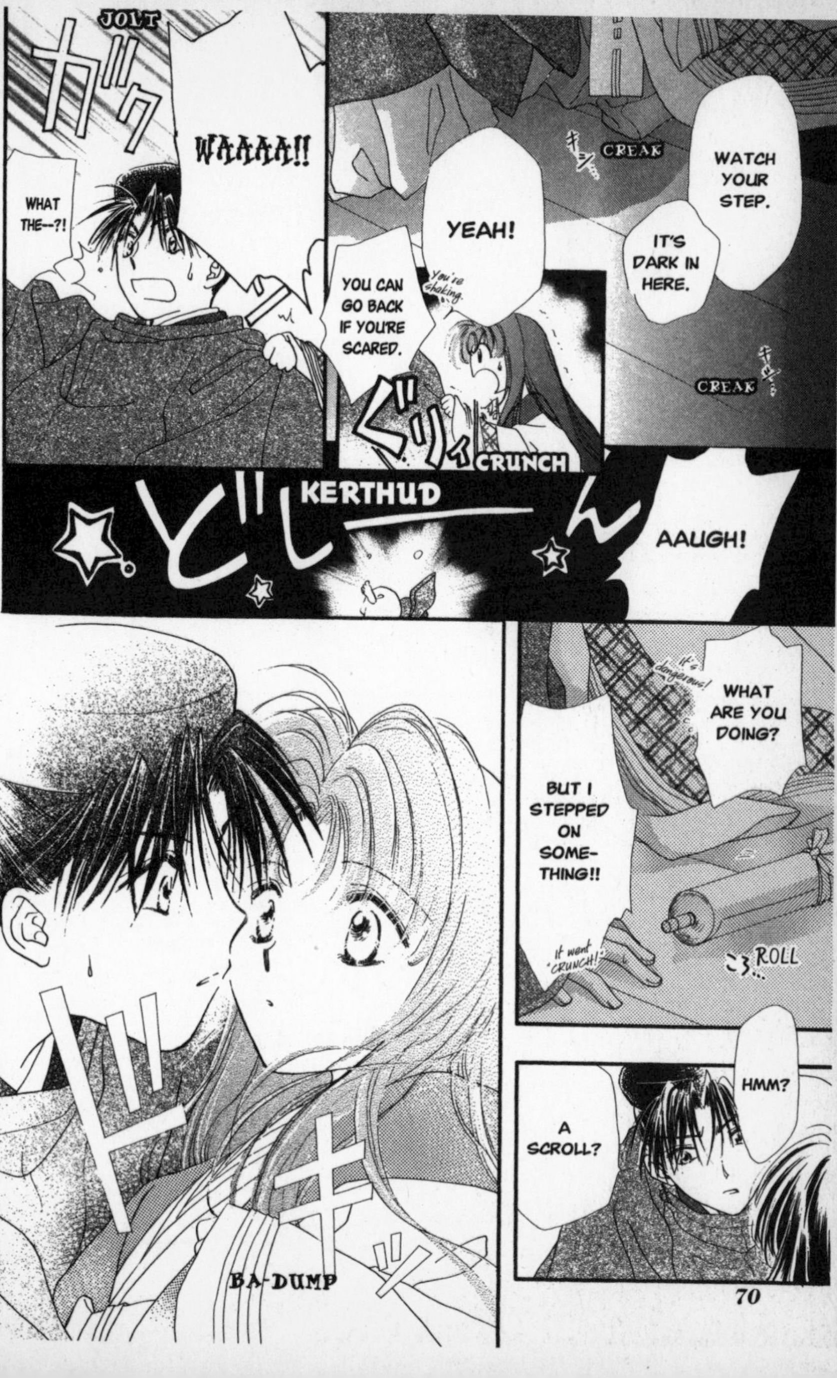
WATCH YOUR STEP.
CREAK
IT'S DARK IN HERE.
CREAK
YEAH!
You're shaking.
YOU CAN GO BACK IF YOU'RE SCARED.
CRUNCH
JOLT
WAAAA!!
WHAT THE--?!
AAUGH!
KERTHUD
It's dangerous!
WHAT ARE YOU DOING?
BUT I STEPPED ON SOMETHING!!
It went "CRUNCH!"
ROLL
HMM?
A SCROLL?
BA-DUMP

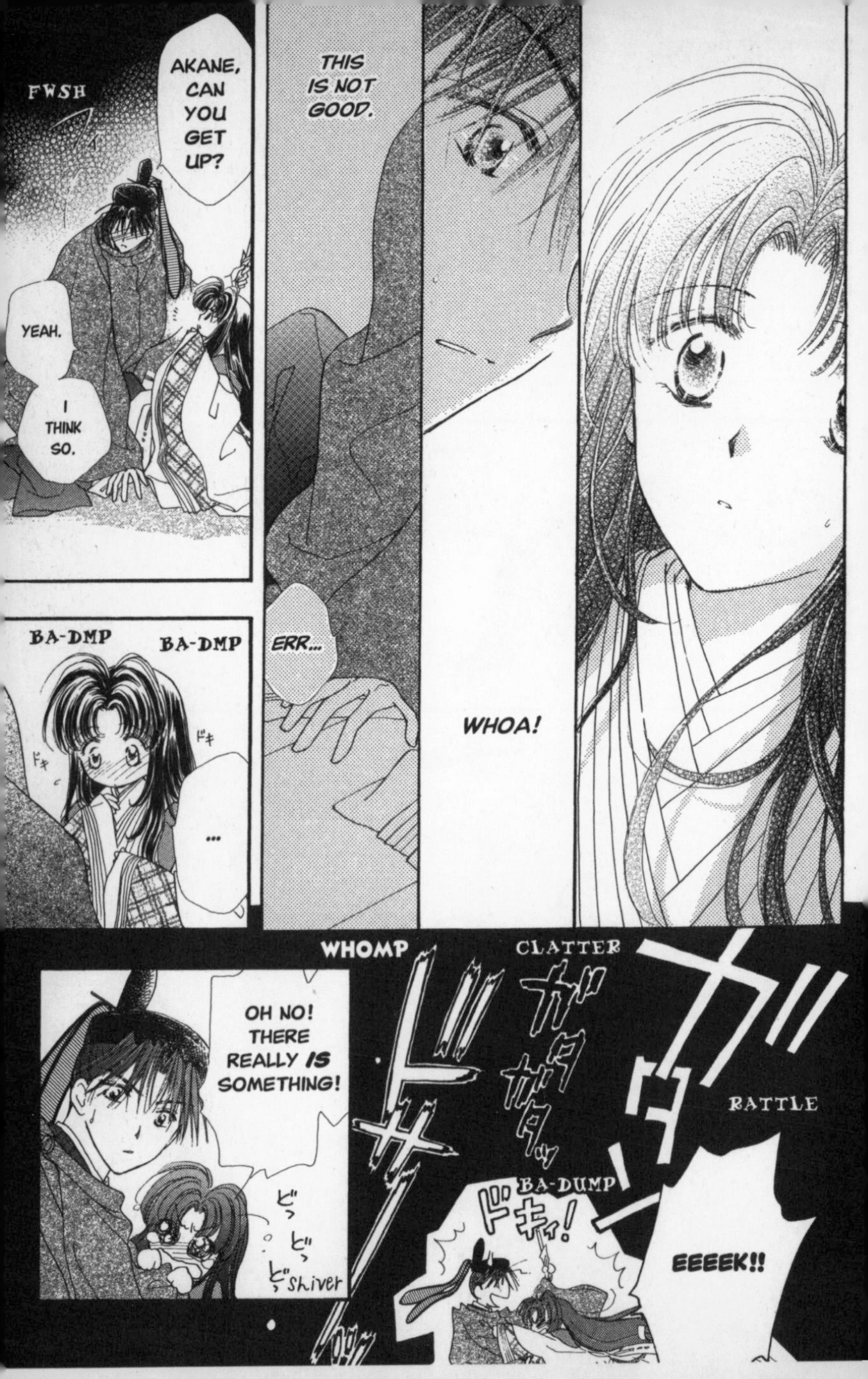
WHOA!
THIS IS NOT GOOD.
ERR...
FWSH
AKANE, CAN YOU GET UP?
YEAH.
I THINK SO.
BA-DMP
BA-DMP
ドキ
ドキ
...
WHOMP
CLATTER
ガタガタッ
RATTLE
BA-DUMP
ドキィ!
EEEEK!!
OH NO! THERE REALLY *IS* SOMETHING!
どっ どっ どっ shiver

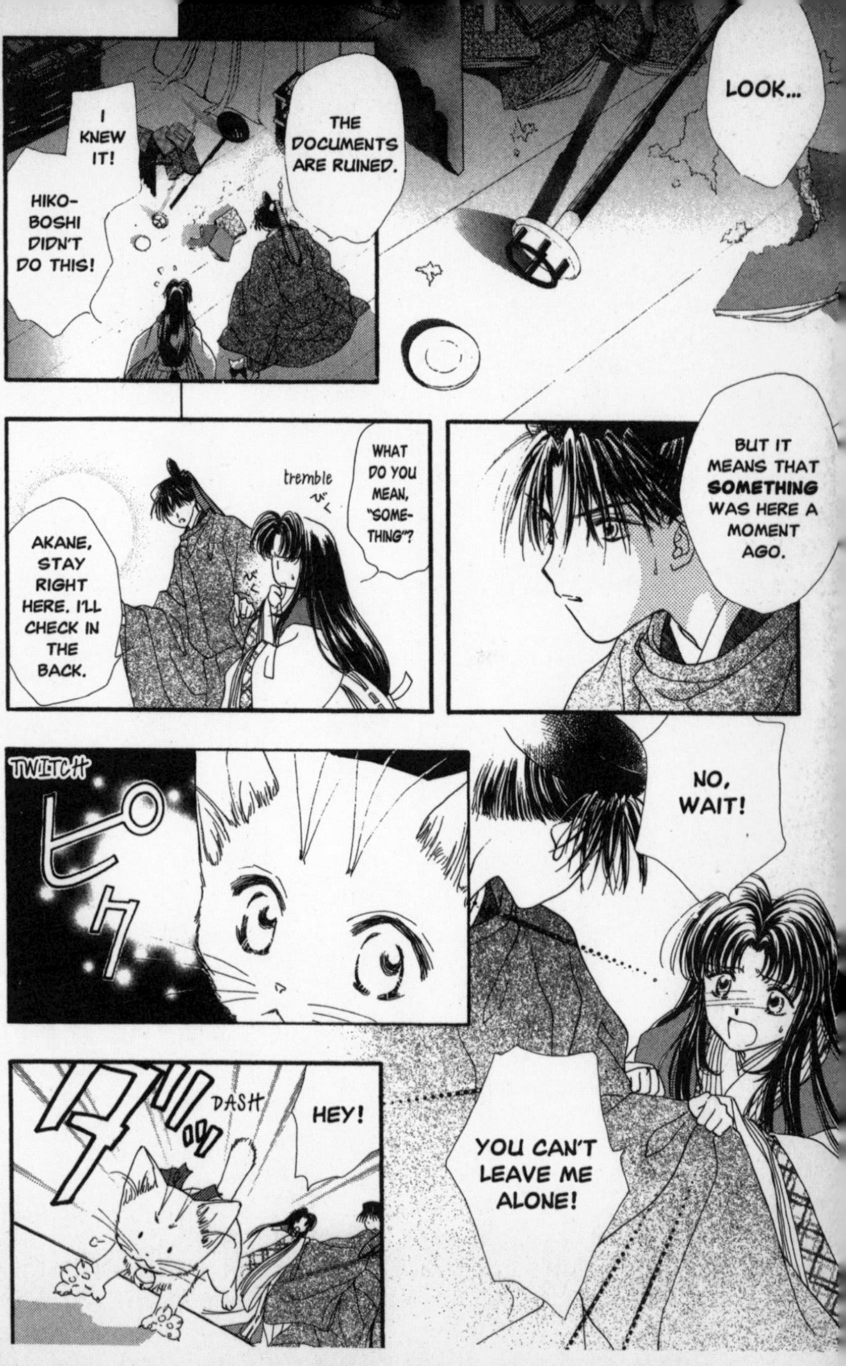
LOOK...
THE DOCUMENTS ARE RUINED.
I KNEW IT!
HIKO-BOSHI DIDN'T DO THIS!
BUT IT MEANS THAT SOMETHING WAS HERE A MOMENT AGO.
WHAT DO YOU MEAN, "SOME-THING"?
tremble
AKANE, STAY RIGHT HERE. I'LL CHECK IN THE BACK.
NO, WAIT!
YOU CAN'T LEAVE ME ALONE!
TWITCH
DASH
HEY!

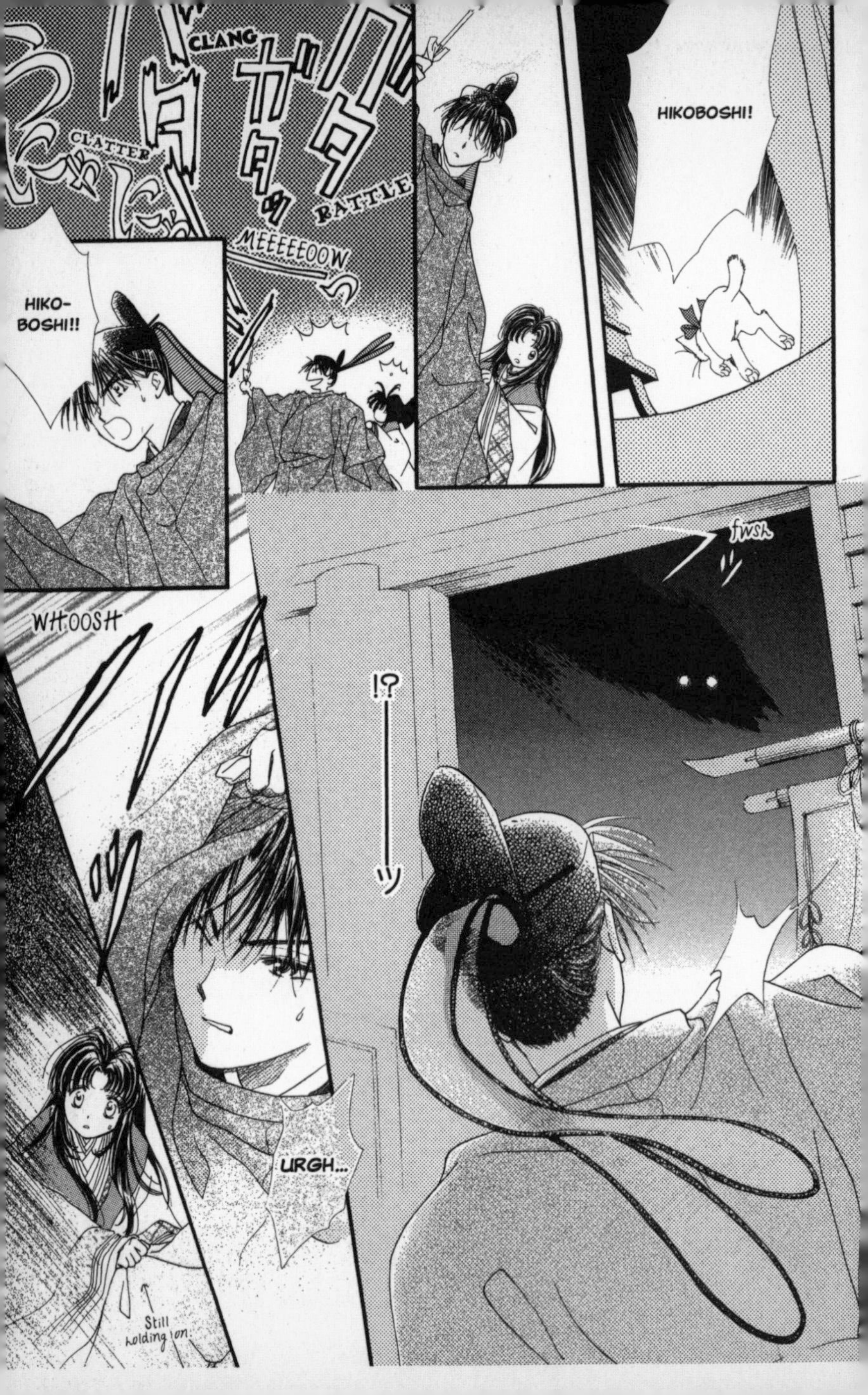
HIKOBOSHI!
CLANG
RATTLE
MEEEEEOOW
CLATTER
HIKO-BOSHI!!
fwsh
!?
WHOOSH
URGH...
Still holding on.

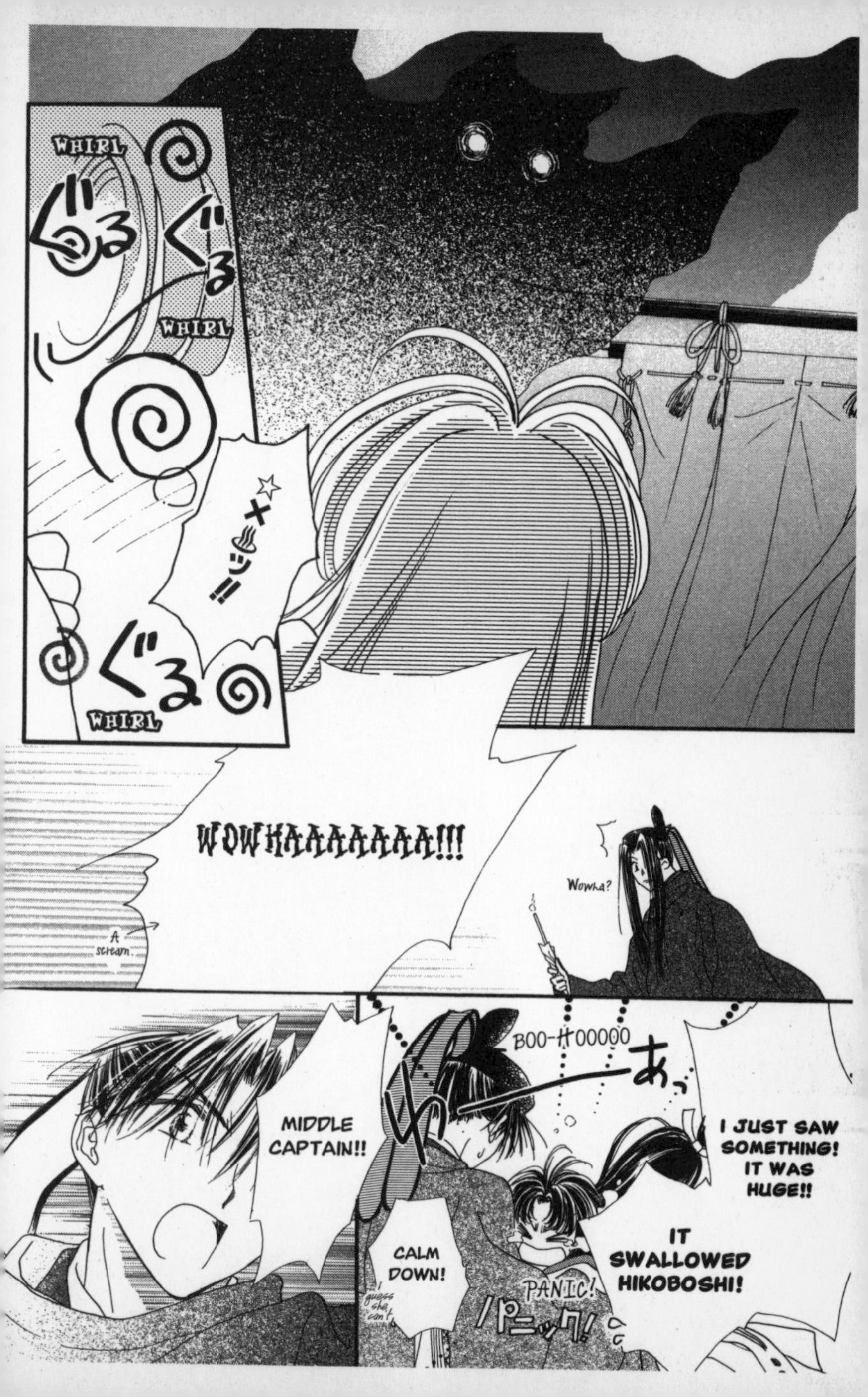
WHIRL
ぐるぐる
WHIRL
☆メ♨ッ!!
ぐる
WHIRL
WOWHAAAAAAAA!!!
A scream.
Wowha?
BOO-HOOOOOO
あっ
I JUST SAW SOMETHING! IT WAS HUGE!!
IT SWALLOWED HIKOBOSHI!
PANIC!
パニック!
CALM DOWN!
I guess she can't
MIDDLE CAPTAIN!!

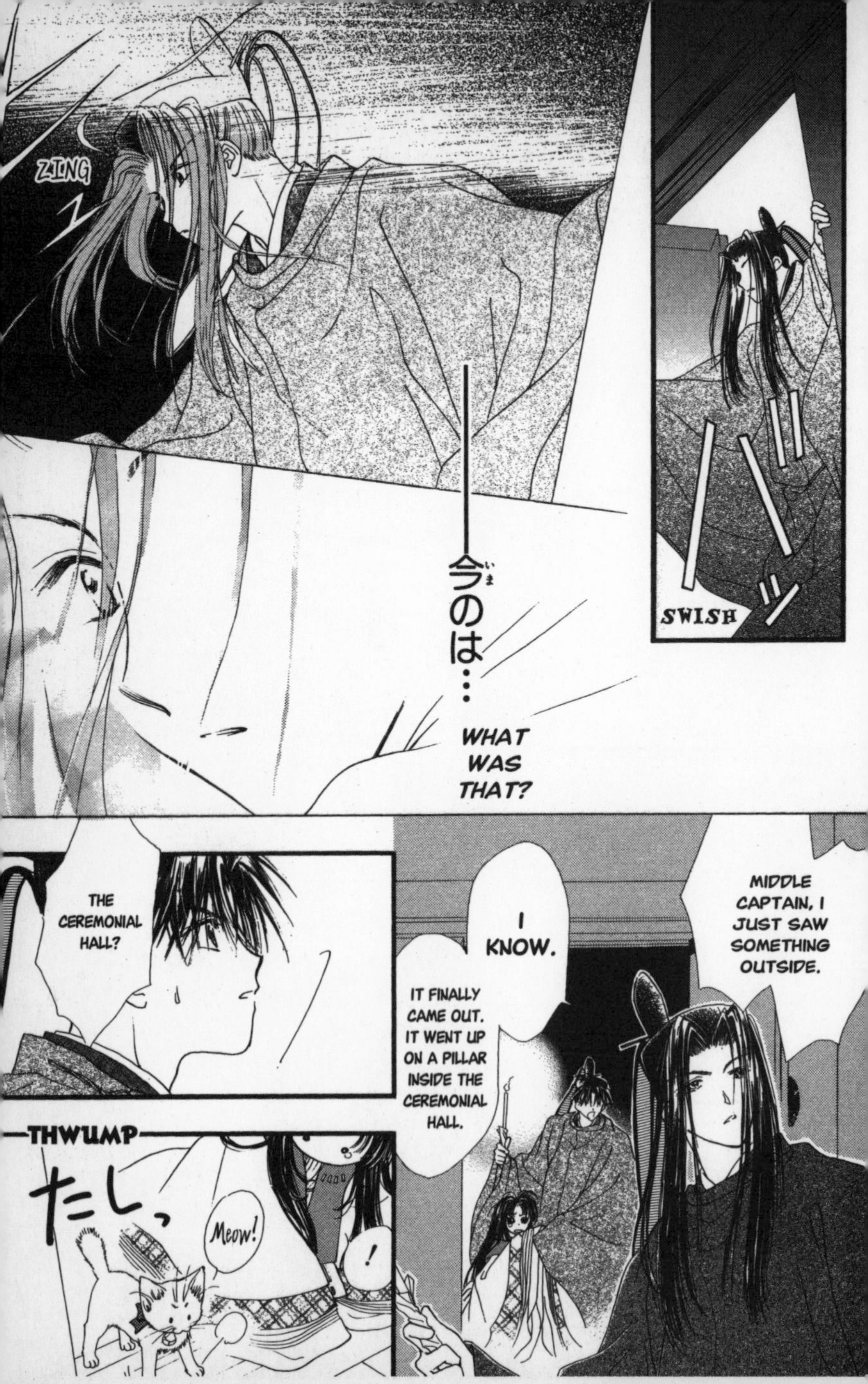
SWISH
ZING
今のは…
WHAT WAS THAT?
MIDDLE CAPTAIN, I JUST SAW SOMETHING OUTSIDE.
I KNOW.
IT FINALLY CAME OUT. IT WENT UP ON A PILLAR INSIDE THE CEREMONIAL HALL.
THE CEREMONIAL HALL?
THWUMP
たしっ
Meow!
!

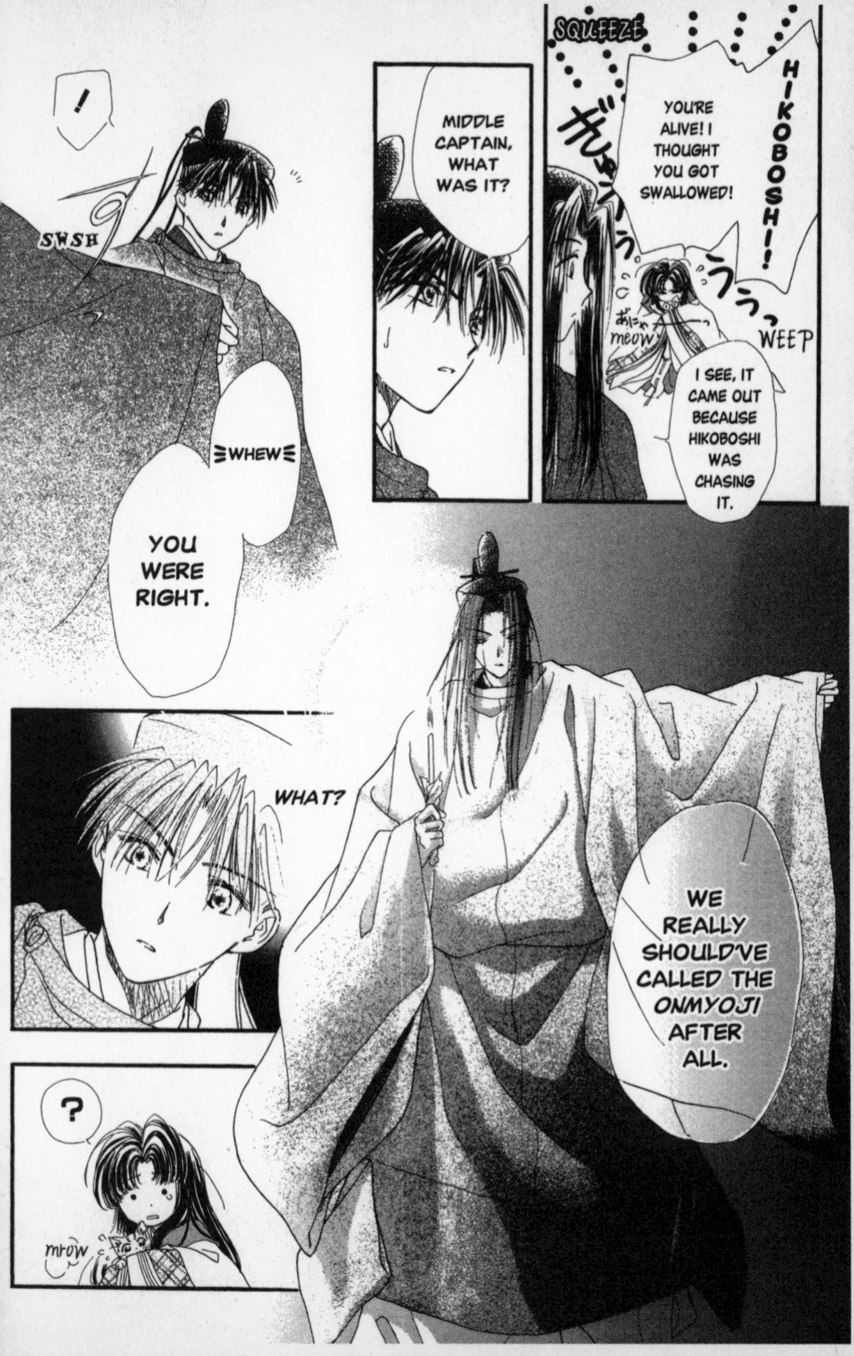
SQUEEZE
HIKOBOSHI!
YOU'RE ALIVE! I THOUGHT YOU GOT SWALLOWED!
WEEP
meow
I SEE, IT CAME OUT BECAUSE HIKOBOSHI WAS CHASING IT.
MIDDLE CAPTAIN, WHAT WAS IT?
!
SWSH
WHEW
YOU WERE RIGHT.
WE REALLY SHOULD'VE CALLED THE ONMYOJI AFTER ALL.
WHAT?
?
mrow

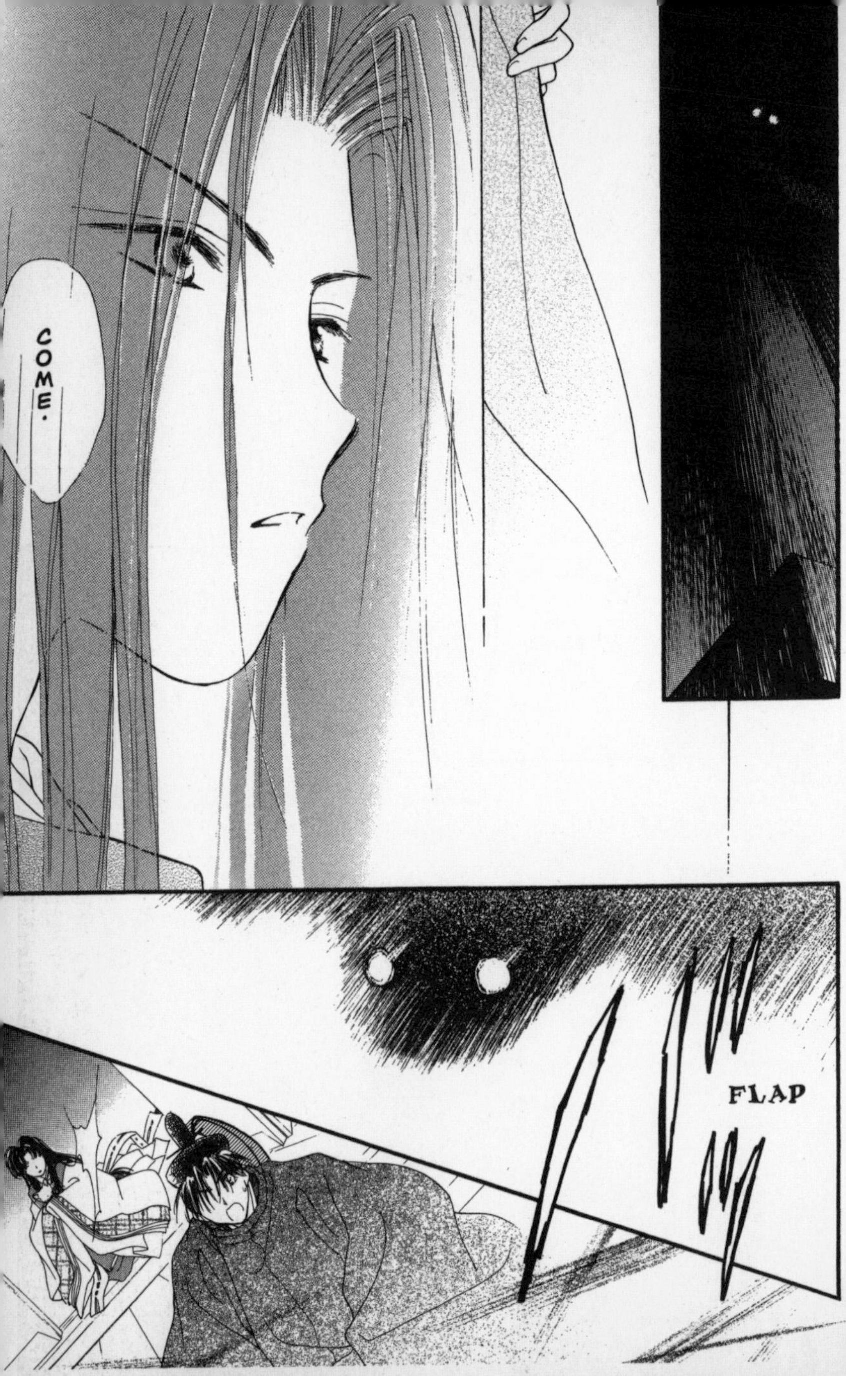
COME.
FLAP

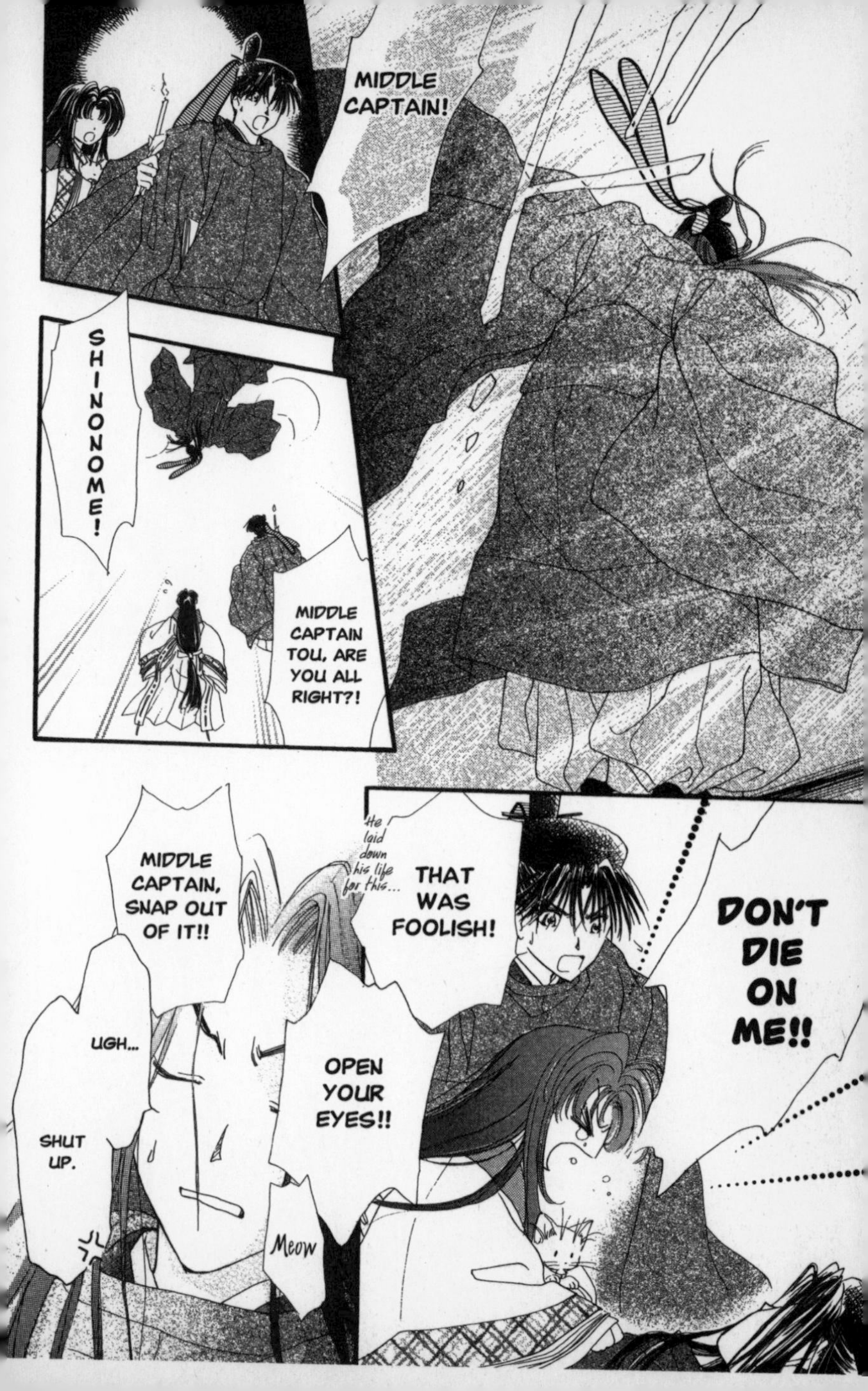
MIDDLE CAPTAIN!
SHINONOME!
MIDDLE CAPTAIN TOU, ARE YOU ALL RIGHT?!
DON'T DIE ON ME!!
......
THAT WAS FOOLISH!
He laid down his life for this...
MIDDLE CAPTAIN, SNAP OUT OF IT!!
OPEN YOUR EYES!!
Meow
UGH...
SHUT UP.

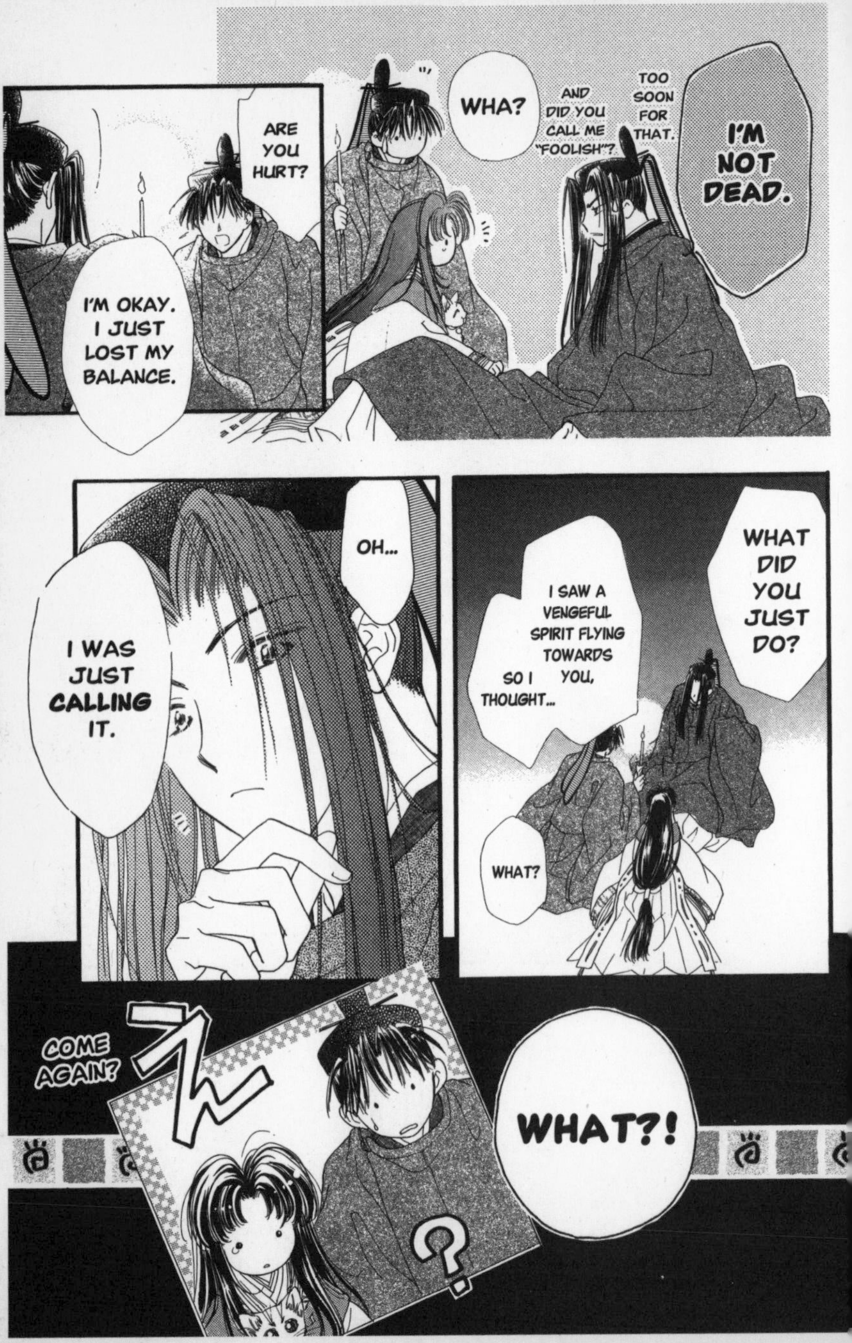
I'M NOT DEAD.
TOO SOON FOR THAT.
AND DID YOU CALL ME "FOOLISH"?
WHA?
ARE YOU HURT?
I'M OKAY. I JUST LOST MY BALANCE.
WHAT DID YOU JUST DO?
I SAW A VENGEFUL SPIRIT FLYING TOWARDS YOU, SO I THOUGHT...
WHAT?
OH...
I WAS JUST CALLING IT.
WHAT?!
COME AGAIN?

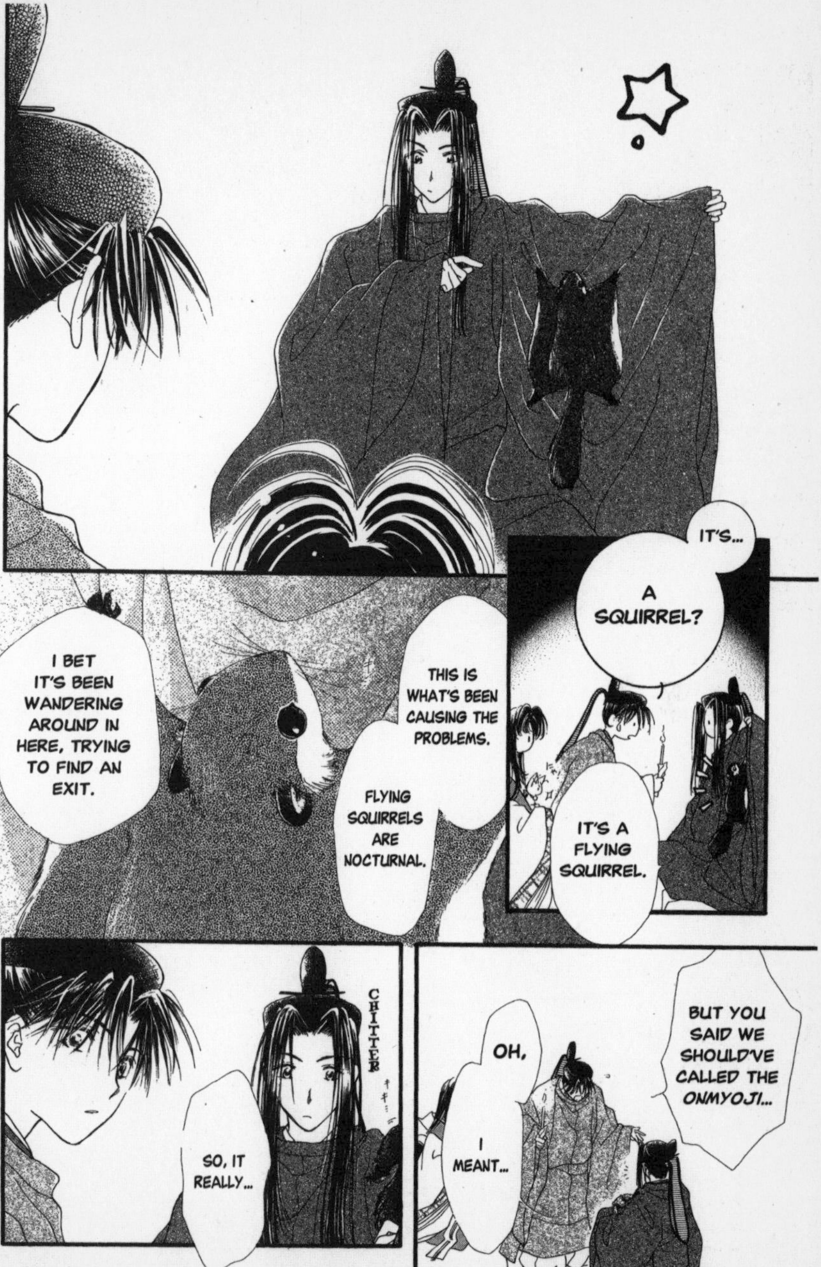
IT'S...
A SQUIRREL?
IT'S A FLYING SQUIRREL.
THIS IS WHAT'S BEEN CAUSING THE PROBLEMS.
FLYING SQUIRRELS ARE NOCTURNAL.
I BET IT'S BEEN WANDERING AROUND IN HERE, TRYING TO FIND AN EXIT.
BUT YOU SAID WE SHOULD'VE CALLED THE ONMYOJI...
OH,
I MEANT...
CHITTER
SO, IT REALLY...

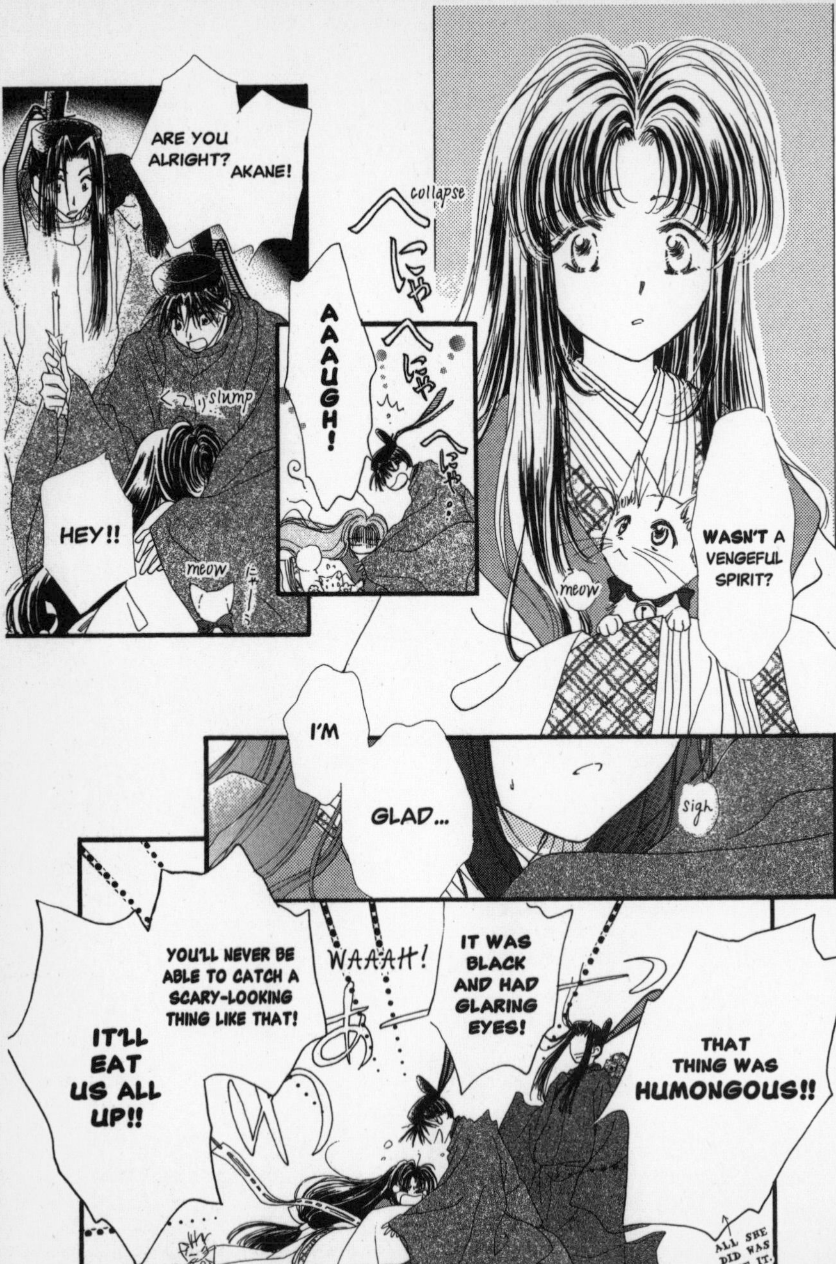
WASN'T A VENGEFUL SPIRIT?
meow
collapse
AAAUGH!
ARE YOU ALRIGHT? AKANE!
slump
HEY!!
meow
I'M
GLAD...
sigh
THAT THING WAS HUMONGOUS!!
IT WAS BLACK AND HAD GLARING EYES!
WAAAH!
YOU'LL NEVER BE ABLE TO CATCH A SCARY-LOOKING THING LIKE THAT!
IT'LL EAT US ALL UP!!
ALL SHE DID WAS SEE IT.

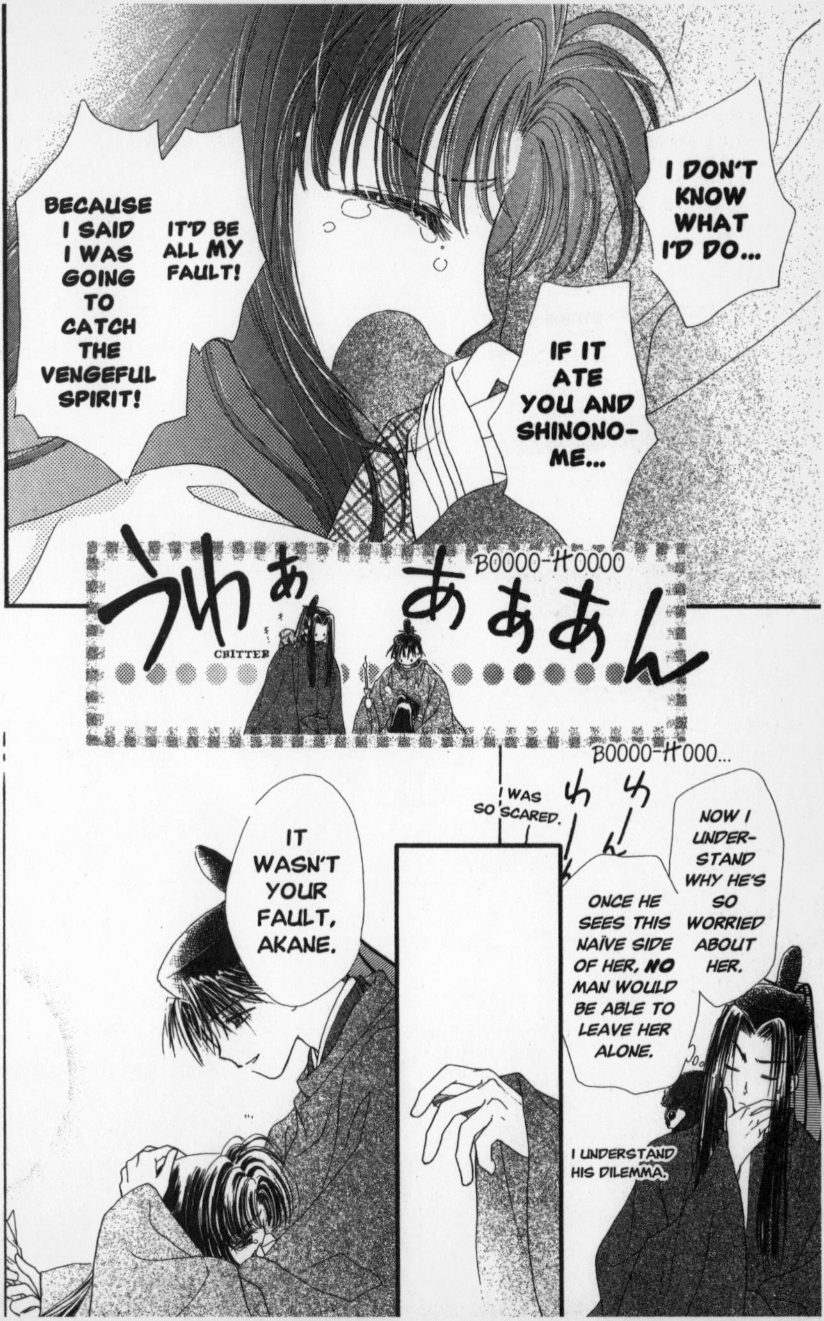

I DON'T KNOW WHAT I'D DO...
IF IT ATE YOU AND SHINONO-ME...
IT'D BE ALL MY FAULT!
BECAUSE I SAID I WAS GOING TO CATCH THE VENGEFUL SPIRIT!
BOOOO-HOOOO
うわぁ あぁあん
CHITTER
BOOOO-HOOO...
わわん
NOW I UNDER-STAND WHY HE'S SO WORRIED ABOUT HER.
ONCE HE SEES THIS NAÏVE SIDE OF HER, NO MAN WOULD BE ABLE TO LEAVE HER ALONE.
I UNDERSTAND HIS DILEMMA.
I WAS SO SCARED.
IT WASN'T YOUR FAULT, AKANE.

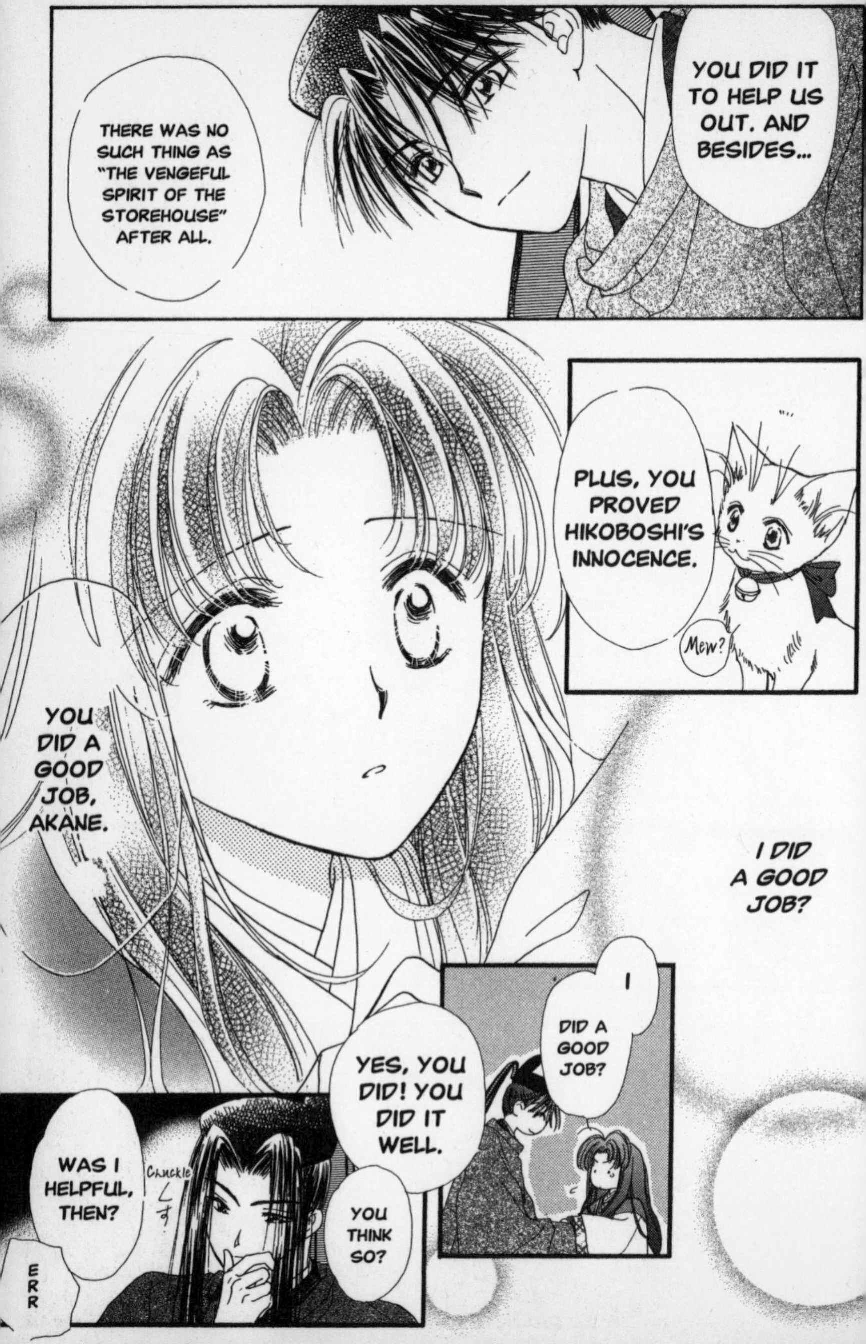
YOU DID IT TO HELP US OUT. AND BESIDES...
THERE WAS NO SUCH THING AS "THE VENGEFUL SPIRIT OF THE STOREHOUSE" AFTER ALL.
PLUS, YOU PROVED HIKOBOSHI'S INNOCENCE.
Mew?
YOU DID A GOOD JOB, AKANE.
I DID A GOOD JOB?
I
DID A GOOD JOB?
YES, YOU DID! YOU DID IT WELL.
YOU THINK SO?
WAS I HELPFUL, THEN?
Chuckle
ERR

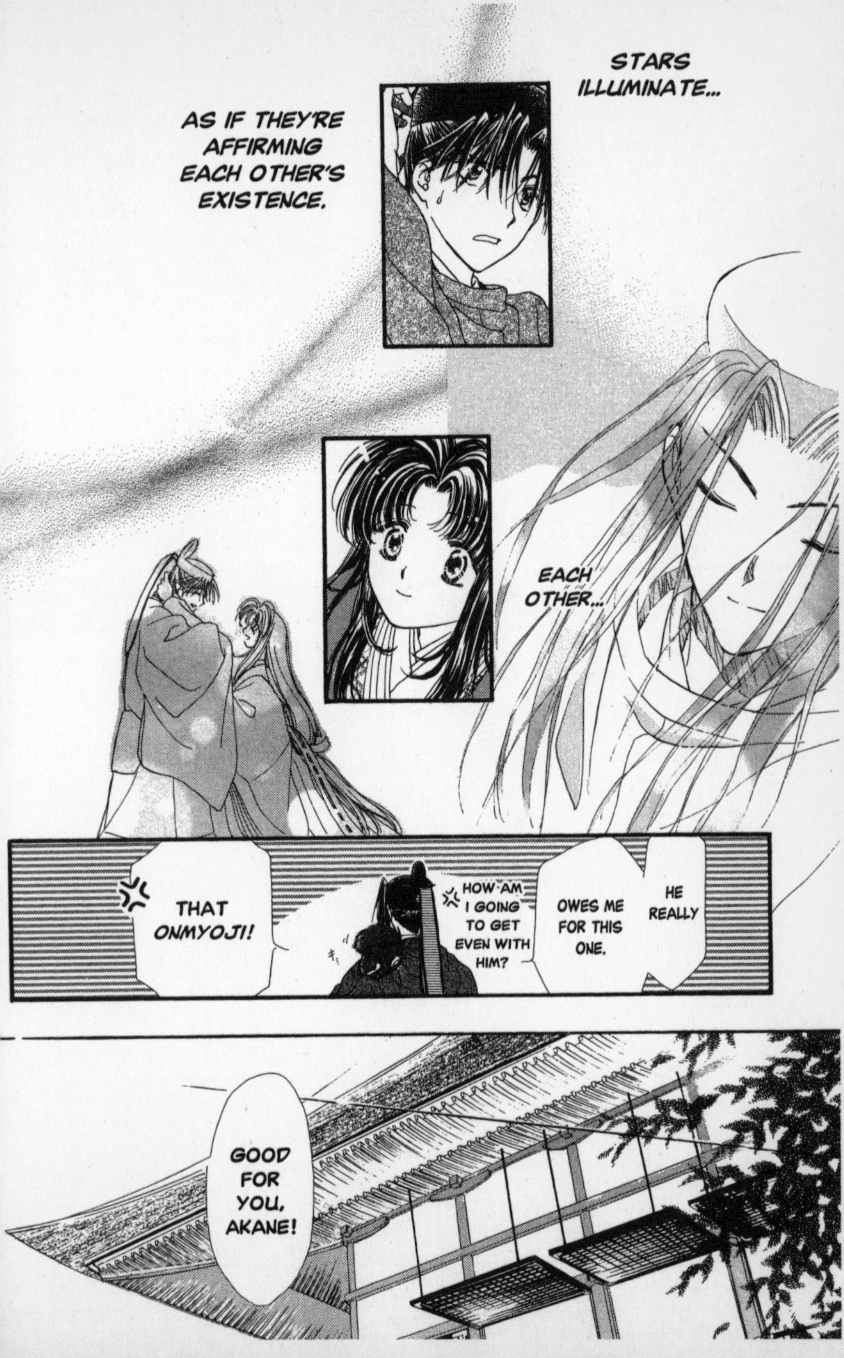
STARS ILLUMINATE...
EACH OTHER...
AS IF THEY'RE AFFIRMING EACH OTHER'S EXISTENCE.
HE REALLY OWES ME FOR THIS ONE.
HOW AM I GOING TO GET EVEN WITH HIM?
THAT ONMYOJI!
GOOD FOR YOU, AKANE!

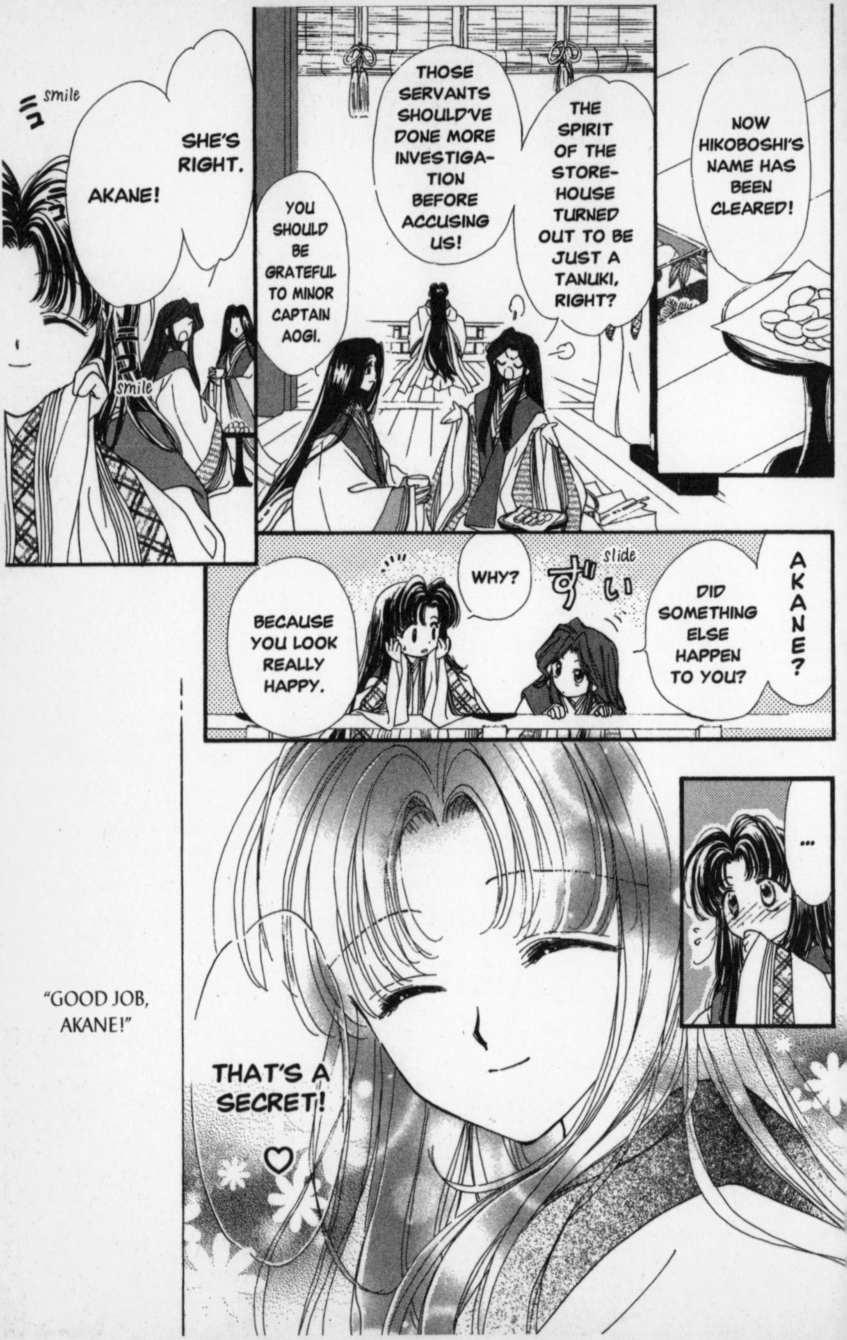
NOW HIKOBOSHI'S NAME HAS BEEN CLEARED!
THE SPIRIT OF THE STOREHOUSE TURNED OUT TO BE JUST A TANUKI, RIGHT?
THOSE SERVANTS SHOULD'VE DONE MORE INVESTIGATION BEFORE ACCUSING US!
YOU SHOULD BE GRATEFUL TO MINOR CAPTAIN AOGI.
SHE'S RIGHT.
AKANE!
smile
smile
AKANE?
DID SOMETHING ELSE HAPPEN TO YOU?
slide
WHY?
BECAUSE YOU LOOK REALLY HAPPY.
...
THAT'S A SECRET! ♡
"GOOD JOB, AKANE!"

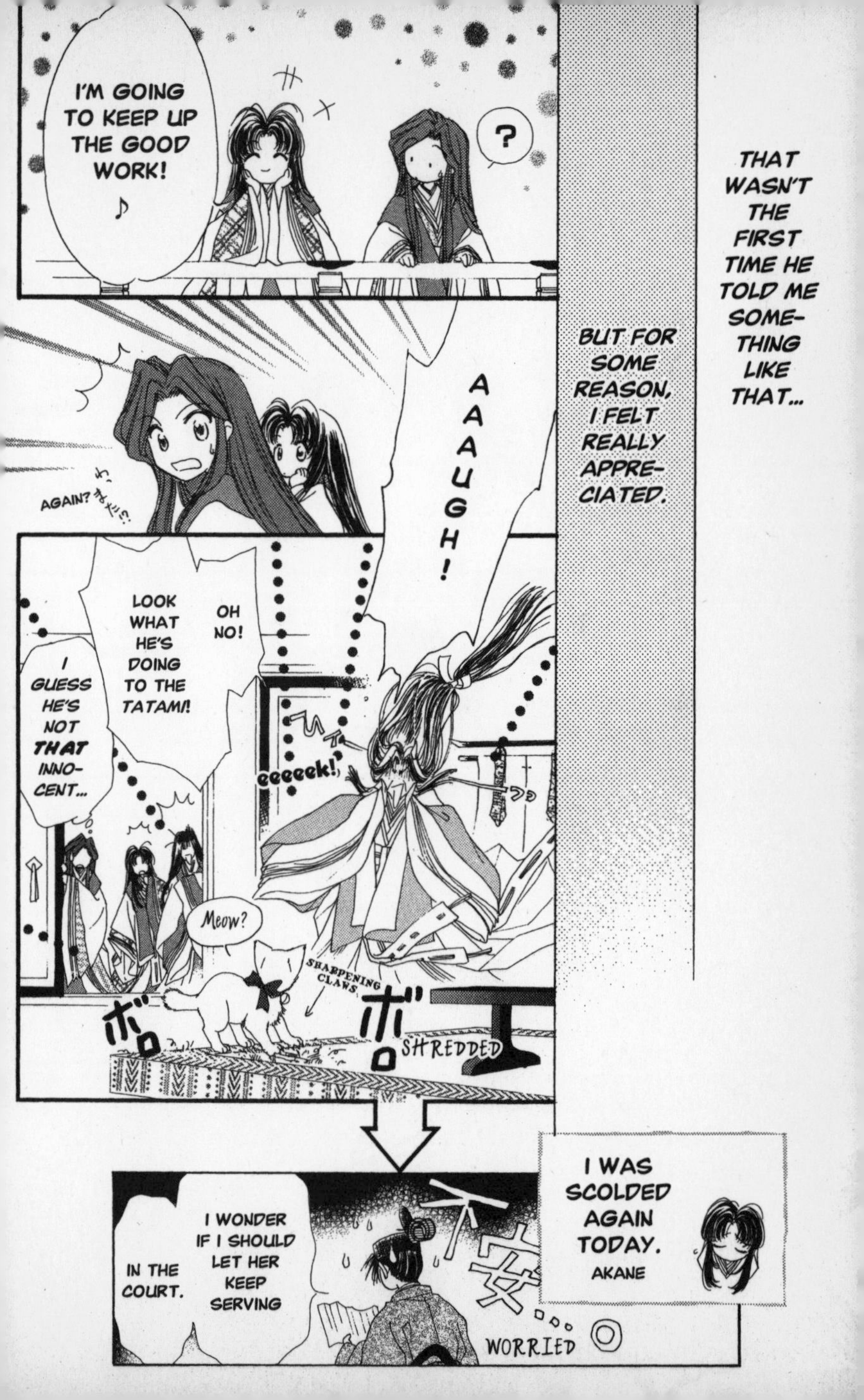
THAT WASN'T THE FIRST TIME HE TOLD ME SOMETHING LIKE THAT...
BUT FOR SOME REASON, I FELT REALLY APPRECIATED.
?
I'M GOING TO KEEP UP THE GOOD WORK! ♪
AAAAUGH!
AGAIN?
eeeeek!
OH NO!
LOOK WHAT HE'S DOING TO THE TATAMI!
I GUESS HE'S NOT **THAT** INNOCENT...
Meow?
SHARPENING CLAWS
SHREDDED
I WAS SCOLDED AGAIN TODAY.
AKANE
I WONDER IF I SHOULD LET HER KEEP SERVING
IN THE COURT.
WORRIED

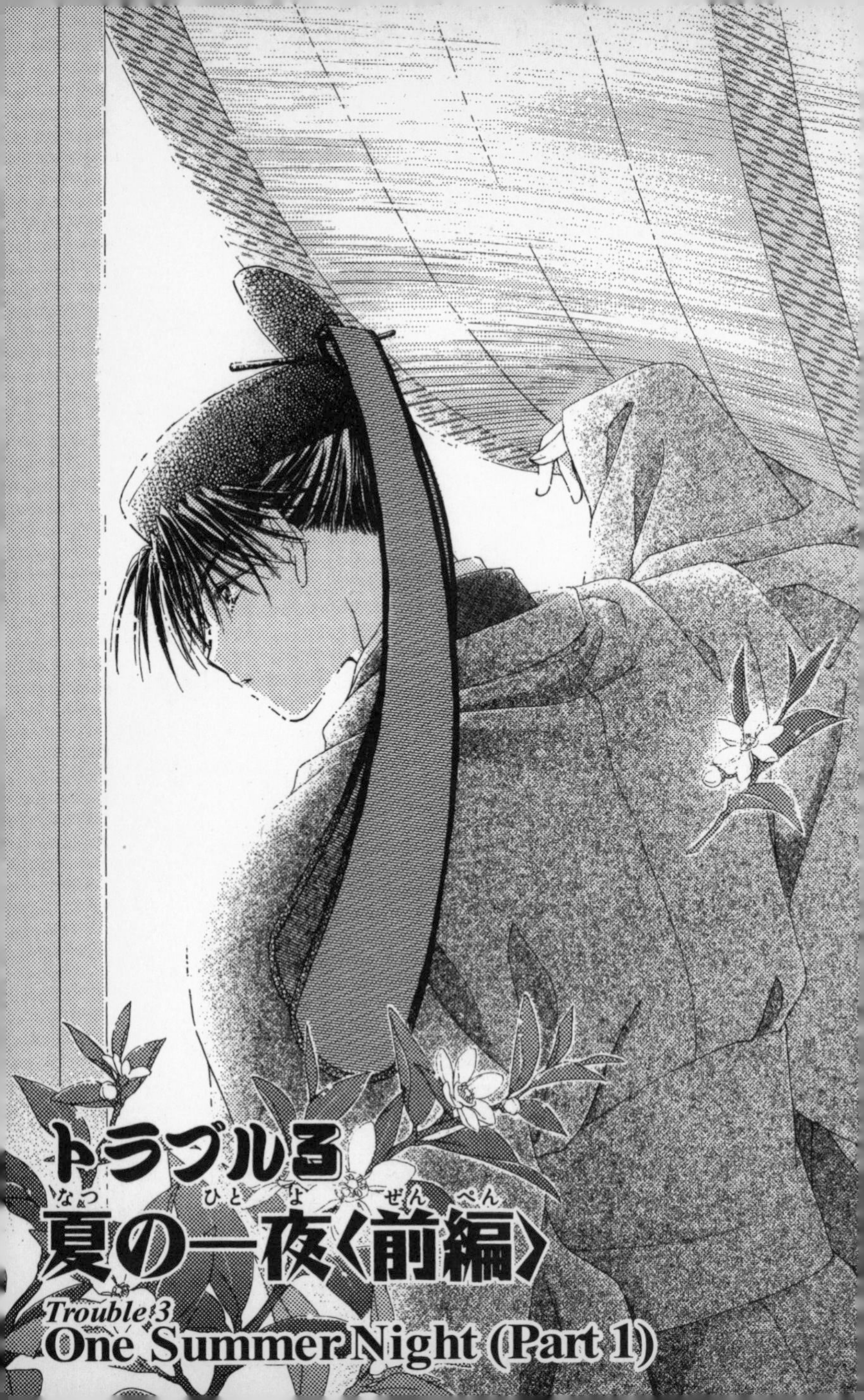
トラブル3
夏の一夜〈前編〉
Trouble 3
One Summer Night (Part 1)

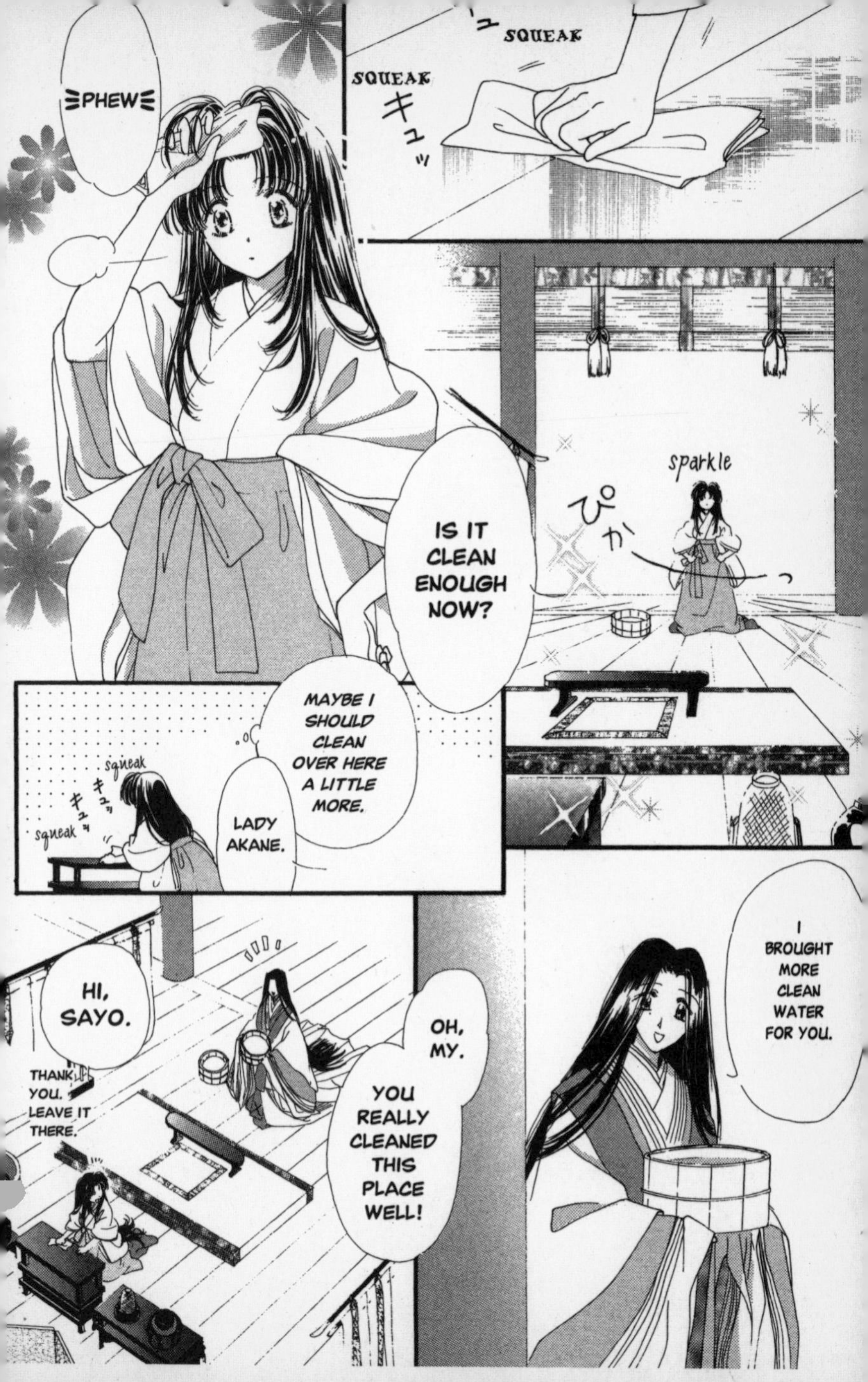

SQUEAK
SQUEAK
キュッ
sparkle
ぴか
PHEW
IS IT CLEAN ENOUGH NOW?
MAYBE I SHOULD CLEAN OVER HERE A LITTLE MORE.
squeak
キュッ
キュッ
squeak
LADY AKANE.
I BROUGHT MORE CLEAN WATER FOR YOU.
OH, MY.
YOU REALLY CLEANED THIS PLACE WELL!
HI, SAYO.
THANK YOU. LEAVE IT THERE.

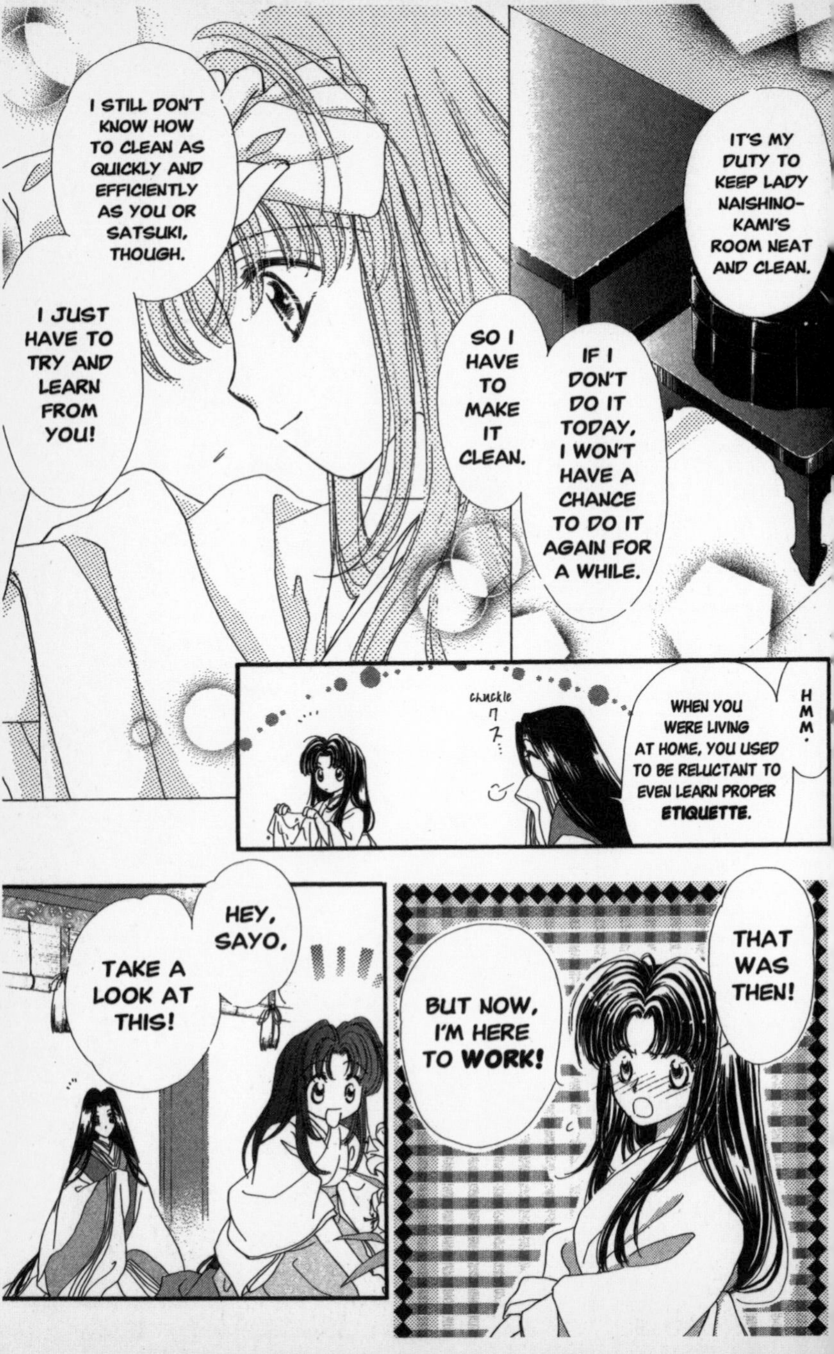
IT'S MY DUTY TO KEEP LADY NAISHINO-KAMI'S ROOM NEAT AND CLEAN.
IF I DON'T DO IT TODAY, I WON'T HAVE A CHANCE TO DO IT AGAIN FOR A WHILE.
SO I HAVE TO MAKE IT CLEAN.
I STILL DON'T KNOW HOW TO CLEAN AS QUICKLY AND EFFICIENTLY AS YOU OR SATSUKI, THOUGH.
I JUST HAVE TO TRY AND LEARN FROM YOU!
HMM.
WHEN YOU WERE LIVING AT HOME, YOU USED TO BE RELUCTANT TO EVEN LEARN PROPER ETIQUETTE.
chuckle
THAT WAS THEN!
BUT NOW, I'M HERE TO WORK!
HEY, SAYO,
TAKE A LOOK AT THIS!

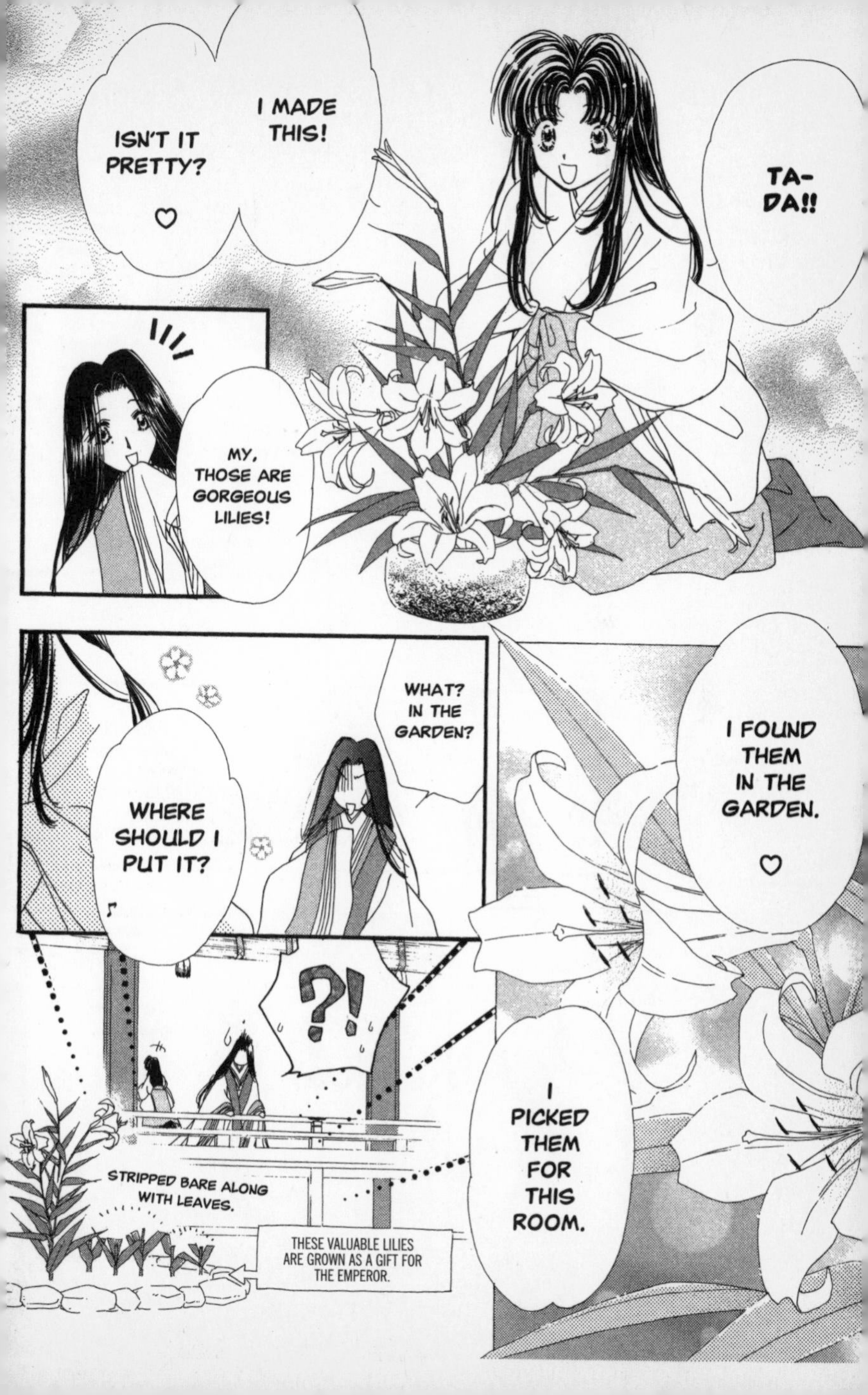
TA-DA!!
I MADE THIS!
ISN'T IT PRETTY? ♡
MY, THOSE ARE GORGEOUS LILIES!
I FOUND THEM IN THE GARDEN. ♡
I PICKED THEM FOR THIS ROOM.
WHAT? IN THE GARDEN?
WHERE SHOULD I PUT IT?
?!
STRIPPED BARE ALONG WITH LEAVES.
THESE VALUABLE LILIES ARE GROWN AS A GIFT FOR THE EMPEROR.

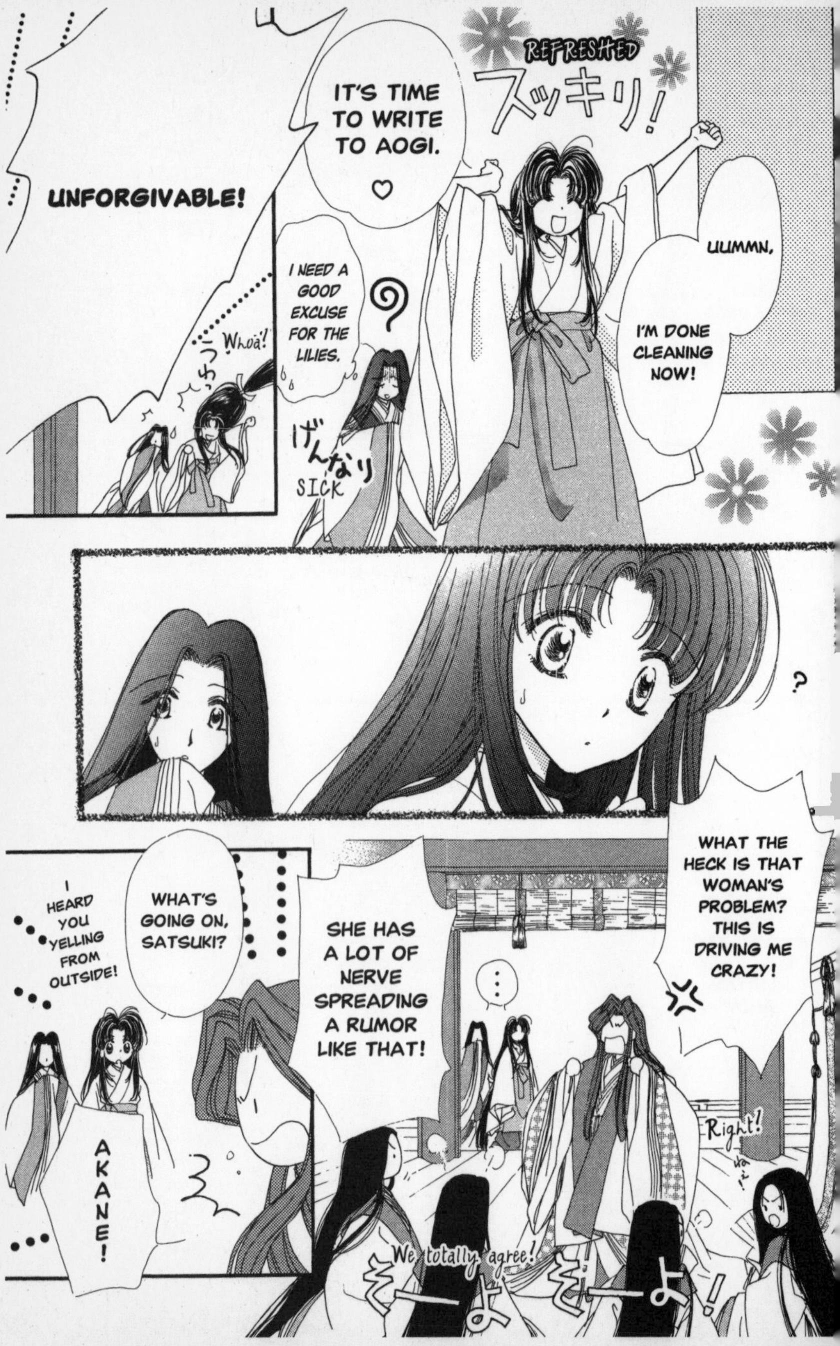
REFRESHED
スッキリ!
UUMMN,
I'M DONE CLEANING NOW!
IT'S TIME TO WRITE TO AOGI. ♡
I NEED A GOOD EXCUSE FOR THE LILIES.
げんなり
SICK
UNFORGIVABLE!
うわっ
Whoa!
?
WHAT THE HECK IS THAT WOMAN'S PROBLEM? THIS IS DRIVING ME CRAZY!
SHE HAS A LOT OF NERVE SPREADING A RUMOR LIKE THAT!
Right!
...
We totally agree!
そーよそーよ!
WHAT'S GOING ON, SATSUKI?
I HEARD YOU YELLING FROM OUTSIDE!
AKANE!

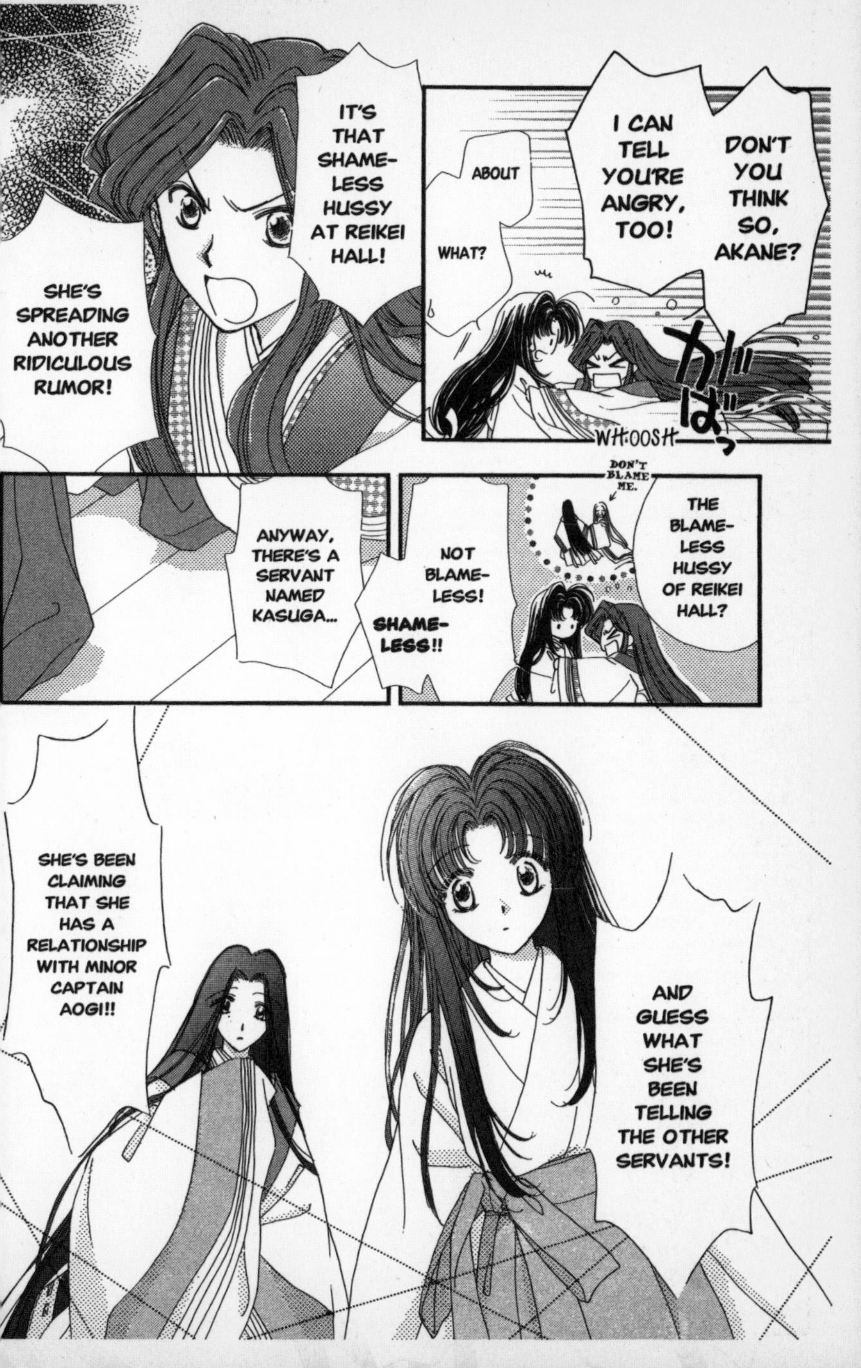
DON'T YOU THINK SO, AKANE?
I CAN TELL YOU'RE ANGRY, TOO!
ABOUT WHAT?
かばっ
WHOOSH
IT'S THAT SHAME-LESS HUSSY AT REIKEI HALL!
SHE'S SPREADING ANOTHER RIDICULOUS RUMOR!
THE BLAME-LESS HUSSY OF REIKEI HALL?
DON'T BLAME ME.
NOT BLAME-LESS!
SHAME-LESS!!
ANYWAY, THERE'S A SERVANT NAMED KASUGA...
AND GUESS WHAT SHE'S BEEN TELLING THE OTHER SERVANTS!
SHE'S BEEN CLAIMING THAT SHE HAS A RELATIONSHIP WITH MINOR CAPTAIN AOGI!!

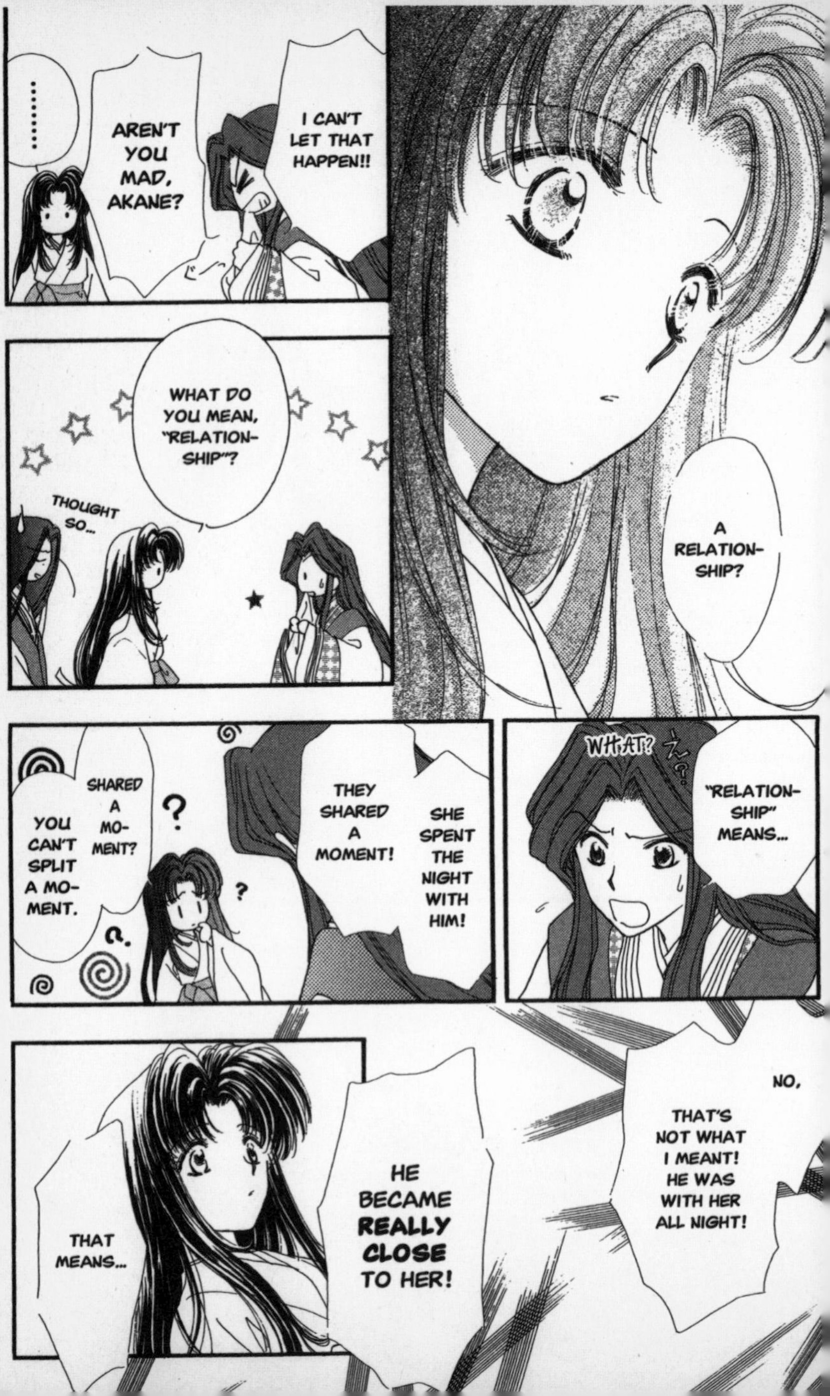
A RELATIONSHIP?
I CAN'T LET THAT HAPPEN!!
AREN'T YOU MAD, AKANE?
....
WHAT DO YOU MEAN, "RELATION-SHIP"?
THOUGHT SO...
WHAT?
"RELATION-SHIP" MEANS...
SHE SPENT THE NIGHT WITH HIM!
THEY SHARED A MOMENT!
SHARED A MO-MENT?
YOU CAN'T SPLIT A MO-MENT.
NO,
THAT'S NOT WHAT I MEANT! HE WAS WITH HER ALL NIGHT!
HE BECAME **REALLY CLOSE** TO HER!
THAT MEANS...

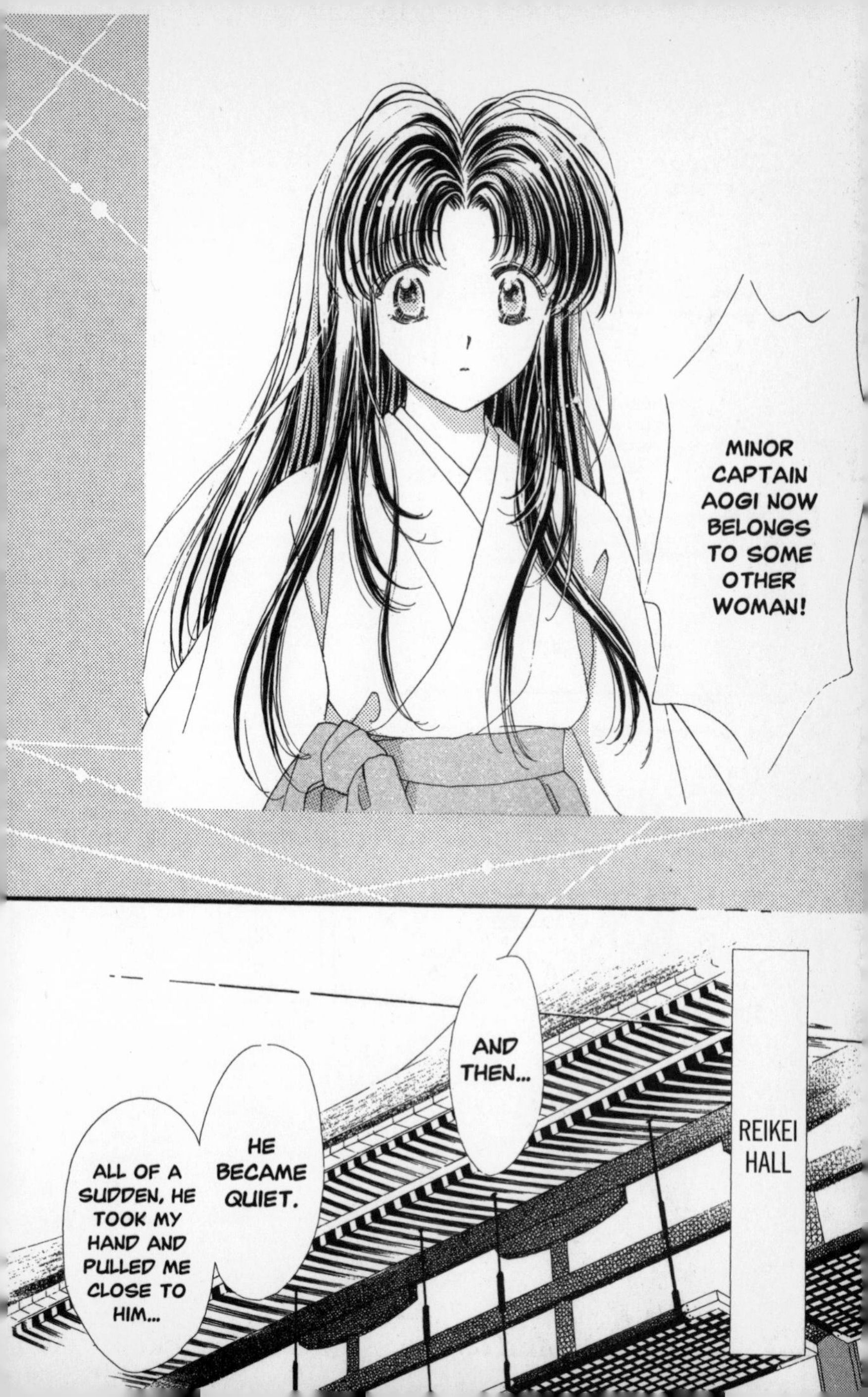
MINOR CAPTAIN AOGI NOW BELONGS TO SOME OTHER WOMAN!
REIKEI HALL
AND THEN...
HE BECAME QUIET.
ALL OF A SUDDEN, HE TOOK MY HAND AND PULLED ME CLOSE TO HIM...

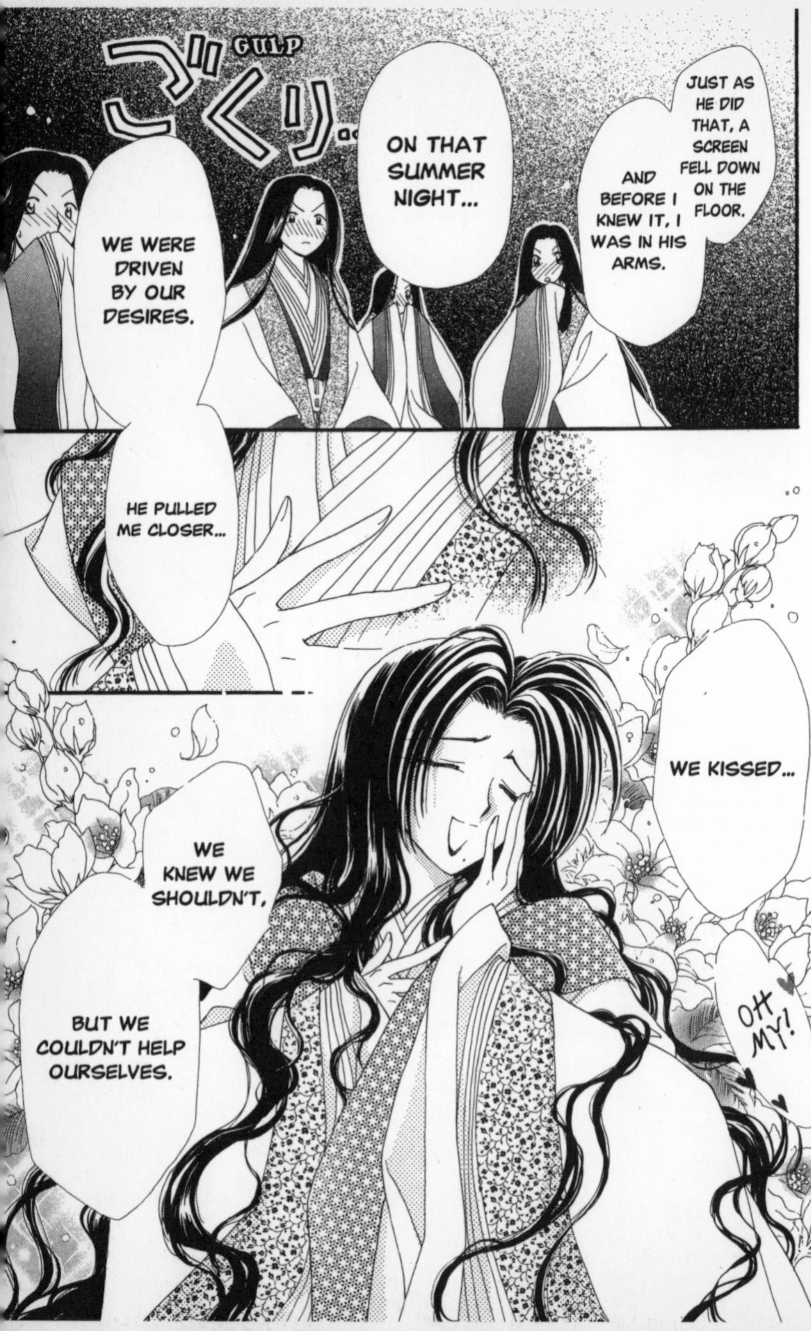
JUST AS HE DID THAT, A SCREEN FELL DOWN ON THE FLOOR.
AND BEFORE I KNEW IT, I WAS IN HIS ARMS.
ON THAT SUMMER NIGHT...
ごくり GULP
WE WERE DRIVEN BY OUR DESIRES.
HE PULLED ME CLOSER...
WE KISSED...
OH MY!
WE KNEW WE SHOULDN'T,
BUT WE COULDN'T HELP OURSELVES.

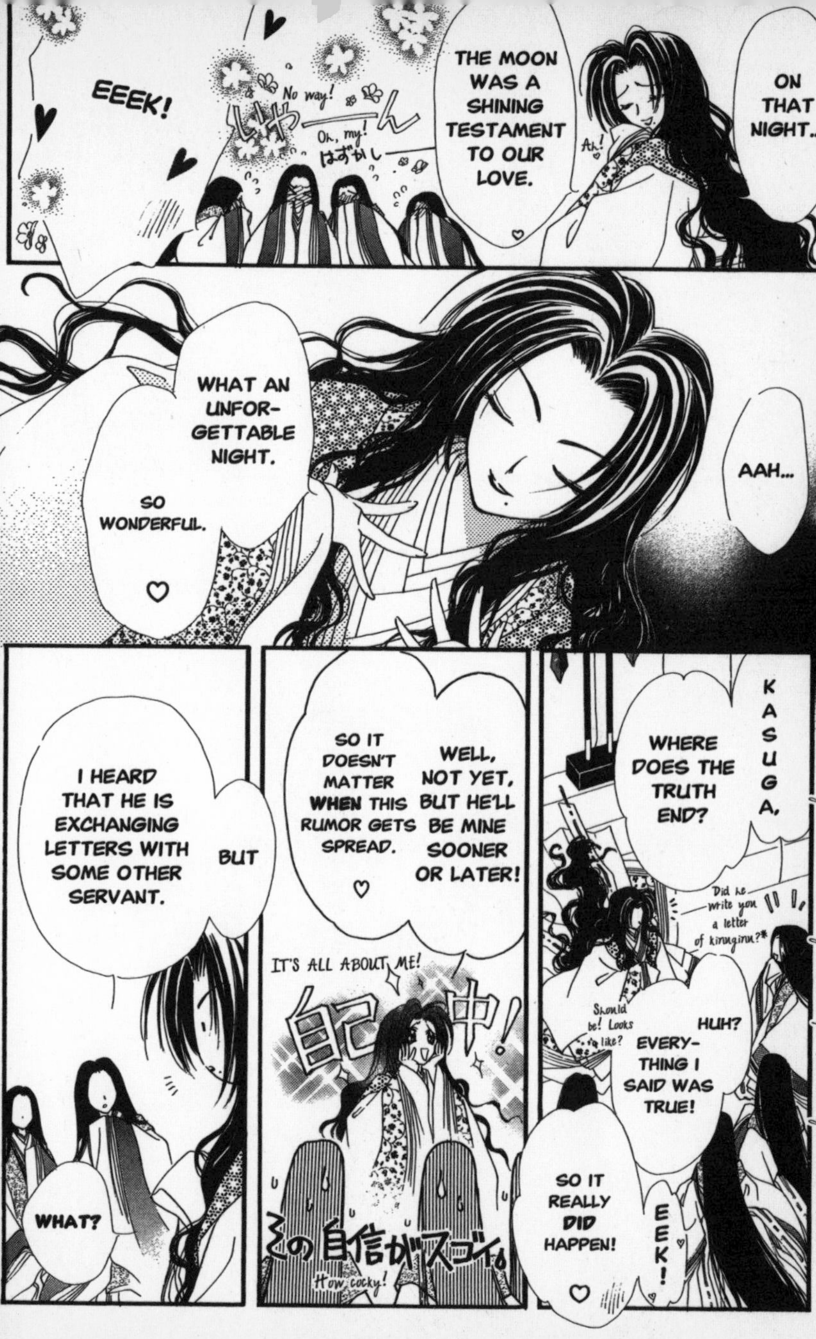
ON THAT NIGHT...
Ah!
THE MOON WAS A SHINING TESTAMENT TO OUR LOVE.
No way!
いやーん
Oh, my!
はずかし
EEEK!
AAH...
WHAT AN UNFORGETTABLE NIGHT.
SO WONDERFUL.
KASUGA,
WHERE DOES THE TRUTH END?
Did he write you a letter of kinuginu?*
HUH? EVERYTHING I SAID WAS TRUE!
Should be! Looks like?
SO IT REALLY DID HAPPEN!
EEK!
WELL, NOT YET, BUT HE'LL BE MINE SOONER OR LATER!
SO IT DOESN'T MATTER WHEN THIS RUMOR GETS SPREAD.
IT'S ALL ABOUT ME!
自己中!
その自信がスゴイ。
How cocky!
I HEARD THAT HE IS EXCHANGING LETTERS WITH SOME OTHER SERVANT.
BUT
WHAT?

•Letter of kinuginu= A letter, usually a romantic poem, written by a man to a woman.

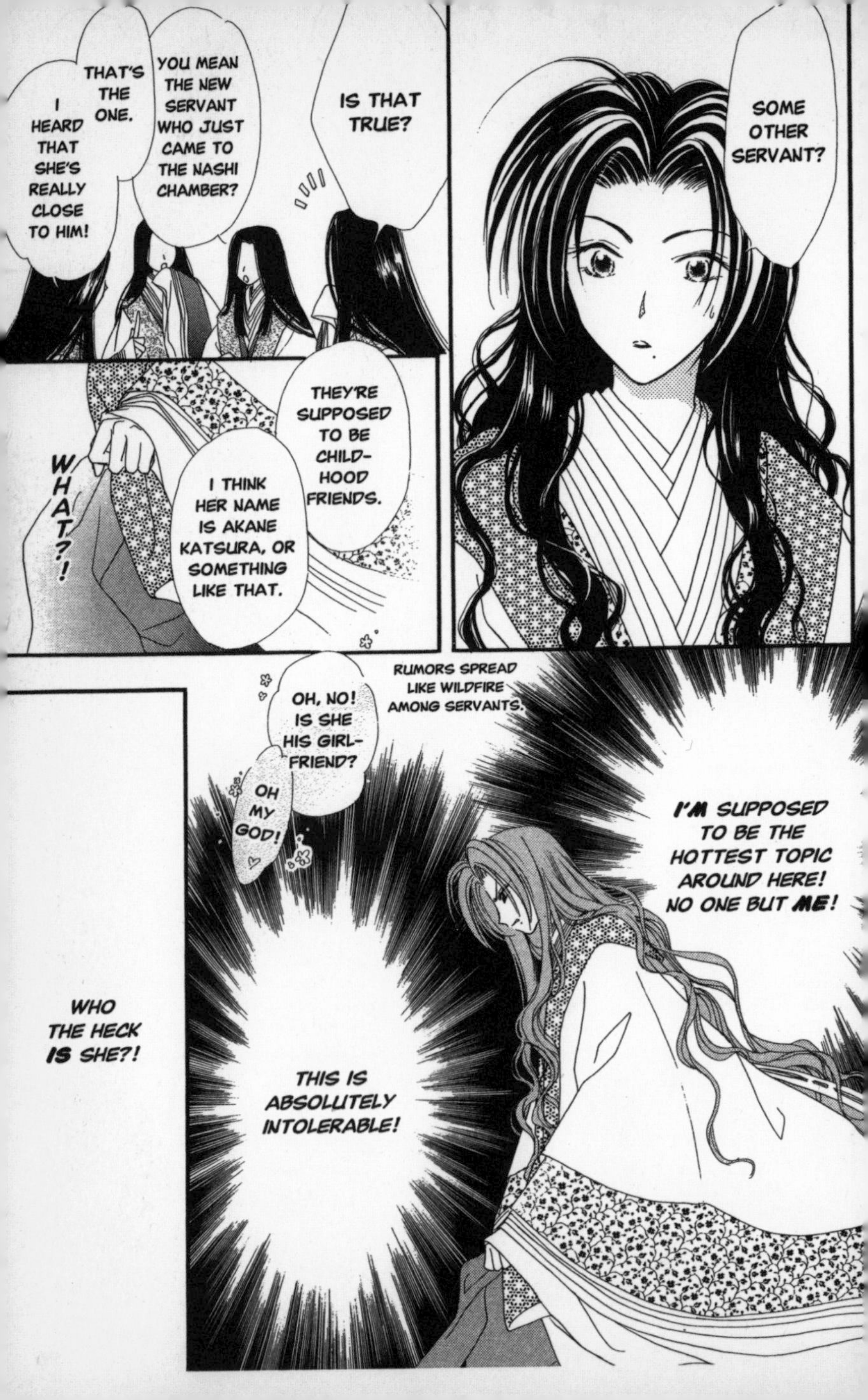
SOME OTHER SERVANT?
IS THAT TRUE?
YOU MEAN THE NEW SERVANT WHO JUST CAME TO THE NASHI CHAMBER?
THAT'S THE ONE.
I HEARD THAT SHE'S REALLY CLOSE TO HIM!
THEY'RE SUPPOSED TO BE CHILD-HOOD FRIENDS.
I THINK HER NAME IS AKANE KATSURA, OR SOMETHING LIKE THAT.
WHAT?!
RUMORS SPREAD LIKE WILDFIRE AMONG SERVANTS.
I'M SUPPOSED TO BE THE HOTTEST TOPIC AROUND HERE! NO ONE BUT ME!
OH, NO! IS SHE HIS GIRL-FRIEND?
OH MY GOD!
THIS IS ABSOLUTELY INTOLERABLE!
WHO THE HECK IS SHE?!

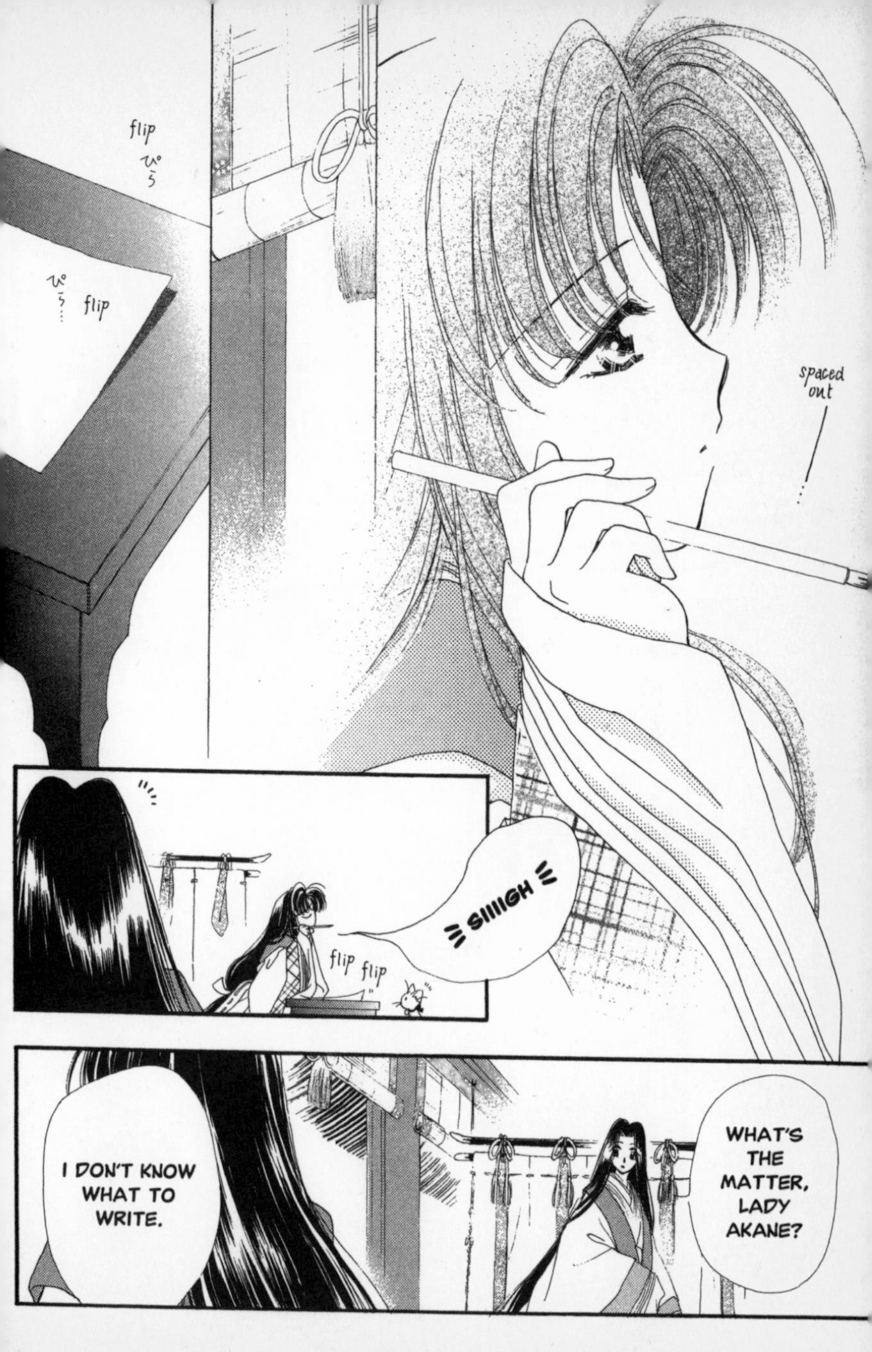
spaced out
flip ぴら
ぴら… flip
SIIIGH
flip flip
WHAT'S THE MATTER, LADY AKANE?
I DON'T KNOW WHAT TO WRITE.

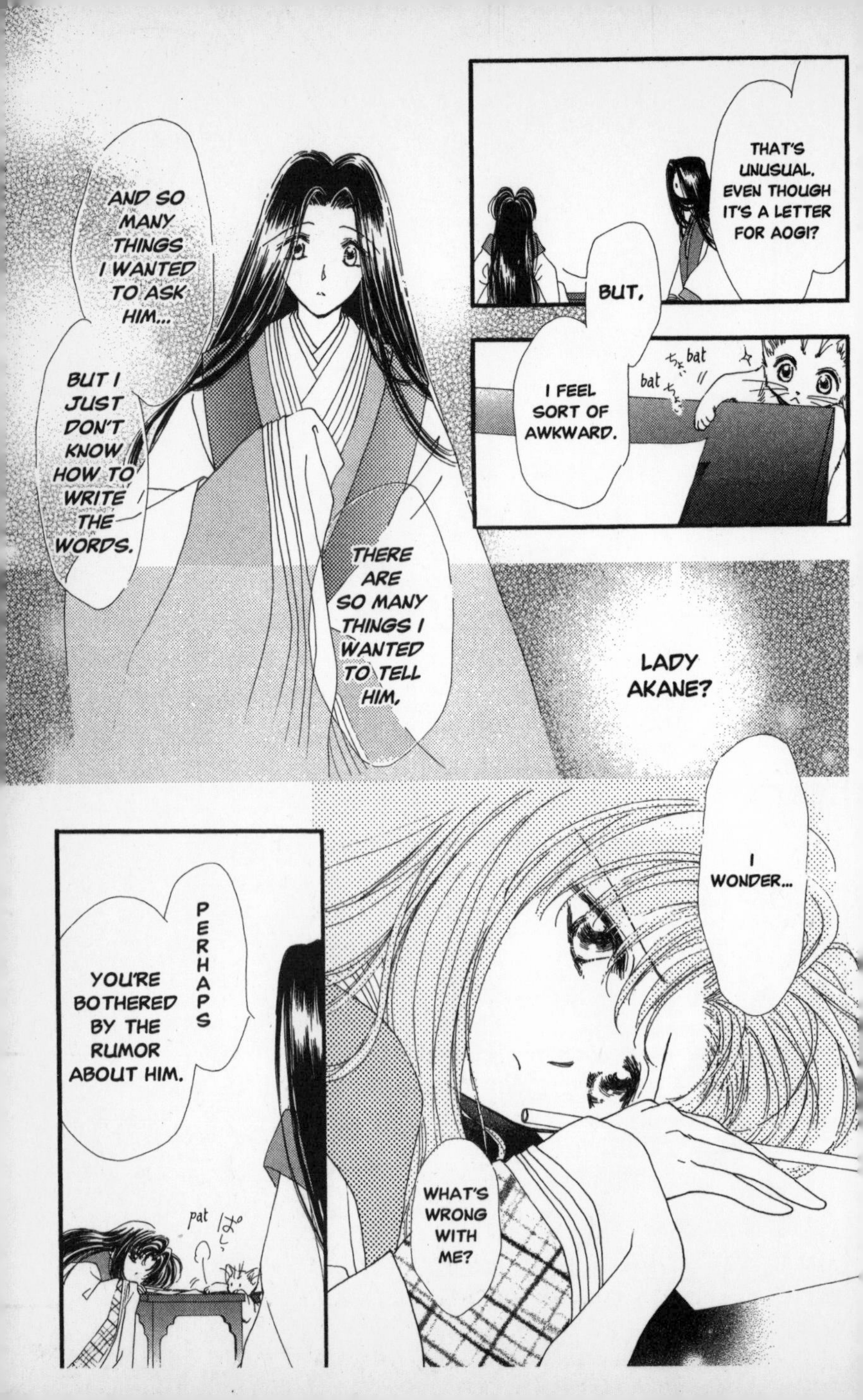
THAT'S UNUSUAL. EVEN THOUGH IT'S A LETTER FOR AOGI?
BUT,
I FEEL SORT OF AWKWARD.
bat
bat
THERE ARE SO MANY THINGS I WANTED TO TELL HIM,
AND SO MANY THINGS I WANTED TO ASK HIM...
BUT I JUST DON'T KNOW HOW TO WRITE THE WORDS.
LADY AKANE?
I WONDER...
WHAT'S WRONG WITH ME?
PERHAPS
YOU'RE BOTHERED BY THE RUMOR ABOUT HIM.
pat

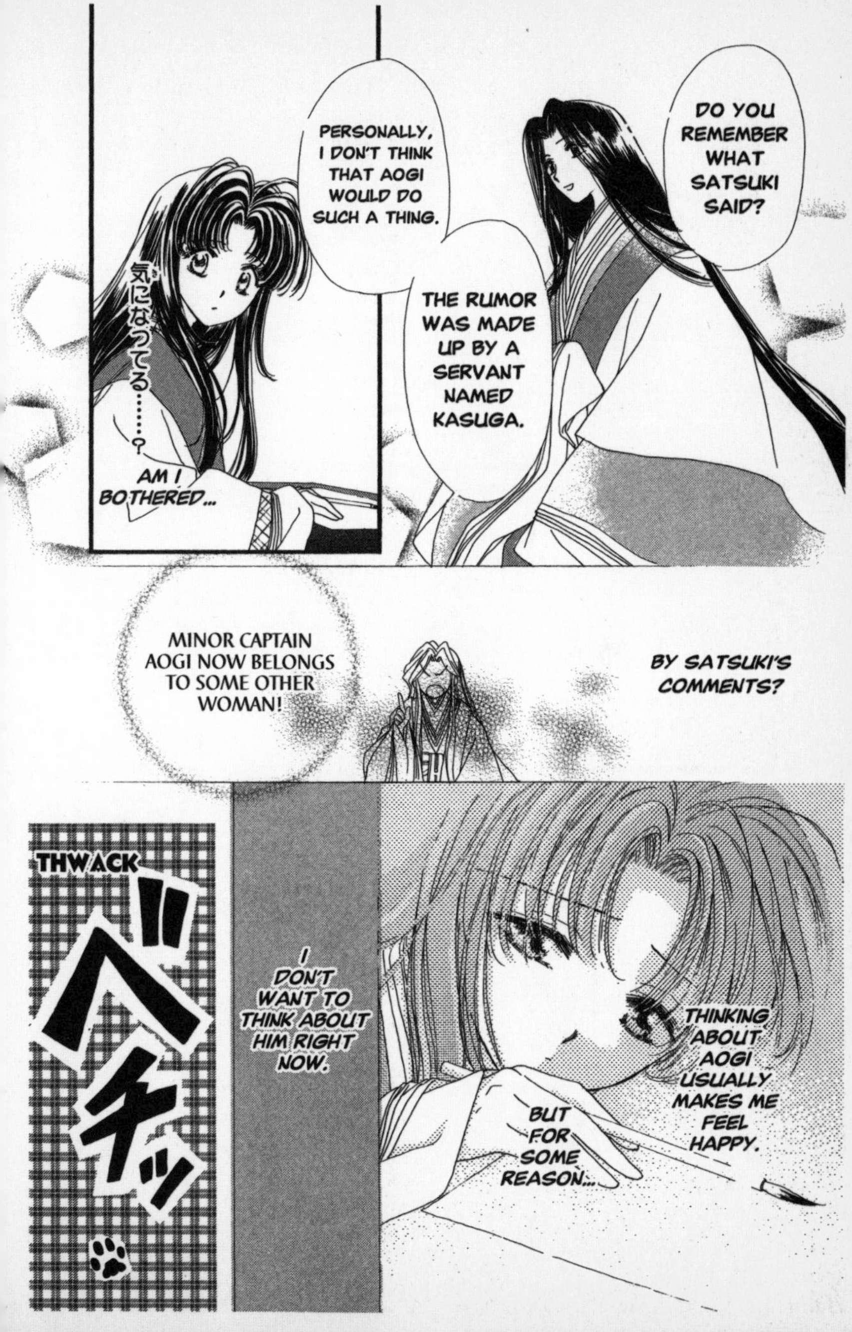
DO YOU REMEMBER WHAT SATSUKI SAID?
THE RUMOR WAS MADE UP BY A SERVANT NAMED KASUGA.
PERSONALLY, I DON'T THINK THAT AOGI WOULD DO SUCH A THING.
気になってる……？
AM I BOTHERED...
BY SATSUKI'S COMMENTS?
MINOR CAPTAIN AOGI NOW BELONGS TO SOME OTHER WOMAN!
THINKING ABOUT AOGI USUALLY MAKES ME FEEL HAPPY.
BUT FOR SOME REASON...
I DON'T WANT TO THINK ABOUT HIM RIGHT NOW.
THWACK
ベチッ

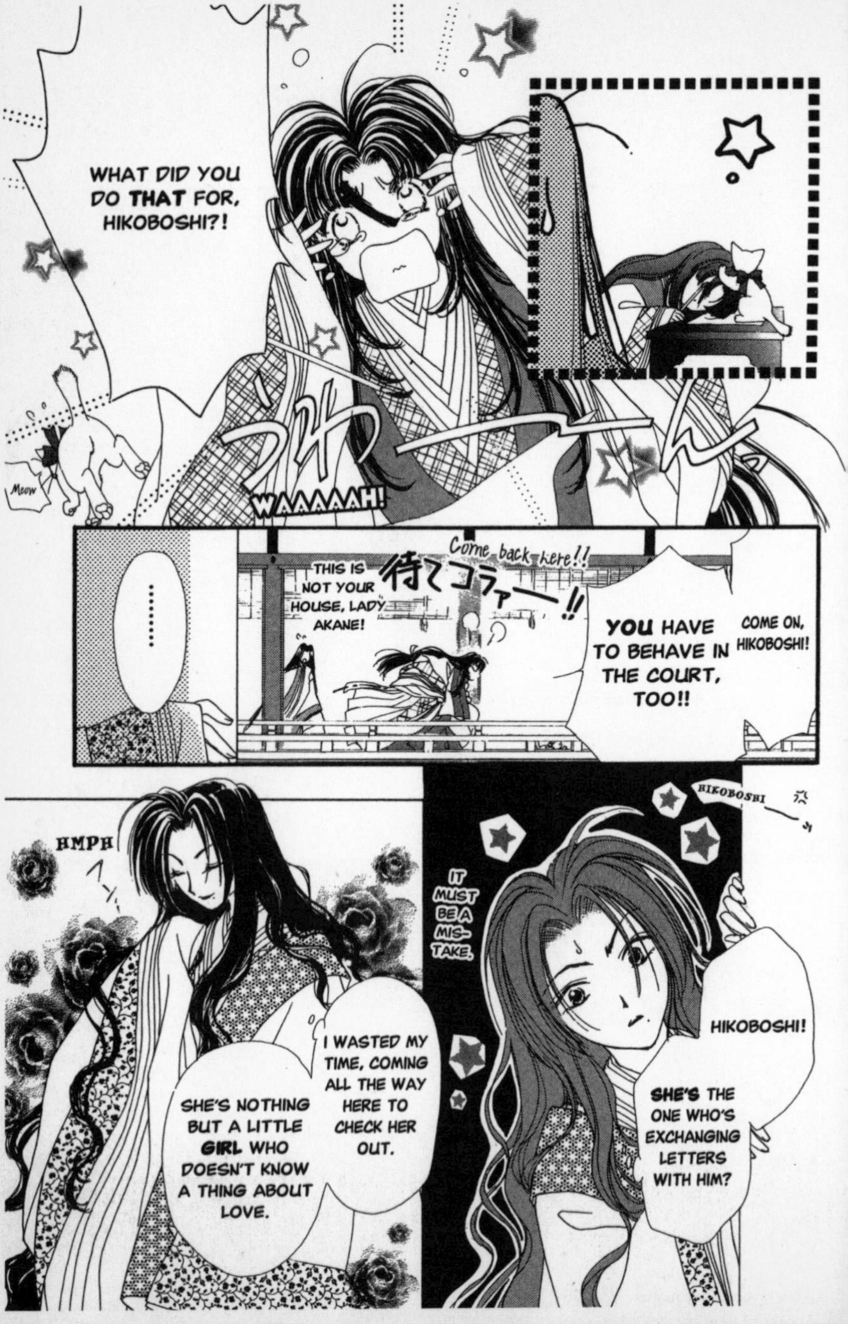
WHAT DID YOU DO **THAT** FOR, HIKOBOSHI?!
うわっーん
WAAAAAH!
Meow
COME ON, HIKOBOSHI!
YOU HAVE TO BEHAVE IN THE COURT, TOO!!
Come back here!!
待てコラァー!!
THIS IS NOT YOUR HOUSE, LADY AKANE!
......
HIKOBOSHI
HIKOBOSHI!
SHE'S THE ONE WHO'S EXCHANGING LETTERS WITH HIM?
IT MUST BE A MIS-TAKE.
I WASTED MY TIME, COMING ALL THE WAY HERE TO CHECK HER OUT.
SHE'S NOTHING BUT A LITTLE **GIRL** WHO DOESN'T KNOW A THING ABOUT LOVE.
HMPH

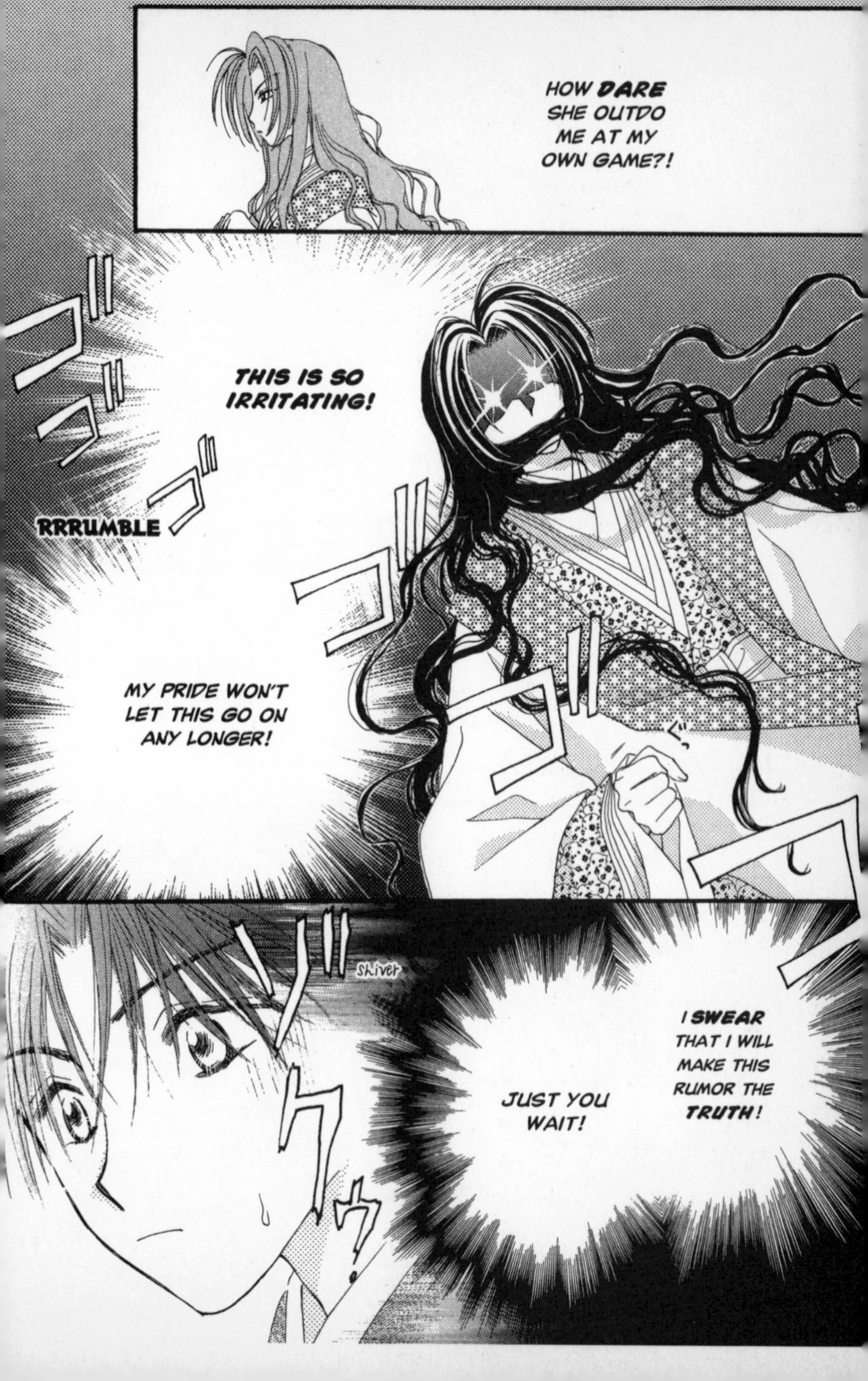
HOW DARE SHE OUTDO ME AT MY OWN GAME?!
THIS IS SO IRRITATING!
RRRUMBLE
MY PRIDE WON'T LET THIS GO ON ANY LONGER!
shiver
I SWEAR THAT I WILL MAKE THIS RUMOR THE TRUTH!
JUST YOU WAIT!

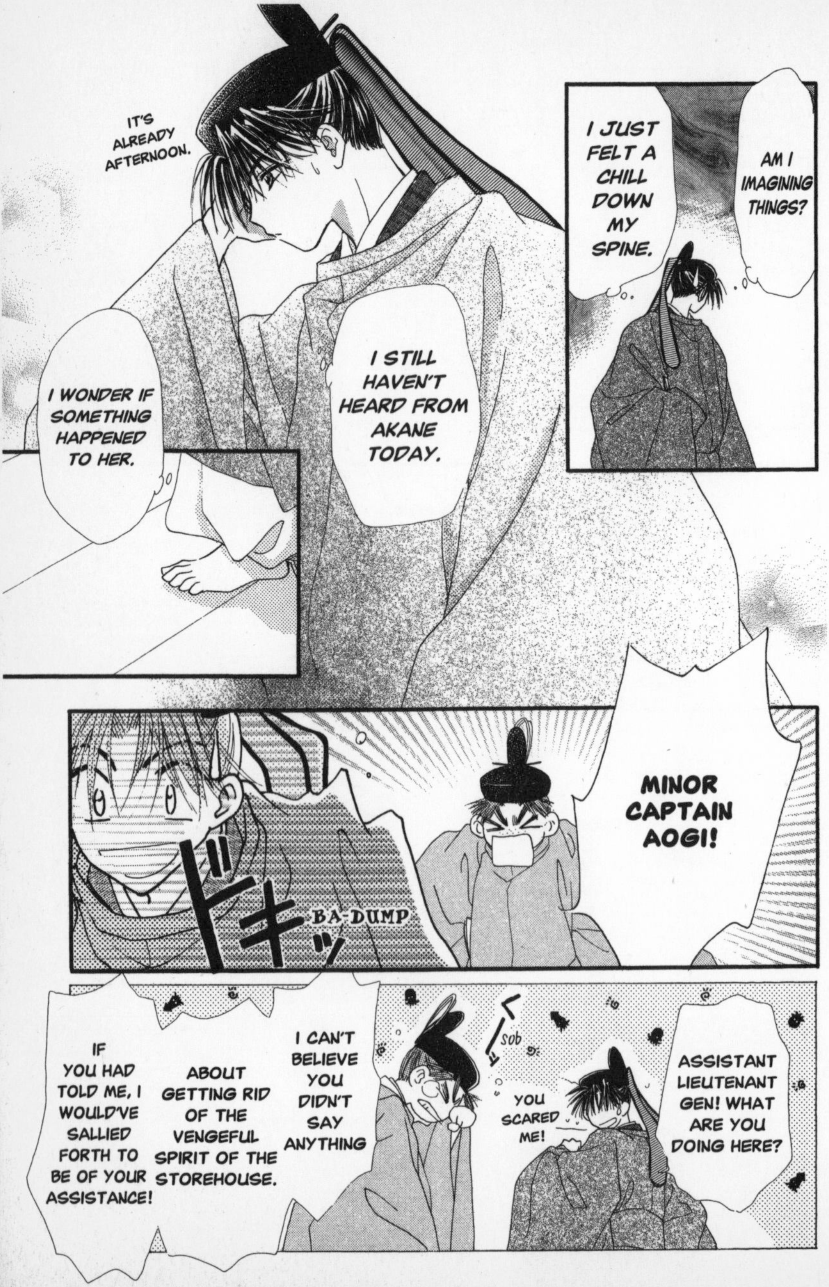
IT'S ALREADY AFTERNOON.
I STILL HAVEN'T HEARD FROM AKANE TODAY.
I WONDER IF SOMETHING HAPPENED TO HER.
AM I IMAGINING THINGS?
I JUST FELT A CHILL DOWN MY SPINE.
MINOR CAPTAIN AOGI!
BA-DUMP
ASSISTANT LIEUTENANT GEN! WHAT ARE YOU DOING HERE?
YOU SCARED ME!
sob
I CAN'T BELIEVE YOU DIDN'T SAY ANYTHING
ABOUT GETTING RID OF THE VENGEFUL SPIRIT OF THE STOREHOUSE.
IF YOU HAD TOLD ME, I WOULD'VE SALLIED FORTH TO BE OF YOUR ASSISTANCE!

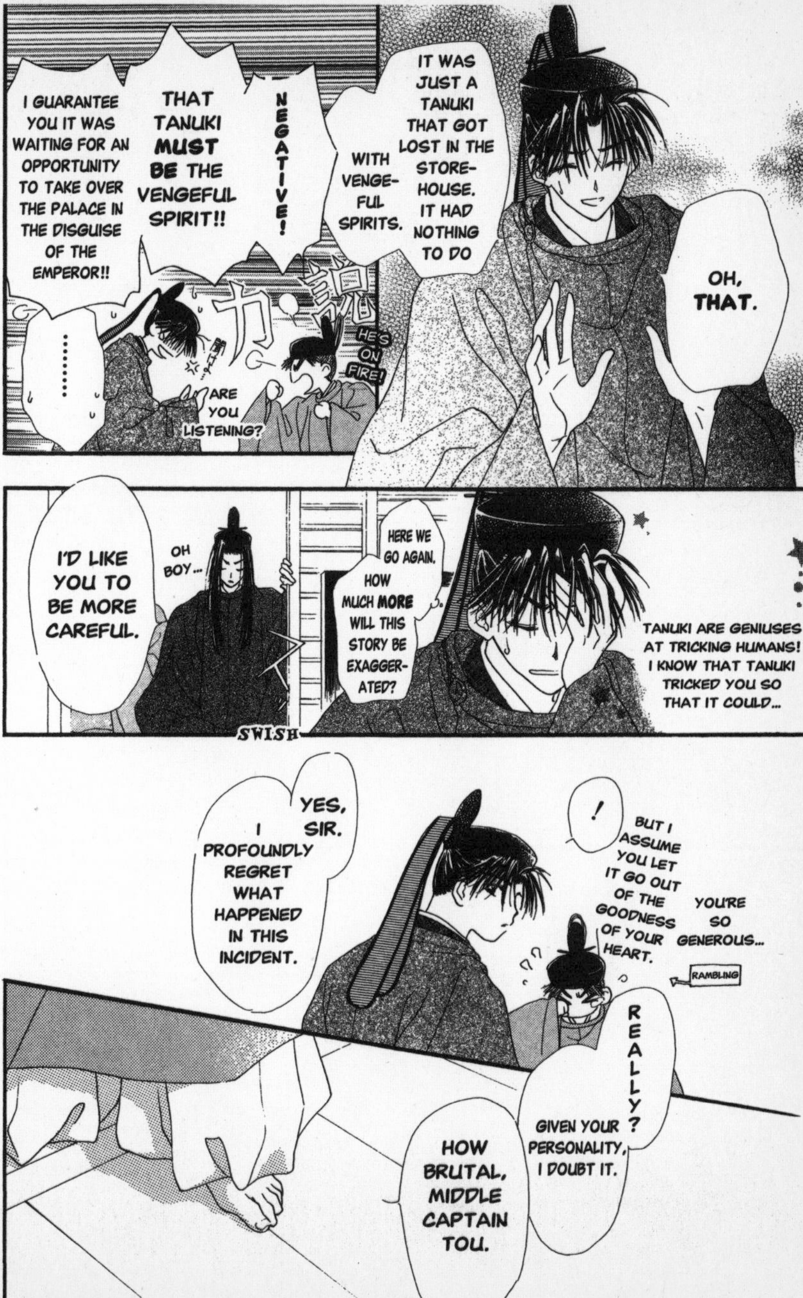
OH, THAT.
IT WAS JUST A TANUKI THAT GOT LOST IN THE STOREHOUSE. IT HAD NOTHING TO DO
WITH VENGEFUL SPIRITS.
NEGATIVE!
THAT TANUKI MUST BE THE VENGEFUL SPIRIT!!
I GUARANTEE YOU IT WAS WAITING FOR AN OPPORTUNITY TO TAKE OVER THE PALACE IN THE DISGUISE OF THE EMPEROR!!
HE'S ON FIRE!
ARE YOU LISTENING?
....
TANUKI ARE GENIUSES AT TRICKING HUMANS! I KNOW THAT TANUKI TRICKED YOU SO THAT IT COULD...
HERE WE GO AGAIN.
HOW MUCH MORE WILL THIS STORY BE EXAGGERATED?
OH BOY...
I'D LIKE YOU TO BE MORE CAREFUL.
SWISH
YOU'RE SO GENEROUS...
RAMBLING
BUT I ASSUME YOU LET IT GO OUT OF THE GOODNESS OF YOUR HEART.
!
YES, SIR.
I PROFOUNDLY REGRET WHAT HAPPENED IN THIS INCIDENT.
REALLY?
GIVEN YOUR PERSONALITY, I DOUBT IT.
HOW BRUTAL, MIDDLE CAPTAIN TOU.

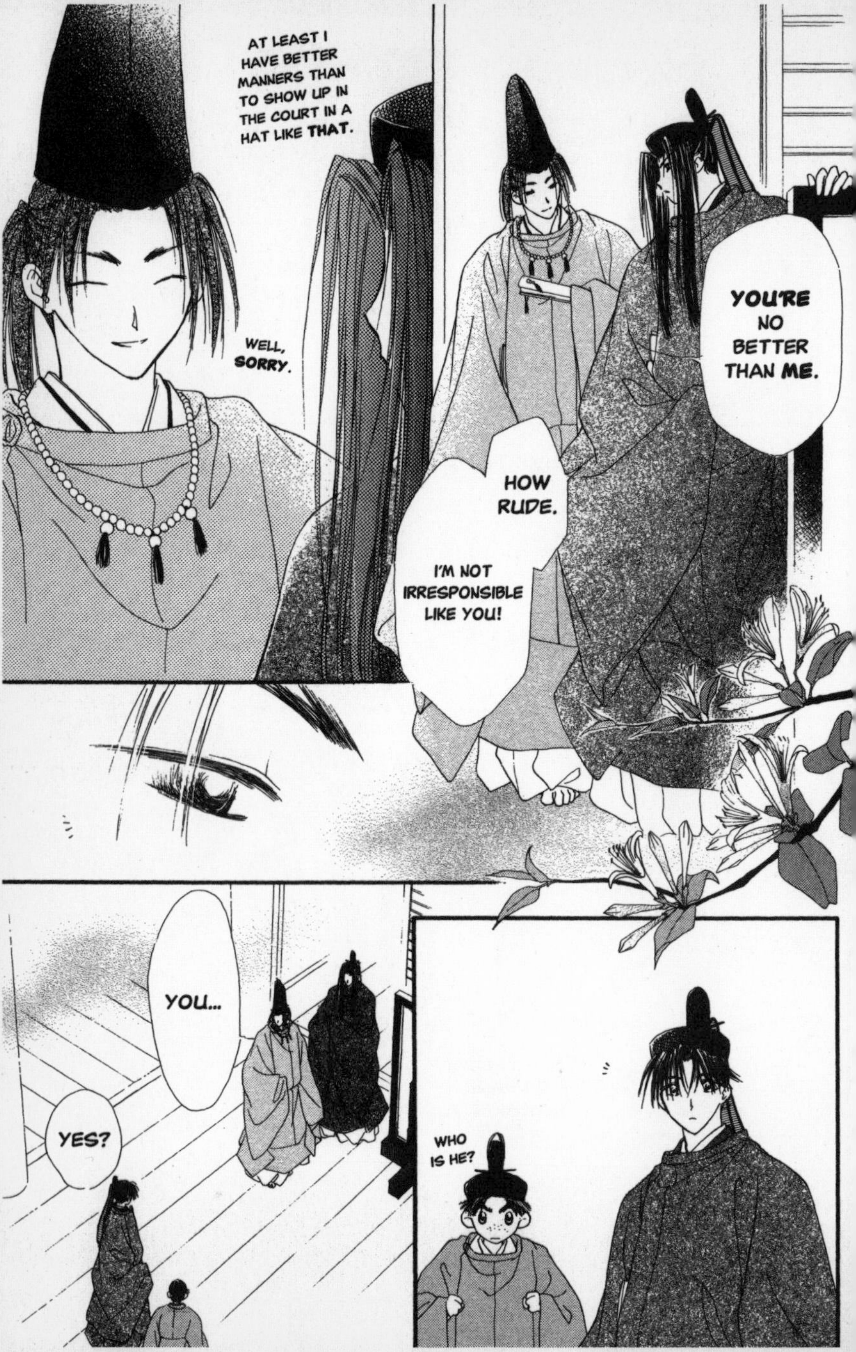
YOU'RE NO BETTER THAN ME.
HOW RUDE.
I'M NOT IRRESPONSIBLE LIKE YOU!
AT LEAST I HAVE BETTER MANNERS THAN TO SHOW UP IN THE COURT IN A HAT LIKE THAT.
WELL, SORRY.
WHO IS HE?
YOU...
YES?

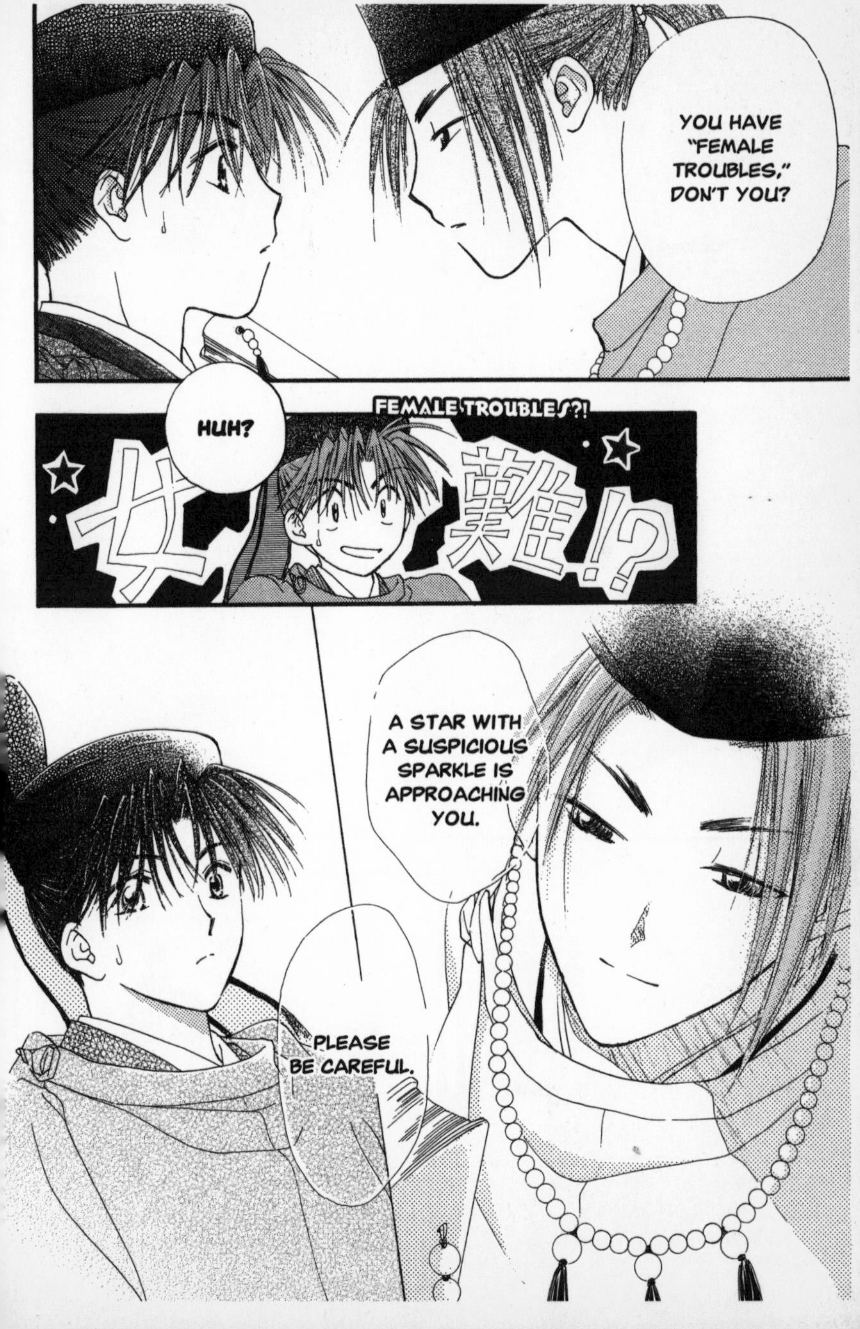
YOU HAVE "FEMALE TROUBLES," DON'T YOU?
FEMALE TROUBLES?!
女難!?
HUH?
A STAR WITH A SUSPICIOUS SPARKLE IS APPROACHING YOU.
PLEASE BE CAREFUL.

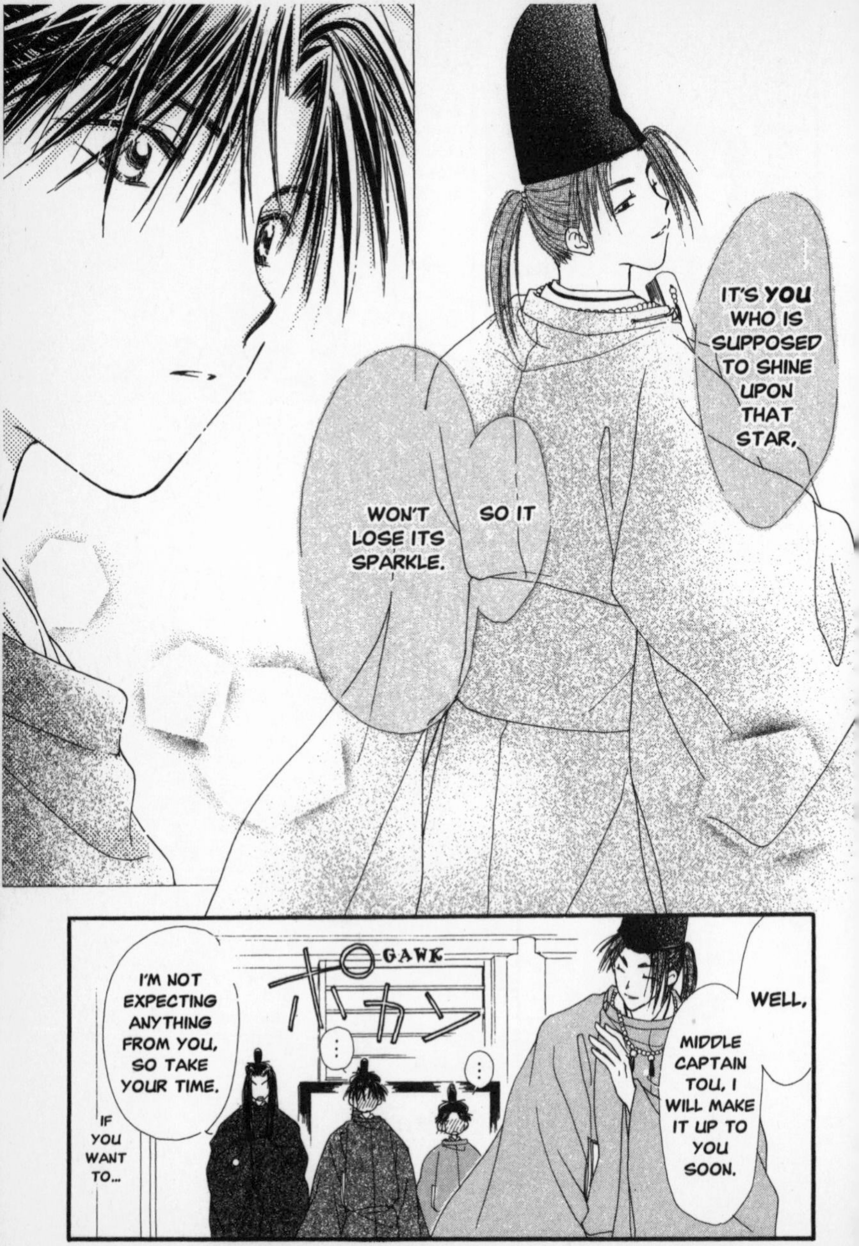
IT'S **YOU** WHO IS SUPPOSED TO SHINE UPON THAT STAR,
SO IT
WON'T LOSE ITS SPARKLE.
WELL,
MIDDLE CAPTAIN TOU, I WILL MAKE IT UP TO YOU SOON.
GAWK
...
...
I'M NOT EXPECTING ANYTHING FROM YOU, SO TAKE YOUR TIME.
IF YOU WANT TO...

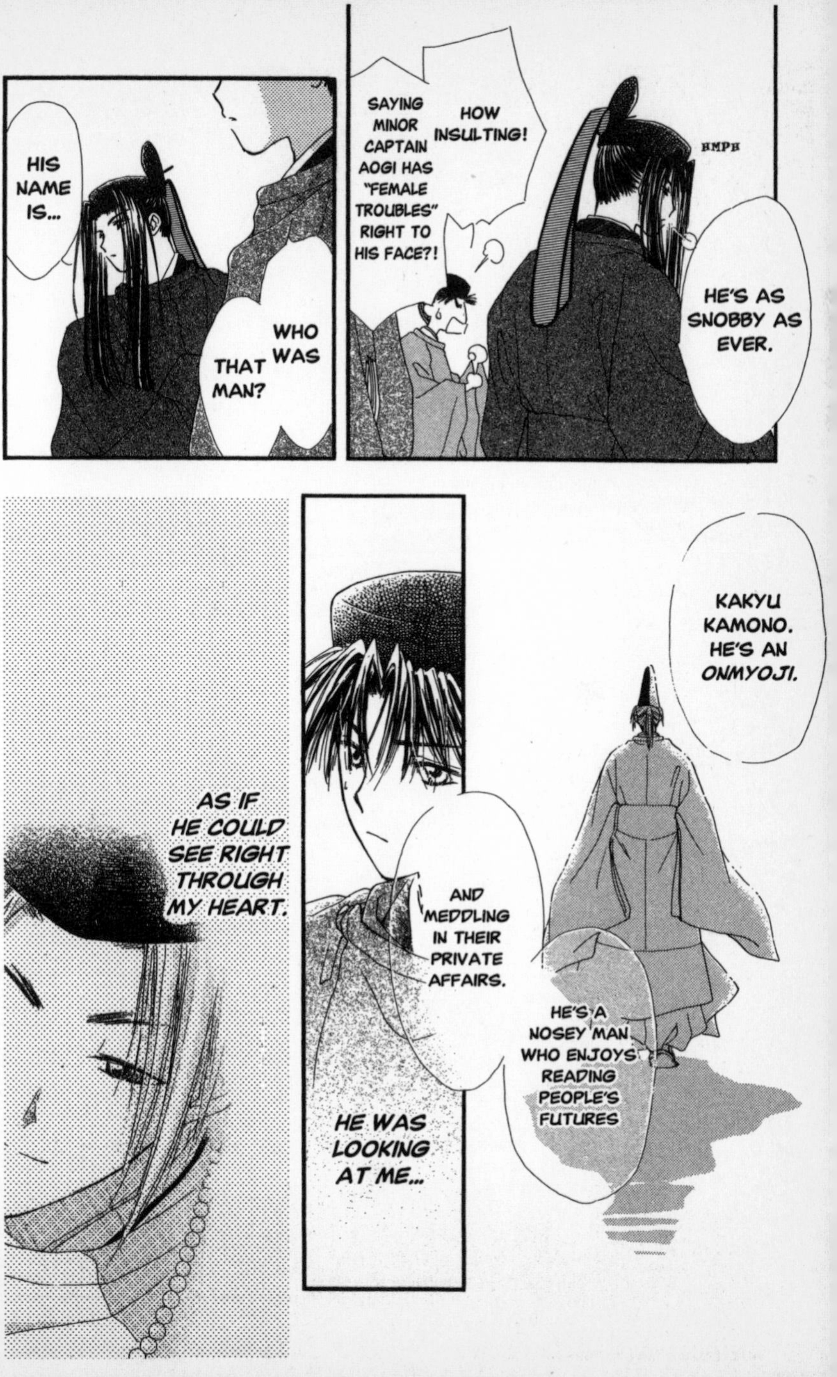
HOW INSULTING!
SAYING MINOR CAPTAIN AOGI HAS "FEMALE TROUBLES" RIGHT TO HIS FACE?!
HMPH
HE'S AS SNOBBY AS EVER.
WHO WAS THAT MAN?
HIS NAME IS...
KAKYU KAMONO. HE'S AN *ONMYOJI.*
HE'S A NOSEY MAN WHO ENJOYS READING PEOPLE'S FUTURES
AND MEDDLING IN THEIR PRIVATE AFFAIRS.
HE WAS LOOKING AT ME...
AS IF HE COULD SEE RIGHT THROUGH MY HEART.

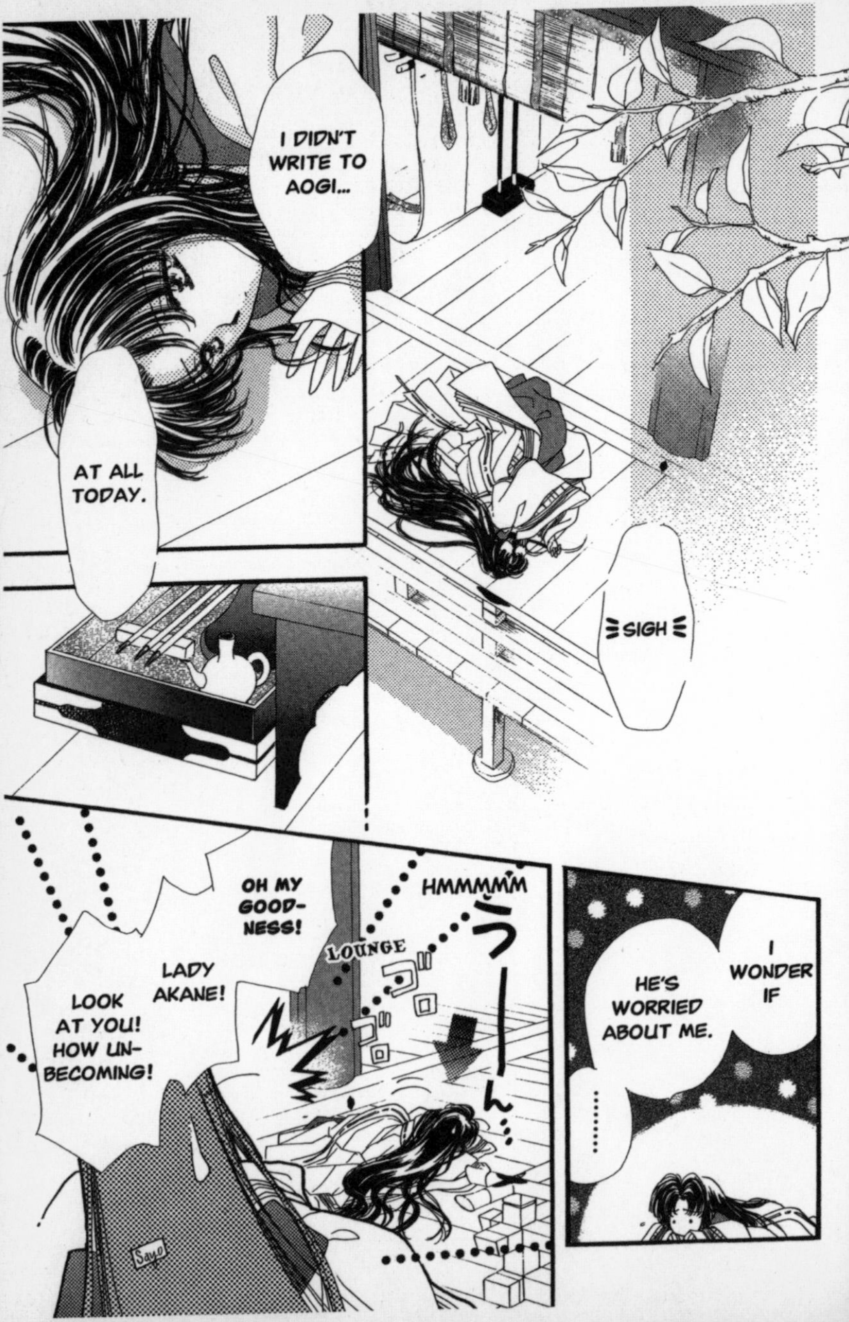
SIGH
I DIDN'T WRITE TO AOGI...
AT ALL TODAY.
I WONDER IF
HE'S WORRIED ABOUT ME.
......
HMMMMM
LOUNGE
OH MY GOOD-NESS!
LADY AKANE!
LOOK AT YOU! HOW UN-BECOMING!
....

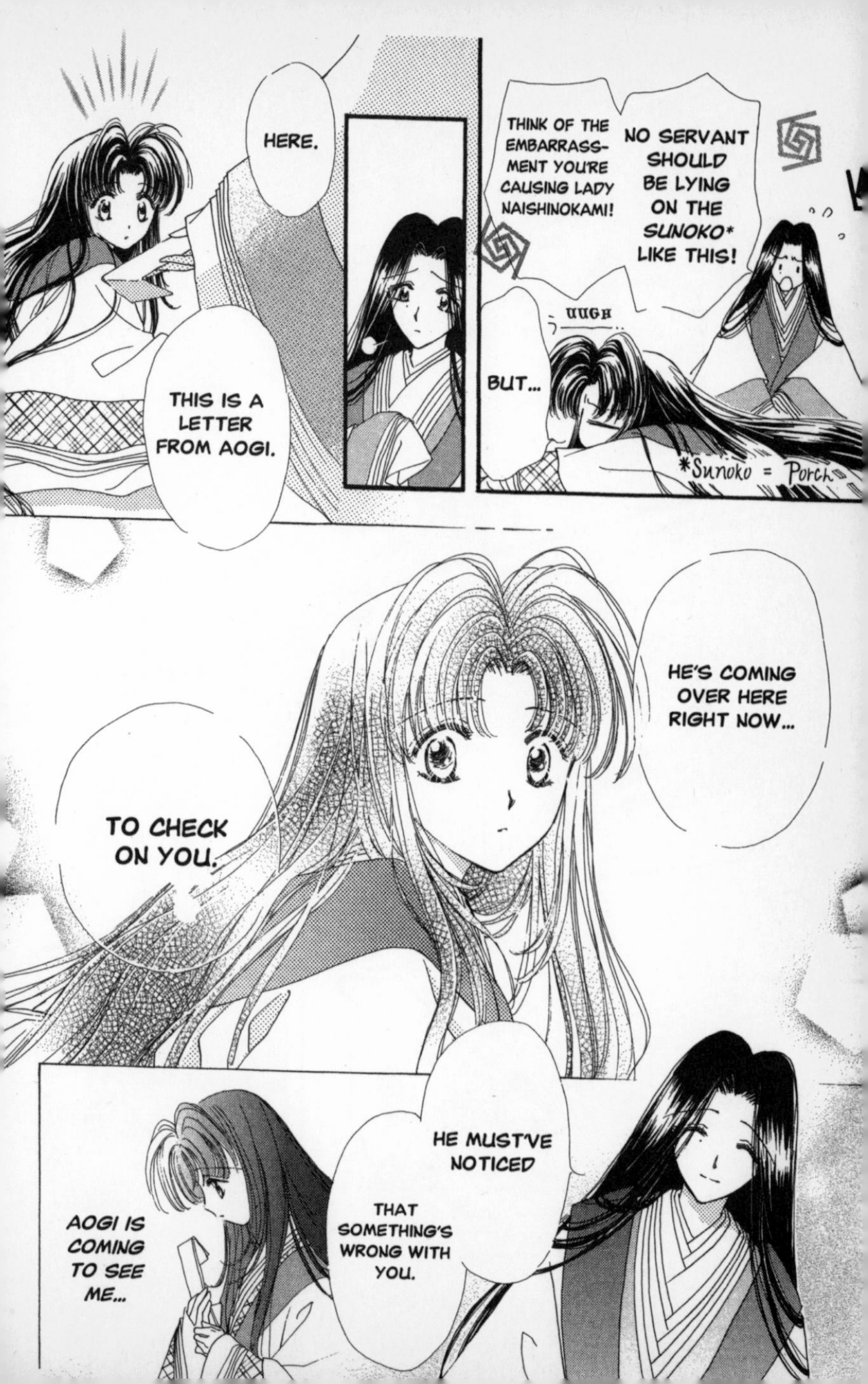
NO SERVANT SHOULD BE LYING ON THE SUNOKO* LIKE THIS!
THINK OF THE EMBARRASSMENT YOU'RE CAUSING LADY NAISHINOKAMI!
UUGH
BUT...
*Sunoko = Porch
HERE.
THIS IS A LETTER FROM AOGI.
HE'S COMING OVER HERE RIGHT NOW...
TO CHECK ON YOU.
HE MUST'VE NOTICED
THAT SOMETHING'S WRONG WITH YOU.
AOGI IS COMING TO SEE ME...

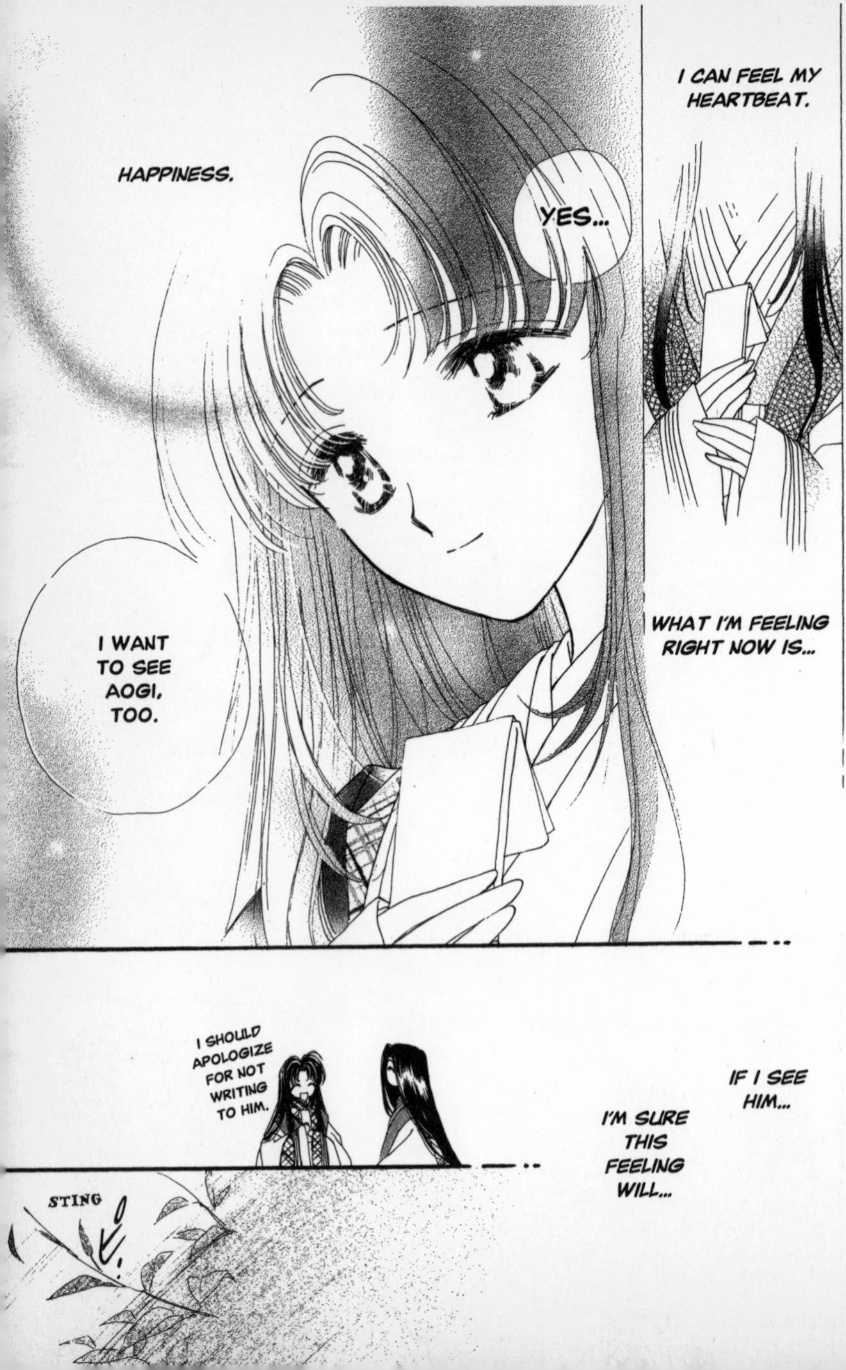
I CAN FEEL MY HEARTBEAT.
WHAT I'M FEELING RIGHT NOW IS...
YES...
HAPPINESS.
I WANT TO SEE AOGI, TOO.
IF I SEE HIM...
I'M SURE THIS FEELING WILL...
I SHOULD APOLOGIZE FOR NOT WRITING TO HIM.
STING

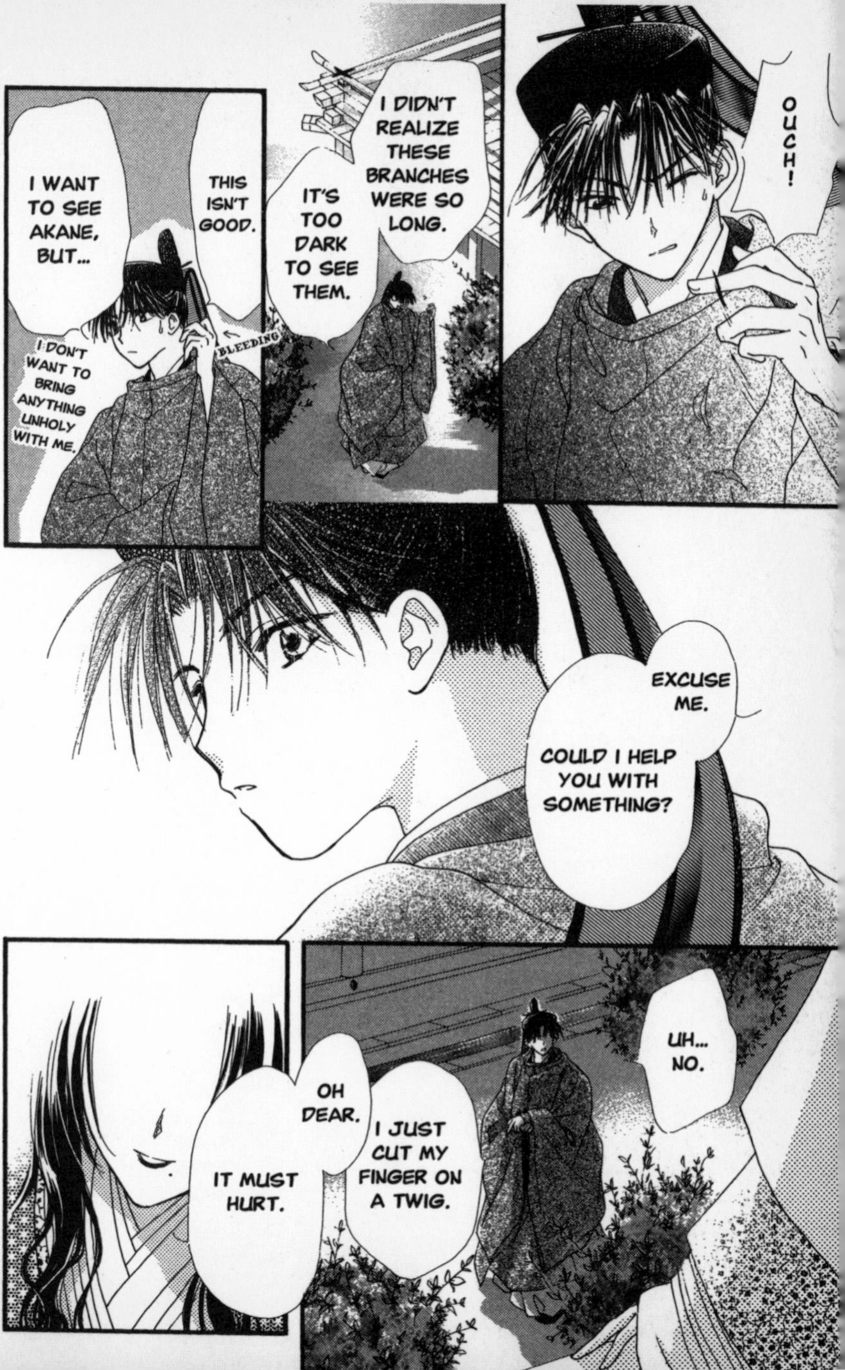
OUCH!
I DIDN'T REALIZE THESE BRANCHES WERE SO LONG.
IT'S TOO DARK TO SEE THEM.
THIS ISN'T GOOD.
BLEEDING
I WANT TO SEE AKANE, BUT...
I DON'T WANT TO BRING ANYTHING UNHOLY WITH ME.
EXCUSE ME.
COULD I HELP YOU WITH SOMETHING?
UH... NO.
I JUST CUT MY FINGER ON A TWIG.
OH DEAR.
IT MUST HURT.

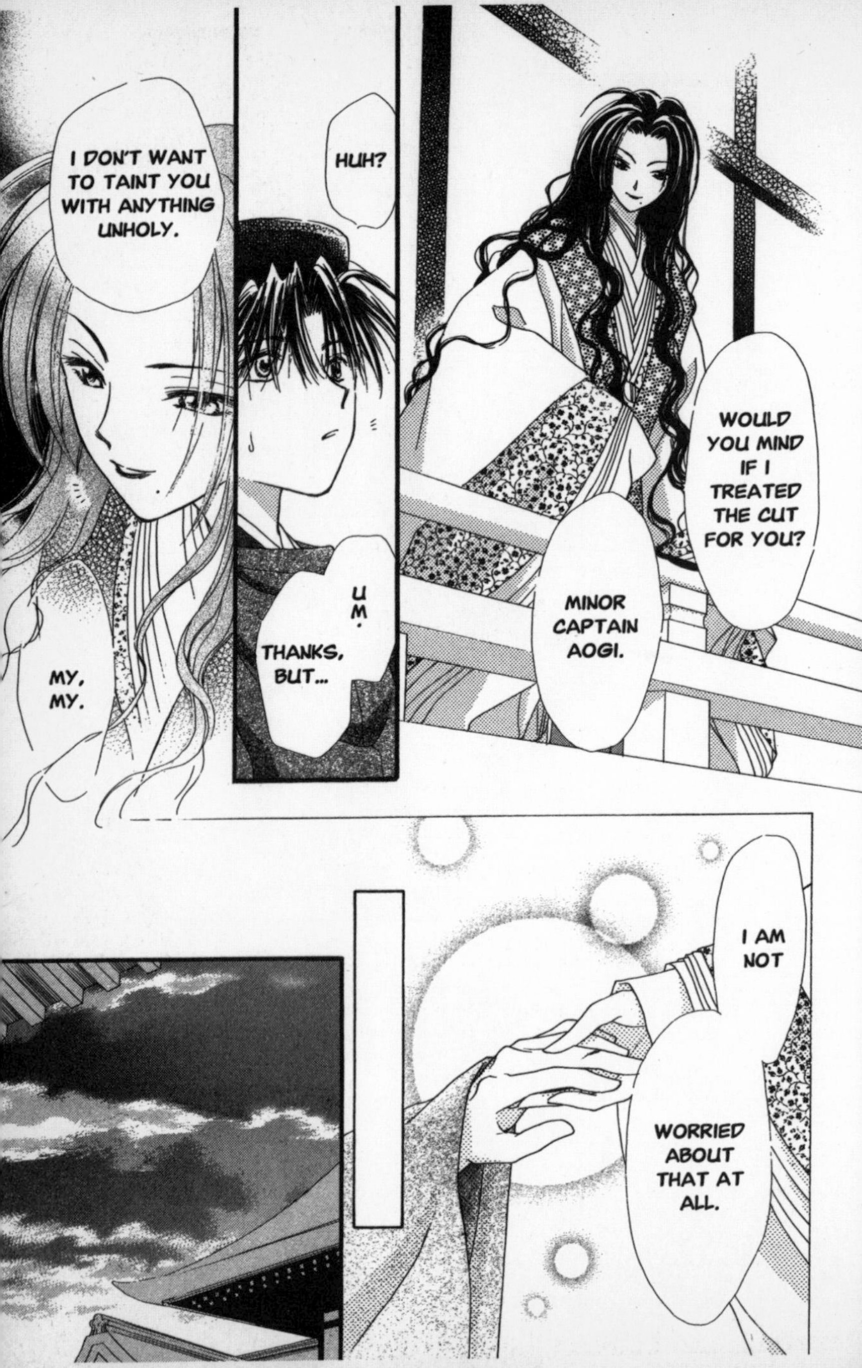
WOULD YOU MIND IF I TREATED THE CUT FOR YOU?
MINOR CAPTAIN AOGI.
HUH?
UM.
THANKS, BUT...
I DON'T WANT TO TAINT YOU WITH ANYTHING UNHOLY.
MY, MY.
I AM NOT
WORRIED ABOUT THAT AT ALL.

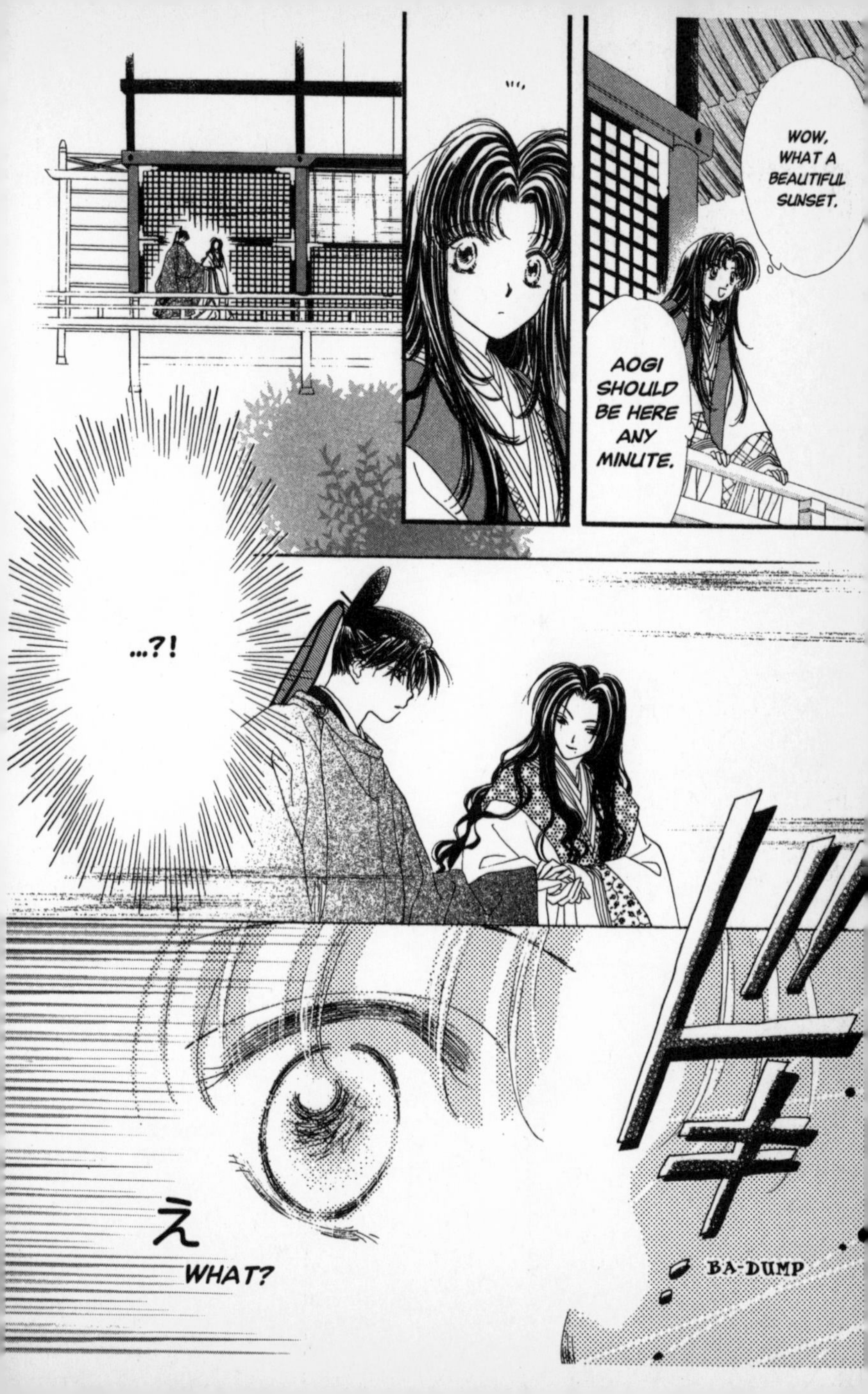
WOW, WHAT A BEAUTIFUL SUNSET.
AOGI SHOULD BE HERE ANY MINUTE.
...
...?!
ドキ
BA-DUMP
え
WHAT?

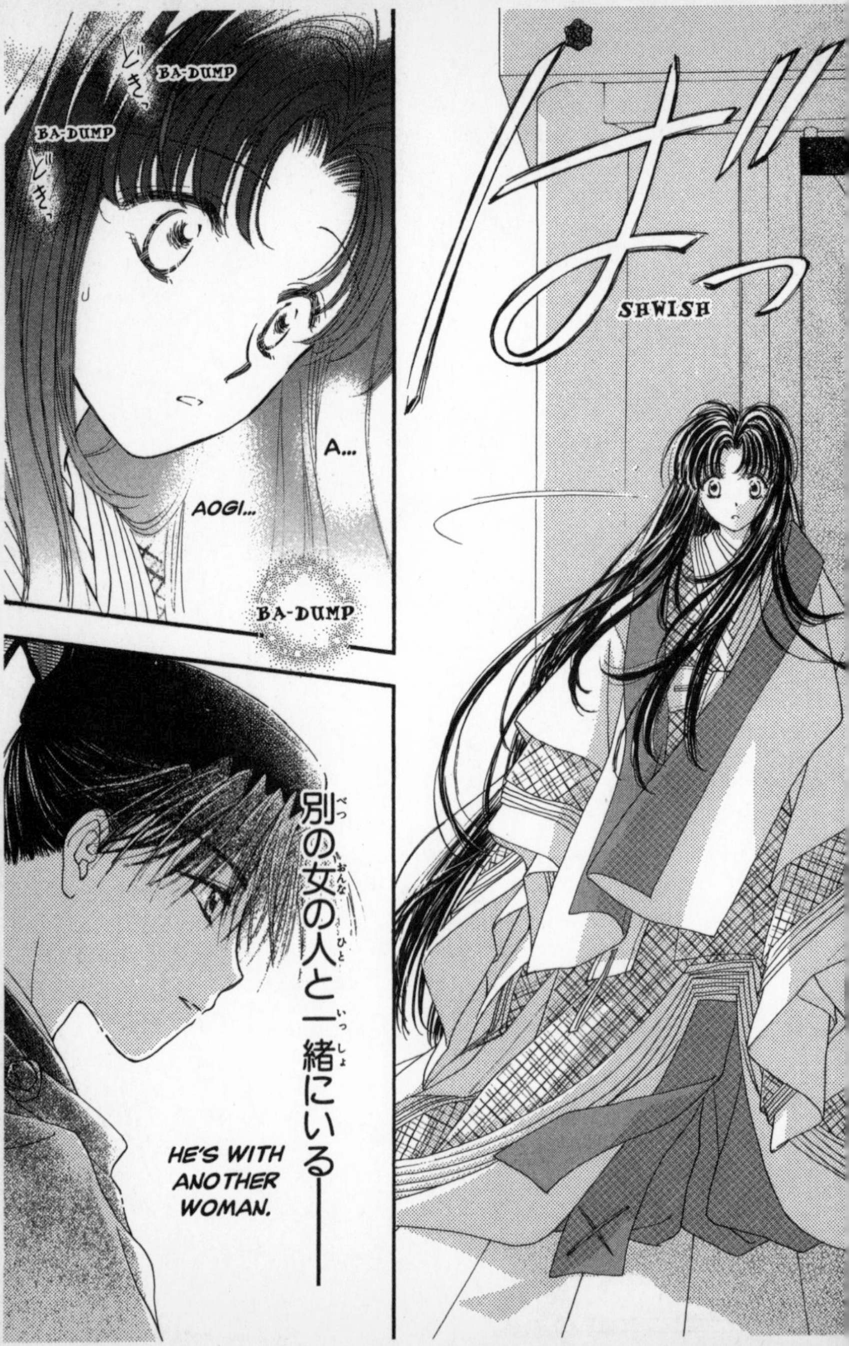
ばっ
SHWISH
どきっ
BA-DUMP
どきっ
BA-DUMP
A...
AOGI...
BA-DUMP
別の女の人と一緒にいる——
HE'S WITH ANOTHER WOMAN.

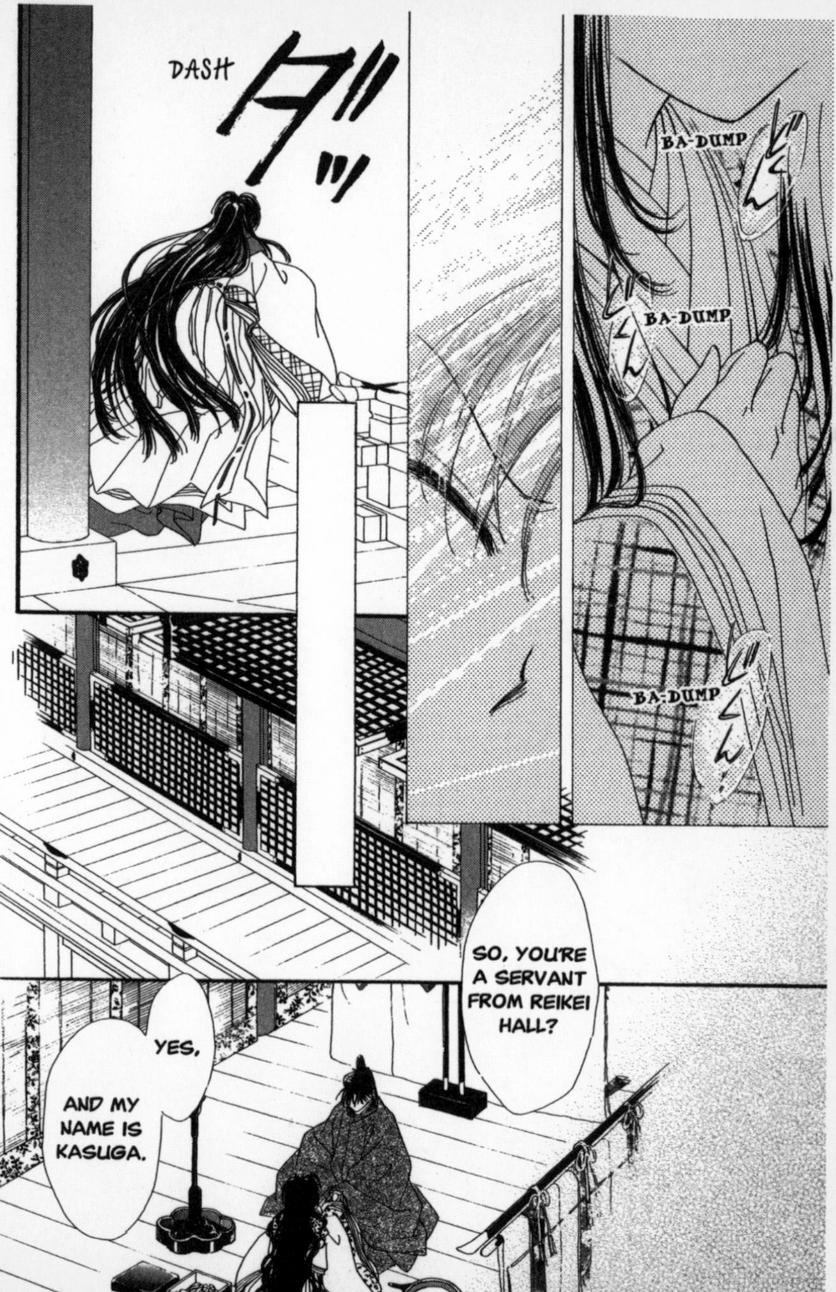
BA-DUMP
BA-DUMP
BA-DUMP
DASH
ダッ
SO, YOU'RE A SERVANT FROM REIKEI HALL?
YES,
AND MY NAME IS KASUGA.

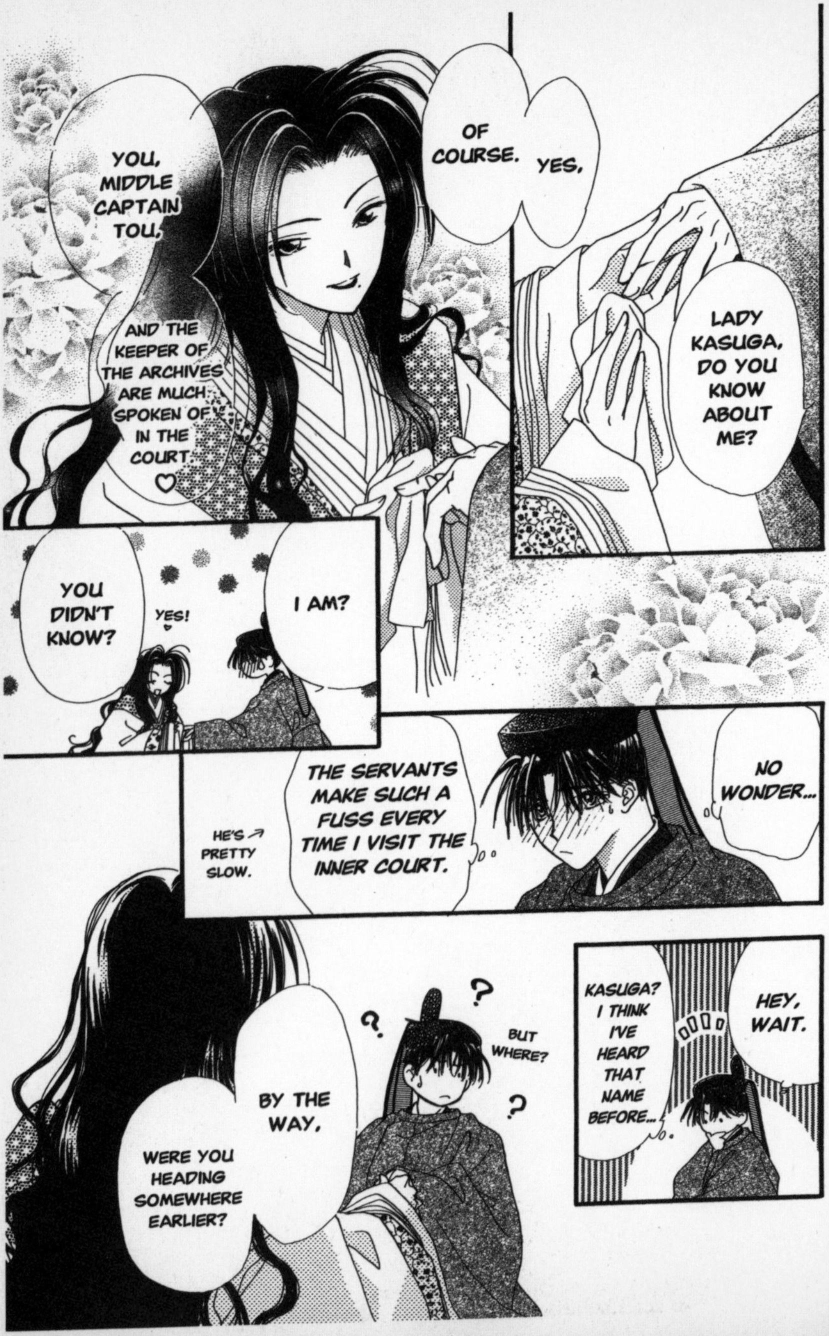
LADY KASUGA, DO YOU KNOW ABOUT ME?
YES,
OF COURSE.
YOU, MIDDLE CAPTAIN TOU,
AND THE KEEPER OF THE ARCHIVES ARE MUCH SPOKEN OF IN THE COURT. ♡
I AM?
YES! ♥
YOU DIDN'T KNOW?
NO WONDER...
THE SERVANTS MAKE SUCH A FUSS EVERY TIME I VISIT THE INNER COURT.
HE'S PRETTY SLOW.
HEY, WAIT.
KASUGA? I THINK I'VE HEARD THAT NAME BEFORE...
BUT WHERE?
BY THE WAY,
WERE YOU HEADING SOMEWHERE EARLIER?

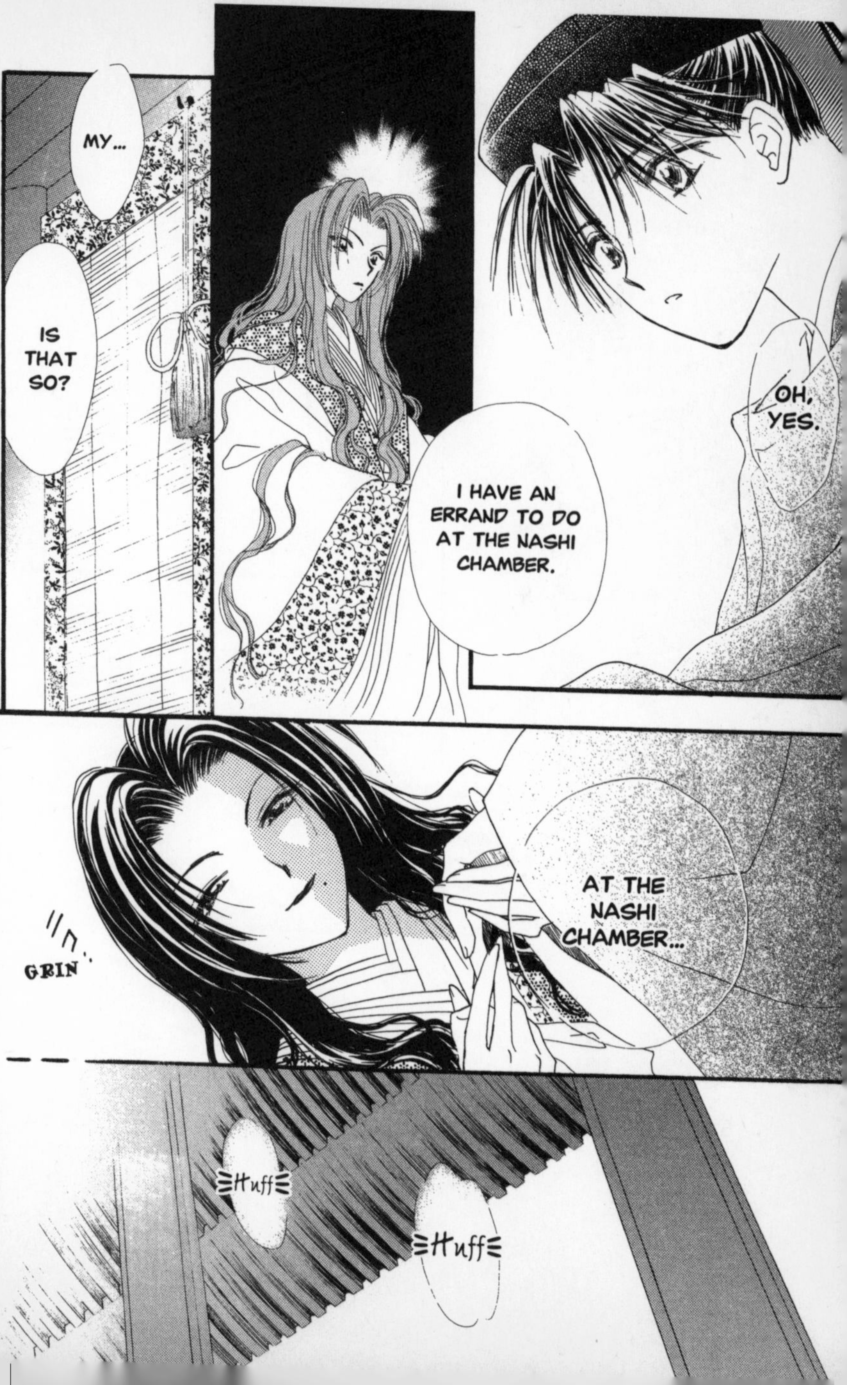
OH, YES.
I HAVE AN ERRAND TO DO AT THE NASHI CHAMBER.
MY...
IS THAT SO?
AT THE NASHI CHAMBER...
GRIN
Huff
Huff

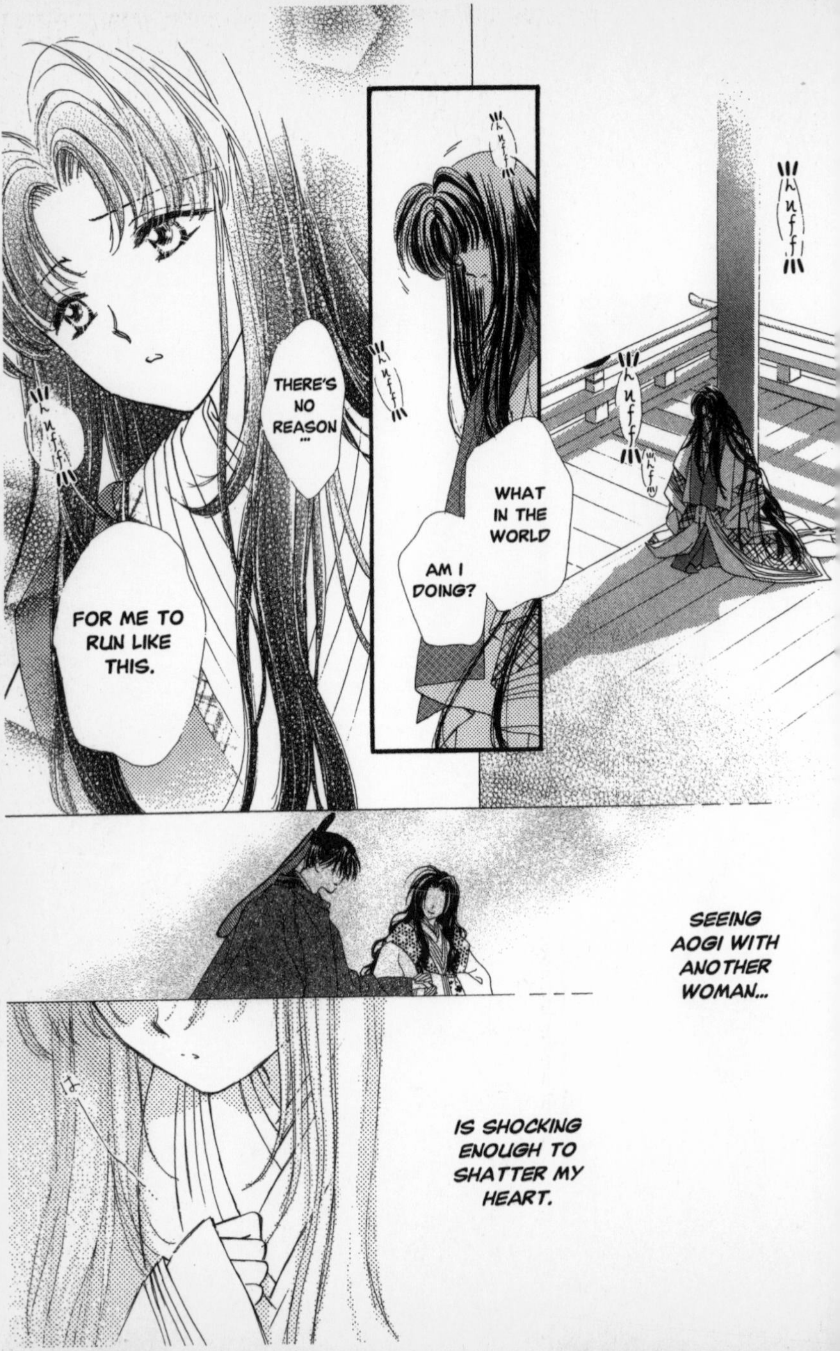
WHAT IN THE WORLD
AM I DOING?
THERE'S NO REASON...
FOR ME TO RUN LIKE THIS.
SEEING AOGI WITH ANOTHER WOMAN...
は
IS SHOCKING ENOUGH TO SHATTER MY HEART.

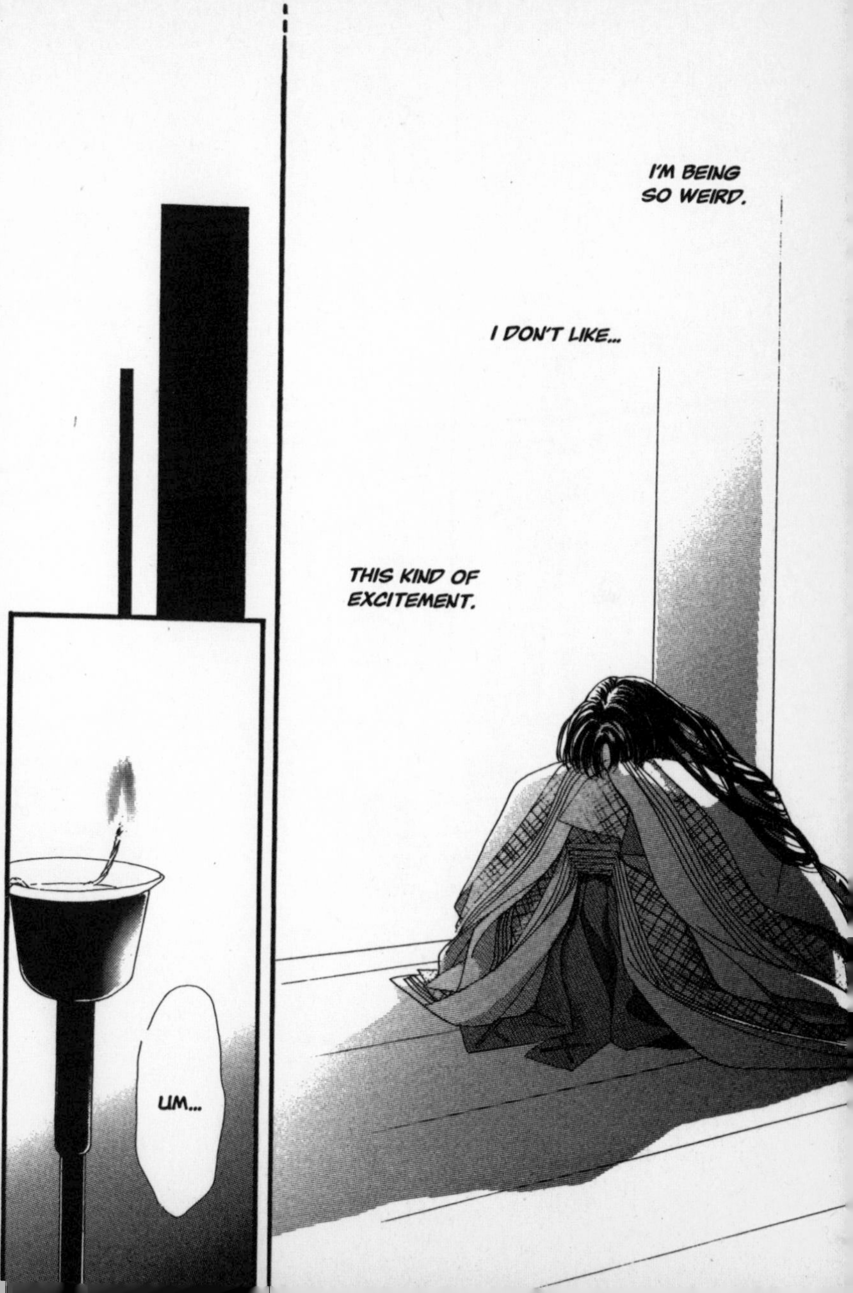
I'M BEING SO WEIRD.
I DON'T LIKE...
THIS KIND OF EXCITEMENT.
UM...

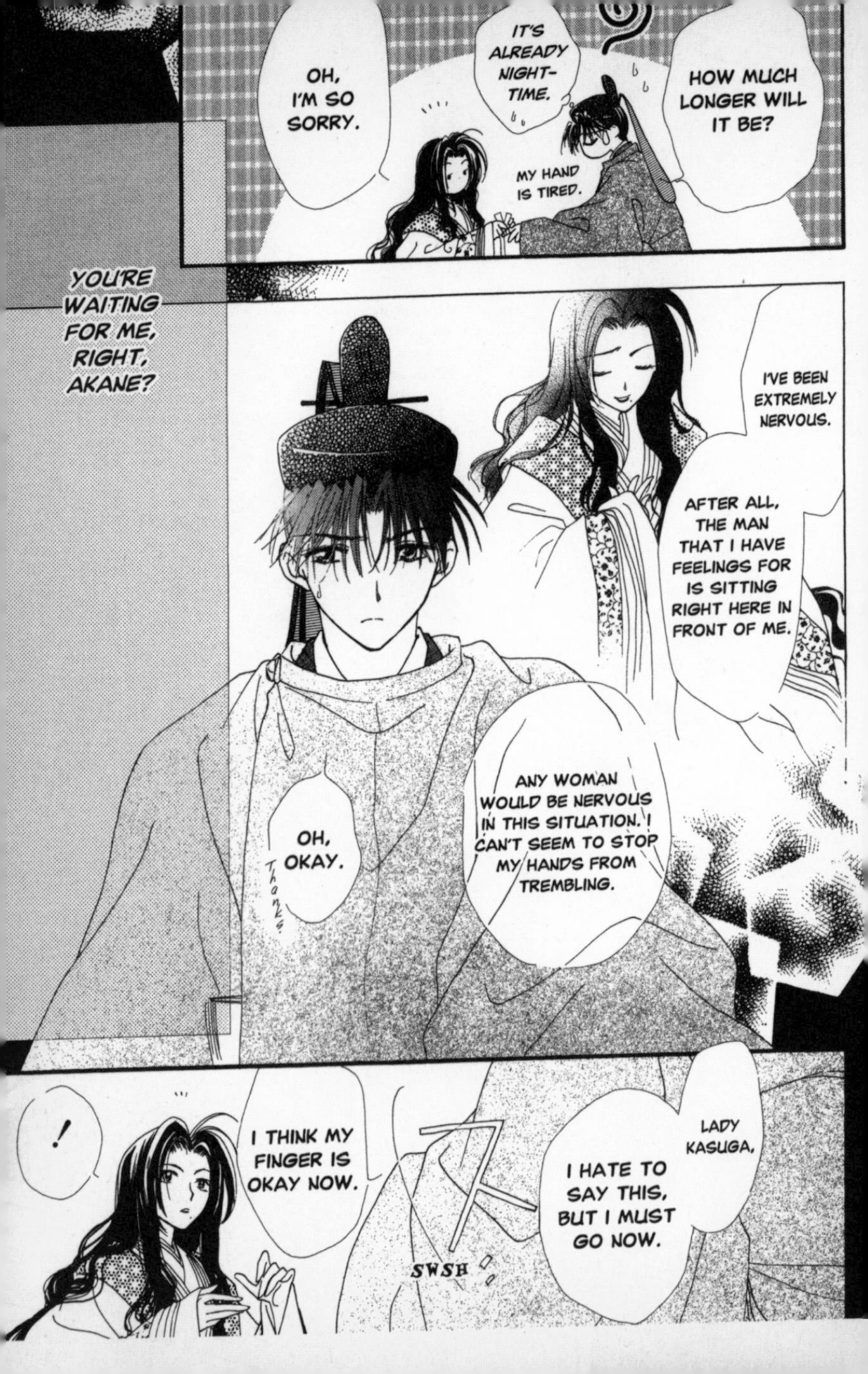
HOW MUCH LONGER WILL IT BE?
IT'S ALREADY NIGHT-TIME.
MY HAND IS TIRED.
OH, I'M SO SORRY.
I'VE BEEN EXTREMELY NERVOUS.
AFTER ALL, THE MAN THAT I HAVE FEELINGS FOR IS SITTING RIGHT HERE IN FRONT OF ME.
ANY WOMAN WOULD BE NERVOUS IN THIS SITUATION. I CAN'T SEEM TO STOP MY HANDS FROM TREMBLING.
OH, OKAY.
Thanks
YOU'RE WAITING FOR ME, RIGHT, AKANE?
LADY KASUGA,
I HATE TO SAY THIS, BUT I MUST GO NOW.
SWSH
I THINK MY FINGER IS OKAY NOW.
!

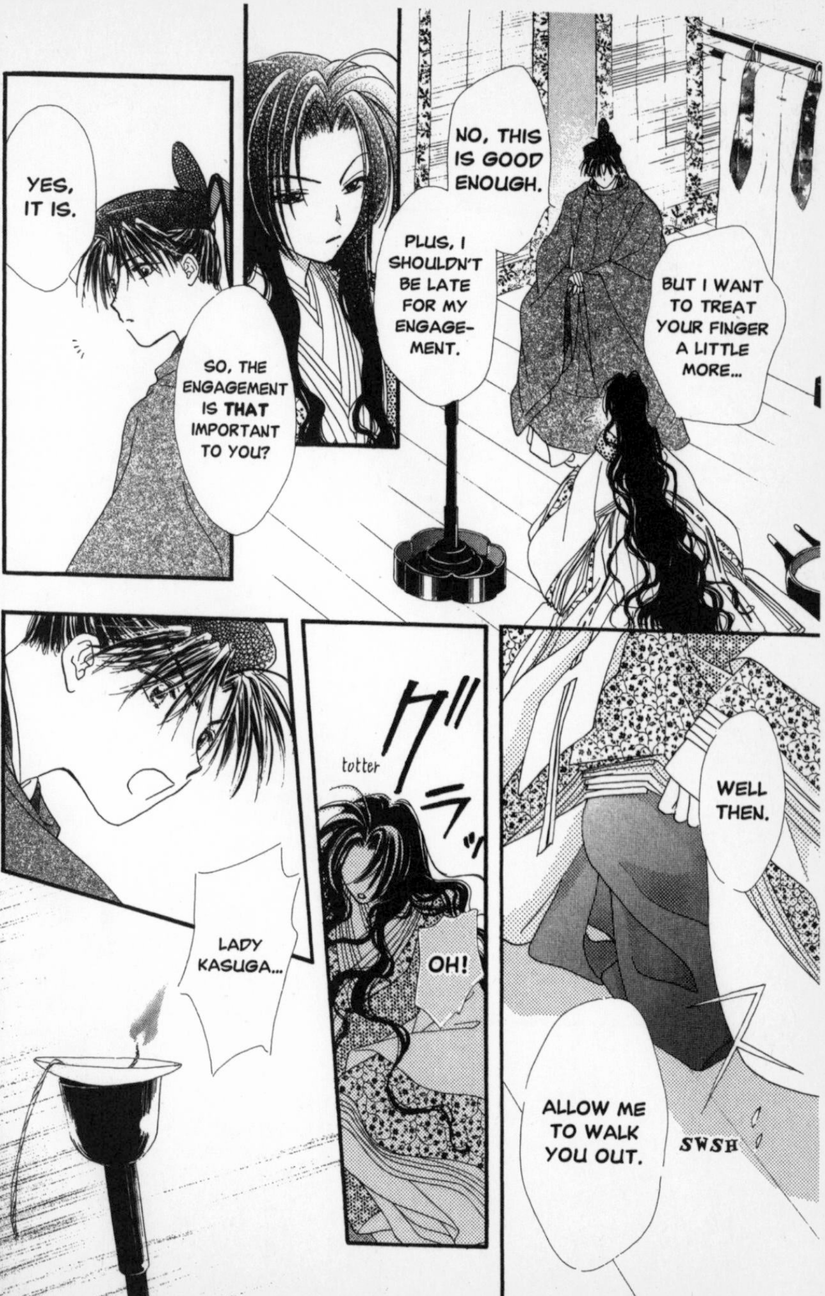
BUT I WANT TO TREAT YOUR FINGER A LITTLE MORE...
NO, THIS IS GOOD ENOUGH.
PLUS, I SHOULDN'T BE LATE FOR MY ENGAGE-MENT.
SO, THE ENGAGEMENT IS **THAT** IMPORTANT TO YOU?
YES, IT IS.
WELL THEN.
ALLOW ME TO WALK YOU OUT.
SWSH
グラッ
totter
OH!
LADY KASUGA...

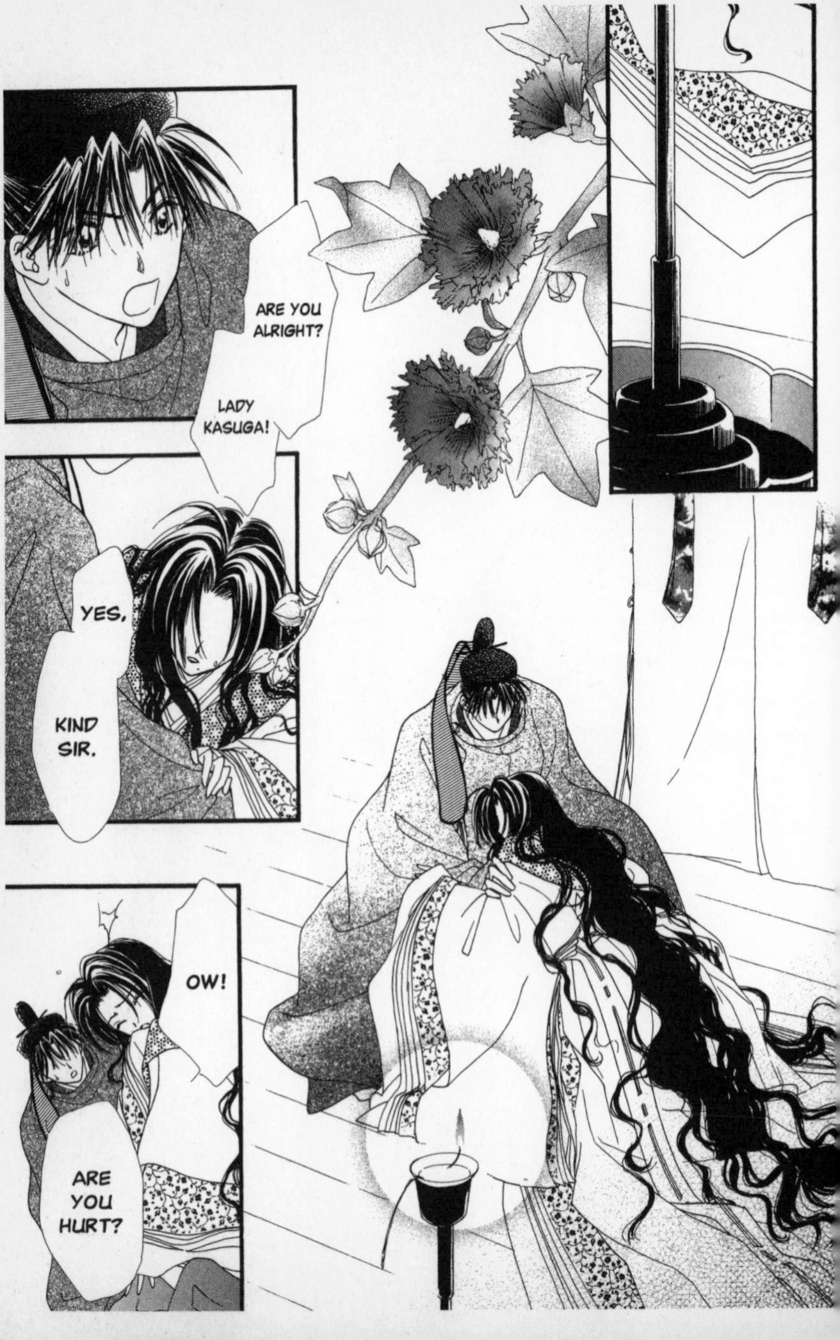
ARE YOU ALRIGHT?
LADY KASUGA!
YES, KIND SIR.
OW!
ARE YOU HURT?

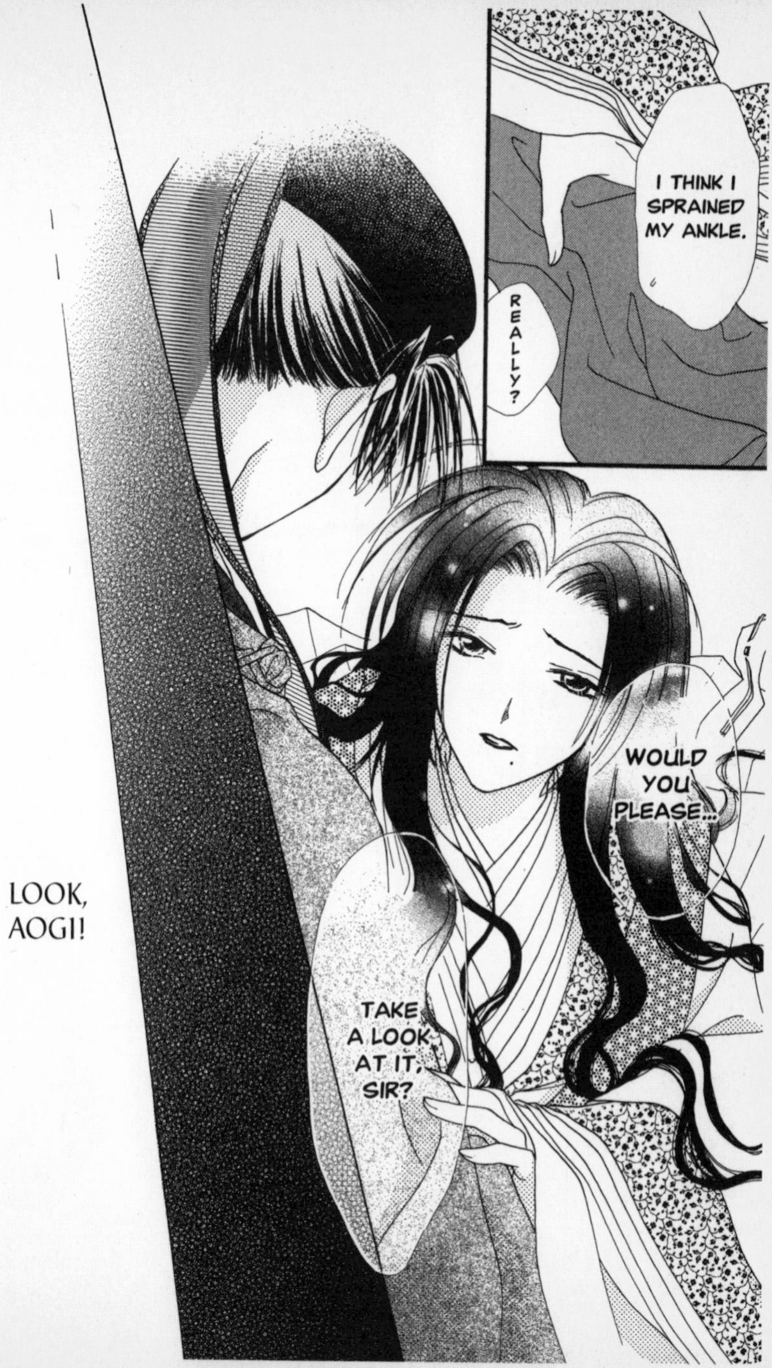
I THINK I SPRAINED MY ANKLE.
REALLY?
WOULD YOU PLEASE...
TAKE A LOOK AT IT, SIR?
LOOK, AOGI!

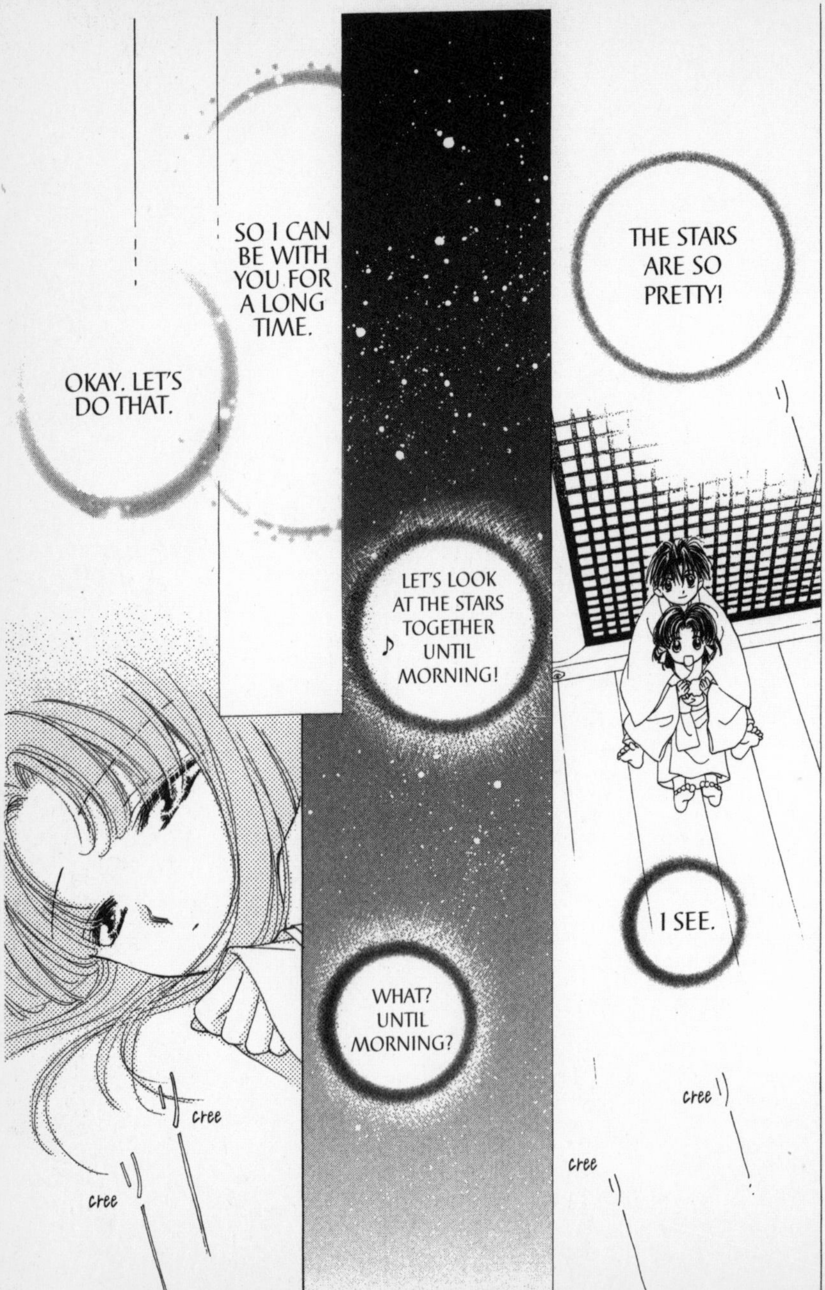
THE STARS ARE SO PRETTY!
I SEE.
cree
cree
LET'S LOOK AT THE STARS TOGETHER UNTIL MORNING! ♪
WHAT? UNTIL MORNING?
SO I CAN BE WITH YOU FOR A LONG TIME.
OKAY. LET'S DO THAT.
cree
cree

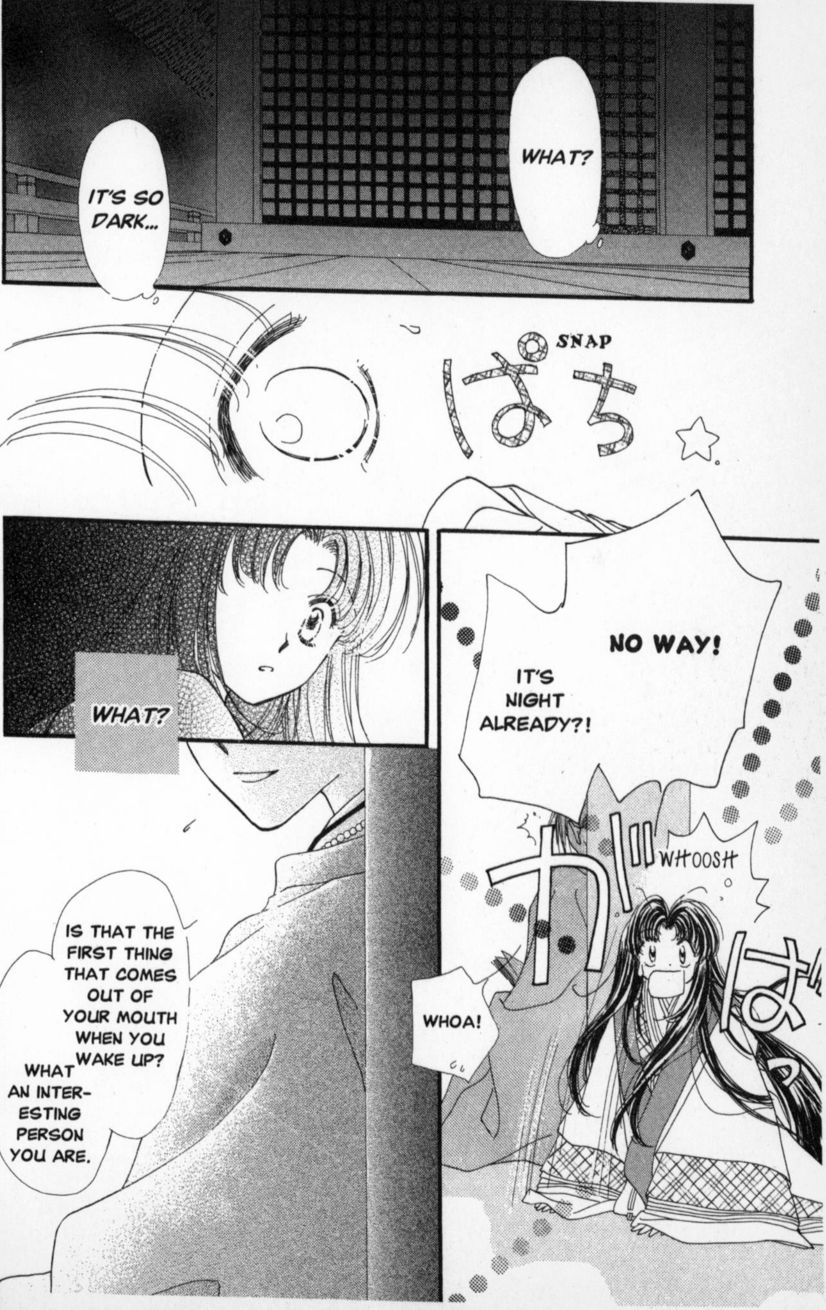
WHAT?
IT'S SO DARK...
SNAP
ぱち
NO WAY! IT'S NIGHT ALREADY?!
WHOOSH
WHOA!
WHAT?
IS THAT THE FIRST THING THAT COMES OUT OF YOUR MOUTH WHEN YOU WAKE UP?
WHAT AN INTER-ESTING PERSON YOU ARE.

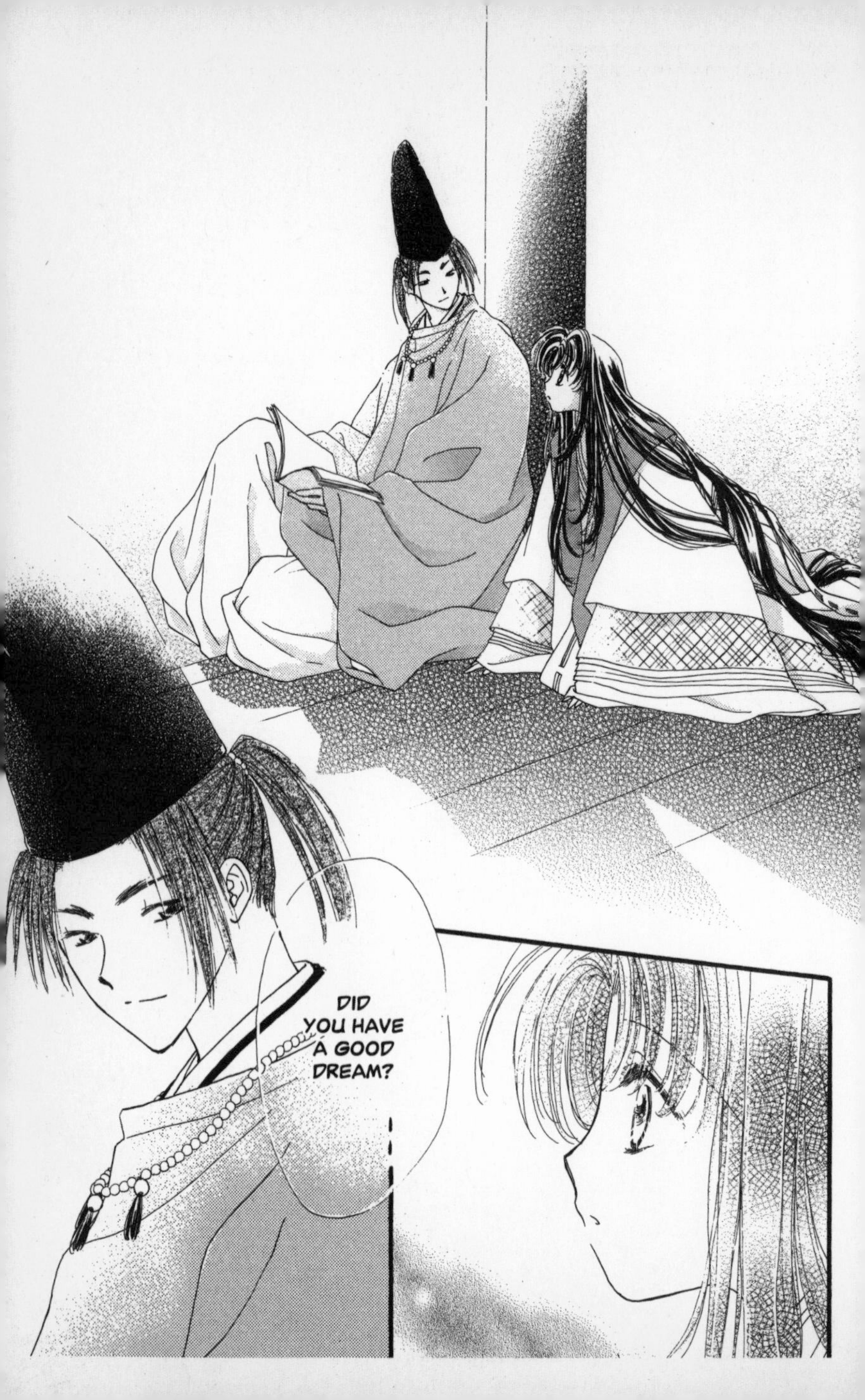
DID YOU HAVE A GOOD DREAM?

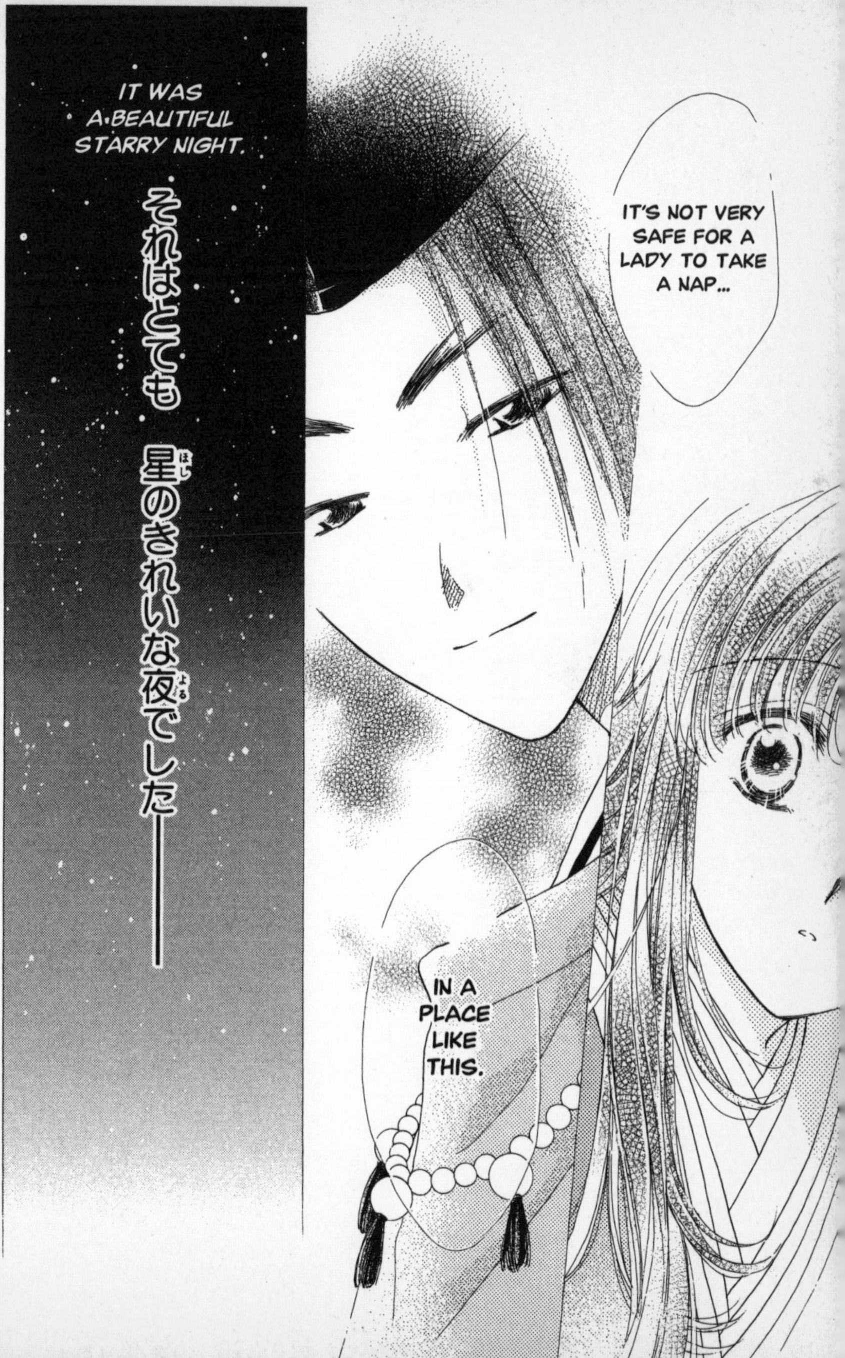
IT'S NOT VERY SAFE FOR A LADY TO TAKE A NAP...
IN A PLACE LIKE THIS.
IT WAS A BEAUTIFUL STARRY NIGHT.
それはとても星のきれいな夜でした——

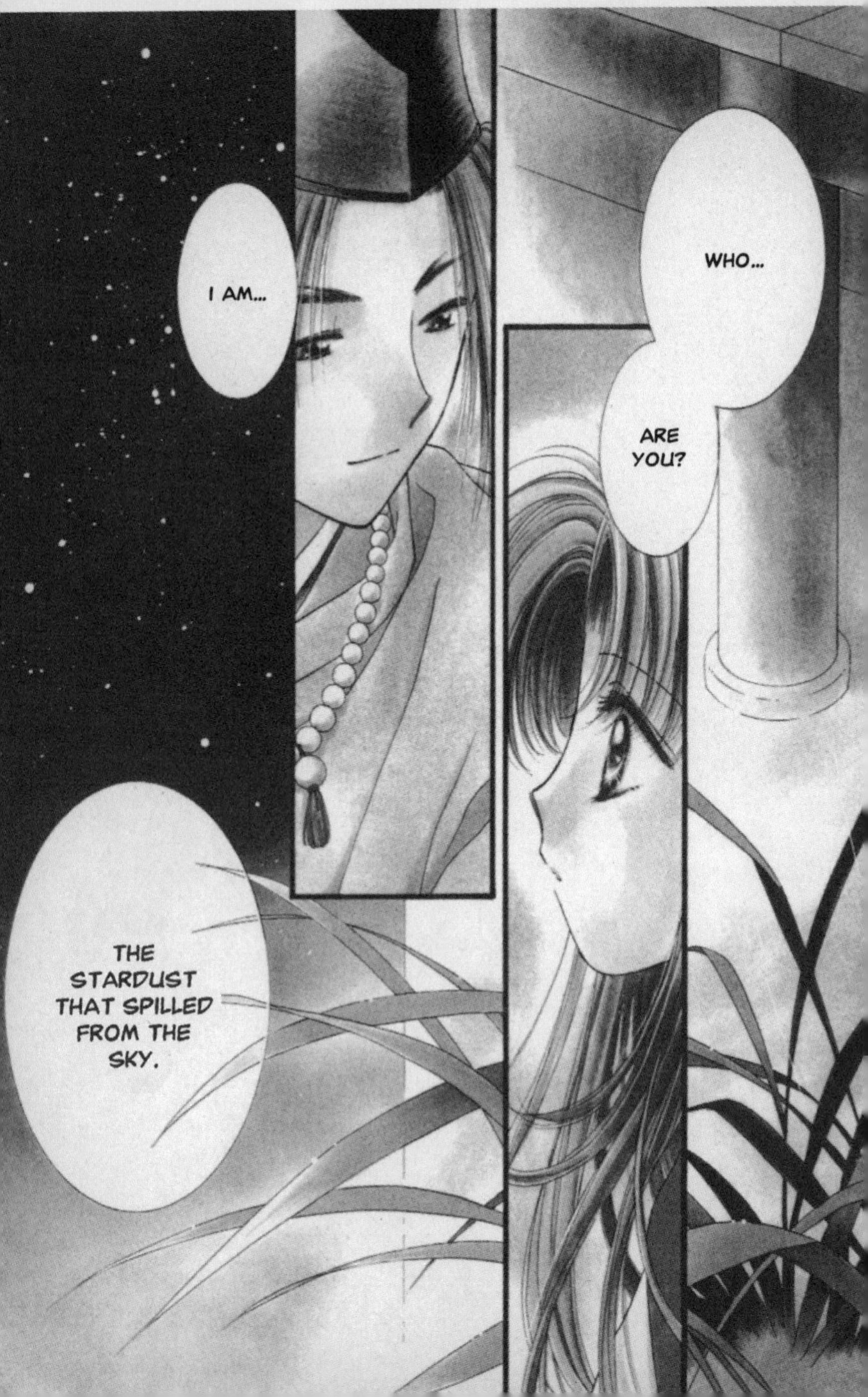
WHO...
ARE YOU?
I AM...
THE STARDUST THAT SPILLED FROM THE SKY.

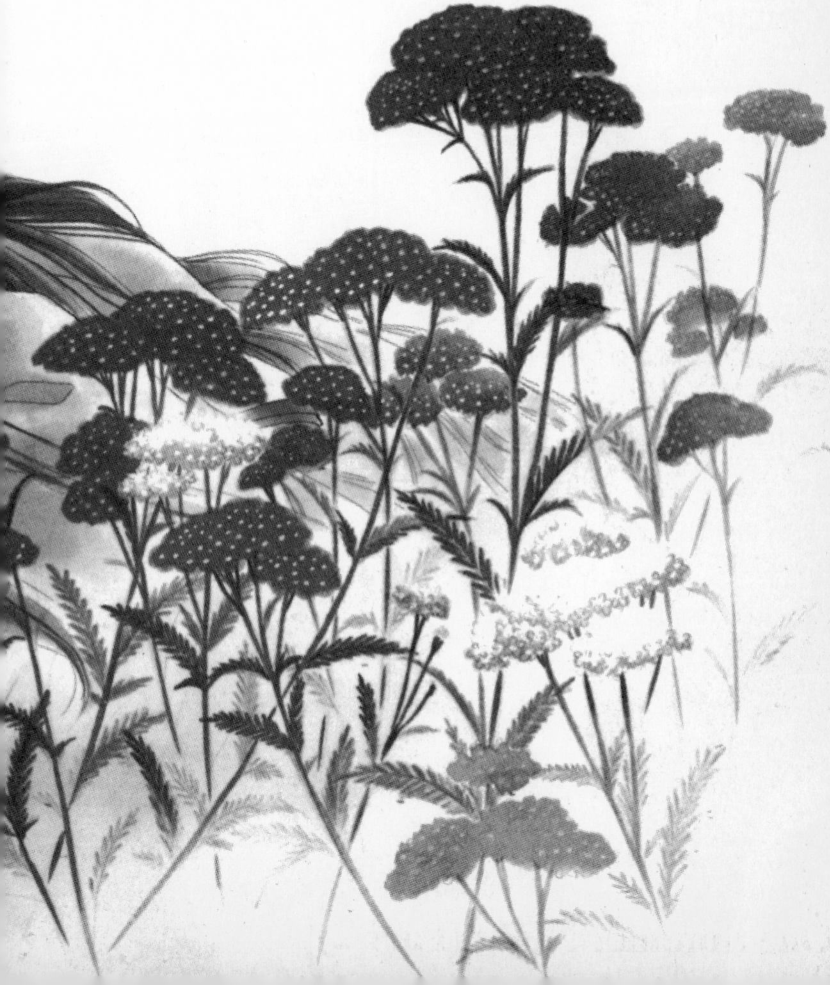

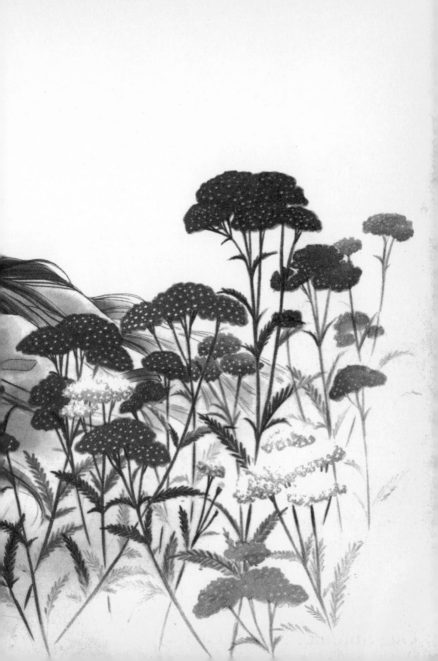

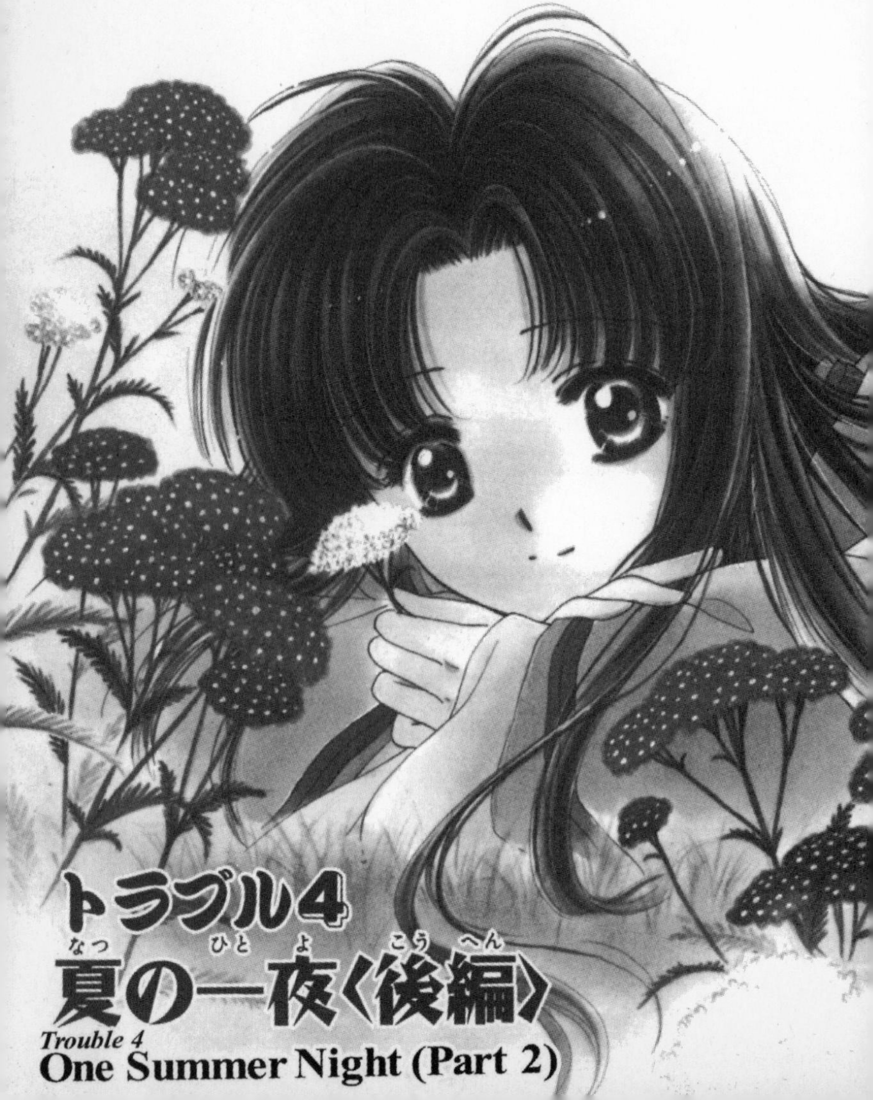
トラブル4
夏の一夜〈後編〉
Trouble 4
One Summer Night (Part 2)

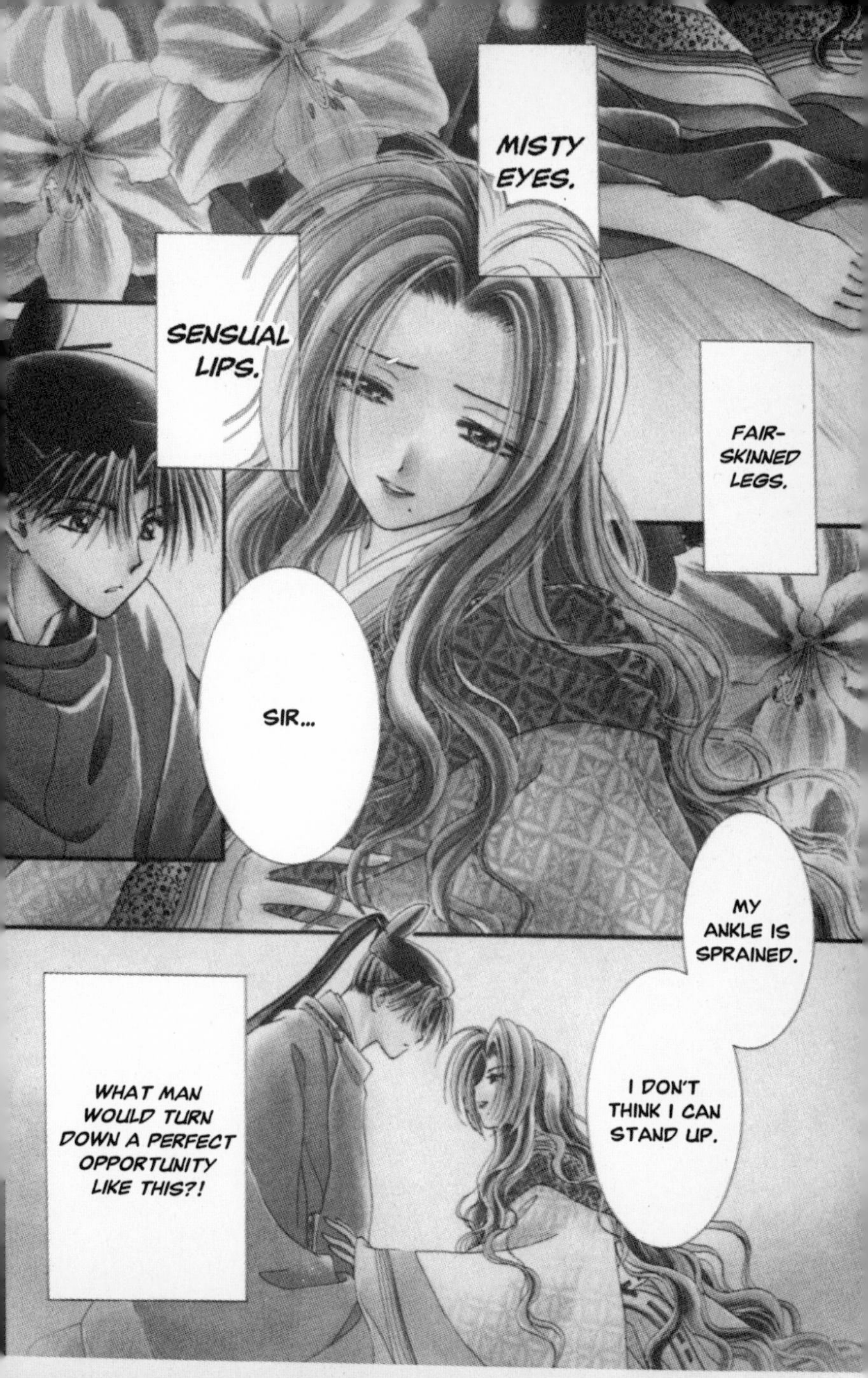
MISTY EYES.
SENSUAL LIPS.
FAIR-SKINNED LEGS.
SIR...
MY ANKLE IS SPRAINED.
I DON'T THINK I CAN STAND UP.
WHAT MAN WOULD TURN DOWN A PERFECT OPPORTUNITY LIKE THIS?!

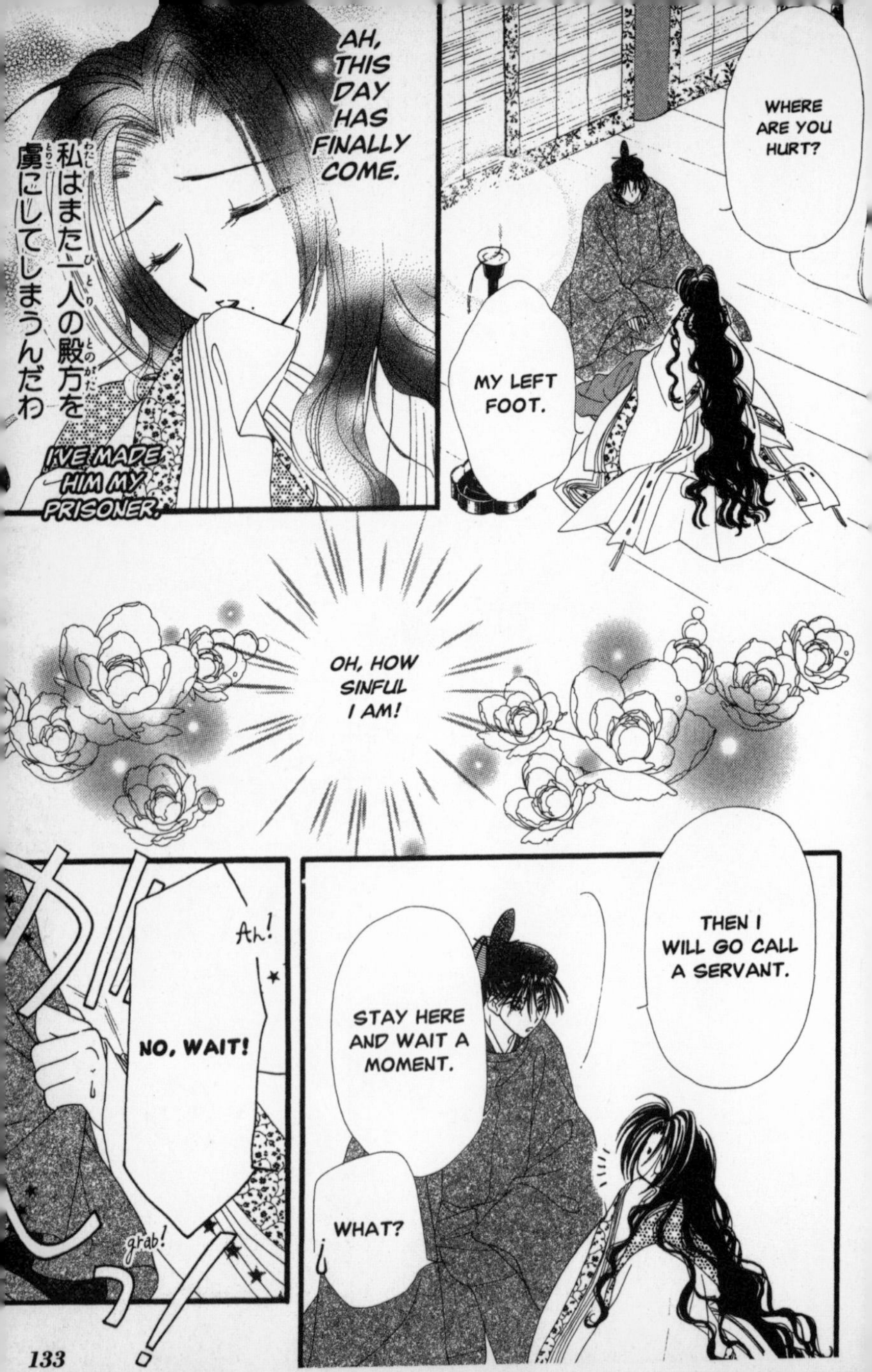
WHERE ARE YOU HURT?
MY LEFT FOOT.
AH, THIS DAY HAS FINALLY COME.
私はまた一人の殿方を虜にしてしまうんだわ
I'VE MADE HIM MY PRISONER.
OH, HOW SINFUL I AM!
THEN I WILL GO CALL A SERVANT.
STAY HERE AND WAIT A MOMENT.
WHAT?
Ah!
NO, WAIT!
grab!

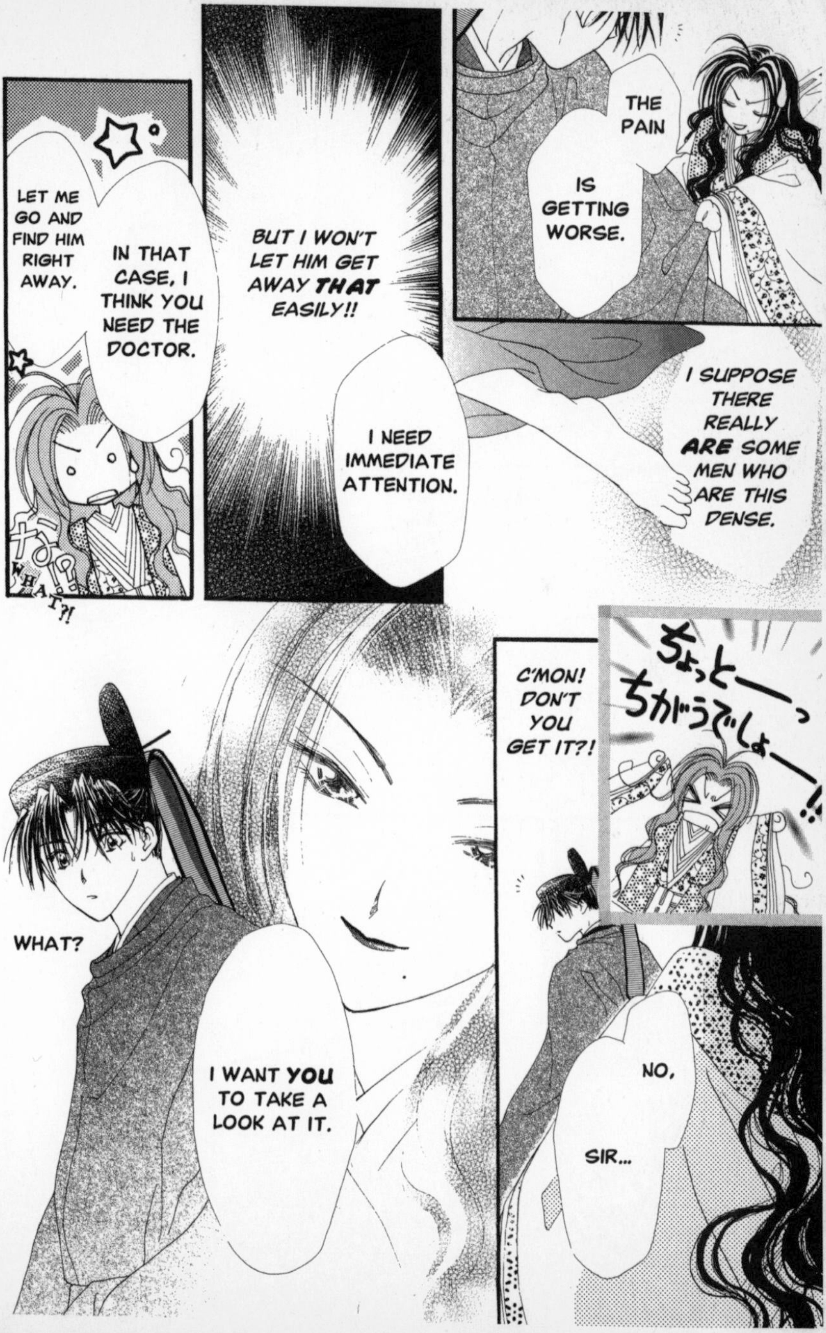
THE PAIN
IS GETTING WORSE.
I NEED IMMEDIATE ATTENTION.
IN THAT CASE, I THINK YOU NEED THE DOCTOR.
LET ME GO AND FIND HIM RIGHT AWAY.
なっ!?
WHAT?!
I SUPPOSE THERE REALLY ARE SOME MEN WHO ARE THIS DENSE.
BUT I WON'T LET HIM GET AWAY THAT EASILY!!
ちょっとーっ ちがうでしょーー!!
C'MON! DON'T YOU GET IT?!
NO,
SIR...
I WANT YOU TO TAKE A LOOK AT IT.
WHAT?

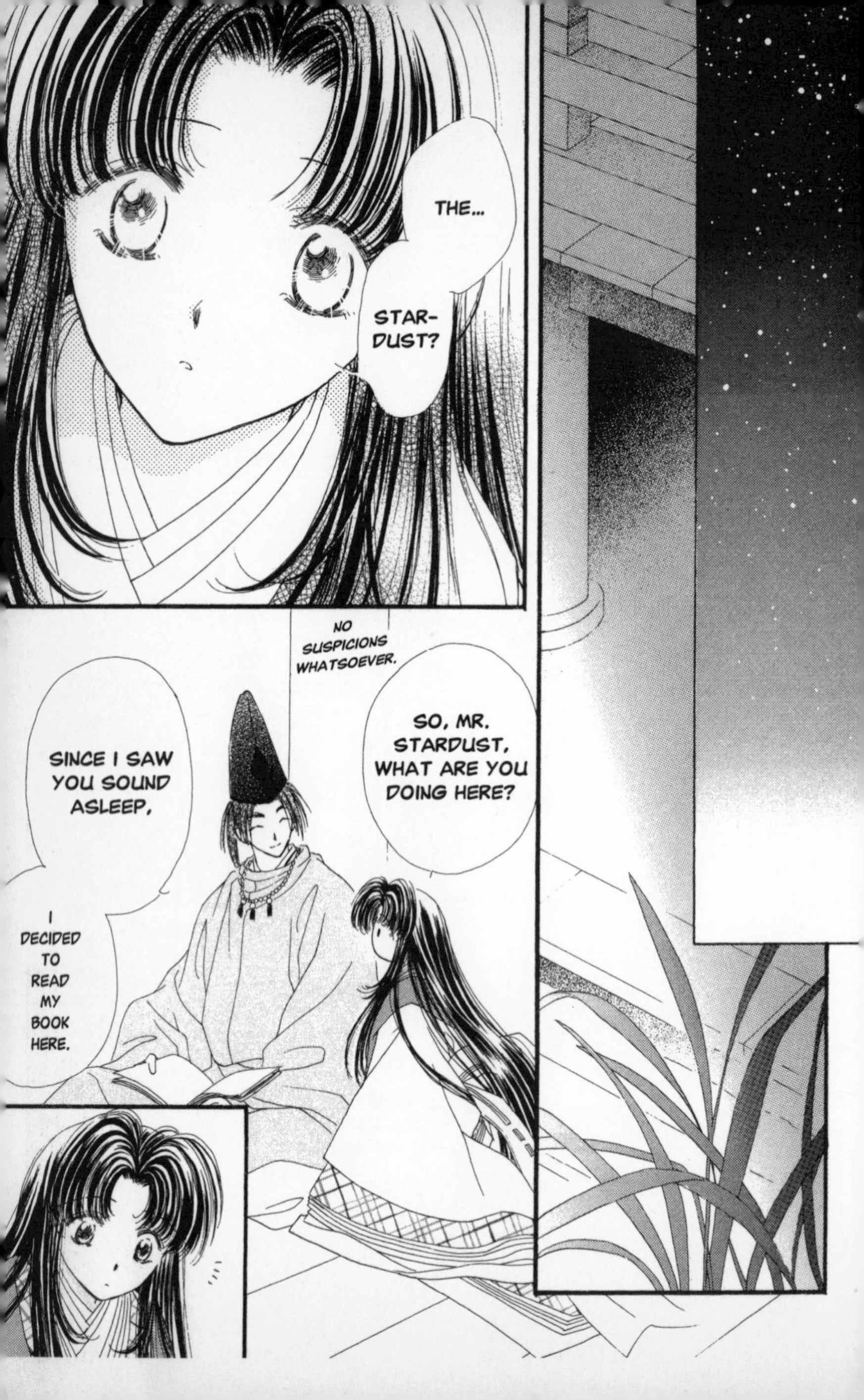
THE...
STAR-DUST?
NO SUSPICIONS WHATSOEVER.
SO, MR. STARDUST, WHAT ARE YOU DOING HERE?
SINCE I SAW YOU SOUND ASLEEP,
I DECIDED TO READ MY BOOK HERE.

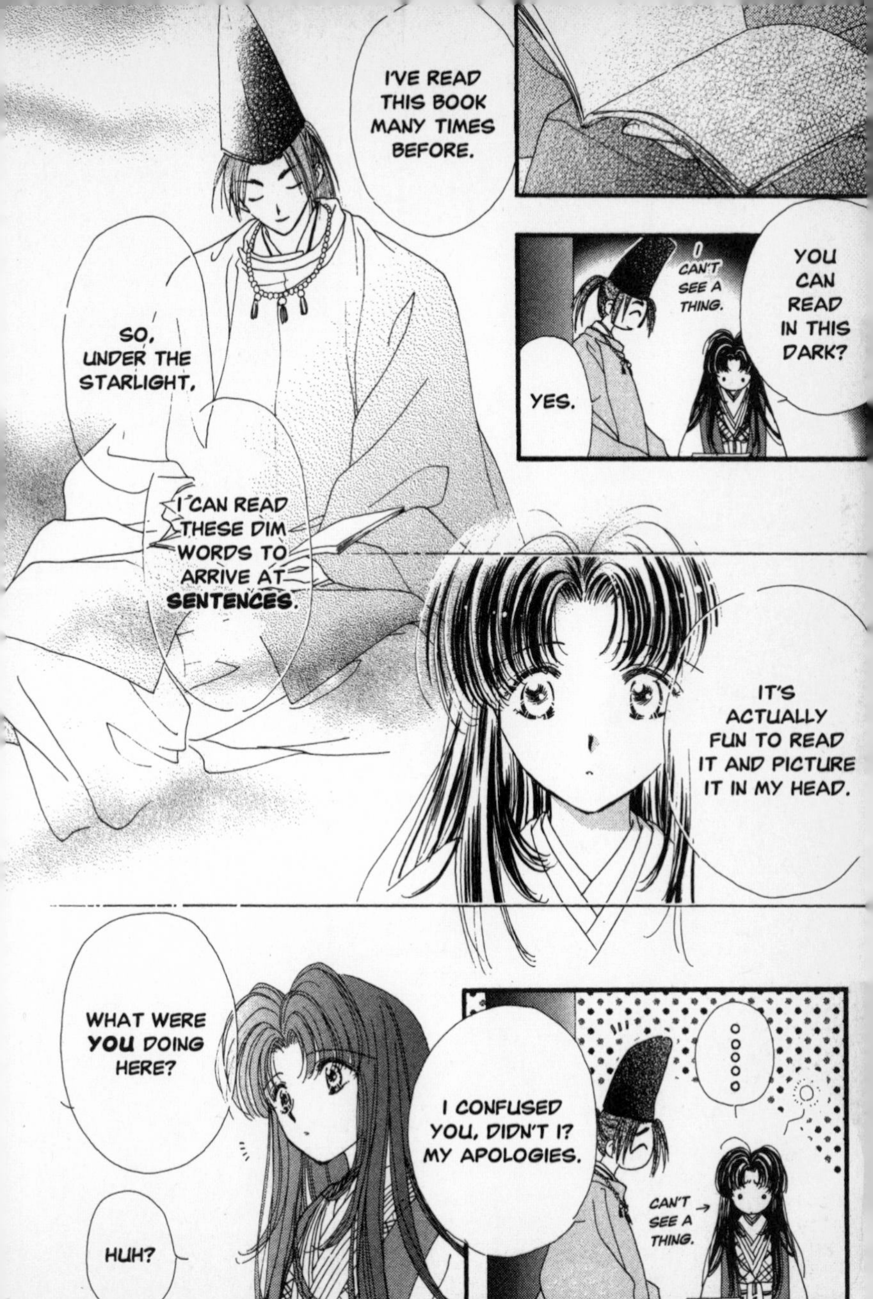
YOU CAN READ IN THIS DARK?
I CAN'T SEE A THING.
YES.
I'VE READ THIS BOOK MANY TIMES BEFORE.
SO, UNDER THE STARLIGHT,
I CAN READ THESE DIM WORDS TO ARRIVE AT **SENTENCES**.
IT'S ACTUALLY FUN TO READ IT AND PICTURE IT IN MY HEAD.
.....
CAN'T SEE A THING.
I CONFUSED YOU, DIDN'T I? MY APOLOGIES.
WHAT WERE **YOU** DOING HERE?
HUH?

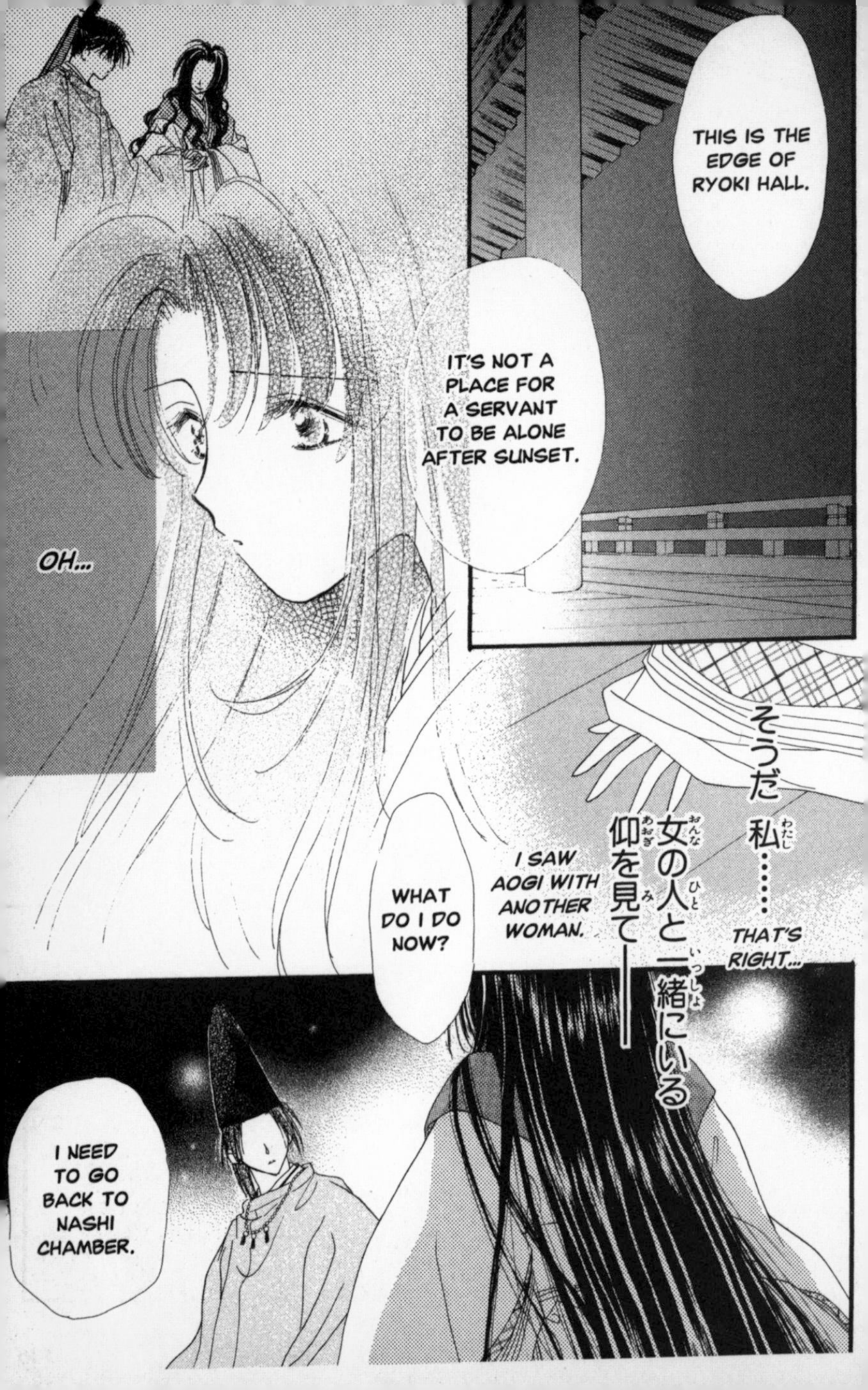
THIS IS THE EDGE OF RYOKI HALL.
IT'S NOT A PLACE FOR A SERVANT TO BE ALONE AFTER SUNSET.
OH...
そうだ 私……
THAT'S RIGHT...
女の人と一緒にいる
仰を見て――
I SAW AOGI WITH ANOTHER WOMAN.
WHAT DO I DO NOW?
I NEED TO GO BACK TO NASHI CHAMBER.

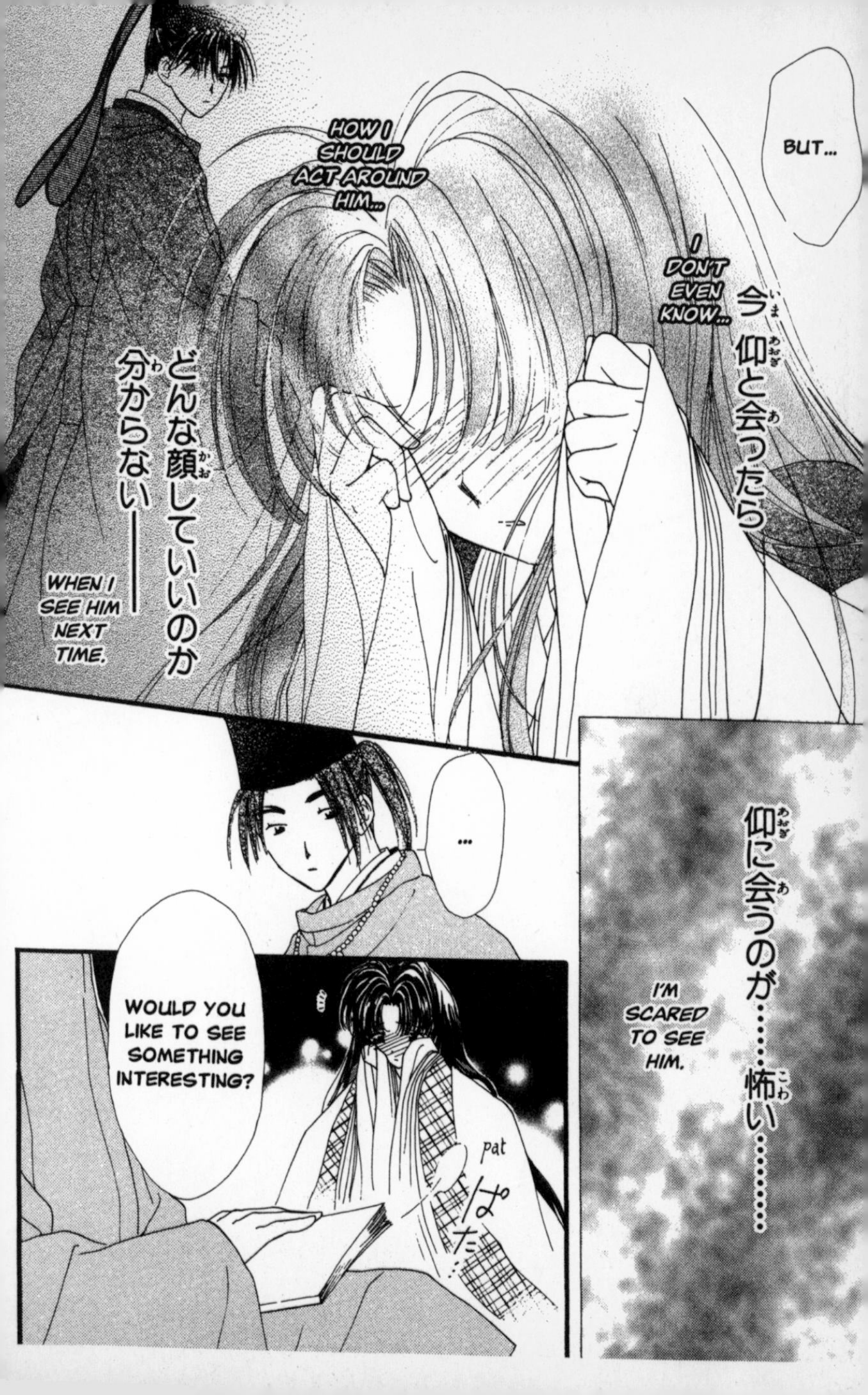
BUT...
今仰と会ったら
I DON'T EVEN KNOW...
HOW I SHOULD ACT AROUND HIM...
どんな顔していいのか
分からないーー
WHEN I SEE HIM NEXT TIME.
仰に会うのが……
怖い………
I'M SCARED TO SEE HIM.
...
WOULD YOU LIKE TO SEE SOMETHING INTERESTING?
pat
ぱた

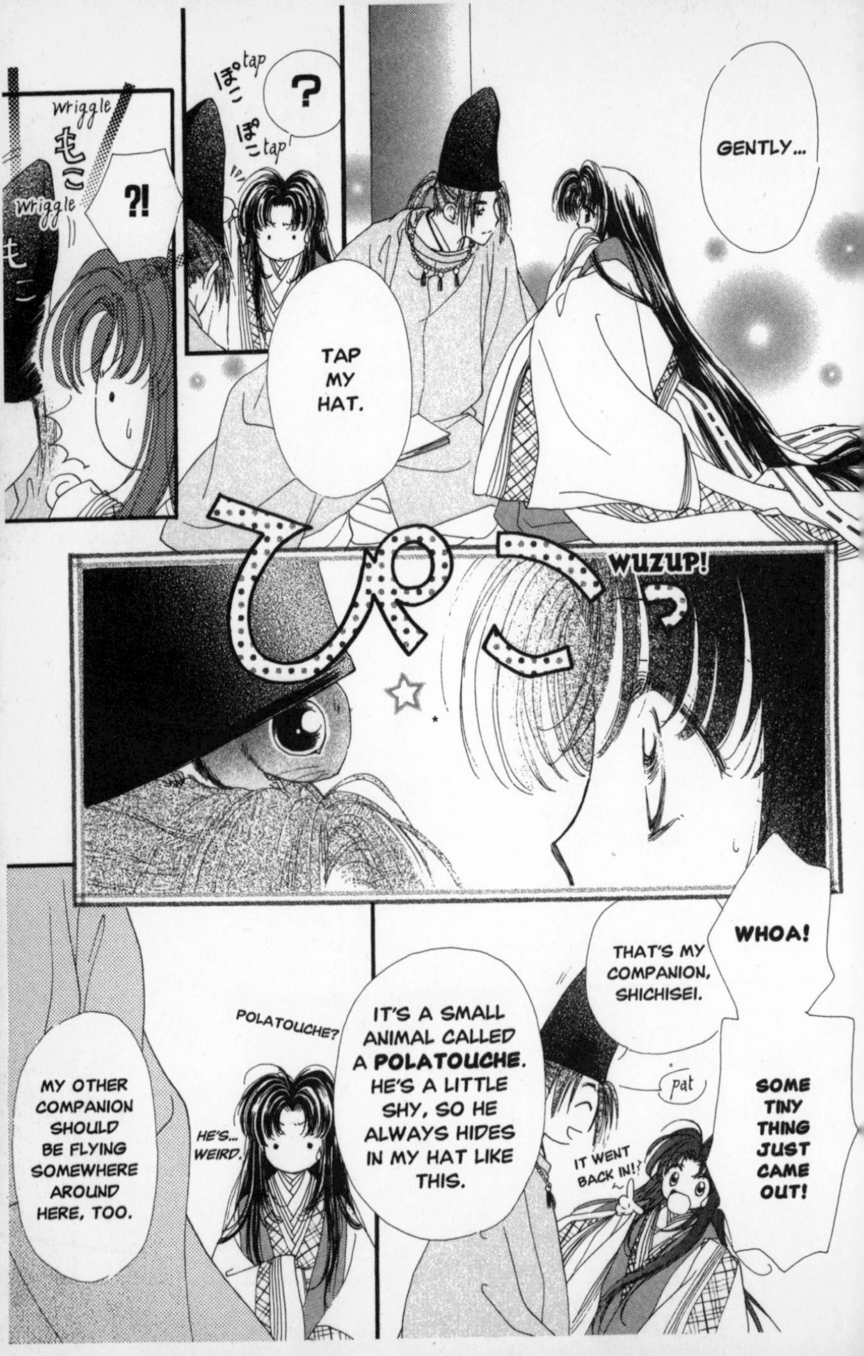
GENTLY...
TAP MY HAT.
ぽこ tap
ぽこ tap
?
wriggle
もこ
wriggle
もこ
?!
WUZUP!
WHOA!
SOME TINY THING JUST CAME OUT!
THAT'S MY COMPANION, SHICHISEI.
pat
IT WENT BACK IN!?
IT'S A SMALL ANIMAL CALLED A **POLATOUCHE**. HE'S A LITTLE SHY, SO HE ALWAYS HIDES IN MY HAT LIKE THIS.
POLATOUCHE?
HE'S... WEIRD.
MY OTHER COMPANION SHOULD BE FLYING SOMEWHERE AROUND HERE, TOO.

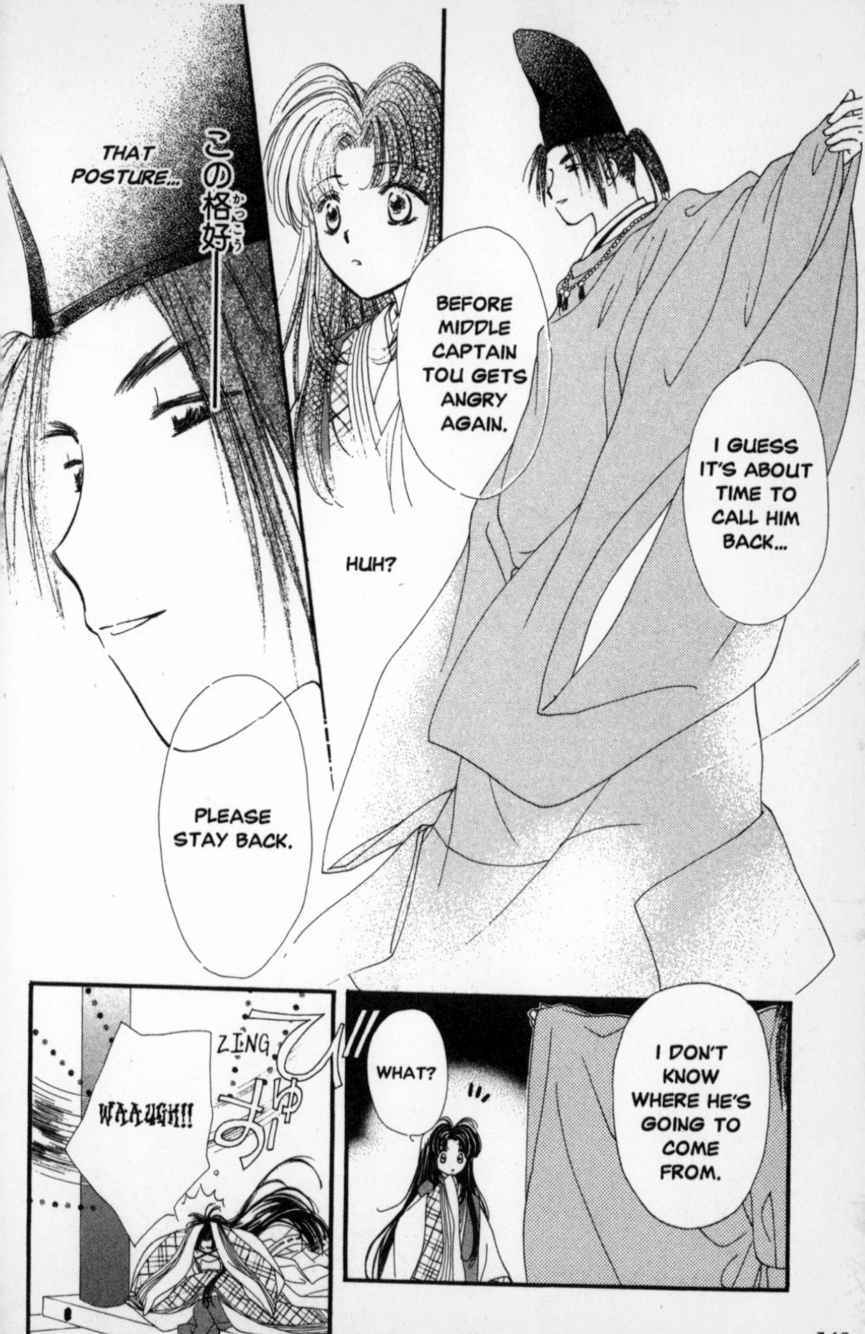
I GUESS IT'S ABOUT TIME TO CALL HIM BACK...
BEFORE MIDDLE CAPTAIN TOU GETS ANGRY AGAIN.
HUH?
THAT POSTURE...
この格好—
PLEASE STAY BACK.
I DON'T KNOW WHERE HE'S GOING TO COME FROM.
WHAT?
ZING
ひゅ〜
WAAUGH!!

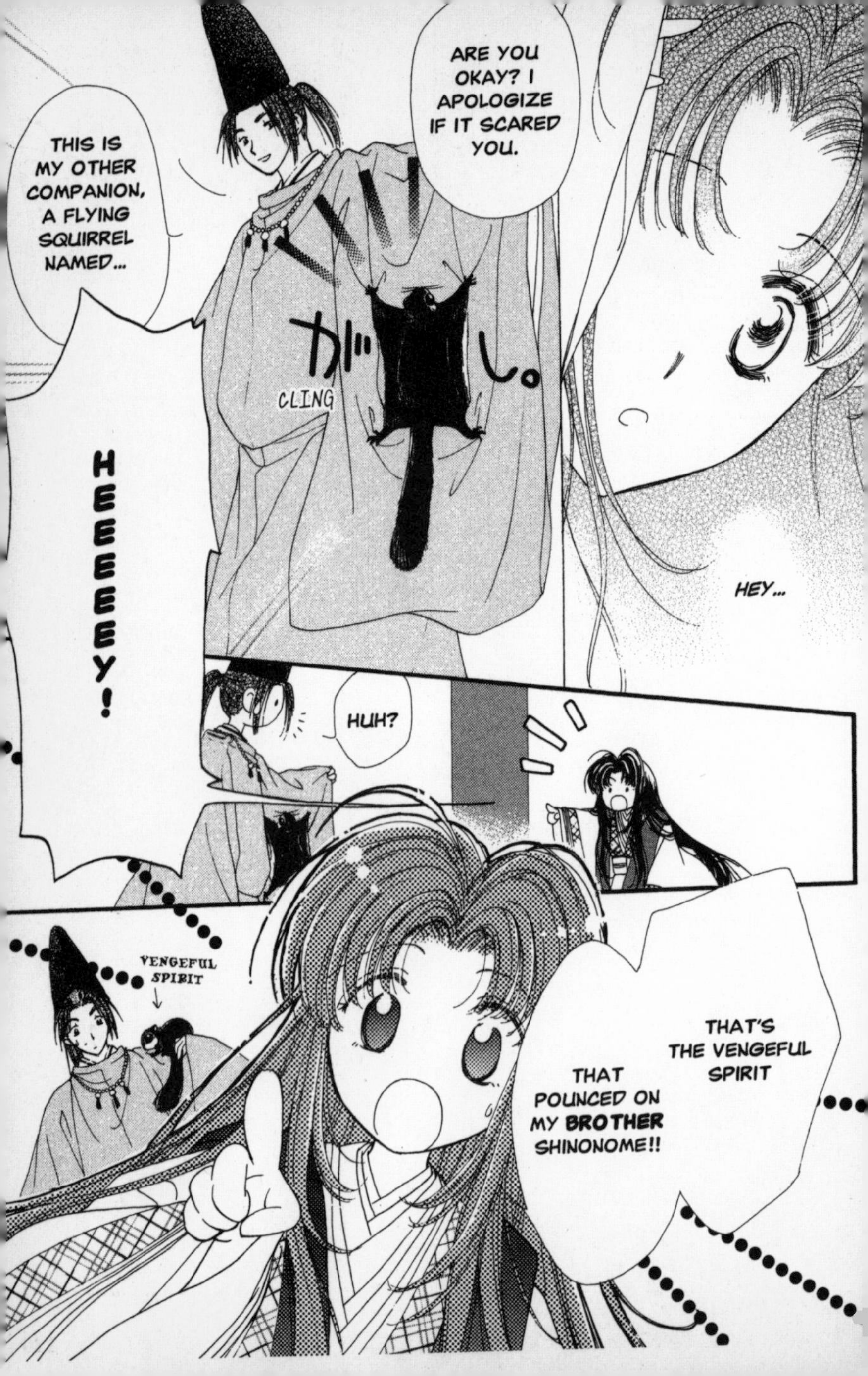

HEY...
ARE YOU OKAY? I APOLOGIZE IF IT SCARED YOU.
THIS IS MY OTHER COMPANION, A FLYING SQUIRREL NAMED...
CLING
HEEEEEEY!
HUH?
THAT'S THE VENGEFUL SPIRIT THAT POUNCED ON MY **BROTHER** SHINONOME!!
VENGEFUL SPIRIT

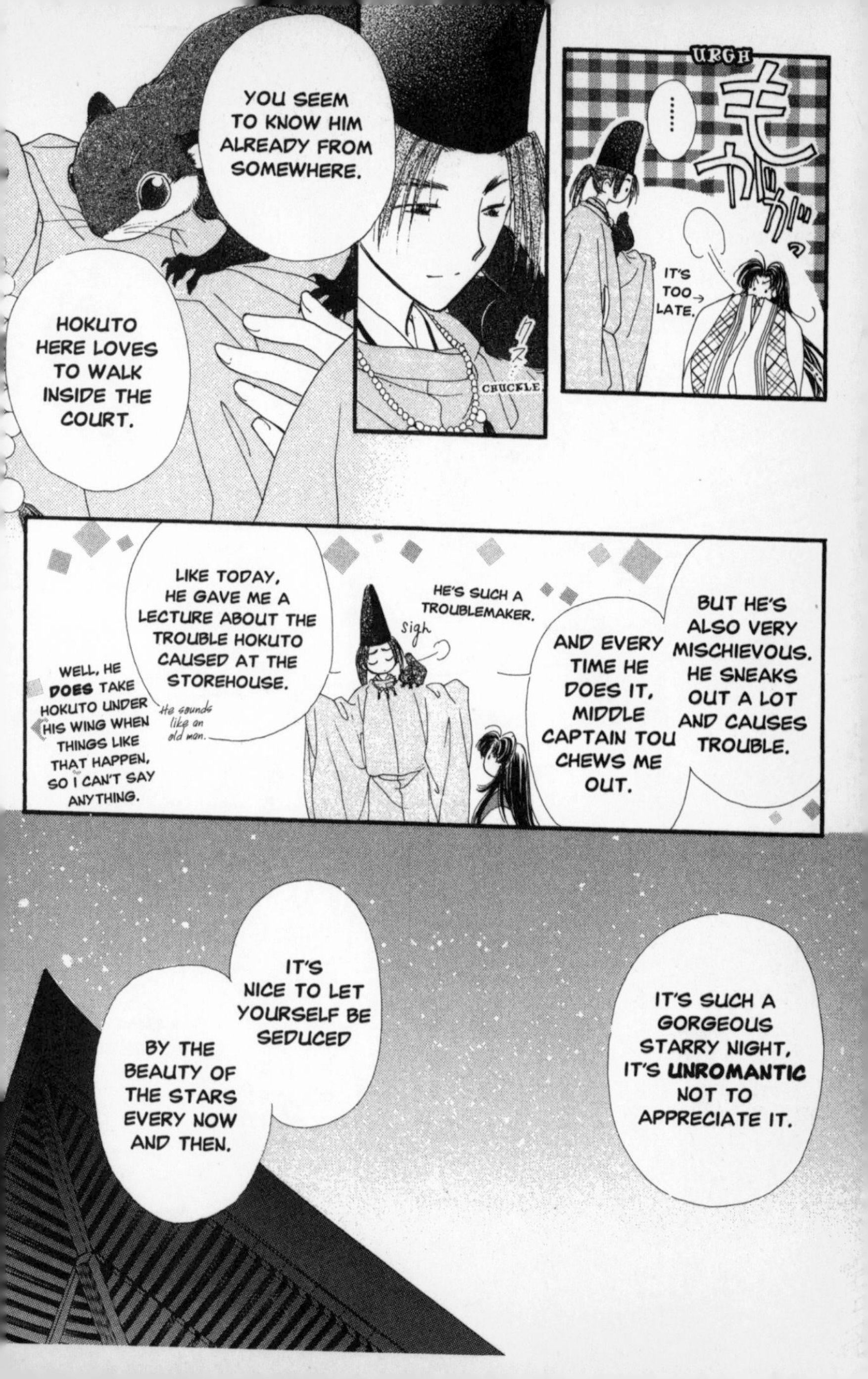
URGH
......
IT'S TOO LATE.
YOU SEEM TO KNOW HIM ALREADY FROM SOMEWHERE.
CHUCKLE
HOKUTO HERE LOVES TO WALK INSIDE THE COURT.
BUT HE'S ALSO VERY MISCHIEVOUS. HE SNEAKS OUT A LOT AND CAUSES TROUBLE.
AND EVERY TIME HE DOES IT, MIDDLE CAPTAIN TOU CHEWS ME OUT.
HE'S SUCH A TROUBLEMAKER.
Sigh
LIKE TODAY, HE GAVE ME A LECTURE ABOUT THE TROUBLE HOKUTO CAUSED AT THE STOREHOUSE.
He sounds like an old man.
WELL, HE **DOES** TAKE HOKUTO UNDER HIS WING WHEN THINGS LIKE THAT HAPPEN, SO I CAN'T SAY ANYTHING.
IT'S SUCH A GORGEOUS STARRY NIGHT, IT'S **UNROMANTIC** NOT TO APPRECIATE IT.
IT'S NICE TO LET YOURSELF BE SEDUCED
BY THE BEAUTY OF THE STARS EVERY NOW AND THEN.

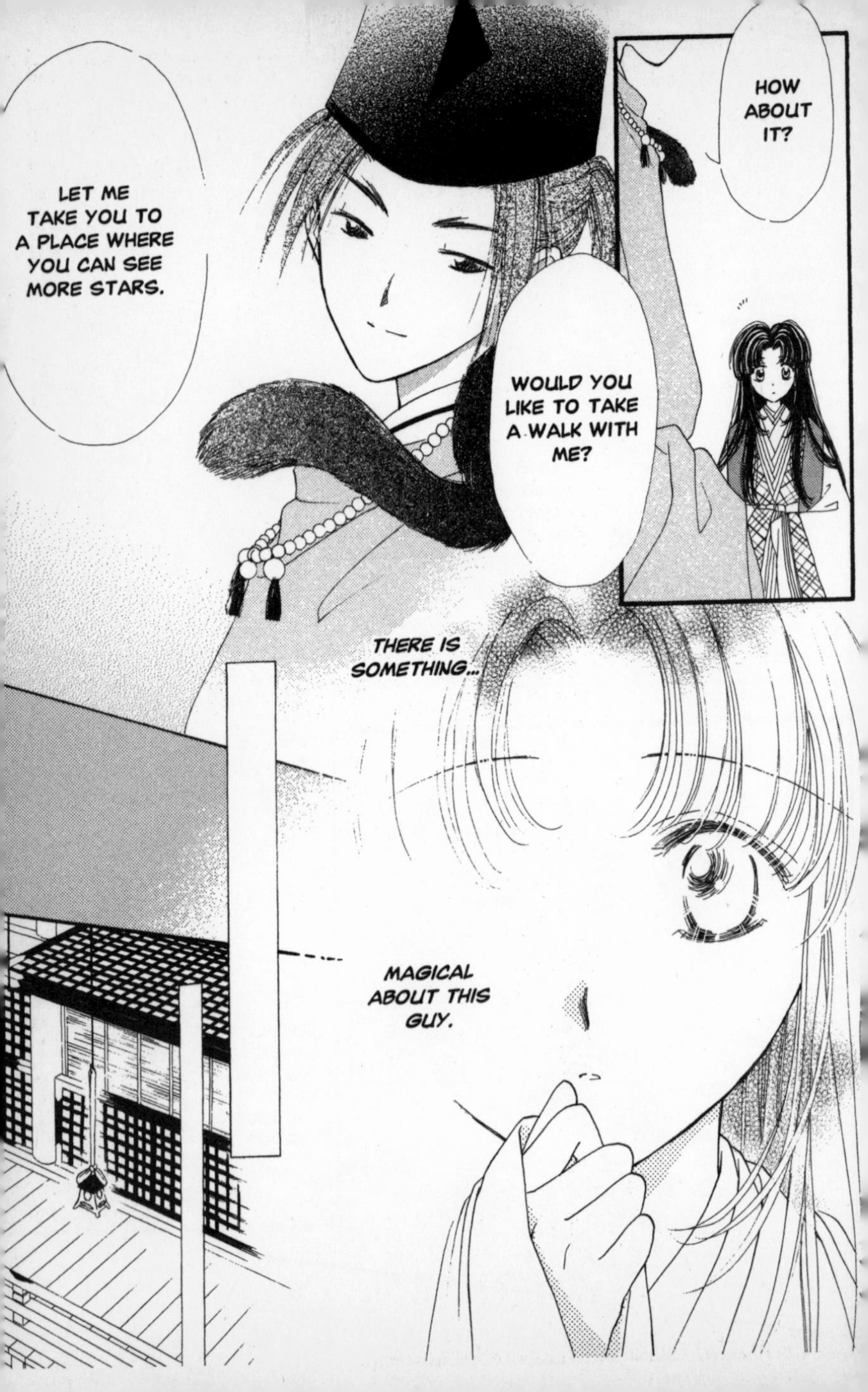
HOW ABOUT IT?
WOULD YOU LIKE TO TAKE A WALK WITH ME?
LET ME TAKE YOU TO A PLACE WHERE YOU CAN SEE MORE STARS.
THERE IS SOMETHING...
MAGICAL ABOUT THIS GUY.

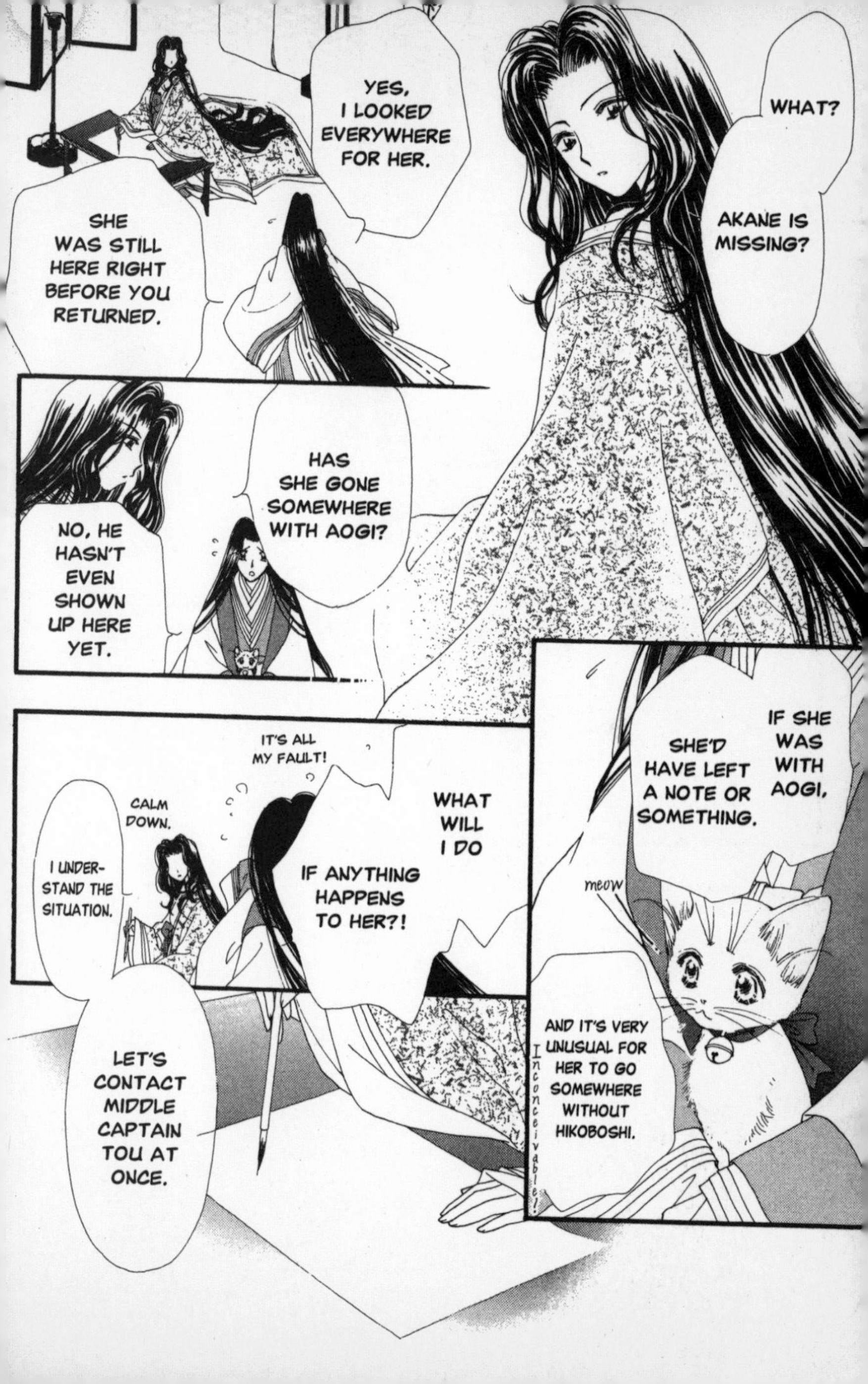
WHAT?
AKANE IS MISSING?
YES, I LOOKED EVERYWHERE FOR HER.
SHE WAS STILL HERE RIGHT BEFORE YOU RETURNED.
HAS SHE GONE SOMEWHERE WITH AOGI?
NO, HE HASN'T EVEN SHOWN UP HERE YET.
IF SHE WAS WITH AOGI,
SHE'D HAVE LEFT A NOTE OR SOMETHING.
meow
AND IT'S VERY UNUSUAL FOR HER TO GO SOMEWHERE WITHOUT HIKOBOSHI.
Inconceivable!
IT'S ALL MY FAULT!
WHAT WILL I DO
IF ANYTHING HAPPENS TO HER?!
CALM DOWN.
I UNDERSTAND THE SITUATION.
LET'S CONTACT MIDDLE CAPTAIN TOU AT ONCE.

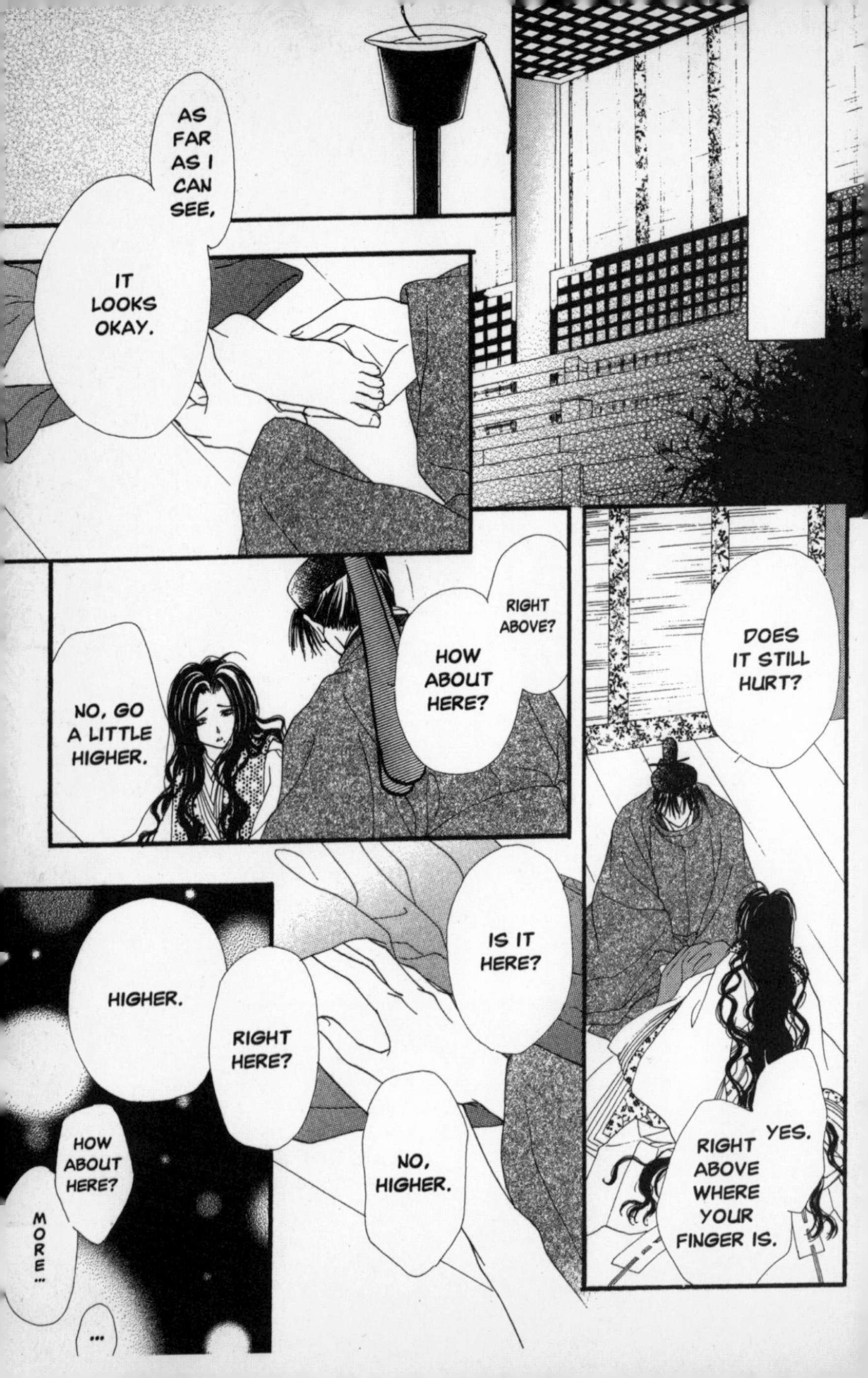
AS FAR AS I CAN SEE, IT LOOKS OKAY.
DOES IT STILL HURT?
YES. RIGHT ABOVE WHERE YOUR FINGER IS.
RIGHT ABOVE?
HOW ABOUT HERE?
NO, GO A LITTLE HIGHER.
IS IT HERE?
NO, HIGHER.
RIGHT HERE?
HIGHER.
HOW ABOUT HERE?
MORE...
...

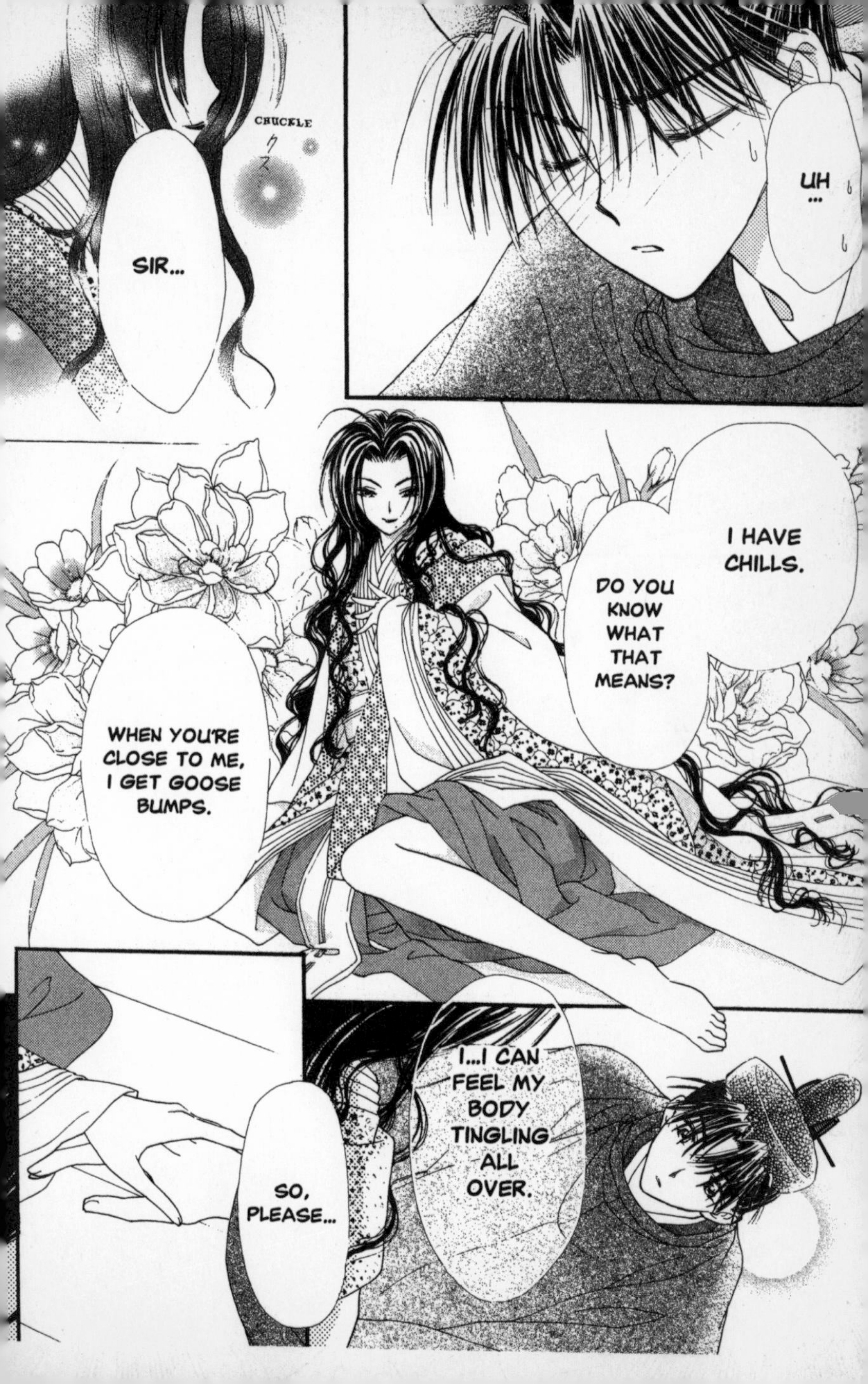
UH...
CHUCKLE クス
SIR...
I HAVE CHILLS.
DO YOU KNOW WHAT THAT MEANS?
WHEN YOU'RE CLOSE TO ME, I GET GOOSE BUMPS.
I...I CAN FEEL MY BODY TINGLING ALL OVER.
SO, PLEASE...

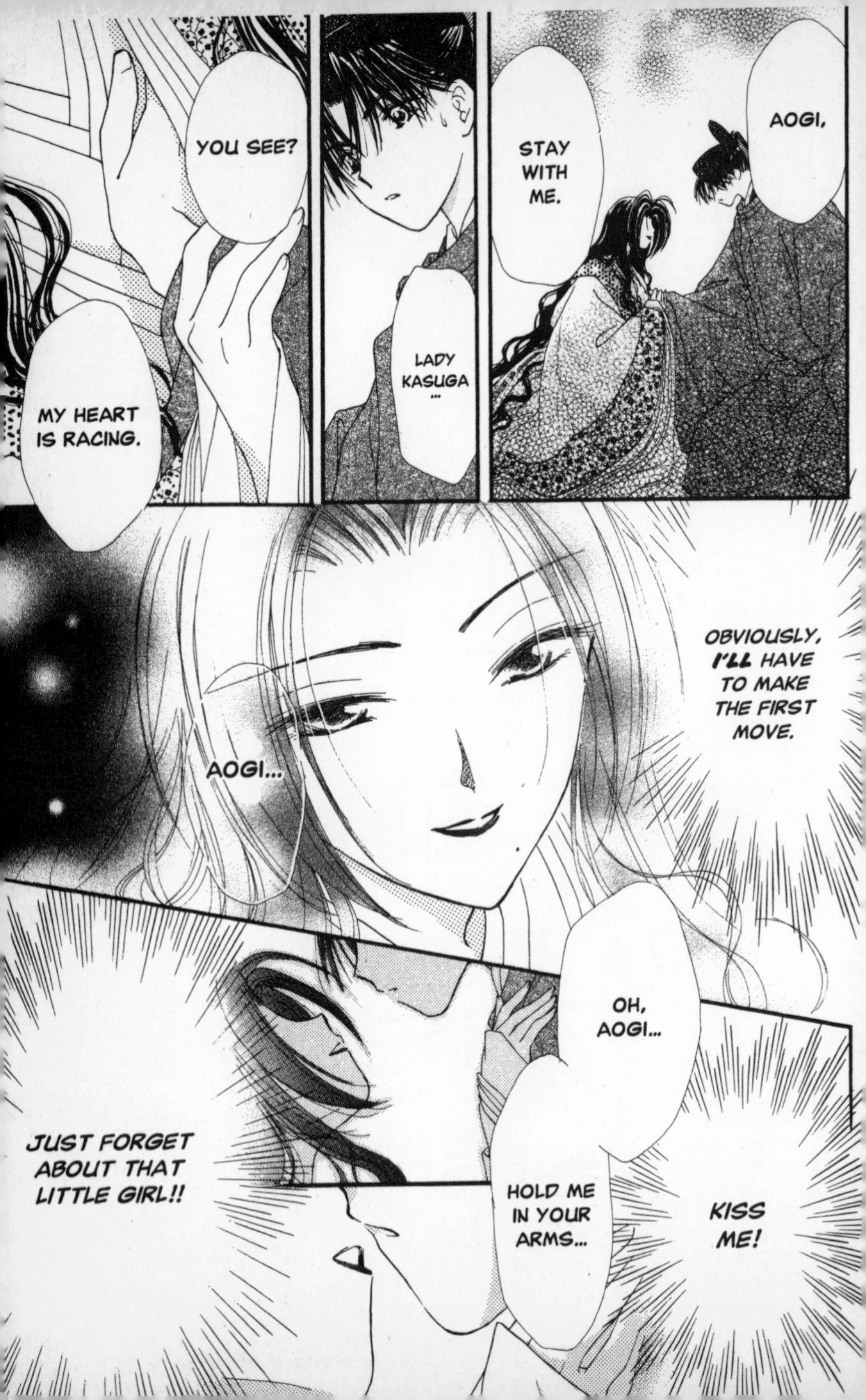
AOGI,
STAY WITH ME.
LADY KASUGA ...
YOU SEE?
MY HEART IS RACING.
OBVIOUSLY, I'LL HAVE TO MAKE THE FIRST MOVE.
AOGI...
OH, AOGI...
KISS ME!
HOLD ME IN YOUR ARMS...
JUST FORGET ABOUT THAT LITTLE GIRL!!

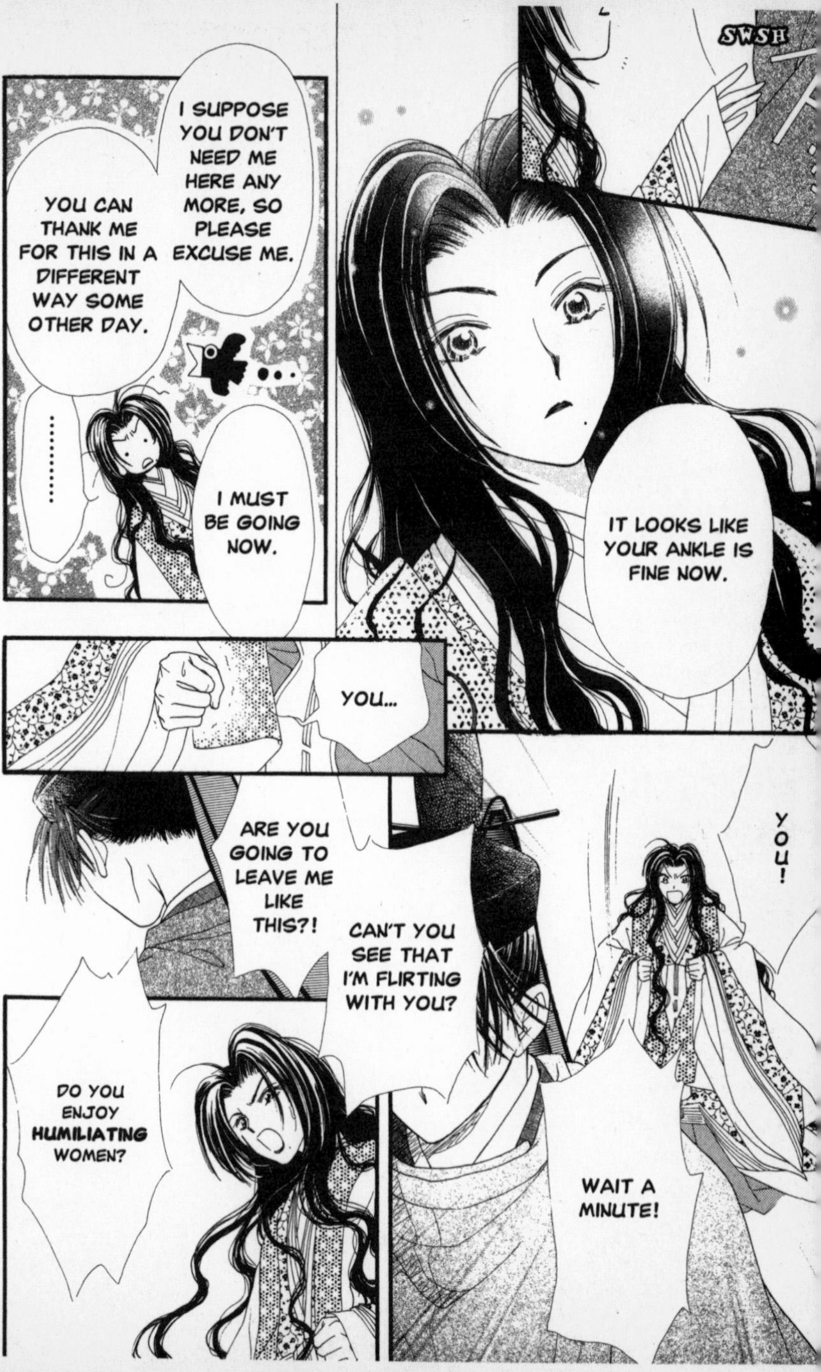
SWSH
IT LOOKS LIKE YOUR ANKLE IS FINE NOW.
I SUPPOSE YOU DON'T NEED ME HERE ANY MORE, SO PLEASE EXCUSE ME.
YOU CAN THANK ME FOR THIS IN A DIFFERENT WAY SOME OTHER DAY.
I MUST BE GOING NOW.
......
YOU...
YOU!
WAIT A MINUTE!
ARE YOU GOING TO LEAVE ME LIKE THIS?!
CAN'T YOU SEE THAT I'M FLIRTING WITH YOU?
DO YOU ENJOY HUMILIATING WOMEN?

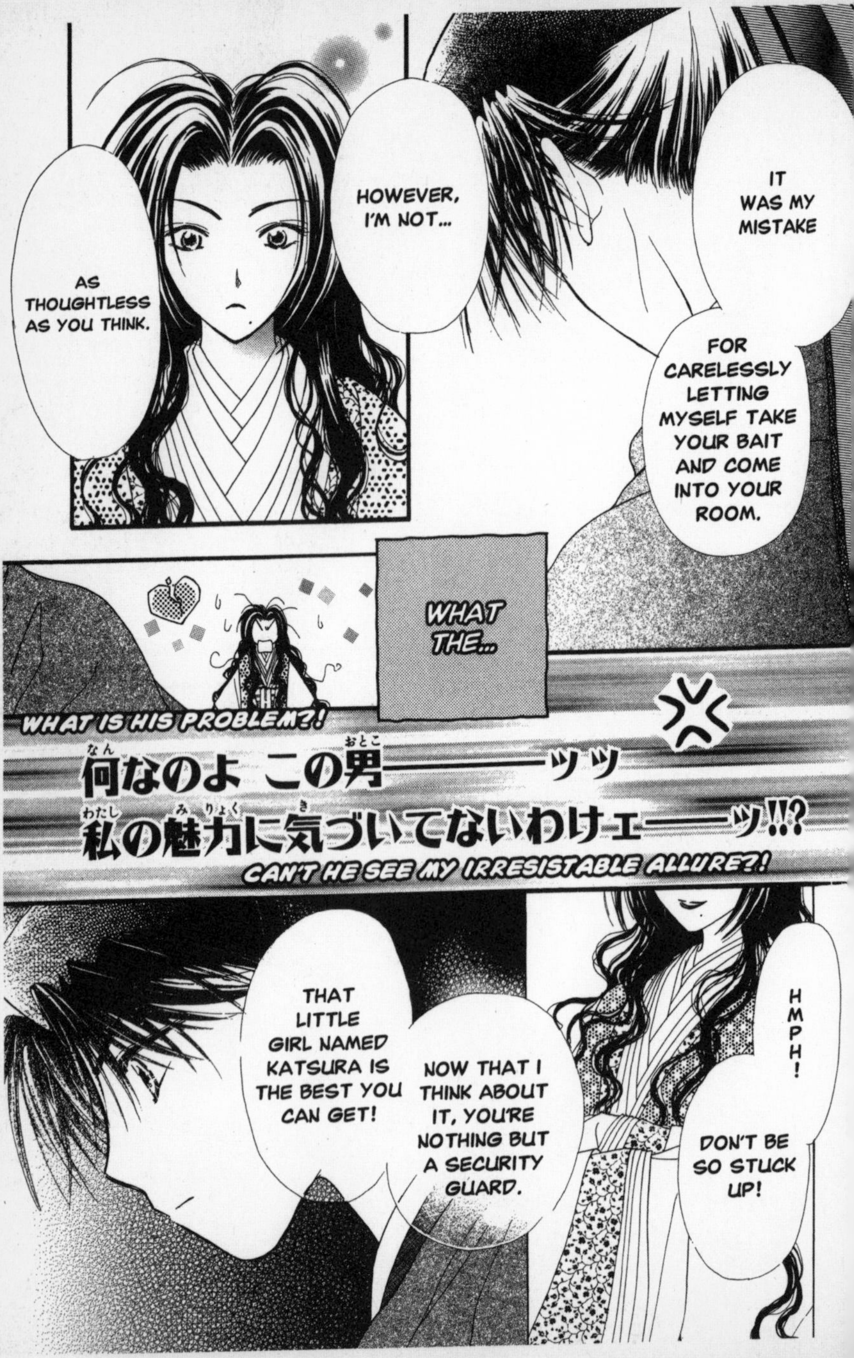
IT WAS MY MISTAKE
FOR CARELESSLY LETTING MYSELF TAKE YOUR BAIT AND COME INTO YOUR ROOM.
HOWEVER, I'M NOT...
AS THOUGHTLESS AS YOU THINK.
WHAT THE...
WHAT IS HIS PROBLEM?!
何なのよ この男――――ッッ
私の魅力に気づいてないわけェ――ッ!!?
CAN'T HE SEE MY IRRESISTABLE ALLURE?!
HMPH!
DON'T BE SO STUCK UP!
NOW THAT I THINK ABOUT IT, YOU'RE NOTHING BUT A SECURITY GUARD.
THAT LITTLE GIRL NAMED KATSURA IS THE BEST YOU CAN GET!

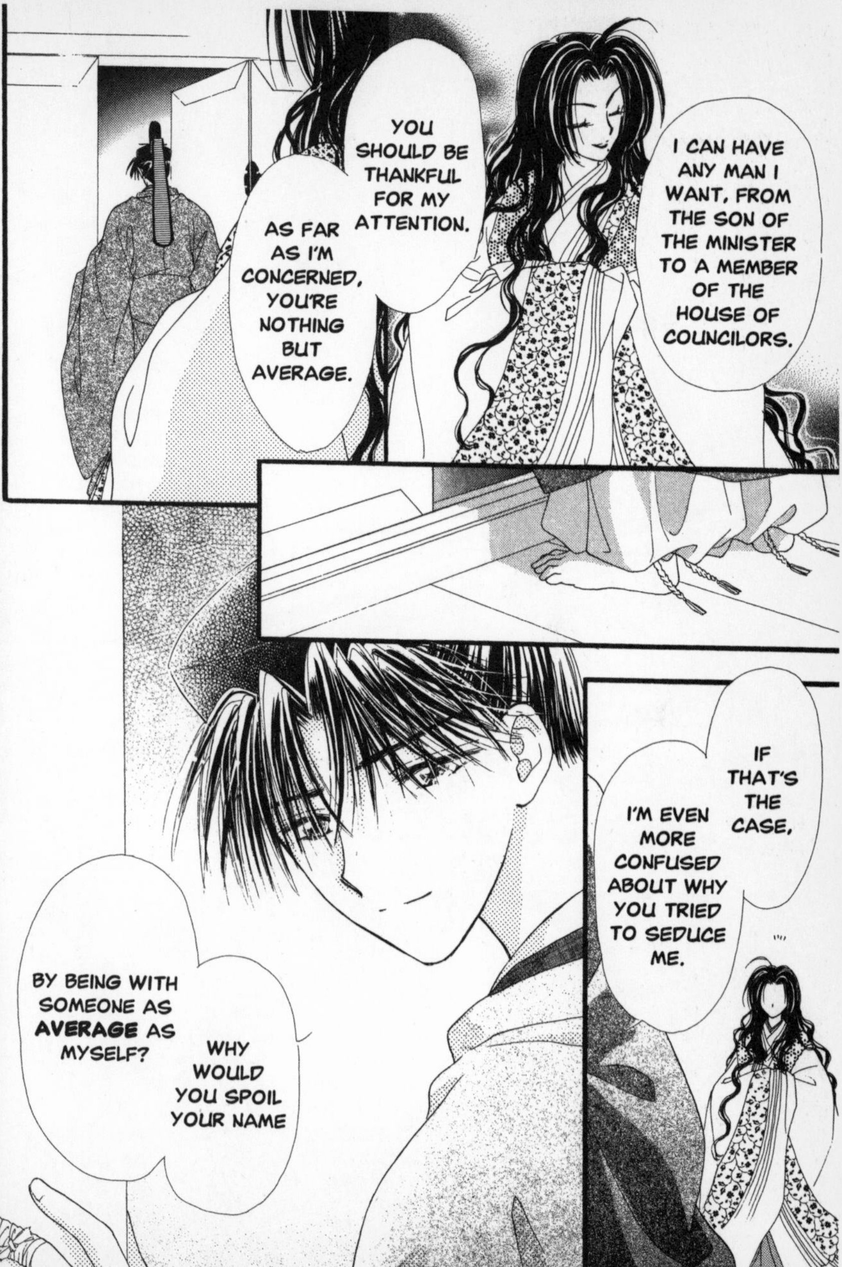
I CAN HAVE ANY MAN I WANT, FROM THE SON OF THE MINISTER TO A MEMBER OF THE HOUSE OF COUNCILORS.
YOU SHOULD BE THANKFUL FOR MY ATTENTION.
AS FAR AS I'M CONCERNED, YOU'RE NOTHING BUT AVERAGE.
IF THAT'S THE CASE,
I'M EVEN MORE CONFUSED ABOUT WHY YOU TRIED TO SEDUCE ME.
WHY WOULD YOU SPOIL YOUR NAME
BY BEING WITH SOMEONE AS **AVERAGE** AS MYSELF?

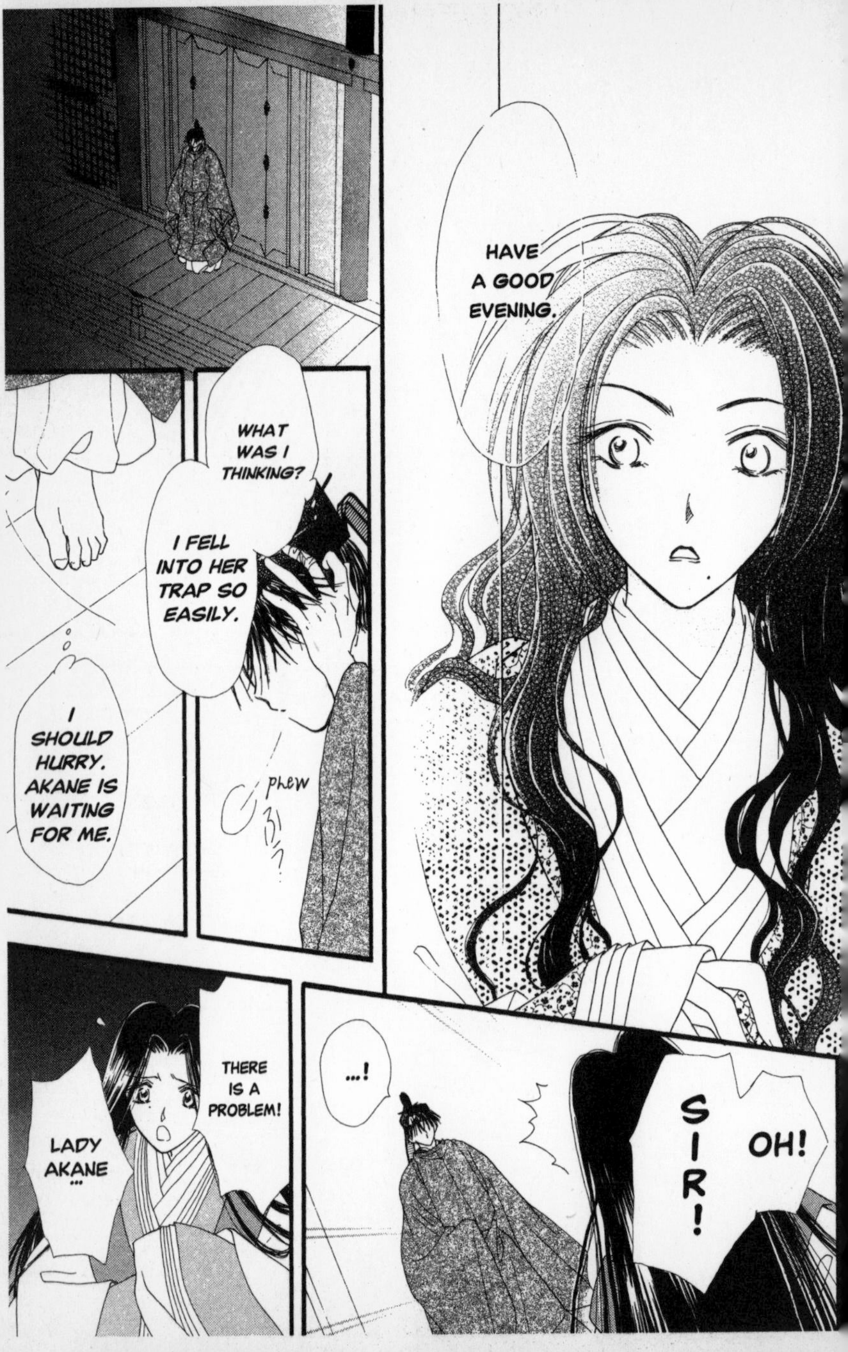
HAVE A GOOD EVENING.
WHAT WAS I THINKING?
I FELL INTO HER TRAP SO EASILY.
phew
I SHOULD HURRY. AKANE IS WAITING FOR ME.
OH!
SIR!
...!
THERE IS A PROBLEM!
LADY AKANE...

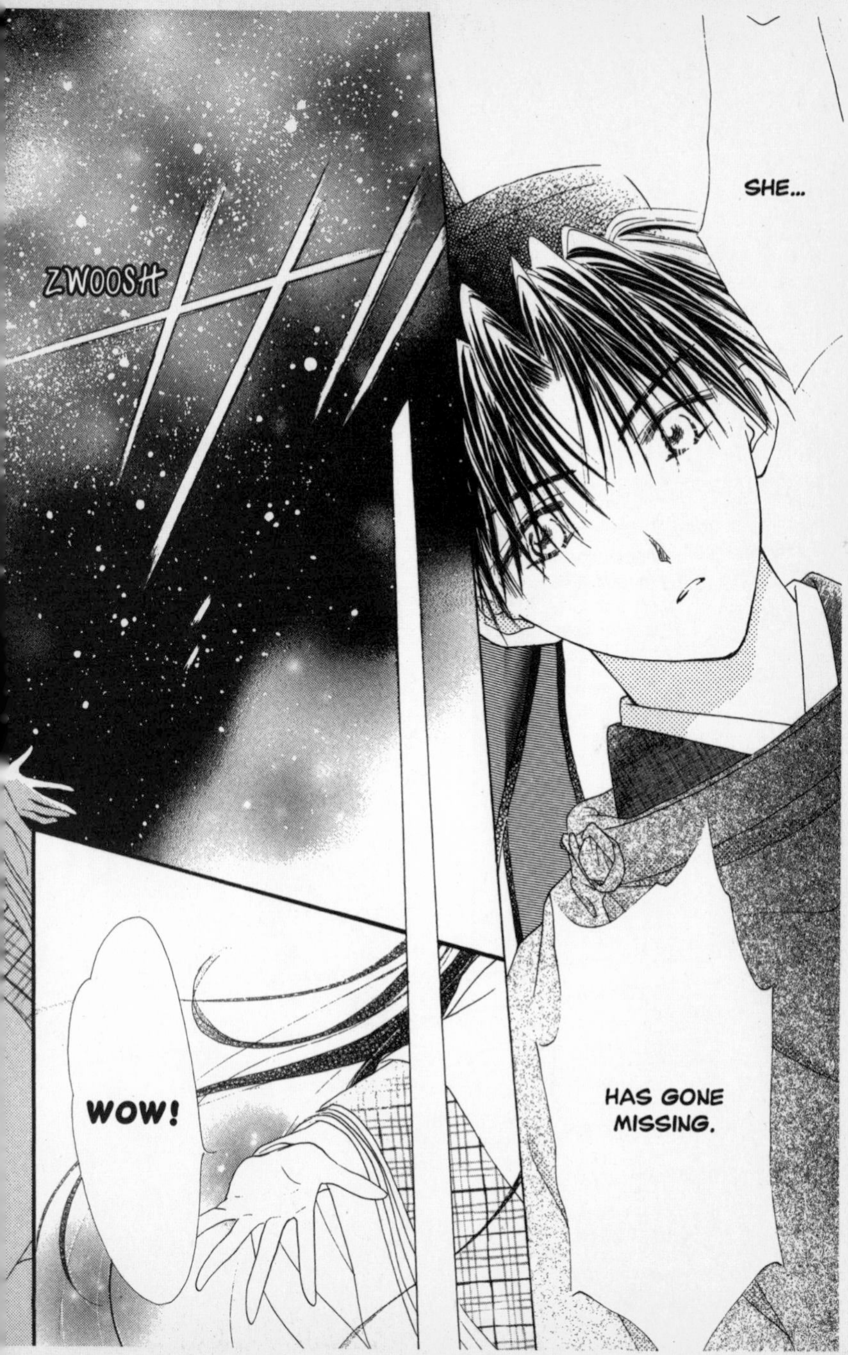
SHE...
HAS GONE MISSING.
ZWOOSH
WOW!

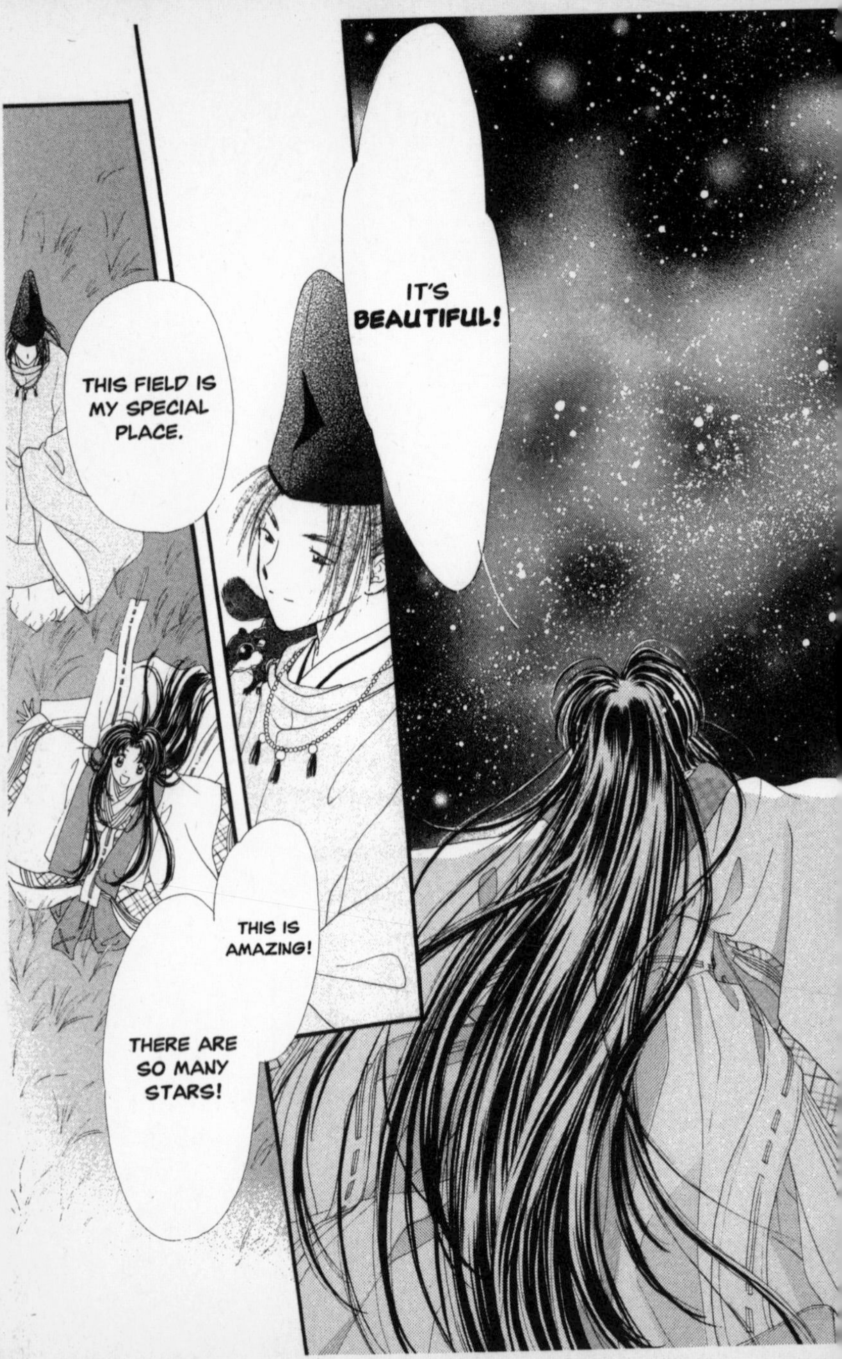
IT'S BEAUTIFUL!
THIS FIELD IS MY SPECIAL PLACE.
THIS IS AMAZING!
THERE ARE SO MANY STARS!

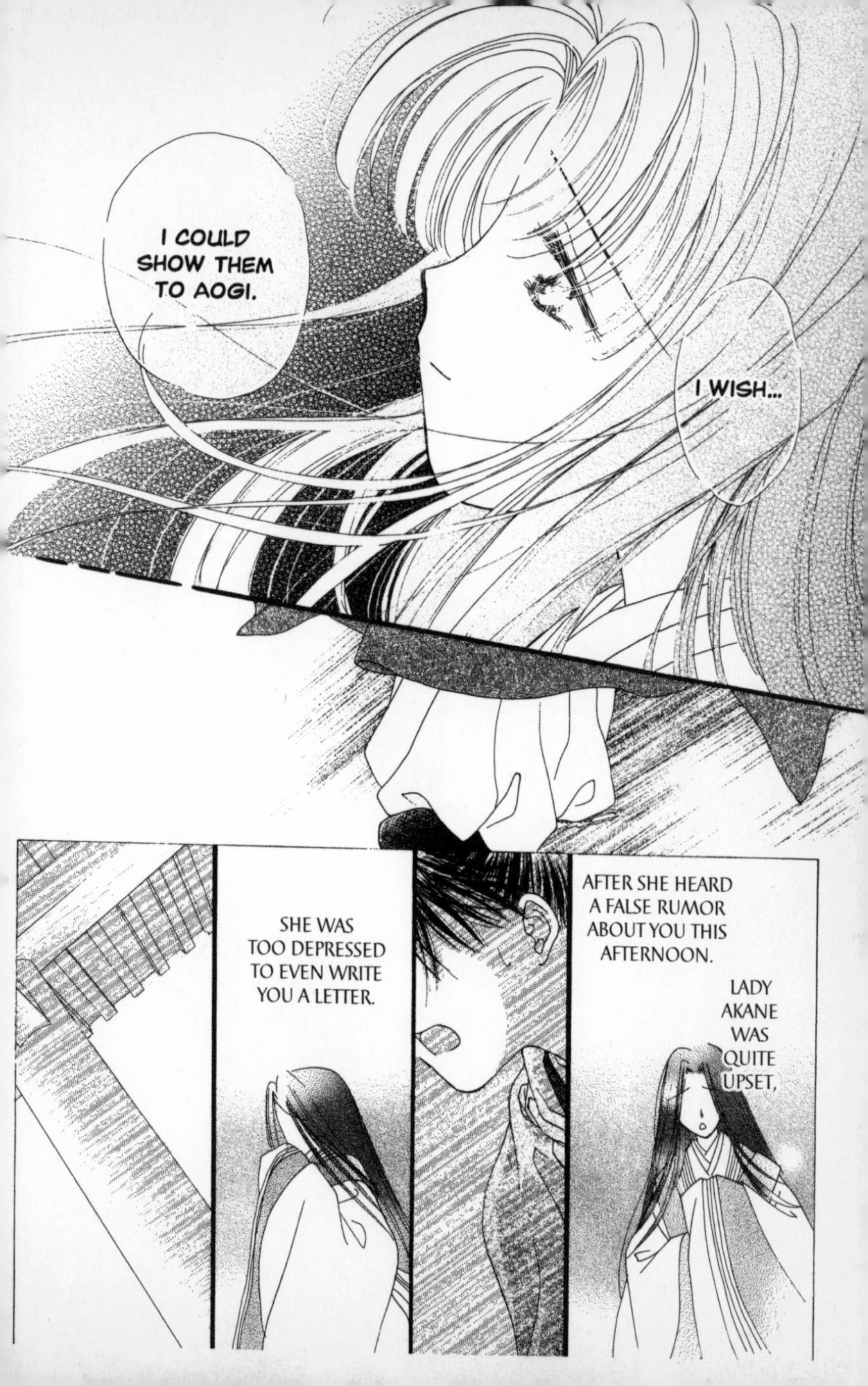
I WISH...
I COULD SHOW THEM TO AOGI.
LADY AKANE WAS QUITE UPSET,
AFTER SHE HEARD A FALSE RUMOR ABOUT YOU THIS AFTERNOON.
SHE WAS TOO DEPRESSED TO EVEN WRITE YOU A LETTER.

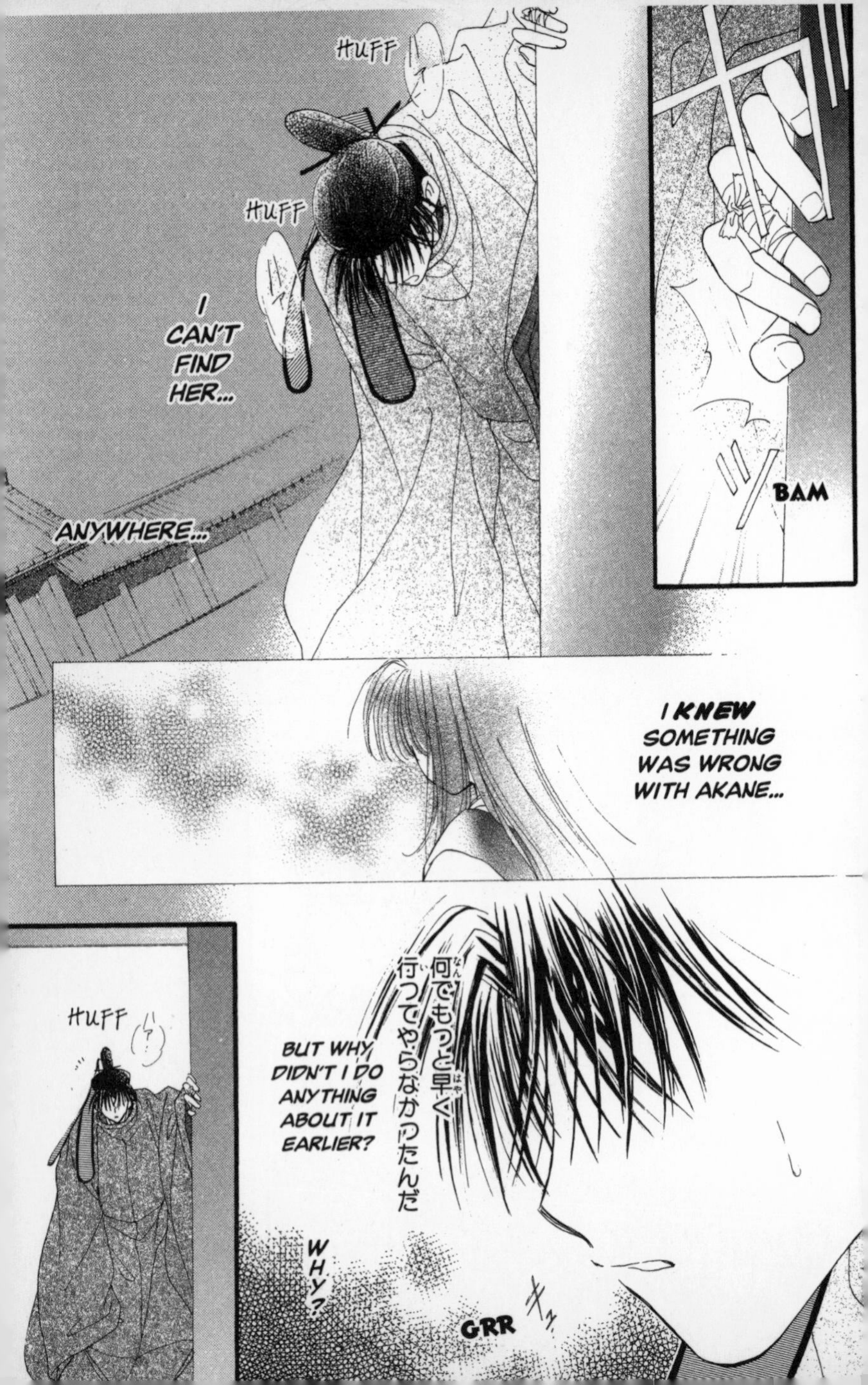
BAM
HUFF
HUFF
I CAN'T FIND HER...
ANYWHERE...
I KNEW SOMETHING WAS WRONG WITH AKANE...
何でもっと早く行ってやらなかったんだ
BUT WHY DIDN'T I DO ANYTHING ABOUT IT EARLIER?
WHY?
GRR
HUFF
?

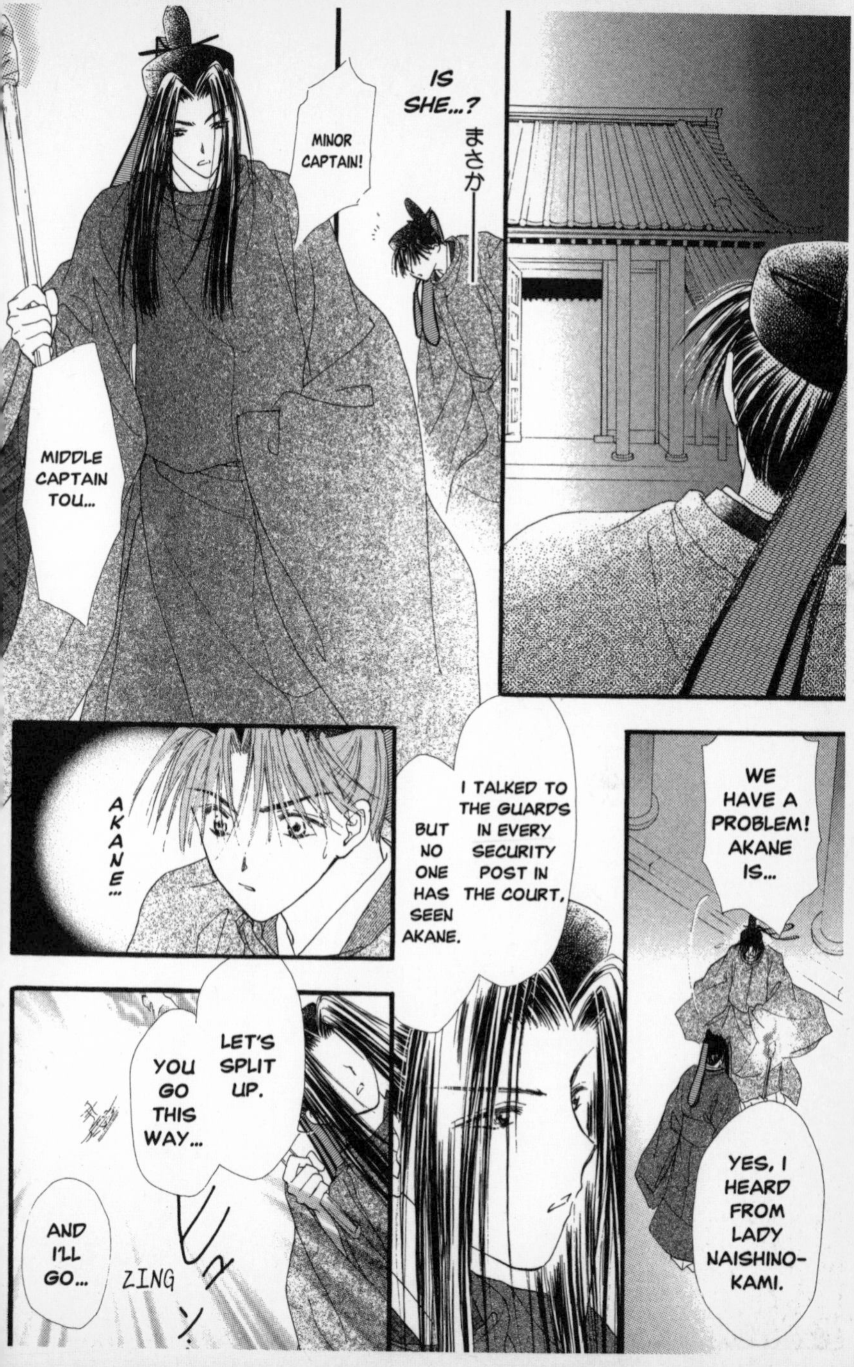
IS SHE...?
まさか—
MINOR CAPTAIN!
MIDDLE CAPTAIN TOU...
WE HAVE A PROBLEM! AKANE IS...
YES, I HEARD FROM LADY NAISHINO-KAMI.
I TALKED TO THE GUARDS IN EVERY SECURITY POST IN THE COURT,
BUT NO ONE HAS SEEN AKANE.
AKANE...
LET'S SPLIT UP.
YOU GO THIS WAY...
AND I'LL GO...
ZING

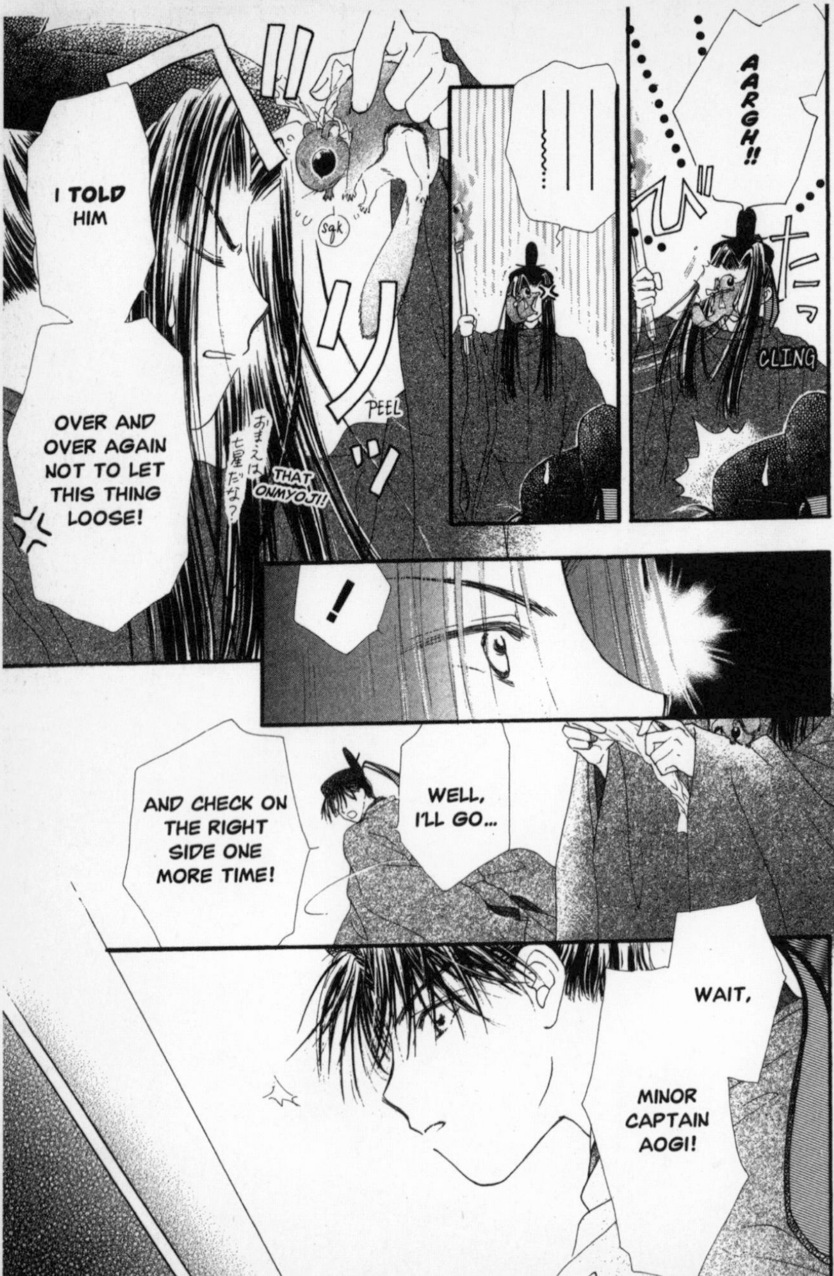

AARGH!!
CLING
……
!
I TOLD HIM
OVER AND OVER AGAIN NOT TO LET THIS THING LOOSE!
sqk
PEEL
おまえは七星だな?
THAT ONMYOJI!
WELL, I'LL GO...
AND CHECK ON THE RIGHT SIDE ONE MORE TIME!
WAIT,
MINOR CAPTAIN AOGI!

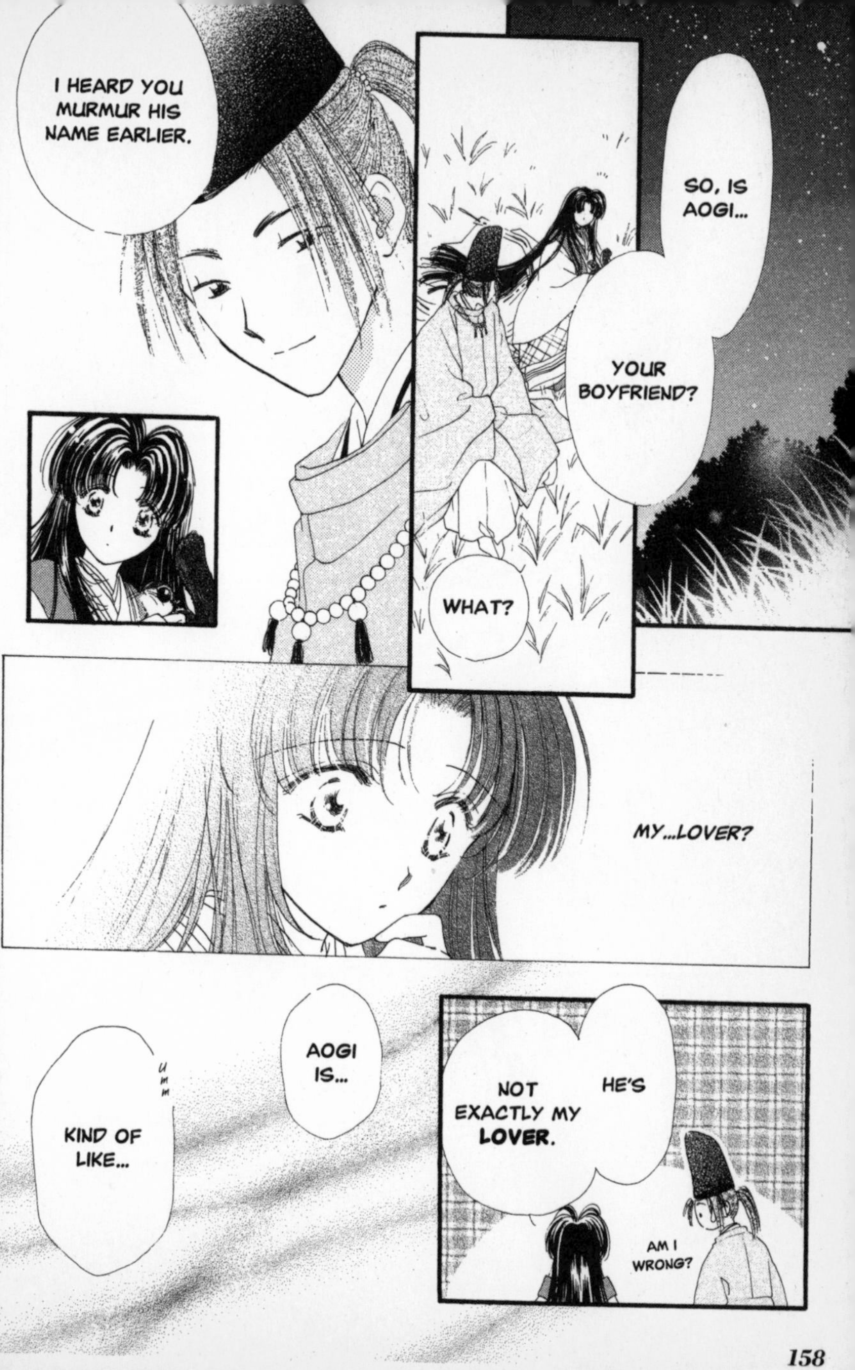

SO, IS AOGI...
YOUR BOYFRIEND?
WHAT?
I HEARD YOU MURMUR HIS NAME EARLIER.
MY...LOVER?
HE'S NOT EXACTLY MY **LOVER**.
AM I WRONG?
AOGI IS...
UMM
KIND OF LIKE...

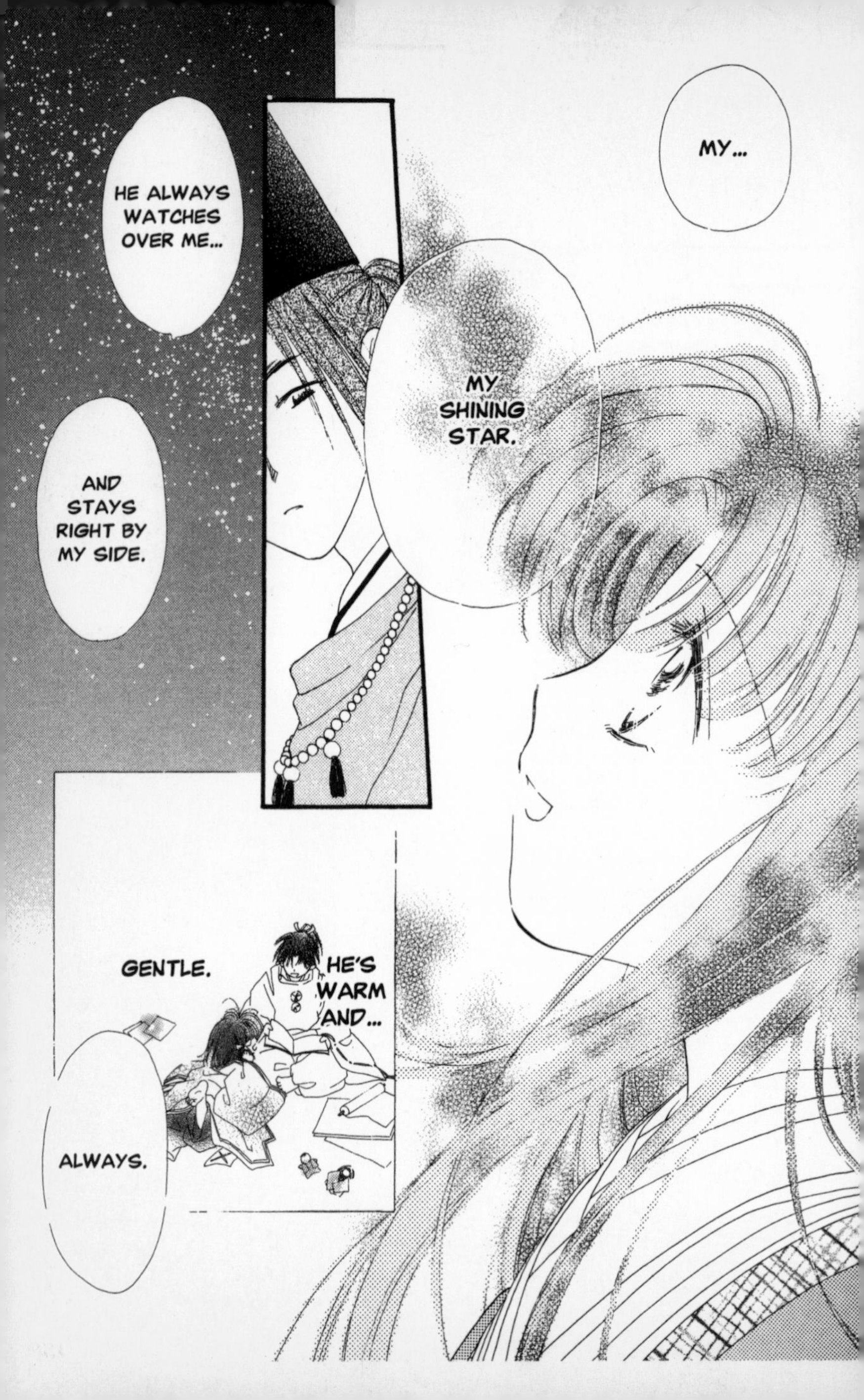
MY...
MY SHINING STAR.
HE ALWAYS WATCHES OVER ME...
AND STAYS RIGHT BY MY SIDE.
HE'S WARM AND...
GENTLE.
ALWAYS.

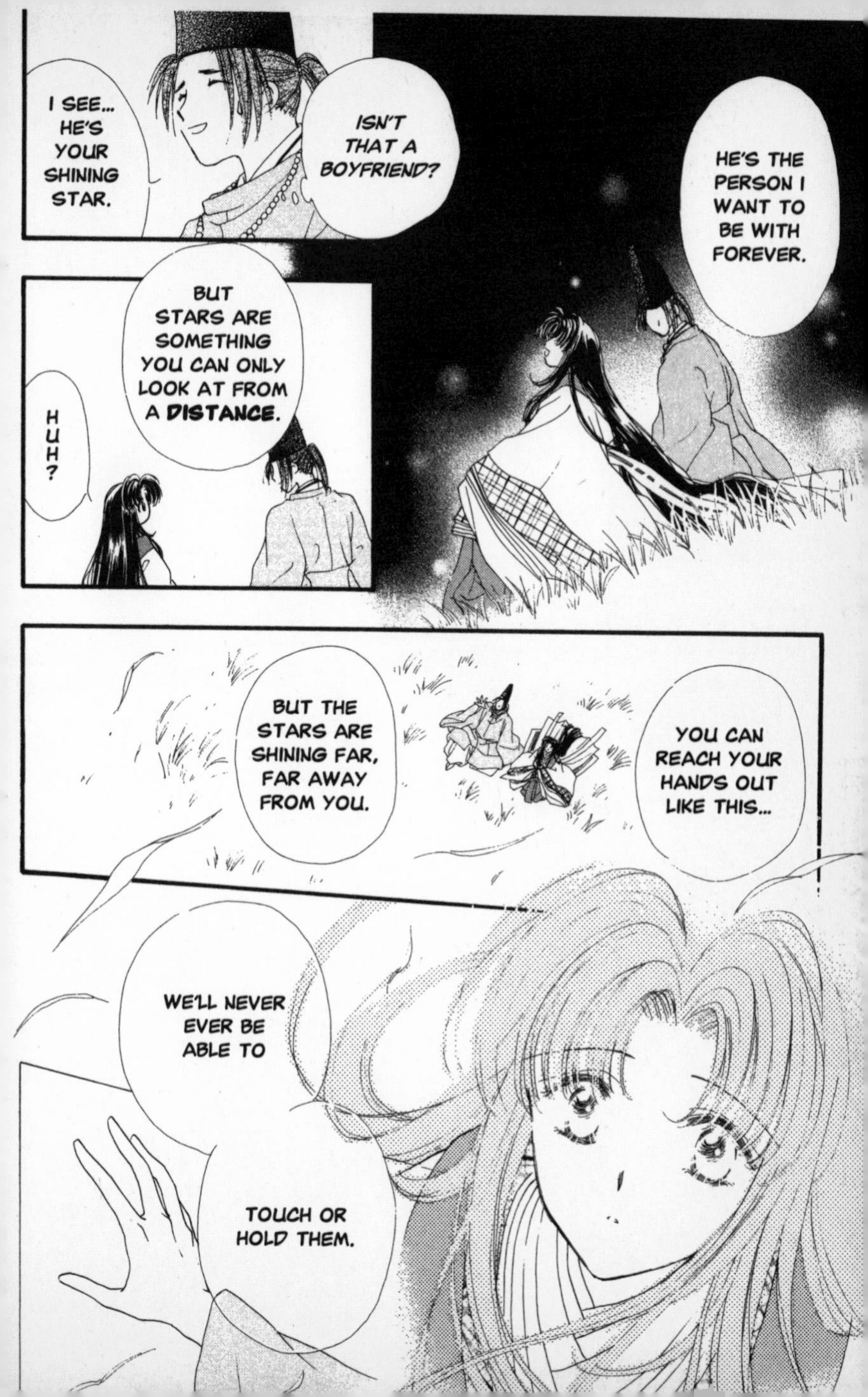
HE'S THE PERSON I WANT TO BE WITH FOREVER.
ISN'T THAT A BOYFRIEND?
I SEE... HE'S YOUR SHINING STAR.
BUT STARS ARE SOMETHING YOU CAN ONLY LOOK AT FROM A **DISTANCE**.
HUH?
YOU CAN REACH YOUR HANDS OUT LIKE THIS...
BUT THE STARS ARE SHINING FAR, FAR AWAY FROM YOU.
WE'LL NEVER EVER BE ABLE TO
TOUCH OR HOLD THEM.

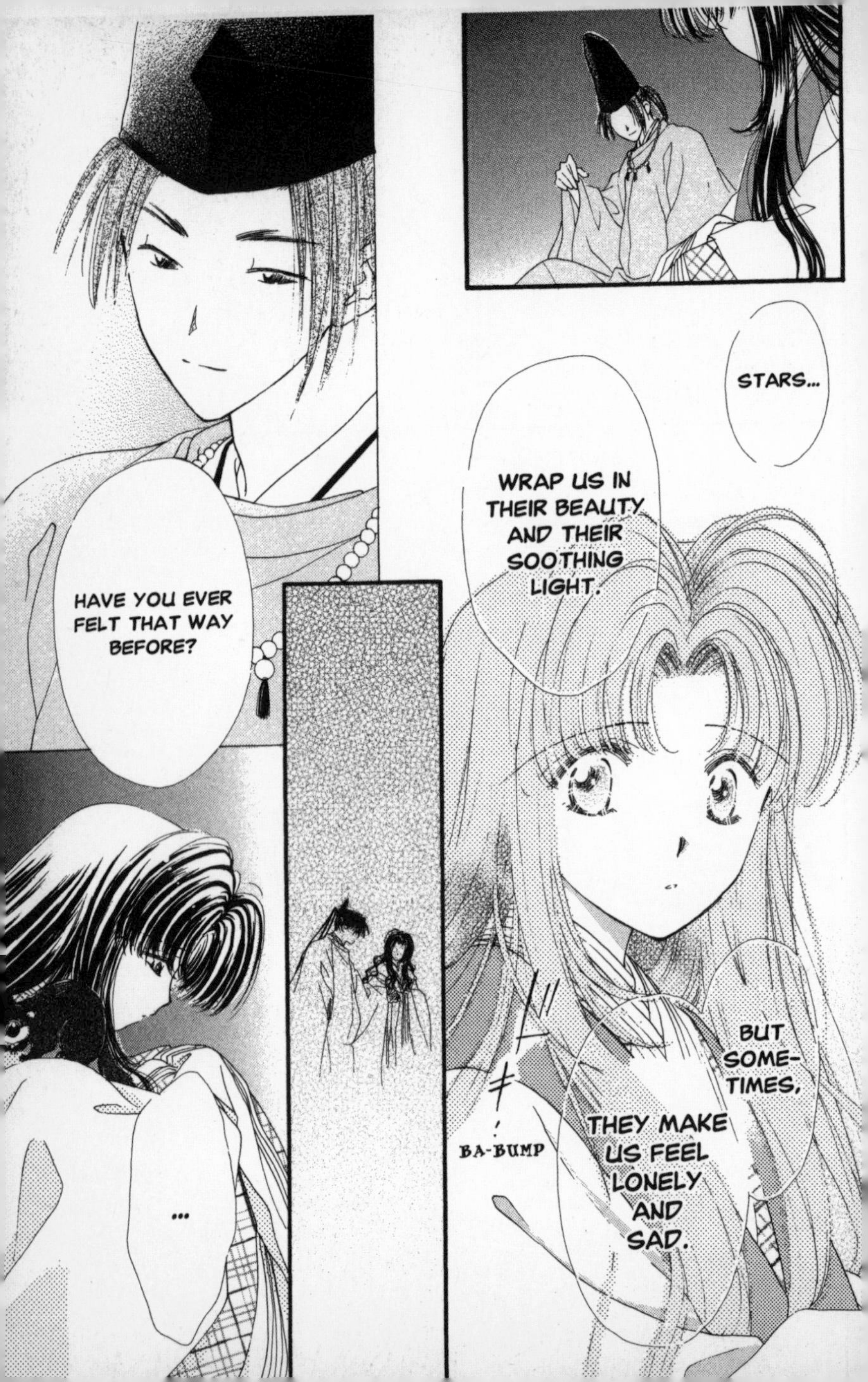
STARS...
WRAP US IN THEIR BEAUTY AND THEIR SOOTHING LIGHT.
BUT SOME-TIMES,
THEY MAKE US FEEL LONELY AND SAD.
BA-BUMP
HAVE YOU EVER FELT THAT WAY BEFORE?
...

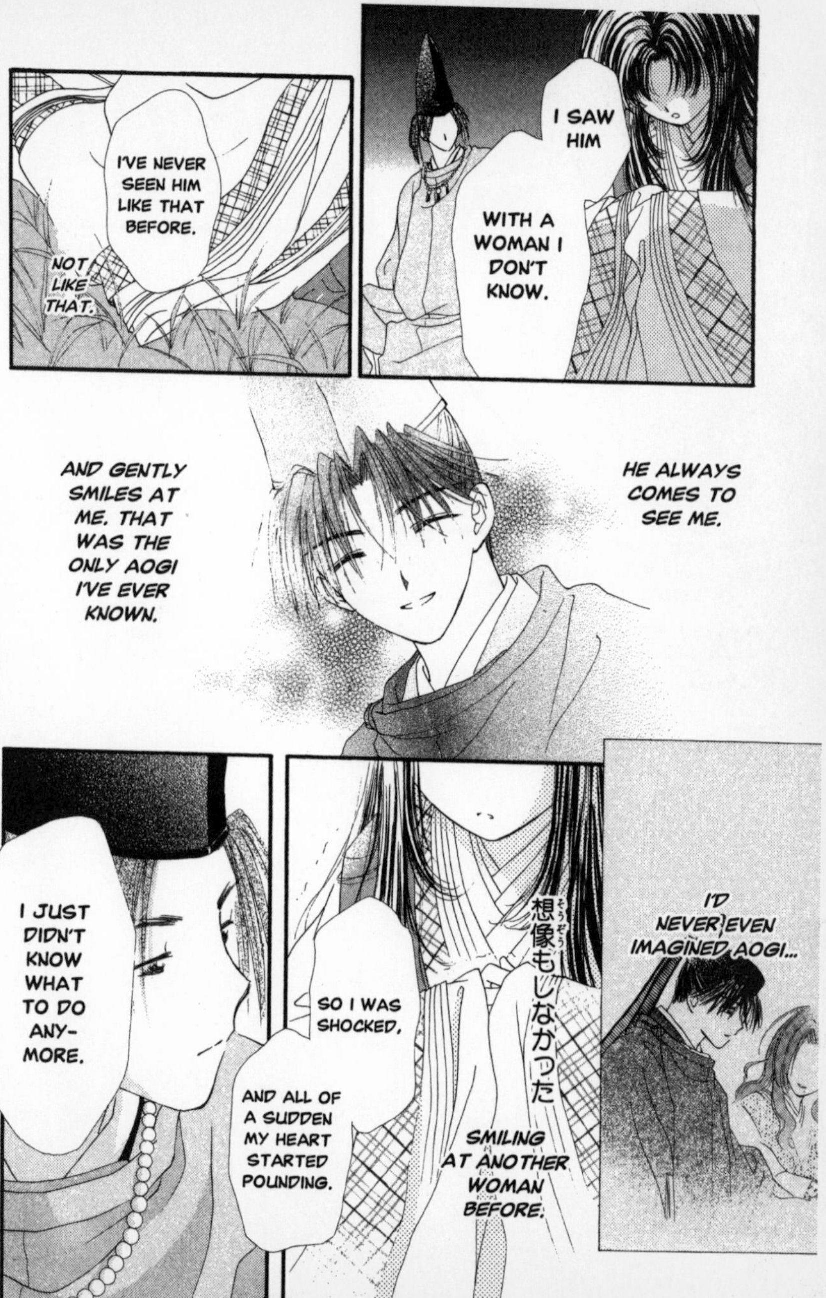
I SAW HIM
WITH A WOMAN I DON'T KNOW.
I'VE NEVER SEEN HIM LIKE THAT BEFORE.
NOT LIKE THAT.
HE ALWAYS COMES TO SEE ME.
AND GENTLY SMILES AT ME. THAT WAS THE ONLY AOGI I'VE EVER KNOWN.
I'D NEVER EVEN IMAGINED AOGI...
想像もしなかった
SMILING AT ANOTHER WOMAN BEFORE.
SO I WAS SHOCKED,
AND ALL OF A SUDDEN MY HEART STARTED POUNDING.
I JUST DIDN'T KNOW WHAT TO DO ANYMORE.

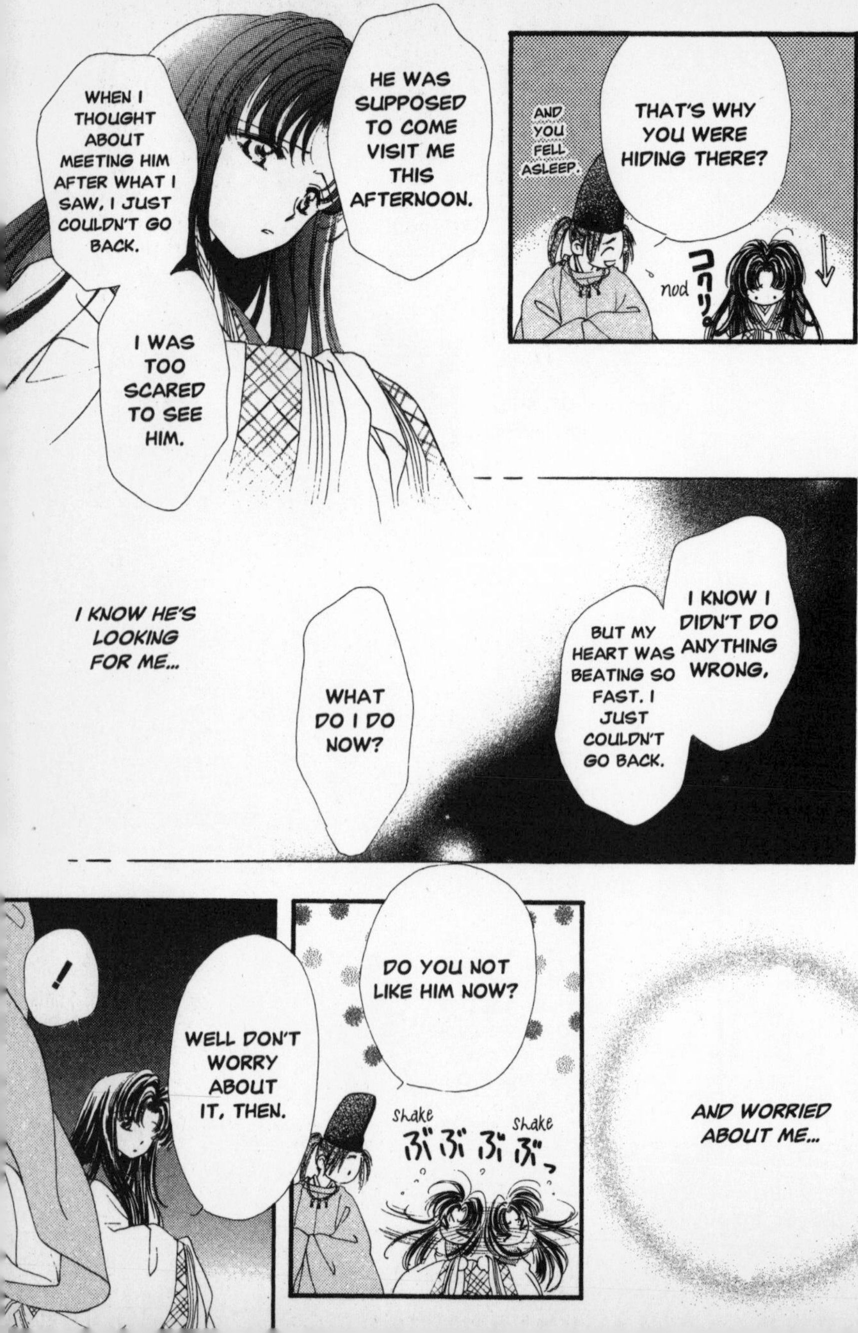
THAT'S WHY YOU WERE HIDING THERE?
AND YOU FELL ASLEEP.
nod
コクリ
HE WAS SUPPOSED TO COME VISIT ME THIS AFTERNOON.
WHEN I THOUGHT ABOUT MEETING HIM AFTER WHAT I SAW, I JUST COULDN'T GO BACK.
I WAS TOO SCARED TO SEE HIM.
I KNOW I DIDN'T DO ANYTHING WRONG,
BUT MY HEART WAS BEATING SO FAST. I JUST COULDN'T GO BACK.
WHAT DO I DO NOW?
I KNOW HE'S LOOKING FOR ME...
AND WORRIED ABOUT ME...
DO YOU NOT LIKE HIM NOW?
shake
ぶぶぶぶっ
shake
!
WELL DON'T WORRY ABOUT IT, THEN.

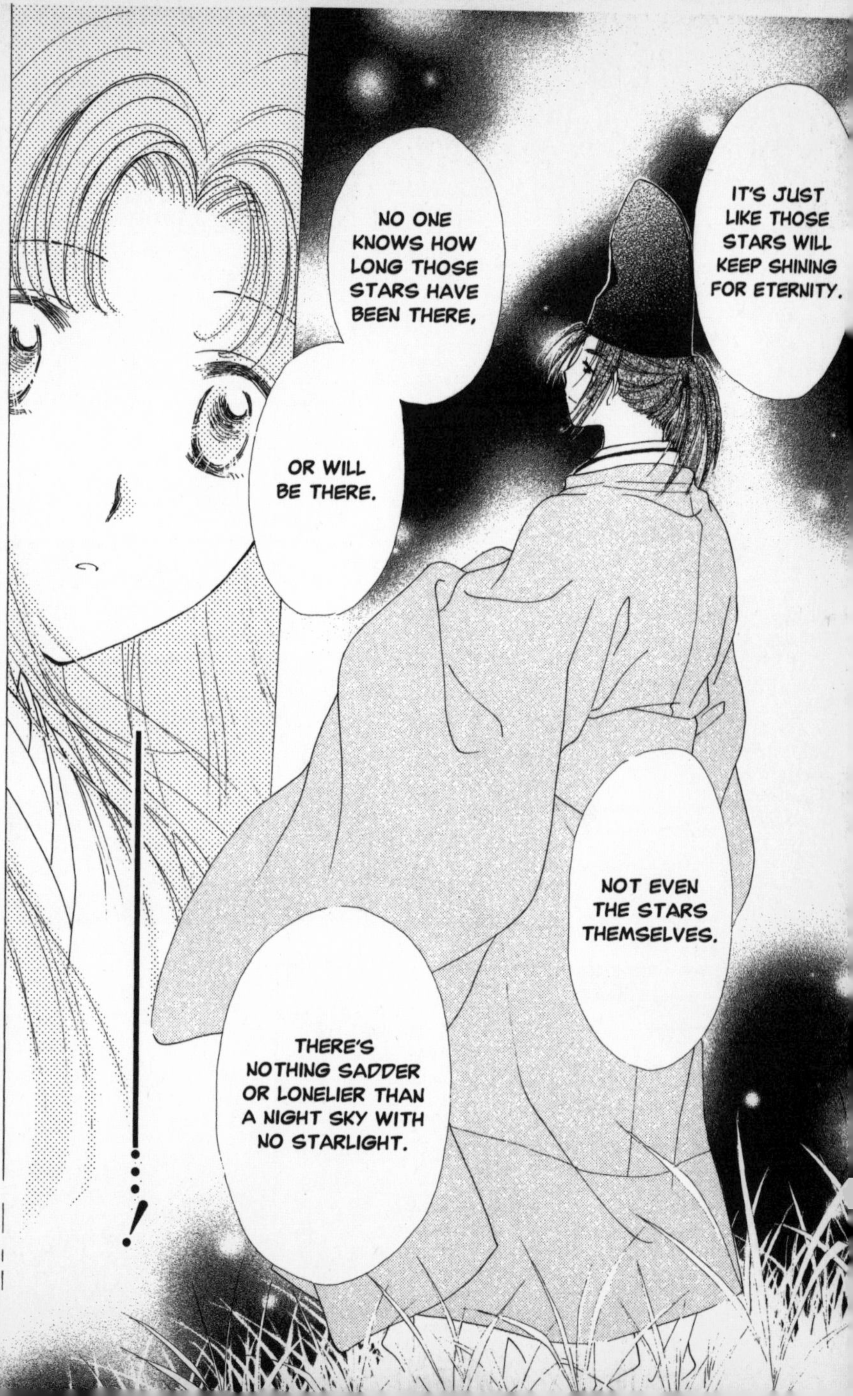

IT'S JUST LIKE THOSE STARS WILL KEEP SHINING FOR ETERNITY.
NO ONE KNOWS HOW LONG THOSE STARS HAVE BEEN THERE,
OR WILL BE THERE.
NOT EVEN THE STARS THEMSELVES.
THERE'S NOTHING SADDER OR LONELIER THAN A NIGHT SKY WITH NO STARLIGHT.
......!

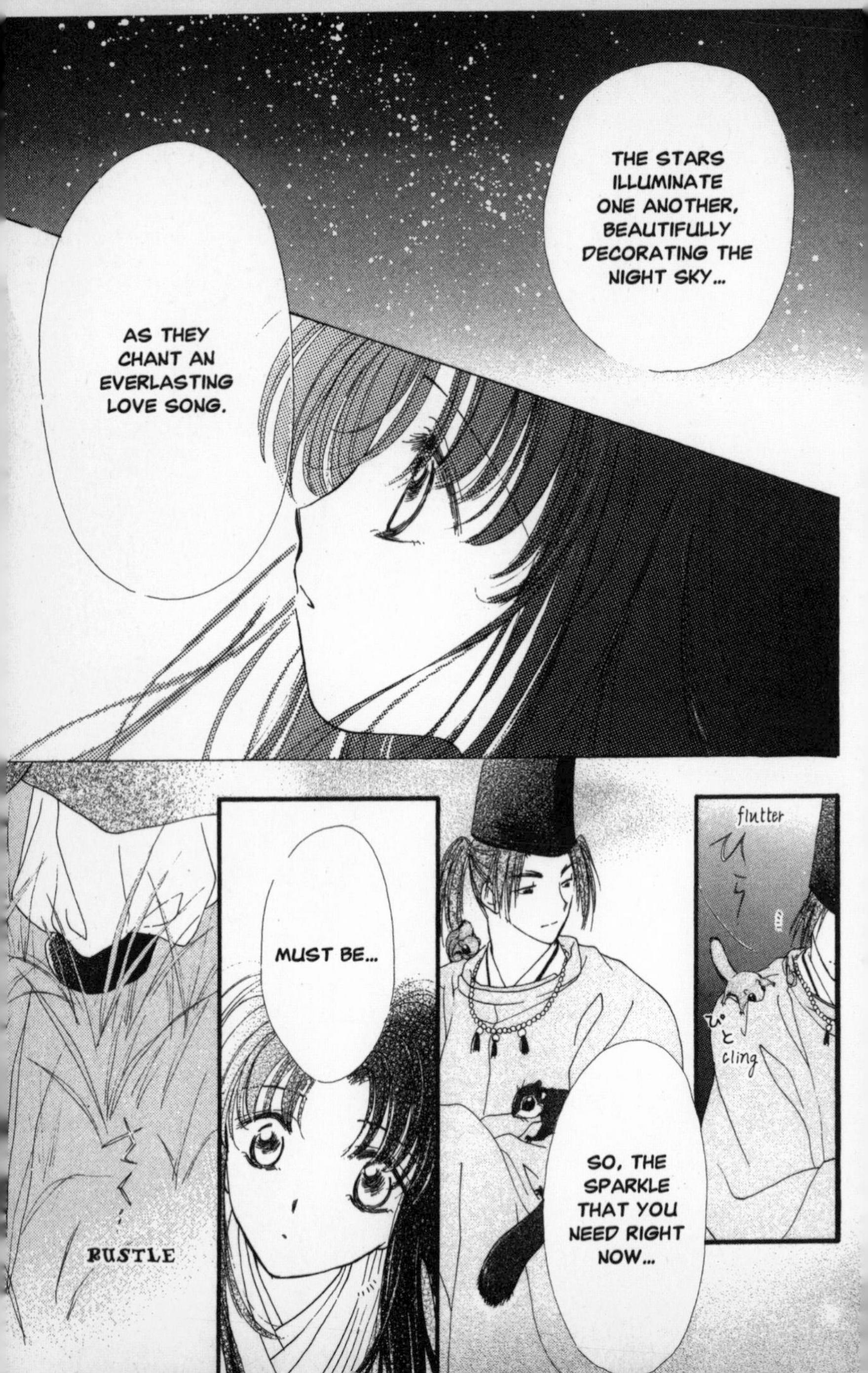
THE STARS ILLUMINATE ONE ANOTHER, BEAUTIFULLY DECORATING THE NIGHT SKY...
AS THEY CHANT AN EVERLASTING LOVE SONG.
ひら
flutter
ひと
cling
SO, THE SPARKLE THAT YOU NEED RIGHT NOW...
MUST BE...
RUSTLE

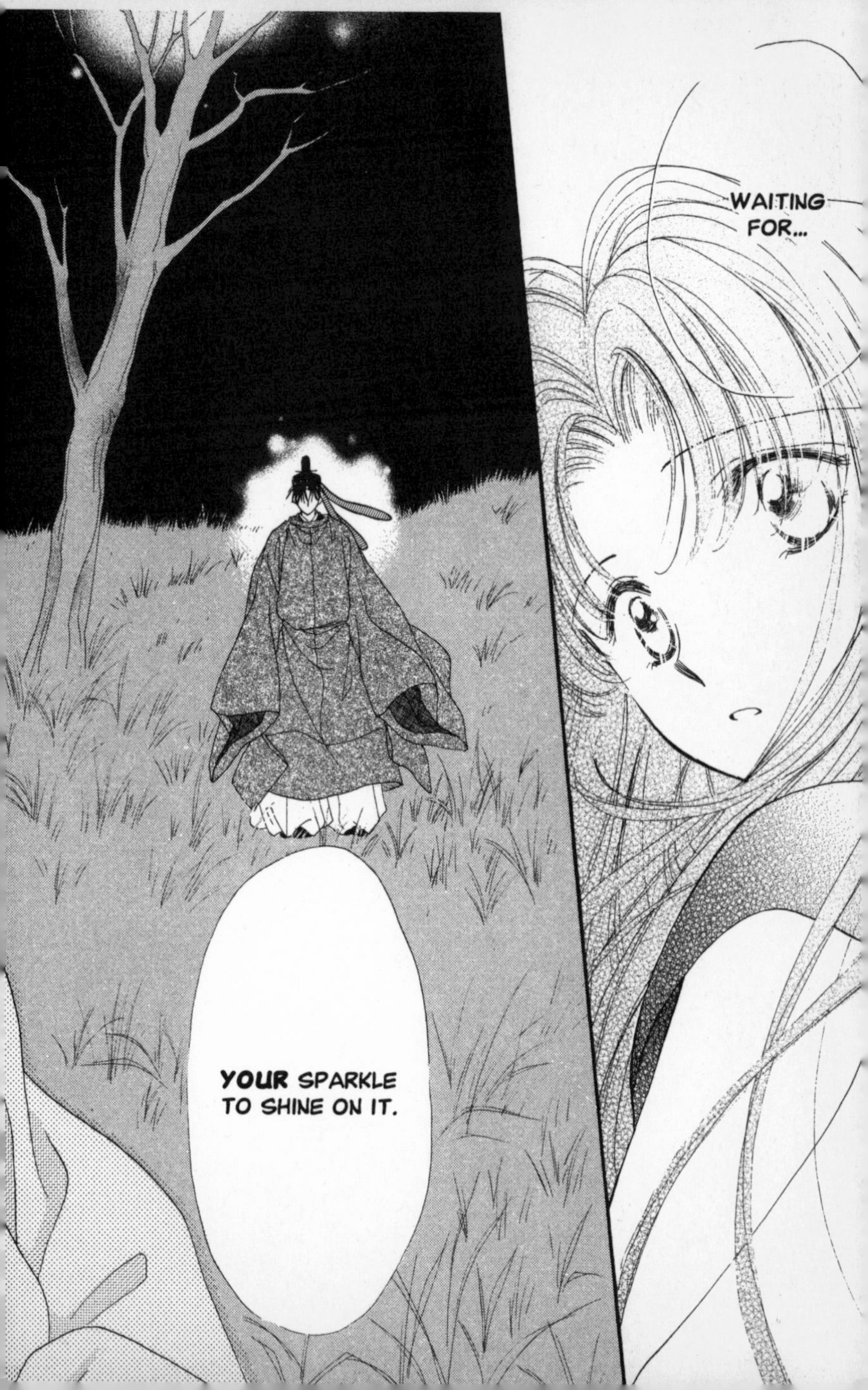
WAITING FOR...
YOUR SPARKLE TO SHINE ON IT.

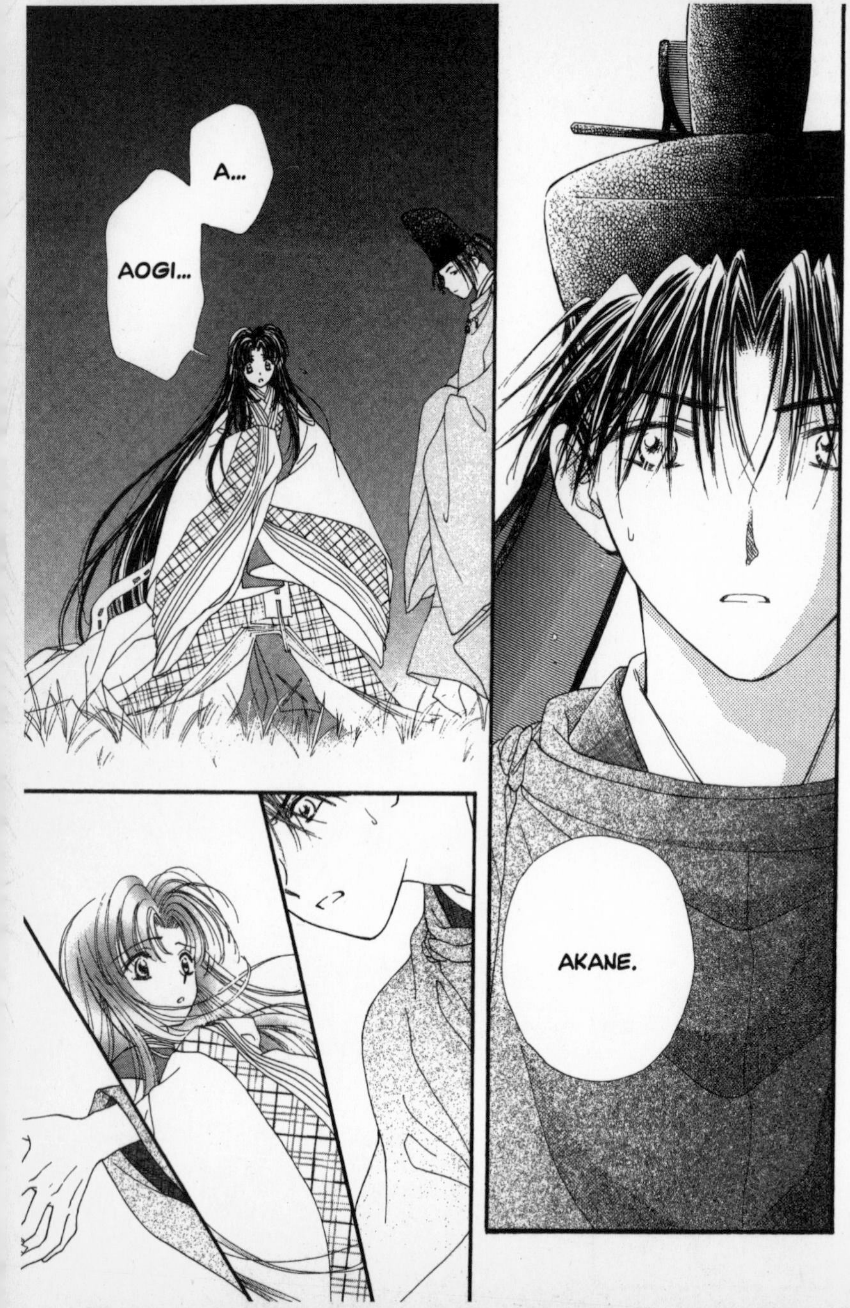
AKANE.
A...
AOGI...

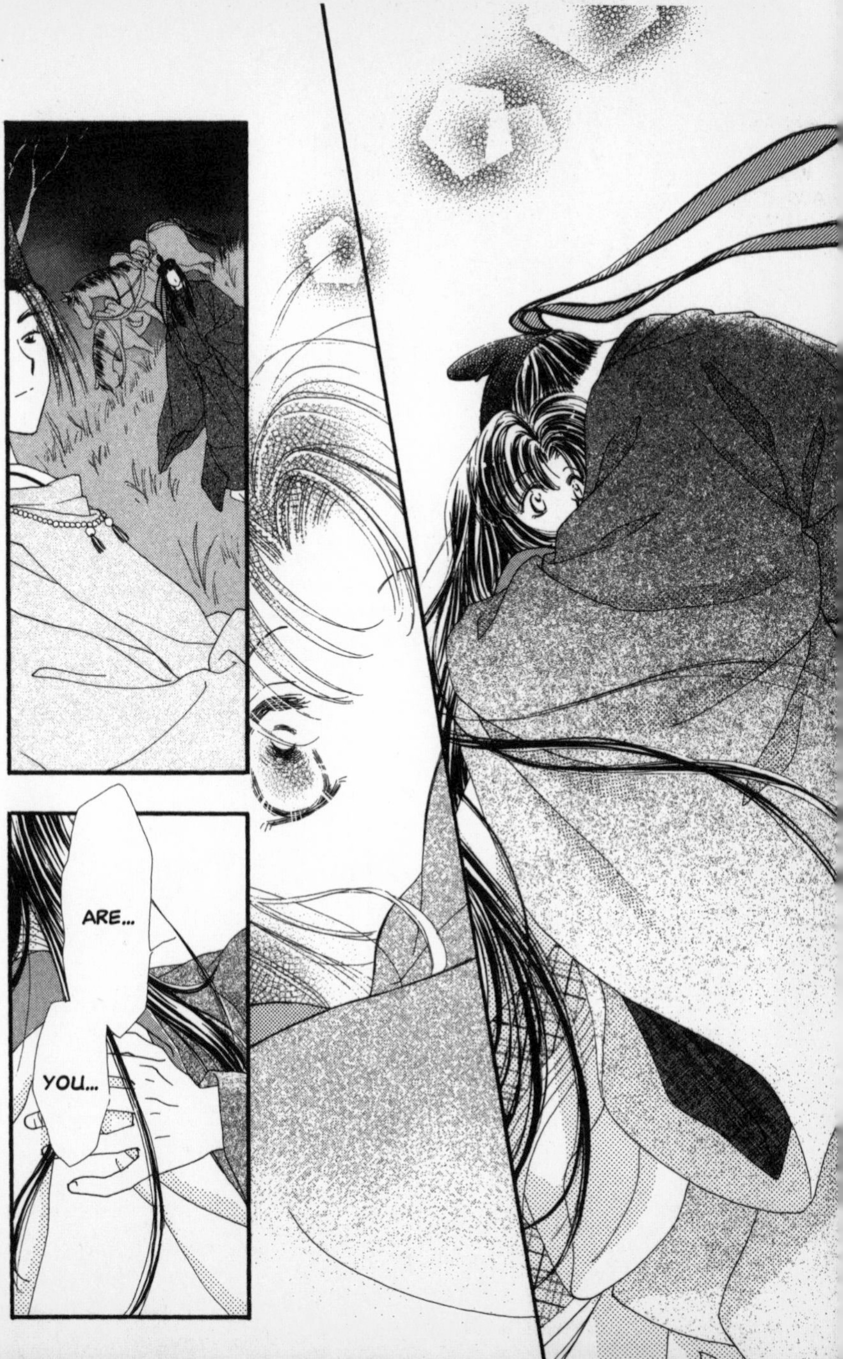
ARE...
YOU...

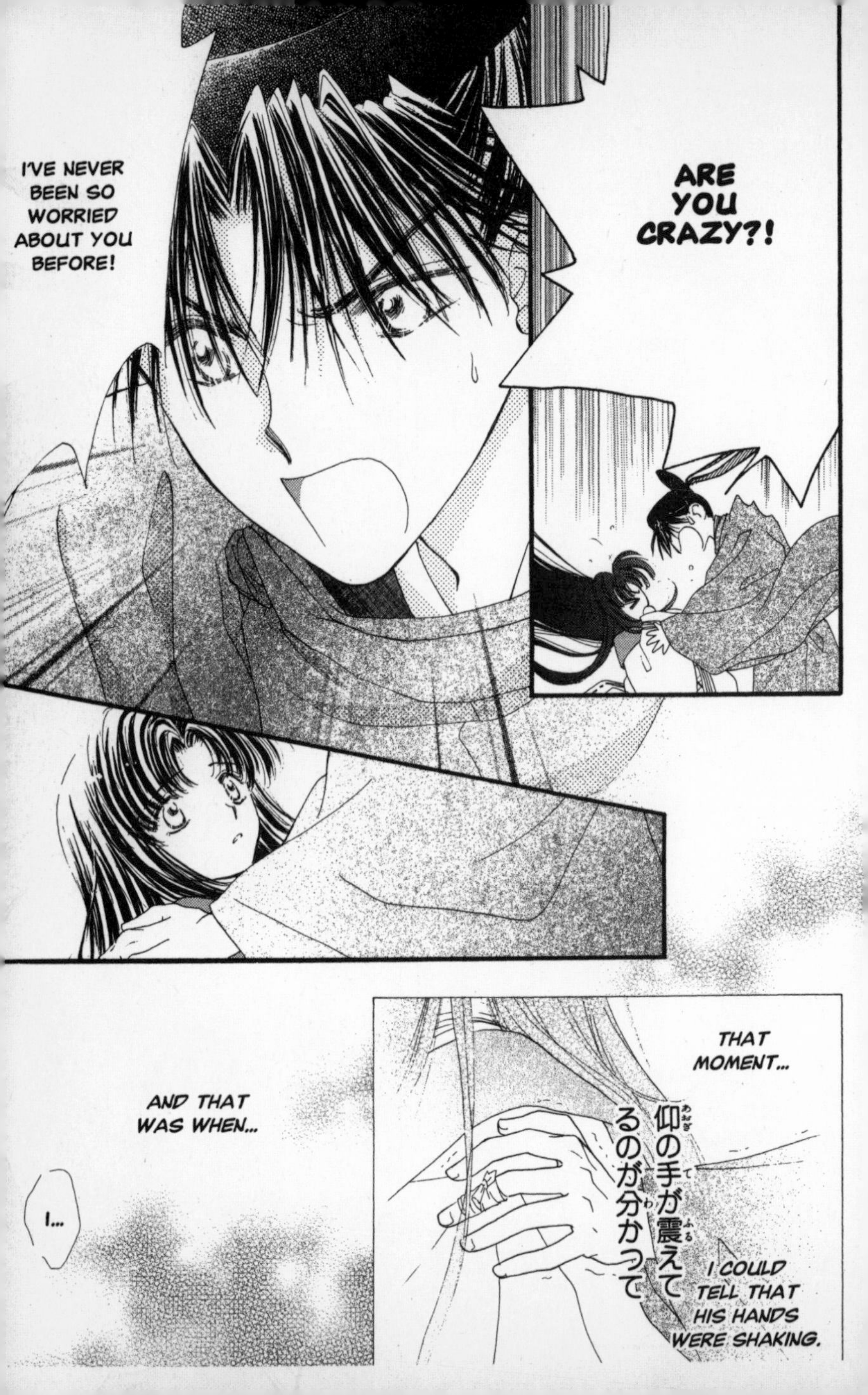
ARE YOU CRAZY?!
I'VE NEVER BEEN SO WORRIED ABOUT YOU BEFORE!
THAT MOMENT...
仰の手が震えてるのが分かって
I COULD TELL THAT HIS HANDS WERE SHAKING.
AND THAT WAS WHEN...
I...

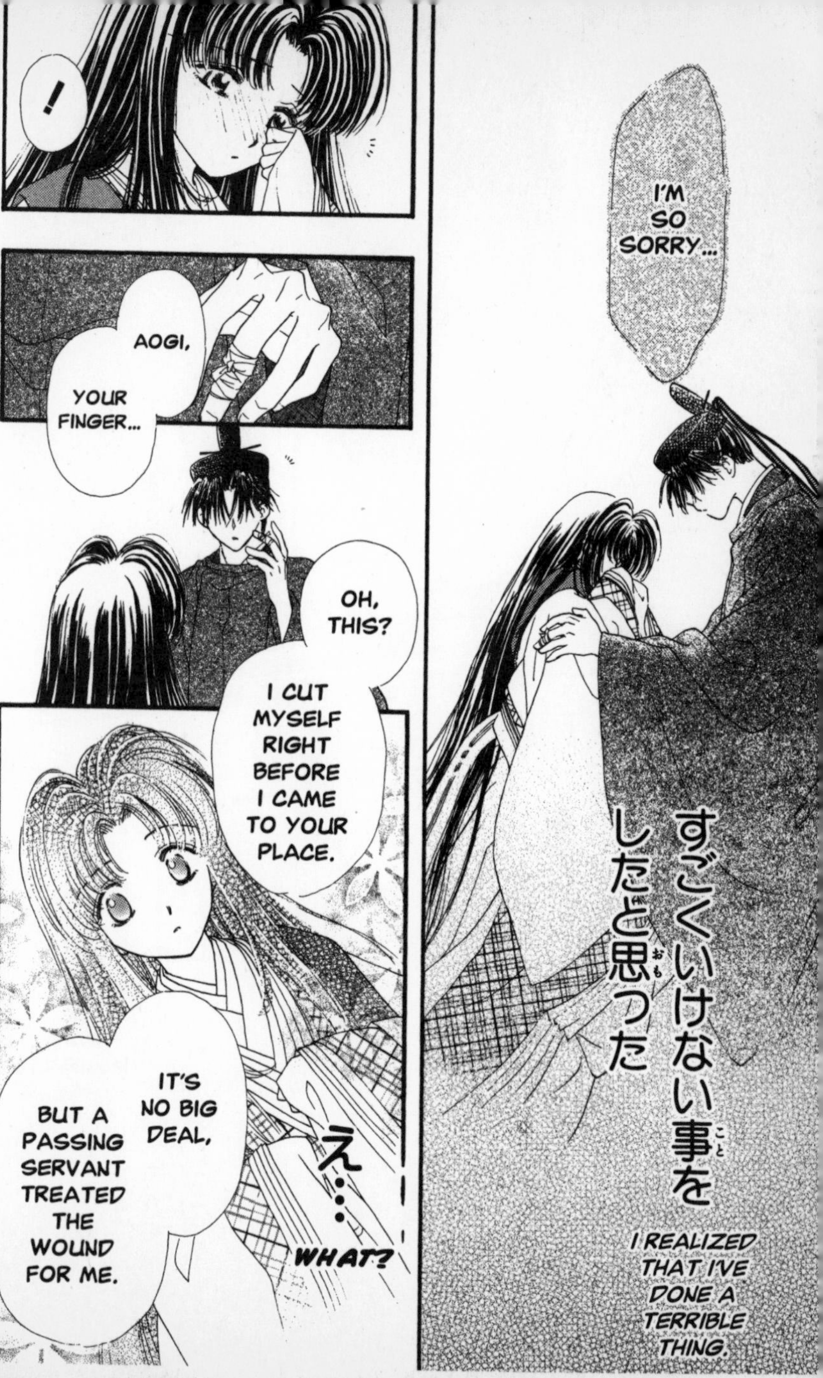

I'M SO SORRY...
すごくいけない事をしたと思った
I REALIZED THAT I'VE DONE A TERRIBLE THING.
!
AOGI,
YOUR FINGER...
OH, THIS?
I CUT MYSELF RIGHT BEFORE I CAME TO YOUR PLACE.
IT'S NO BIG DEAL,
BUT A PASSING SERVANT TREATED THE WOUND FOR ME.
え…
WHAT?

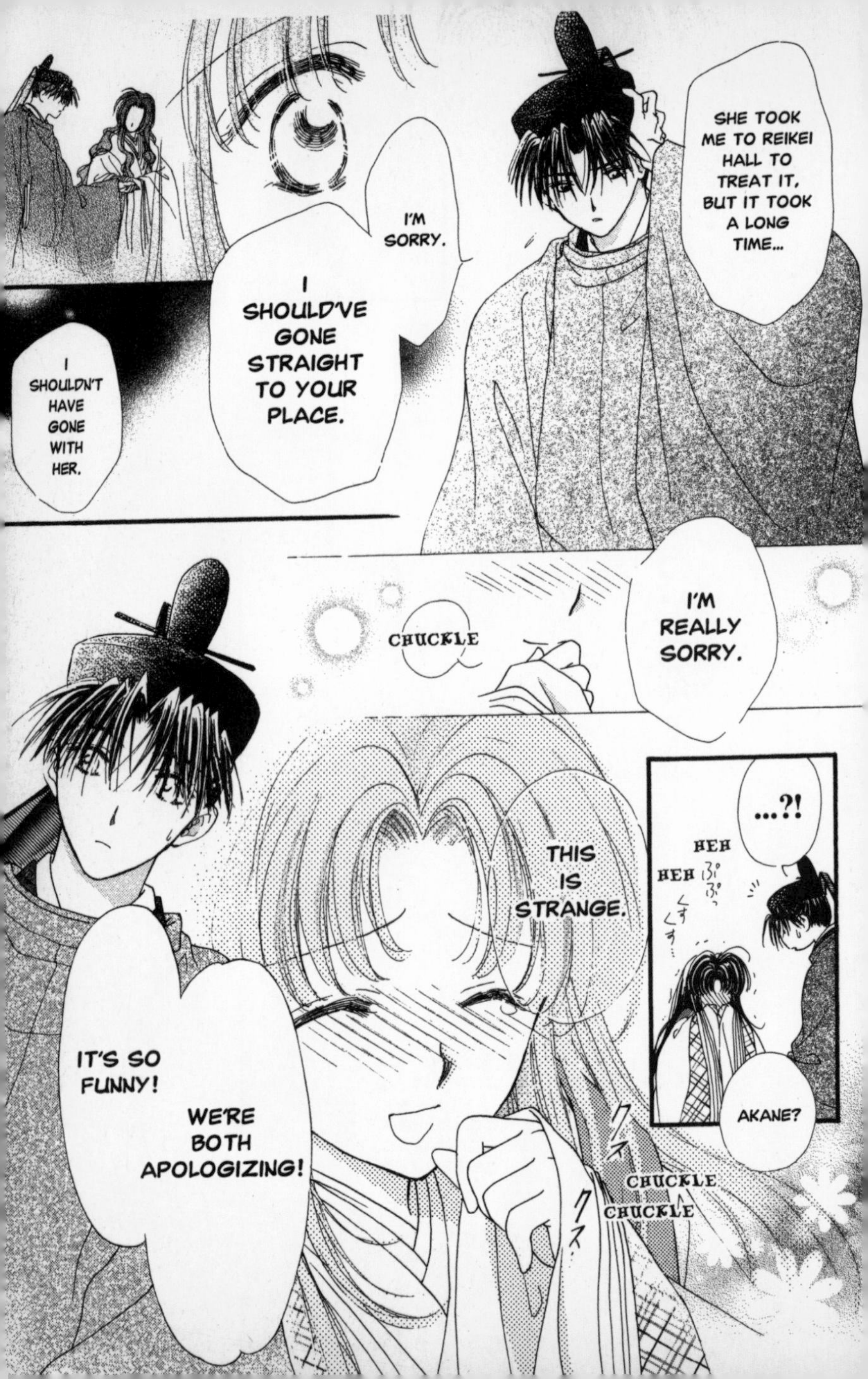
SHE TOOK ME TO REIKEI HALL TO TREAT IT, BUT IT TOOK A LONG TIME...
I'M SORRY.
I SHOULD'VE GONE STRAIGHT TO YOUR PLACE.
I SHOULDN'T HAVE GONE WITH HER.
I'M REALLY SORRY.
CHUCKLE
...?!
HEH HEH
AKANE?
THIS IS STRANGE.
IT'S SO FUNNY!
WE'RE BOTH APOLOGIZING!
CHUCKLE CHUCKLE

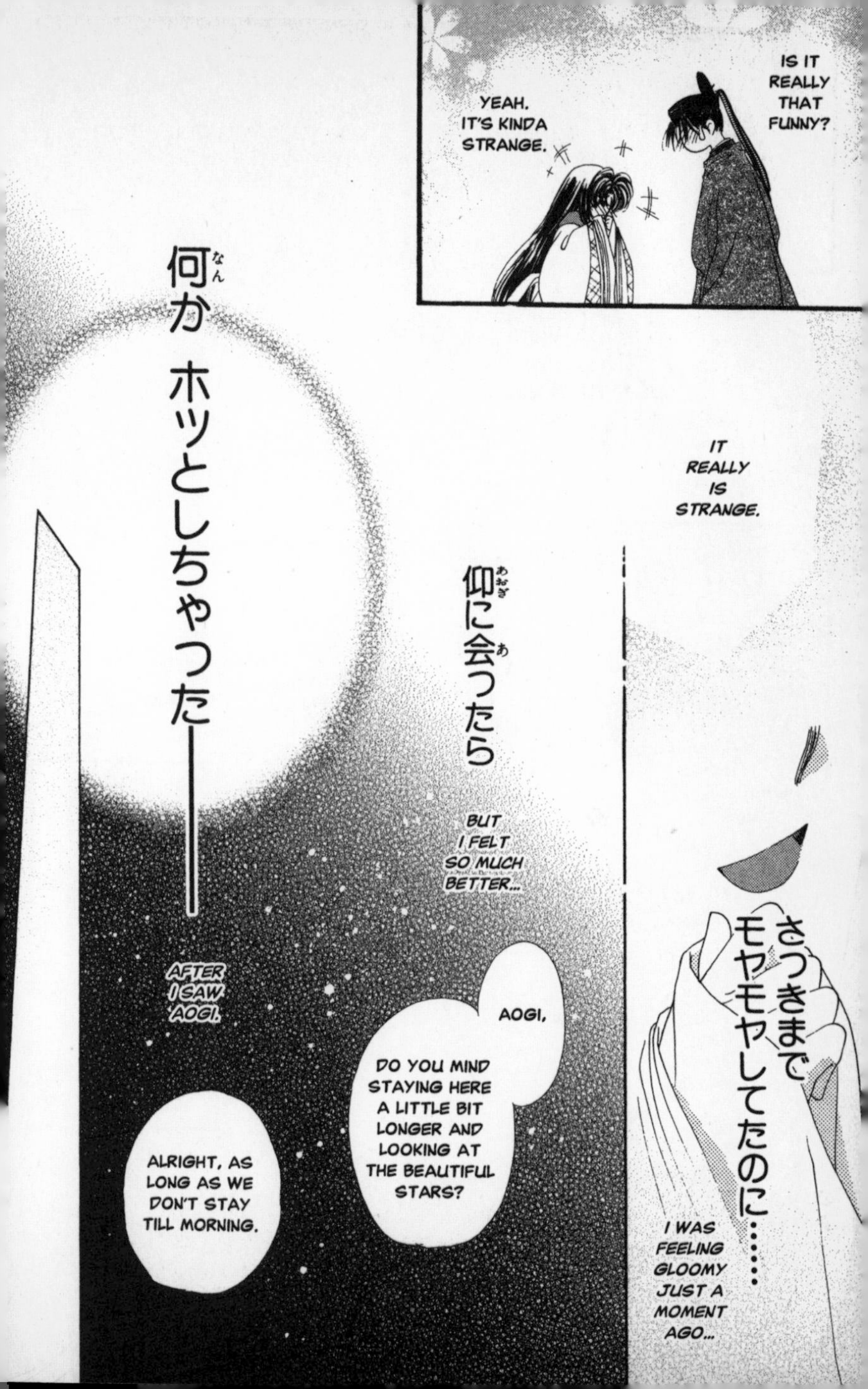
IS IT REALLY THAT FUNNY?
YEAH. IT'S KINDA STRANGE.
IT REALLY IS STRANGE.
さっきまでモヤモヤしてたのに……
I WAS FEELING GLOOMY JUST A MOMENT AGO...
仰に会ったら
BUT I FELT SO MUCH BETTER...
何かホッとしちゃった——
AFTER I SAW AOGI.
AOGI,
DO YOU MIND STAYING HERE A LITTLE BIT LONGER AND LOOKING AT THE BEAUTIFUL STARS?
ALRIGHT, AS LONG AS WE DON'T STAY TILL MORNING.

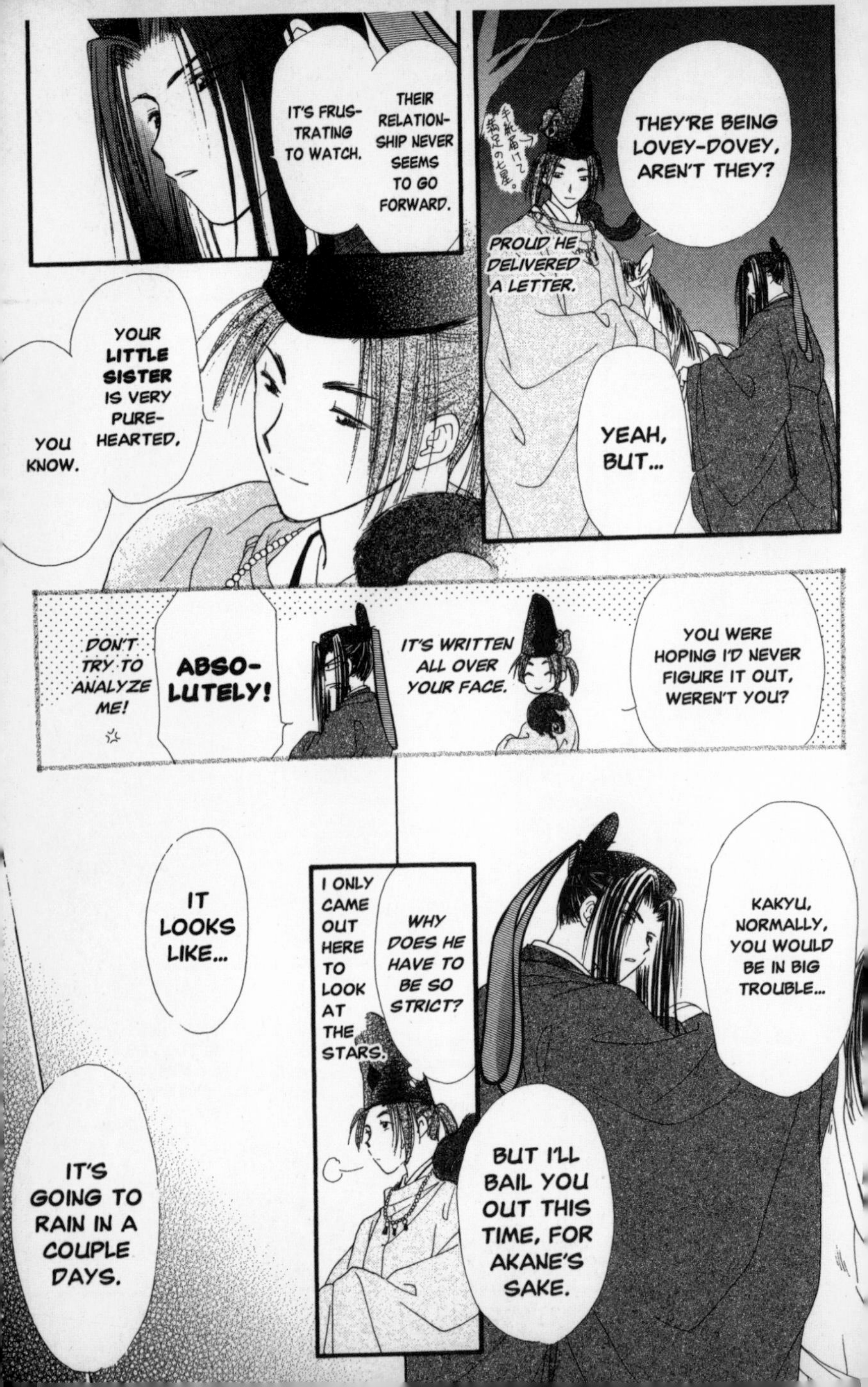
THEY'RE BEING LOVEY-DOVEY, AREN'T THEY?
手紙届けて満足の七星。
PROUD HE DELIVERED A LETTER.
YEAH, BUT...
THEIR RELATION-SHIP NEVER SEEMS TO GO FORWARD.
IT'S FRUS-TRATING TO WATCH.
YOUR LITTLE SISTER IS VERY PURE-HEARTED,
YOU KNOW.
YOU WERE HOPING I'D NEVER FIGURE IT OUT, WEREN'T YOU?
IT'S WRITTEN ALL OVER YOUR FACE.
ABSO-LUTELY!
DON'T TRY TO ANALYZE ME!
KAKYU, NORMALLY, YOU WOULD BE IN BIG TROUBLE...
BUT I'LL BAIL YOU OUT THIS TIME, FOR AKANE'S SAKE.
WHY DOES HE HAVE TO BE SO STRICT?
I ONLY CAME OUT HERE TO LOOK AT THE STARS.
IT LOOKS LIKE...
IT'S GOING TO RAIN IN A COUPLE DAYS.

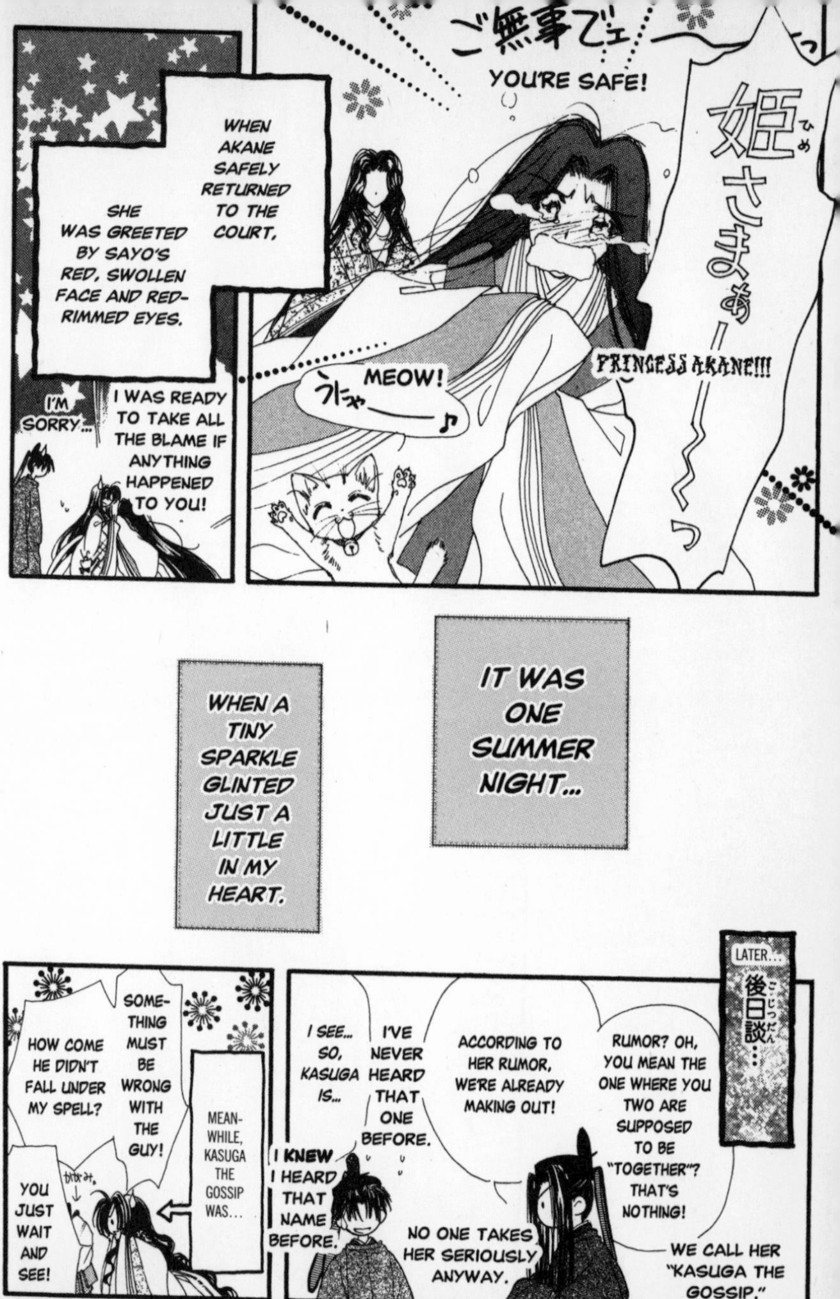
姫さまぁ〜〜っ
PRINCESS AKANE!!!
ご無事でェっ
YOU'RE SAFE!
うにゃ— ♪
MEOW!
WHEN AKANE SAFELY RETURNED TO THE COURT,
SHE WAS GREETED BY SAYO'S RED, SWOLLEN FACE AND RED-RIMMED EYES.
I WAS READY TO TAKE ALL THE BLAME IF ANYTHING HAPPENED TO YOU!
I'M SORRY...
IT WAS ONE SUMMER NIGHT...
WHEN A TINY SPARKLE GLINTED JUST A LITTLE IN MY HEART.
後日談…
LATER...
RUMOR? OH, YOU MEAN THE ONE WHERE YOU TWO ARE SUPPOSED TO BE "TOGETHER"? THAT'S NOTHING!
ACCORDING TO HER RUMOR, WE'RE ALREADY MAKING OUT!
I'VE NEVER HEARD THAT ONE BEFORE.
I SEE... SO, KASUGA IS...
WE CALL HER "KASUGA THE GOSSIP."
NO ONE TAKES HER SERIOUSLY ANYWAY.
I KNEW I HEARD THAT NAME BEFORE.
SOMETHING MUST BE WRONG WITH THE GUY!
HOW COME HE DIDN'T FALL UNDER MY SPELL?
MEANWHILE, KASUGA THE GOSSIP WAS...
YOU JUST WAIT AND SEE!

MORE STARLIGHT TO YOUR HEART VOLUME 1 END

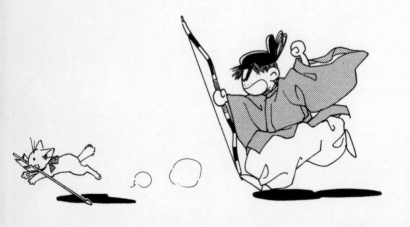

PINECONE H.M. NEWS SERVICE [COMIC EDITION] 7

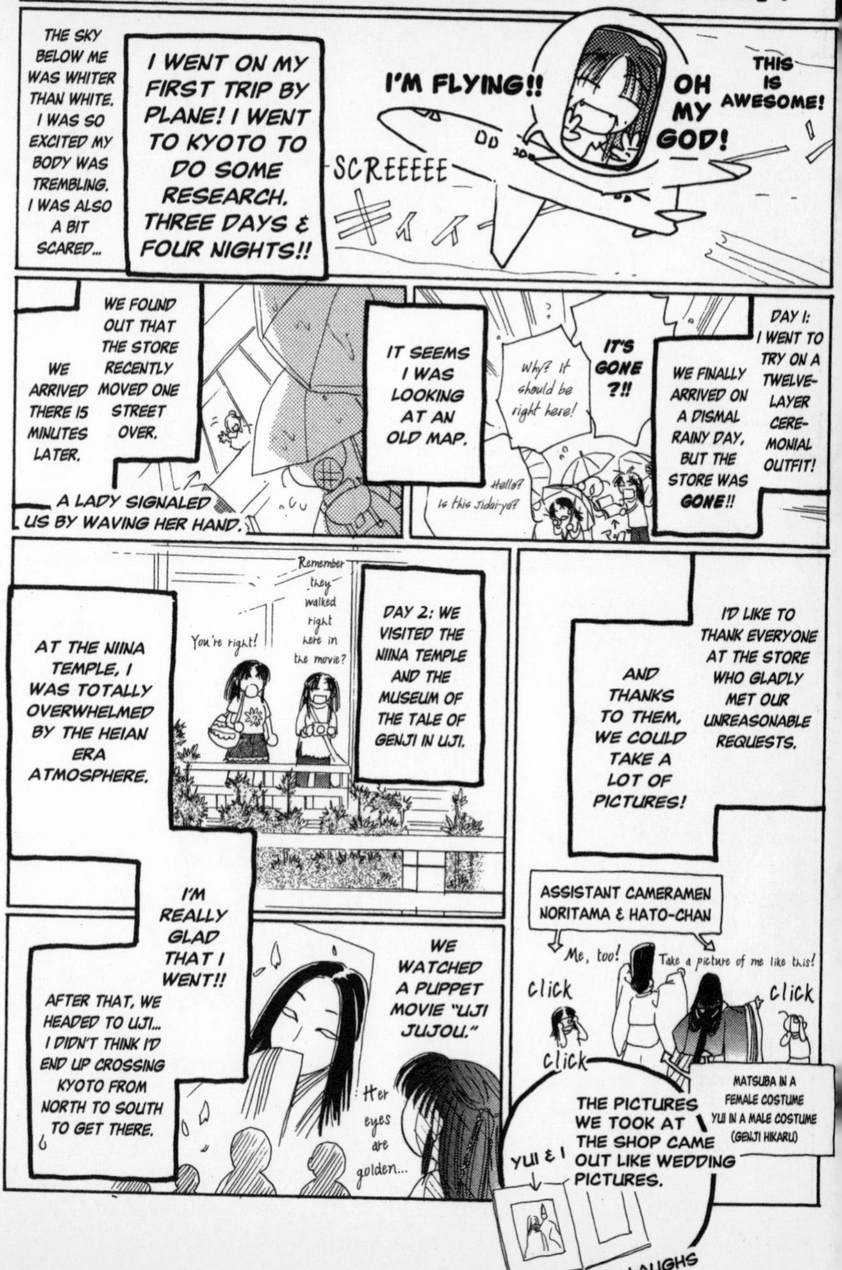
THIS IS AWESOME!
OH MY GOD!
I'M FLYING!!
I WENT ON MY FIRST TRIP BY PLANE! I WENT TO KYOTO TO DO SOME RESEARCH. THREE DAYS & FOUR NIGHTS!!
THE SKY BELOW ME WAS WHITER THAN WHITE. I WAS SO EXCITED MY BODY WAS TREMBLING. I WAS ALSO A BIT SCARED...
SCREEEEE
DAY 1: I WENT TO TRY ON A TWELVE-LAYER CEREMONIAL OUTFIT!
WE FINALLY ARRIVED ON A DISMAL RAINY DAY, BUT THE STORE WAS GONE!!
IT'S GONE?!!
Why? It should be right here!
Hello? Is this Jidai-ya?
IT SEEMS I WAS LOOKING AT AN OLD MAP.
WE FOUND OUT THAT THE STORE RECENTLY MOVED ONE STREET OVER.
WE ARRIVED THERE 15 MINUTES LATER.
A LADY SIGNALED US BY WAVING HER HAND.
I'D LIKE TO THANK EVERYONE AT THE STORE WHO GLADLY MET OUR UNREASONABLE REQUESTS.
AND THANKS TO THEM, WE COULD TAKE A LOT OF PICTURES!
ASSISTANT CAMERAMEN NORITAMA & HATO-CHAN
Take a picture of me like this!
Me, too!
Click
Click
Click
MATSUBA IN A FEMALE COSTUME YUI IN A MALE COSTUME (GENJI HIKARU)
THE PICTURES WE TOOK AT THE SHOP CAME OUT LIKE WEDDING PICTURES.
YUI & I
LAUGHS
DAY 2: WE VISITED THE NIINA TEMPLE AND THE MUSEUM OF THE TALE OF GENJI IN UJI.
Remember they walked right here in the movie?
You're right!
AT THE NIINA TEMPLE, I WAS TOTALLY OVERWHELMED BY THE HEIAN ERA ATMOSPHERE.
WE WATCHED A PUPPET MOVIE "UJI JUJOU."
I'M REALLY GLAD THAT I WENT!!
Her eyes are golden...
AFTER THAT, WE HEADED TO UJI... I DIDN'T THINK I'D END UP CROSSING KYOTO FROM NORTH TO SOUTH TO GET THERE.

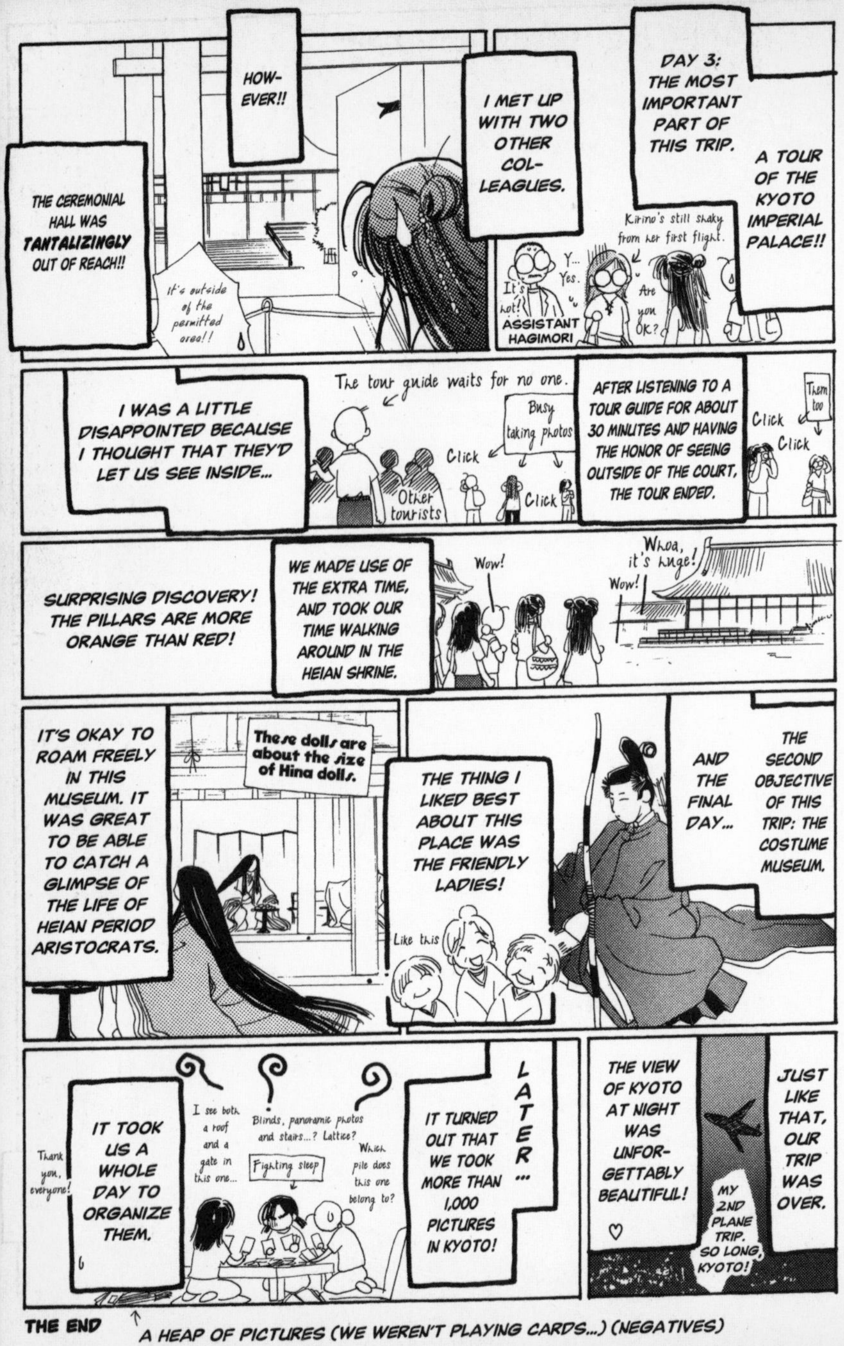
DAY 3: THE MOST IMPORTANT PART OF THIS TRIP.
A TOUR OF THE KYOTO IMPERIAL PALACE!!
Kirino's still shaky from her first flight.
Are you OK?
Y... Yes.
It's hot!
ASSISTANT HAGIMORI
I MET UP WITH TWO OTHER COL-LEAGUES.
HOW-EVER!!
THE CEREMONIAL HALL WAS TANTALIZINGLY OUT OF REACH!!
It's outside of the permitted area!!
AFTER LISTENING TO A TOUR GUIDE FOR ABOUT 30 MINUTES AND HAVING THE HONOR OF SEEING OUTSIDE OF THE COURT, THE TOUR ENDED.
Them too
Click
Click
The tour guide waits for no one.
Busy taking photos
Click
Click
Other tourists
I WAS A LITTLE DISAPPOINTED BECAUSE I THOUGHT THAT THEY'D LET US SEE INSIDE...
Whoa, it's huge!
Wow!
Wow!
WE MADE USE OF THE EXTRA TIME, AND TOOK OUR TIME WALKING AROUND IN THE HEIAN SHRINE.
SURPRISING DISCOVERY! THE PILLARS ARE MORE ORANGE THAN RED!
THE SECOND OBJECTIVE OF THIS TRIP: THE COSTUME MUSEUM.
AND THE FINAL DAY...
THE THING I LIKED BEST ABOUT THIS PLACE WAS THE FRIENDLY LADIES!
Like this
These dolls are about the size of Hina dolls.
IT'S OKAY TO ROAM FREELY IN THIS MUSEUM. IT WAS GREAT TO BE ABLE TO CATCH A GLIMPSE OF THE LIFE OF HEIAN PERIOD ARISTOCRATS.
JUST LIKE THAT, OUR TRIP WAS OVER.
MY 2ND PLANE TRIP. SO LONG, KYOTO!
THE VIEW OF KYOTO AT NIGHT WAS UNFOR-GETTABLY BEAUTIFUL!
LATER...
IT TURNED OUT THAT WE TOOK MORE THAN 1,000 PICTURES IN KYOTO!
Which pile does this one belong to?
Blinds, panoramic photos and stairs...? Lattice?
I see both a roof and a gate in this one...
Fighting sleep
IT TOOK US A WHOLE DAY TO ORGANIZE THEM.
Thank you, everyone!
THE END
A HEAP OF PICTURES (WE WEREN'T PLAYING CARDS...) (NEGATIVES)

More Starlight To Your Heart
VOLUME 1

© Hiro Matsuba 2002

All rights reserved.
First published in 2002 by MAG Garden Corporation.
English translation rights arranged with MAG Garden Corporation.

Translator **KAY BERTRAND**
Lead Translator/Translation Supervisor **JAVIER LOPEZ**
ADV Manga Translation Staff **JOSH COLE, AMY FORSYTH, BRENDAN FRAYNE,
HARUKA KANEKO-SMITH, EIKO McGREGOR AND MADOKA MOROE**

Print Production/Art Studio Manager **LISA PUCKETT**
Pre-press Manager **KLYS REEDYK**
Art Production Manager **RYAN MASON**
Senior Designer/Creative Manager **JORGE ALVARADO**
Graphic Designer/Group Leader **SHANNON RASBERRY**
Graphic Designer **CHRIS LAPP**
Graphic Artists **CHY LING, NATALIA MORALES,
LISA RAPER, GEORGE REYNOLDS AND NANAKO TSUKIHASHI**
Graphic Intern **MARK MEZA**

International Coordinator **TORU IWAKAMI**
International Coordinator **ATSUSHI KANBAYASHI**

Publishing Editor **SUSAN ITIN**
Assistant Editor **MARGARET SCHAROLD**
Editorial Assistant **VARSHA BHUCHAR**
Proofreaders **SHERIDAN JACOBS AND STEVEN REED**
Editorial Intern **JENNIFER VACCA**

Research/Traffic Coordinator **MARSHA ARNOLD**

Executive VP, CFO, COO **KEVIN CORCORAN**

President, CEO & Publisher **JOHN LEDFORD**

Email: editor@adv-manga.com
www.adv-manga.com
www.advfilms.com

For sales and distribution inquiries please call 1.800.282.7202

ADV MANGA™ is a division of A.D. Vision, Inc.
10114 W. Sam Houston Parkway, Suite 200, Houston, Texas 77099

English text © 2004 published by A.D. Vision, Inc. under exclusive license.
ADV MANGA is a trademark of A.D. Vision, Inc.

ISBN: 1-4139-0206-5
First printing, December 2004
10 9 8 7 6 5 4 3 2 1
Printed in Canada

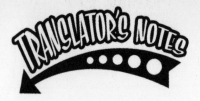

More Starlight To Your Heart Vol. 01

PG. 3   **Heian Period**   The Heian period of Japanese history lasted from 794, when Kyoto became the capital of Japan, to 1185. It is often considered the golden age of Japanese culture and literature, and the imperial court reached its height at this time.

PG. 7   **Lady Naishinokami**   Naishinokami is not her name, but it is her title. The Naishinokami is in charge of all administrative matters in the inner palace. She works closely with the emperor, and could even become his wife.

PG. 62   **Onmyo**   *Onmyodo*, or the Onmyo Way, is historically an extension of Chinese Taoism in Japan, which focused on astrology and the Taoist five elements (wood, fire, earth, metal, and water) theory. It developed into a formalized ritualistic practice (which actually combined beliefs from multiple disciplines) as early as the Heian period (794 – 1185). The services of *Onmyodo* practitioners, or *Onmyoji* were called upon in state and religious ceremonies as well as for divining and other matters related to the supernatural.

PG. 85   **Tanuki**   The tanuki is a real animal native to Japan, and they are sometimes called "raccoon dogs." They look something like a large raccoon, but they are members of the dog family and are not related to raccoons. In Japanese folklore, they are said to be mischievous and possess magical powers. They can transform into anything they want, including humans. They are also famous for their love of saké, and they are often depicted with a saké bottle in one hand and large, round bellies. Today it's common to see ceramic statues of tanuki outside restaurants and bars, beckoning drinkers and diners inside.

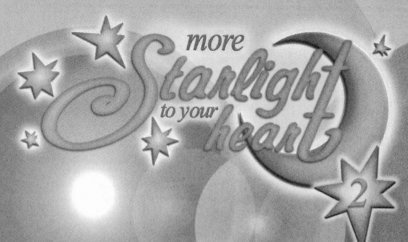

more Starlight to your heart

2

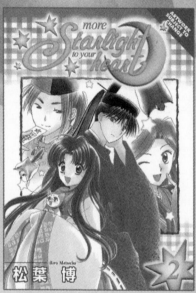

more Starlight to your heart

ARTWORK SUBJECT TO CHANGE

Hiro Matsuba

松葉 博

2

Akane is slowly adjusting to the life of a servant, and under the guiding eye of her mother, she's actually having fun with her true love, Aogi. But trouble awaits the happy couple. Stolen moments with him are few, and could end altogether if her father has any say in the matter. But overcoming her old man's scheming is not quite as time-consuming as a little drama in the palace court!

A happily-ever-after for Akane and Aogi is once again put on hold for another twist of fate in <u>More Starlight To Your Heart, Volume 2</u>.

ADV MANGA™
www.adv-manga.com

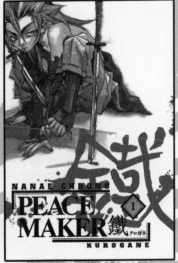
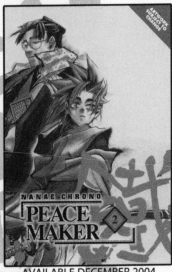

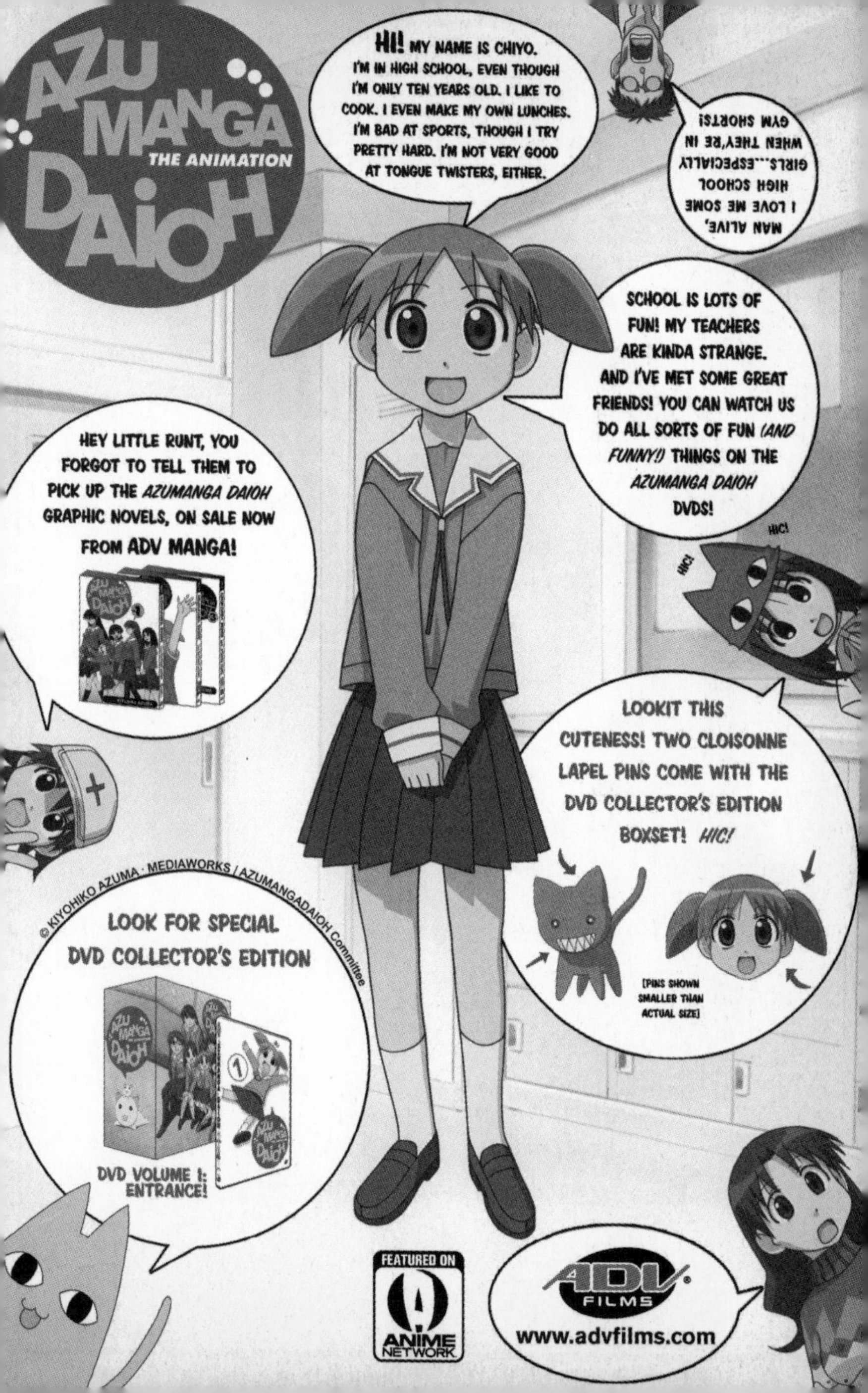
AZUMANGA DAIOH
THE ANIMATION
HI! MY NAME IS CHIYO. I'M IN HIGH SCHOOL, EVEN THOUGH I'M ONLY TEN YEARS OLD. I LIKE TO COOK. I EVEN MAKE MY OWN LUNCHES. I'M BAD AT SPORTS, THOUGH I TRY PRETTY HARD. I'M NOT VERY GOOD AT TONGUE TWISTERS, EITHER.
MAN ALIVE, I LOVE ME SOME HIGH SCHOOL GIRLS...ESPECIALLY WHEN THEY'RE IN GYM SHORTS!
SCHOOL IS LOTS OF FUN! MY TEACHERS ARE KINDA STRANGE. AND I'VE MET SOME GREAT FRIENDS! YOU CAN WATCH US DO ALL SORTS OF FUN *(AND FUNNY!)* THINGS ON THE *AZUMANGA DAIOH* DVDS!
HEY LITTLE RUNT, YOU FORGOT TO TELL THEM TO PICK UP THE *AZUMANGA DAIOH* GRAPHIC NOVELS, ON SALE NOW FROM ADV MANGA!
HIC!
HIC!
LOOKIT THIS CUTENESS! TWO CLOISONNE LAPEL PINS COME WITH THE DVD COLLECTOR'S EDITION BOXSET! *HIC!*
[PINS SHOWN SMALLER THAN ACTUAL SIZE]
© KIYOHIKO AZUMA · MEDIAWORKS / AZUMANGADAIOH Committee
LOOK FOR SPECIAL DVD COLLECTOR'S EDITION
DVD VOLUME 1: ENTRANCE!
FEATURED ON ANIME NETWORK
ADV FILMS
www.advfilms.com

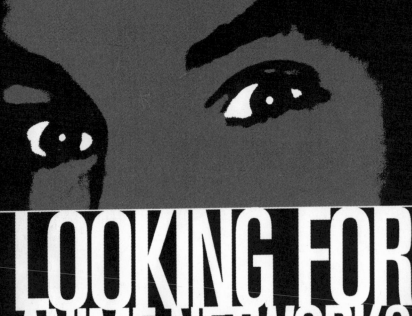

LOOKING FOR ANIME NETWORK?

THIS GUY WAS, THEN HE CALLED HIS LOCAL
CABLE PROVIDER AND DEMANDED HIS ANIME!

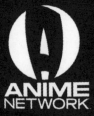

FOR MORE INFO LOG ON TO
WWW.THEANIMENETWORK.COM

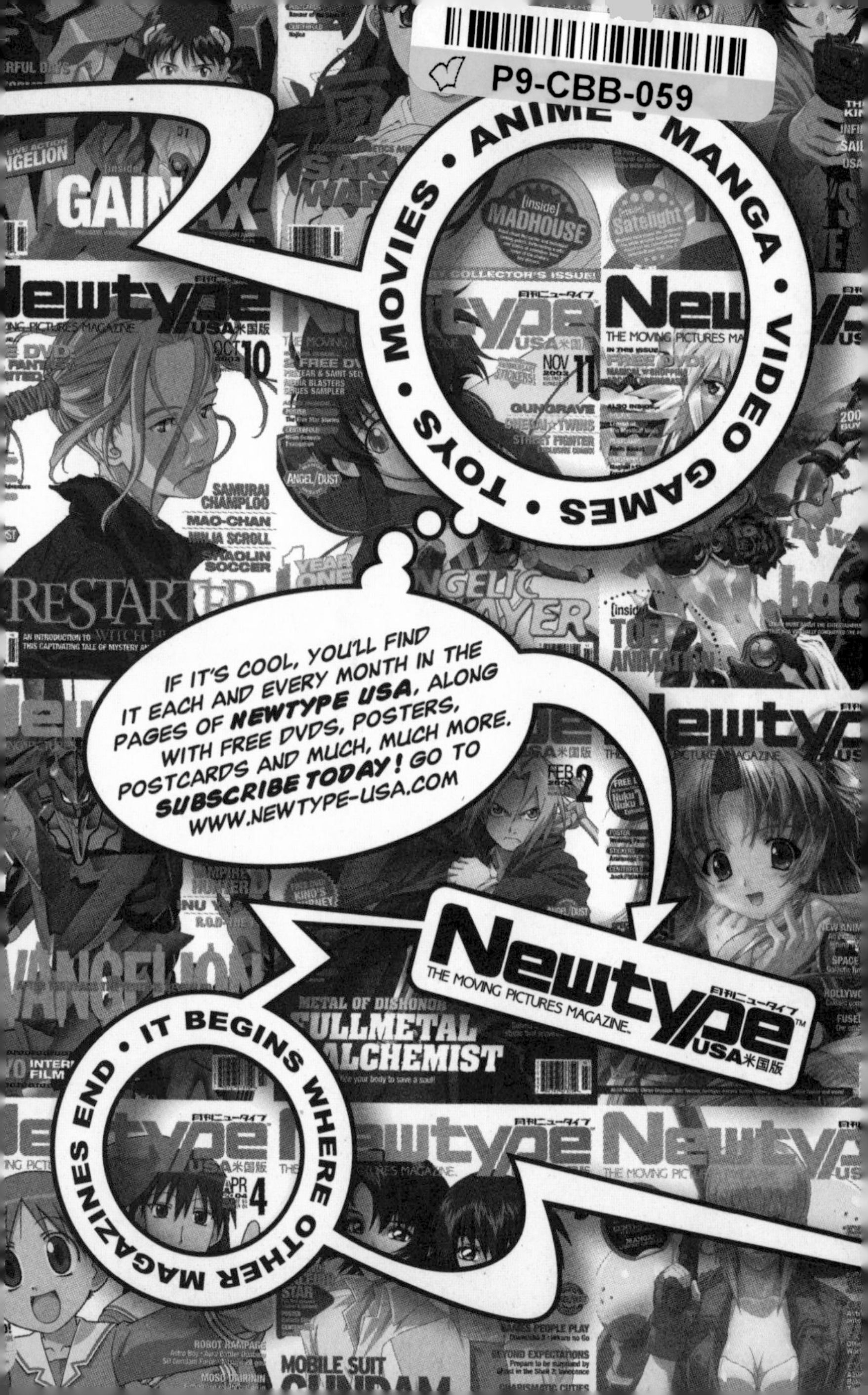MOVIES • ANIME • MANGA • VIDEO GAMES • TOYS •
IF IT'S COOL, YOU'LL FIND IT EACH AND EVERY MONTH IN THE PAGES OF NEWTYPE USA, ALONG WITH FREE DVDS, POSTERS, POSTCARDS AND MUCH, MUCH MORE. SUBSCRIBE TODAY! GO TO WWW.NEWTYPE-USA.COM
Newtype
THE MOVING PICTURES MAGAZINE.
USA米国版
月刊ニュータイプ
IT BEGINS WHERE OTHER MAGAZINES END •